High-tech Entrepreneurship

Managing innovation, variety and uncertainty

Edited by

**Michel Bernasconi, Simon Harris
and Mette Moensted**

Routledge
Taylor & Francis Group

LONDON AND NEW YORK

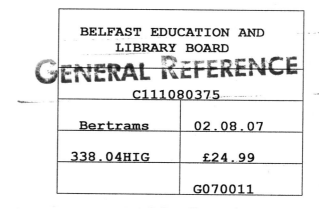
First published 2006
by Routledge
2 Park Square, Milton Park, Abingdon, Oxon OX14 4RN

Simultaneously published in the USA and Canada
by Routledge
270 Madison Ave, New York, NY 10016

Routledge is an imprint of the Taylor & Francis Group, an informa business

Typeset in Perpetua and Bell Gothic by
HWA Text and Data Management, Tunbridge Wells
Printed and bound in Great Britain by
MPG Books Ltd, Bodmin

British Library Cataloguing in Publication Data
A catalogue record for this book is available from the British Library

Library of Congress Cataloging-in-Publication Data
High-tech entrepreneurship : managing innovation, variety and uncertainty / edited by
Michel Bernasconi, Simon Harris, and Mette Moensted.
    p. cm.
Includes bibliographical references and index.
1. High technology industries–Management. 2. Technological innovations–Management.
I. Bernasconi, Michel. II. Harris, Simon. III. Moensted, Mette.
HD62.37.H535 2006
658.4'21–dc22   2006011813

ISBN10: 0–415–38058–8 (hbk)   ISBN13: 978–0–415–38058–4 (hbk)
ISBN10: 0–415–38059–6 (pbk)   ISBN13: 978–0–415–38059–1 (pbk)

Contents

List of illustrations   ix
Contributors   xi
Preface   xiil

1   High-tech entrepreneurship: managing innovation in a world of
    variety and uncertainty   1
    Michel Bernasconi, Simon Harris and Mette Moensted

**PART I   UNCERTAINTY AND INNOVATION IN
               ENTREPRENEURSHIP   11**
    Mette Moensted

2   High-tech, uncertainty and innovation:
    the opportunity for high-tech entrepreneurship   15
    Mette Moensted

3   For high-tech small is beautiful: why small firms can handle
    complexity better   33
    Ludovic Dibiaggio

4   Engineers as high-tech entrepreneurs: French engineers' paths to
    entrepreneurship   50
    Alain Fayolle

5   Collective learning processes in high-tech firms: enablers and
    barriers to the innovation process   69
    Valérie-Inès de La Ville

CONTENTS

**PART II   DIFFERENT ENTREPRENEURIAL WAYS OF FACING
UNCERTAINTY   87**
Simon Harris

6   High-tech clusters: network richness in Sophia Antipolis and
Silicon Valley   93
Michel Bernasconi, Ludovic Dibiaggio and Michel Ferrary

7   Network relationships in different cultures: high-tech globalization
meets local cultures   112
Simon Harris

8   Technology business incubation management: lessons of
experience   131
Philippe Albert and Lynda Gaynor

9   Strategy development processes: the importance of considering
integration and timing   144
Franck Moreau

10   University spin-out firms: patterns of development based on
expertise   158
Céline Druilhe and Elizabeth Garnsey

11   Creation processes as evolving projects: high-tech firms as
emerging systems   174
Michel Bernasconi

PART III   MANAGING INNOVATIVE HIGH-TECH FIRMS   187
Michel Bernasconi

12   Marketing technological innovations: the challenges of creating
markets   189
Paul Millier

13   Creating competitive intelligence: competing technologies come
from anywhere   207
Gil Ayache

14   Evaluating technology development projects: a multiplexity of
controllability and uncontrollability   225
Dominique Jolly

15   Networking for innovation: managing through networks   242
      Mette Moensted

References   262
Index   286

Illustrations

FIGURES

2.1	Project selection, decision and outcomes	18
2.2	The importance of decisions and the knowledge basis for decisions	19
2.3	Latour's Janus dictum	25
4.1	Trajectories and entrepreneurial paths of engineers	59
4.2	Positioning the engineer-entrepreneur types	62
4.3	Characteristics of engineer-entrepreneurs	63
4.4	'Managerial' engineer-entrepreneurs (Type X)	65
4.5	'Technical' engineer-entrepreneurs (Type Y)	66
4.6	'Super-technical' engineer-entrepreneurs (Type Z)	67
7.1	Four different categories of network ties	122
8.1	Evaluating the trilogy	140
9.1	A typology of start-up development modes	148
9.2	Operational model of 'simple' company development	149
9.3	Operational model of traditional development	150
9.4	Operational model of complex development	152
9.5	Operational model of chaotic development	154
10.1	Typology of academic spin-outs activities	165
11.1	The five elements of the system	180
11.2	Evolving process of company creation	182
11.3	Progression of interactions between the different dimensions of the project	184
12.1	A proliferation of applications	195
12.2	Proliferation, segmentation, focus	197
12.3	Segmentation matrix	198
12.4	Diagnosis of the marketing situation of the firm	199
13.1	Building up knowledge through the 'Mandala of creativity'	213
13.2	Integrating knowledge through a project	213
13.3	The strategic threshold of anticipation	217
13.4	A process as part of the strategy	218
13.5	From competitive intelligence to technological resources management	219
13.6	The basic process of competitive intelligence	220

14.1 Definition of technology   227
14.2 The company's technology portfolio map   237
15.1 Dyads and triads   245
15.2 Value-loaded networks   245
15.3 Segmented networks   246
15.4 The virtuous circle of trust   250
15.5 Structural holes in strategic networks   253
15.6 Network forces   255
15.7 Power positions in networks   256

TABLES

 1.1 Variety and uncertainty in the contributions to this volume   6
 2.1 Comparing conventional wisdom with a modern biotechnology study   21
 2.2 Conditions for, and the need for trust   30
 4.1 Key features about the three types of engineer-entrepreneurs   64
 6.1 Comparison Silicon Valley – Sophia Antipolis   102
 6.2 Silicon Valley   103
 6.3 Sophia Antipolis   104
 7.1 Values orientations in France, the Netherlands and Great Britain   123
 7.2 Entrepreneurs' network ties in the three countries   125
 7.3 Network ties of institutionally different types of entrepreneurs   128
 8.1 Sponsors of business technology incubation: objectives and contribution 135
 8.2 Examples of incubators specializing in different technologies   136
10.1 Categorization of spin-outs in the literature   161
14.1 Evaluating technological attractiveness   232
14.2 Evaluating technological competitiveness   234

Contributors

Albert, Philippe, Consultant, France. philippe-albert@wanadoo.fr

Ayache, Gil, Chief Executive, Marseille-Provence Technologies, Marseille, France. gil.ayache@club-internet.fr

Bernasconi, Michel, High-Tech Entrepreneurship Center, Sophia Antipolis, France. michel.bernasconi@ceram.fr

Dibiaggio, Ludovic, Professor of Economics at CERAM Sophia Antipolis, France. ludovic.dibiaggio@ceram.fr

Druilhe, Céline, Research Associate, Centre for Business Research, University of Cambridge, UK. cd224@cam.ac.uk

Fayolle, Alain, Director of the Entrepreneurship Centre of EM Lyon and Associate Professor at INP, Grenoble, France. alain.fayolle@esisar.inpg.fr

Ferrary, Michel, Professor in Management and Human Resources at CERAM Sophia Antipolis, France. michel.ferrary@ceram.fr

Garnsey, Elizabeth, Reader, Institute for Manufacturing, University of Cambridge, Department of Engineering, Cambridge, UK. ewg11@cam.ac.uk

Gaynor, Lynda, Consultant, Sapitwa Consulting, Dublin, Eire. lynda.gaynor@sapitwa.com

Harris, Simon, Reader in International Strategic Management, University of Strathclyde, Glasgow, Scotland. simon.harris@strath.ac.uk

Jolly, Dominique, Professor in Strategic Management at CERAM Sophia Antipolis, France. dominique.jolly@ceram.fr

de La Ville, Valérie-Inès, Associate Professor of Management at IAE Poitiers, France. delaville@cuc.univ.poitiers.fr

Millier, Paul, Professor in Industrial Marketing at EM Lyon, France. millier@em-lyon.com

Moensted, Mette, Professor in Knowledge Management at the Department of Management, Politics and Philosophy, Copenhagen Business School, Frederiksberg, Denmark. mm.lpf@cbs.dk

Moreau, Franck, Professor in Strategic Management at CERAM Sophia Antipolis, France. franck.moreau@ceram.fr

Preface

One impetus for this volume is an explosion of interest in high-tech entrepreneurship, reflected amongst other things in a burgeoning in the number of courses on the subject offered around the world at undergraduate, postgraduate and post experience level. The other is a dissatisfaction with existing texts which tend to fall into one of two camps. Some present a 'top-down' description of the phenomenon of high-tech entrepreneurship, with little insight into the managerial issues involved.

Others often present clear and comprehensible models of the managerial issues, but these invariably ignore the deep complexities involved, complexities that arise from the variety of forms of high-technology entrepreneurship and from the extraordinary uncertainties which pervade the world of high-technology entrepreneurship. Our focus in this book is on the management of high-tech entrepreneurship, and our central themes are the variety and the uncertainty within the process of doing it.

Our desire, then, was to assemble a team that would rise to this challenging task, and contribute to a research-led book that reflected not only deep scholarship on the subject, but deep experience as well. We have been extraordinarily fortunate. The different chapters are contributed by leading people in the field throughout Europe. Nearly all the authors have some strong connection with Sophia Antipolis, Europe's largest high-tech business park near Nice in the South of France. Their backgrounds, however, like the subject that is examined, are varied, some being internationally acknowledged on grounds of their scholarship, and others similarly acknowledged on grounds of their experience in the process of high-technology entrepreneurship.

The outcome is a book that deals with the subject with different voices, and from different perspectives, from the academically rigorous born of scholarship and careful examination of real cases, to the direct voice of the experienced practitioner richly enriched with real examples. All are valued, and all contribute, with examples throughout, to a rich and complex tapestry that begins to describe a rich and complex, but immensely important, phenomenon.

Michel Bernasconi
Simon Harris
Mette Moensted
Sophia Antipolis, June 2005

Chapter 1

High-tech entrepreneurship
Managing innovation in a world of variety and uncertainty

Michel Bernasconi, Simon Harris and Mette Moensted

For economies to achieve growth in an increasingly technologically advanced and borderless world, the creative talents of its residents need to be marshalled into successful businesses. This has ever been so. It has been witnessed in Europe, for example, from the times of the Roman Empire, through the age of the Holy Roman Empire, when some countries and regions achieved phenomenal economic success through the entrepreneurial activities of individuals and groups who translated technological and merchant opportunity into the creation of wealth. In this book, we call this process high-tech entrepreneurship.

We are, once again, entering a period of global economic liberation, running in parallel with significant technological advance. This is, inevitably, leading to questions from policy makers with local, regional, national and supranational economic concern as to how this process can be fostered. Managers of firms, whether in their own businesses or professional managers of larger firms, ask how it may be managed. Individuals with innovative intentions ask how they may be able to achieve their dreams: the dreams upon which the future economic welfare of us all, and of future generations, will depend.

So many types of people share an interest in the subject of this book, but do so from different standpoints. Technicians with innovations in their heads and in their hearts seek to understand the process of developing ideas into businesses. Entrepreneurs look to see how they can increase the impact of their innovations, financially or in other ways. Owners and managers of established firms from the small to the very large are seeking ways that they can gain or regain the innovative and entrepreneurial dynamism that characterizes the growth business. Managers and administrators of that environment, from the managers of business incubators, to local support and advice agencies, to the managers of venture capital bodies, wish to learn how they can make a constructive difference, in part by understanding how others do so. Political interests are concerned with how government policies can improve the environment they set for the high-tech entrepreneurship process, and how the environment can impair that process. And students of management, who may be in, or may develop into, one of these roles benefit from an understanding of the processes involved. From in-house executive programmes to specialist MBA and masters programmes, for science and for business specialists, at postgraduate and at undergraduate level, the number of courses offered in the area of high-tech entrepreneurship has exploded.

One outcome of this interest has been a plethora of books that purport to show how it is done; the 'how-to' books. Typically, these give models of the high-tech entrepreneurship process that are clear and logical and, usually, on the face of it at least, reasonably complete. They appear to give us what we want. They make it look straightforward. They present us with certainty. Follow their linear template, they suggest, and we can also do it. As we shall see, this is not a realistic proposition: high-tech entrepreneurship, like life, is more difficult than that.

A WORLD OF VARIETY AND UNCERTAINTY

First, let us define what we mean. Following Jolly and Thérin (1996), we define technology to be any original and protected combination of scientific knowledge, technical knowledge and know-how, mastered by a firm (or firms), and incorporated into a product, service, production process, information system or management method, for an economic purpose. Taking the marketing standpoint that Paul Millier presents in Chapter 12, we regard a high-tech product to be a product or service which is a breakthrough in upsetting its market to a point where the market can no longer be considered in the same way.

High-tech entrepreneurship is the creation of value from technical innovation through success in business. It is not a person, nor is it an idea; rather, it is a process. It is a process of building new companies based on technologies. It is not the only way to innovate, and is not necessary best way to innovate, but as Ludovic Dibiaggio argues in Chapter 3, it is a way that is well adapted to complex situations.

The first thing that we know – this is a research-led text – as Mette Moensted presents in Chapter 2, is that the world of and the process of high-tech entrepreneurship is highly complex. This book will attempt to embrace the complexity that we know to be involved, in two aspects. First, the contexts in which managers are 'doing' high-tech entrepreneurship are highly diverse, and the ways in which they do it vary greatly. Second, they are also doing all this in environments of extreme uncertainty.

Variety in high-technology entrepreneurship

The context within which high-technology entrepreneurship takes place is varied. First, it is geographically varied. The relationship between high-tech firms and the national or regional context is an important theme, since we must remain aware that 'it is not the same everywhere'. Second, the institutional setting for high-tech entrepreneurship is also varied. It can involve young start-ups led by technologically advanced individuals, but it is also commonly practised by existing companies, big or small, research and development centres, universities, private inventors and government departments and agencies.

Technological innovation comes mainly from scientists and technologists, but it is not only the realization of the work and dreams of individuals. As Valérie-Inès de La Ville shows us in Chapter 5, it is also a collective creation, and one that develops over time. The transformation of these people into entrepreneurs, the process examined by Alain Fayolle in Chapter 4, is complex to define, culturally grounded, and the result of personal trajectories. High-tech entrepreneurship requires many different skills that are not available in one person, and as Céline Druilhe and Elizabeth Garnsey show us in Chapter 10, and Michel Bernasconi shows in Chapter 11, entrepreneurial teams are, of necessity, made up of people who complement the founders. All the individuals involved are embedded in social networks, and as Michel Bernasconi and his colleagues show us in Chapter 6, these are not only essential for the success of the entrepreneurial process, but are a key element of the environment in which the firms are created. Such networks are, as Mette Moensted shows us in Chapter 16, an essential element of the innovation process to create access to diversity, but as Simon Harris cautions in Chapter 7, we cannot simply dictate our networks, since they are highly dependent on the cultural heritage.

This all leads us to see each high-tech entrepreneurial context to be at least highly varied, and often infinitely varied. All these factors do not only create complexity, but complexity that itself differs from manager to manager and from management situation to management situation.

Uncertainty in high-technology entrepreneurship

Management in high-technology entrepreneurial contexts has, however, one other dominant trait: uncertainty. This includes risk, differences between contexts, and evaluation of the unknowable. Uncertainty and complexity, innovation and advanced technology is what makes it difficult to use the usual linear business economic models and planning, and makes it necessary to reflect on how to cope with management under these entrepreneurial conditions.

Our analysis of uncertainty in high-tech entrepreneurship, however, is made difficult by there having been so many efforts to define the concept of uncertainty, some including various related concepts, such as opportunity, risk, ignorance, bias or ambiguity, and some discriminating it from these concepts. We are helped by Van de Ven and Grazman's definitions of uncertainty and ambiguity, which by seeing innovation more as a journey than as a well planned and scheduled programmed process, matches our 'process' vision of high-tech entrepreneurship:

> Much of an innovation journey involves an adaptive learning process to deal with conditions of ambiguity (i.e. where it is not clear what specific preferences or objectives should be pursued to reach a vague super ordinate goal) and uncertainty (i.e. where it is not clear what means of actions will achieve desired outcome goals)
>
> (Van de Ven and Grazman 1997: 279)

Julien and Marchesnay (1996) identify uncertainty as a condition for entrepreneurship: an uncertain context is open for new interpretations and for new actions, creating opportunities through innovation. Innovation and entrepreneurship are based on creating new ideas and new knowledge. But a number of aspects of high-tech contexts make the issue of uncertainty even greater than in other entrepreneurial environments.

First, we are faced with intrinsic characteristics of the context. Technologies, especially in early phases, are not yet proven, and the ability of the technology to deliver its promise, and the time this will take, is also uncertain. New markets, especially in radical innovation areas, tend to be novel as well, and do not just fit into an existing market. The time scales for these future developments of technology and markets are unknowable.

Second, lack of control is an important dimension of the uncertainty involved. In high-tech environments there is a greater dependence on skills and other resources which are outside the control of the managers themselves. This creates great demands on communication and learning on the part of those in control of those other resources. In high-tech environments, this is a difficulty. Much of this communication may well be with culturally different people. Some of the lack of communication between high-tech entrepreneurs and financial investors, for example, may be associated with them knowing too little about each other, which is exacerbated by the intrinsic uncertainty of the projects noted before. Others in the support system can see aspects like the uncertainties embedded in an innovation, the opportunities involved and the risks in very different ways.

Third, in high-tech entrepreneurship, stories do not repeat themselves, and even if analysis of earlier experience is important for some creation of meaning, it does not predict the future. This challenges the conceptualizations and strategic models that are typically based on projection of patterns observed earlier and elsewhere. When exploring new ideas, and when developing ideas into innovations, our perspectives on what we know, and our understanding of the models of stable development need to change as well.

So in high-tech entrepreneurship, it is the norm rather than the exception for factors to be unpredictable, and is it the norm rather than the exception for most important factors also to be outside managerial control. Nevertheless, important decisions have to be made, but as we must now recognize, this will be without the possibility of straightforward and clear analysis based on established models of development. That is what we mean by uncertainty.

VARIETY AND COMPLEXITY IN THIS BOOK

We can now begin to see why it is necessary for us to disappoint those who might have wanted us to present a simple, new and all-encompassing 'model' of high-tech entrepreneurship. Whenever faced with contexts of uncertainty and complexity, we can expect calls for solutions, strategies or 'saviour-recipes' (Stacey 1996), as managers in a human way seek meaning and linear causality. The purpose of these is to create 'a sense of certainty', but one that we would now recognize to be an illusion. Such an exercise, therefore, would be both foolish and dangerous.

First, the implicit decision-making structures do not address environments that are either different from those implicit structures, or which are intrinsically diverse. The models which implicitly assume the structure of a Silicon Valley start-up may be irrelevant for a German university spin-out, or for a Swedish government department, even though all may be doing high-tech entrepreneurship.

Second, these business models are embedded with implicit certainties. The simple models, simply, will not do. For example, models based on earlier experience with sectors can overlook new opportunities, and only allow understanding of 'me-too' technologies, not real innovations.

Third, these simplistic models do not show the interacting and organizing conditions of the high-tech entrepreneurial firms. The organization of resources to combine skills for developing technology and markets, which requires communication and negotiation to persuade other firms and agents, is critical. The environmental conditions allow entrepreneurs to recruit supporters such as partners, subcontractors, customers, and investors. Those based on personal traits, for example, overlook the interactive setting, and negotiated influence to form an innovative context. In the simple models this complexity is not transformed into simple indicators but is lost.

The evidence of research into what managers actually do is that in this environment these simple business models do not work. Managers do not use them, and the approaches that they do adopt are highly diverse. The special features of technological innovation, uncertainty in particular, make high-tech entrepreneurship a non-linear process. In this book we will see a diversity and variety of approach: there is not a universalistic 'one way' to manage in this environment. So we have a strong case for recognizing diversity in the high-tech entrepreneurship process, and to begin the process of understanding it by seeing it in many different ways. That is what we do in this book, and Table 1.1(below) shows how we do it.

This book cannot hope to describe all the variety and uncertainty that pervades the high-tech entrepreneurial firm, but it does cover a lot. Part I takes a holistic approach to the issue, and the chapters present a range of different perspectives to

Table 1.1 *Variety and uncertainty in the contributions to this volume*

Chapter	Variety in:	Uncertainty in or from:
PART I: UNDERSTANDING INNOVATION AND ENTREPRENEURSHIP		
2: Mette Moensted High-tech, uncertainty and innovation	Levels of uncertainty; how trust is used in innovation and entrepreneurship	From the environment, from technological changes, and from the market
3: Ludovic Dibiaggio Small is beautiful for high-tech firms	The dynamics of learning and knowledge creation; organizational structures	In firms' innovation processes; from the complexity of the environment and dynamic problems
4: Alain Fayolle Engineers as high-tech entrepreneurs	Within and between countries in the entrepreneurial orientation and the career paths of engineers	In who become entrepreneurs; from their own as well as others' expectations
5: Valérie-Inès de La Ville Collective learning in high-tech firms	The ways in which people interact with one another, a necessary element of innovation	In the processes of interaction between people in innovation, and from the necessity of improvization
PART II: DIFFERENT ENTREPRENEURIAL WAYS OF FACING UNCERTAINTY		
6: Michel Bernasconi, Ludovic Dibiaggio, and Michel Ferrary High-tech clusters	The characteristics of the local milieu; in the communities of practice and social networks	The presence and effectiveness of communities of practice, and the levels of interaction between them
7: Simon Harris Network relationships in different cultures	The national and institutional cultural assumptions underlying business activity and network relationships	The behaviour and wishes of others in network relationships
8: Philippe Albert and Lynda Gaynor Technology business incubation management	The stakeholders, objectives, profiles and practices of technology business incubators	The interaction between incubators stakeholders, management, and the technology firms
9: Franck Moreau Strategy development processes	In the dynamics and models of high-tech start-up development	The unknowables in and interactions between development aspects
10: Céline Druilhe and Elizabeth Garnsey University spin-out firms	How university scientific/ technical capabilities and developments can be commercially exploited	The necessary technical and managerial capabilities available and required
11: Michel Bernasconi Creation processes as evolving projects	The industries, the entrepreneur(s) and the local milieu involved; in all the elements of the projects	In the technologies involved, the market acceptance, and the economic model
PART III: MANAGING INNOVATIVE HIGH-TECH FIRMS		
12: Paul Millier Marketing technological innovations	The specific innovation mechanisms and the former industrial experiences	In customers, markets, competitors and regulatory environments
13: Gil Ayache Creating competitive intelligence	The sources and nature of information; in organizational skills	In markets, technologies and competitors
14: Dominique Jolly Evaluating technology development projects	External technological factors and companies' internal technological resources (skills and competences)	In the markets, the competitors, the technologies and the standards that are demanded
15: Mette Moensted Networking for innovation	Resources and people; how projects are created across boundaries	Know-who to get access to know-why

show different angles on this variety and uncertainty. Part II uses empirical research on different types of high-tech entrepreneurs to show the very different approaches adopted by different types of entrepreneurs. Part III looks at the different managerial functions of high-tech firms, and outlines different approaches to these functions.

ANALOGIES OF HIGH-TECH ENTREPRENEURSHIP

So we are not going to give a standard model. Such standard solutions may be good in stable conditions, but uncertainty and turbulence may call for other methods and tools that are related to this kind of context. The need for sense making, however, remains; we are only human after all. In these circumstances, some kind of structure is needed, or failing that, a narrative with dialogues and narratives that can create images and metaphors as analogies for action (Steyaert 1995). We will now conclude this introduction by drawing on the various contributions in this book to look at this complex world through two analogies.

The world of high-tech as a field of icebergs

We can envisage the environment of the high-tech firm as a field of icebergs in an inhospitable and dangerous sea. What are these icebergs? The first is the high-tech entrepreneur himself. Above the surface we see the expression of an idea, possibly a business plan. But it is what is below the surface that matters: not only the entrepreneur's skills, but character, drive, network of friends, and abilities in the face of uncertainty, setback or potential disaster.

Then we can consider the innovation, and the technology involved. Above the surface we might see an apparently coherent and definable technology. High-tech entrepreneurs, however, rarely succeed on the technology they start with: they nearly always have to change, adapt and augment their technological base. Once again, it is what is below the surface of the technology that really matters: for example, the availability of complementary technologies, and of suppliers of them, and the ability of the entrepreneurial team to combine different technologies into a value creating proposition.

Then we might think of the incubator. The incubator is one important element of the environment (or milieu) for high-tech entrepreneurship. Above the surface we have an office, perhaps some buildings, and some facilities. These may well be of value, but it is what lies below the surface that really matters: for example, the skills and experience of those involved, their networks, and their understanding of the complexities involved. We can also consider the financier. Above the surface we see an individual with access to finance, but below the surface we see a rich array of abilities and relationships that can be the difference between success and failure for the high-tech entrepreneur.

In each 'iceberg' we are dealing with things that we can see, and therefore, it is easy to think that we know. But in each case, we are only seeing the surface, the top, that which reveals itself to the travellers on the sea. There is more, much, much more, below the surface, which is difficult to see. So we are dealing with a situation of asymmetric information. Those in each 'iceberg' know that their own operation – and 'iceberg' – is full of complexities, subtle nuances, and dynamic changes that they find difficult enough to manage themselves. Each iceberg has agendas, cultures and perspectives or 'ways of thinking' that are very different to one another.

What of our environment, our sea is the environment of high-tech entrepreneurship, our 'milieu'. It can be benign, or it can be hostile. A benign environment is a clear sea, so that you can see the depth of the icebergs, and the different parties involved are able to see what they are dealing with and can make better decisions on that basis. They all need to be able to gain knowledge and understanding of the different parties involved, and the different factors involved.

From outside the 'icebergs', it is very difficult to see those agendas, and even if one is told them, to understand them because they may well be embedded within cultures, perspectives, and 'ways of thinking' that are very different to one's own. This lack of understanding, this difficulty of comprehension, generates the massive uncertainty which we emphasize in this book. The consequence of this is that there is a tremendous risk of proceeding on courses of action that will not work out, because that course of action is predicated on assumptions born of observations of the top of the 'icebergs' and without an understanding of the vast complexities that lie beneath the surface.

The world of high-tech as a tropical forest

We can also see the world of high-tech as a tropical forest. Why should we do that? It is because there are a number of features of a tropical forest that seem to hold parallels with the world that we are examining in this book; by using that analogy, we can draw some important lessons. Looked from the sky, a tropical forest can seem to be a flat green carpet; a simple world. On the face of it, the world that we are examining can also be so simple. Expressions such as 'its just a matter of putting the money together with the idea', and 'market research will establish the demand' seem to reflect this apparent simplicity.

We do not, however, have the luxury of floating about above the forest. We have to land. Having penetrated the canopy, we find a strange, dense, dark, complex, exiting, dangerous world that is rich in variety and complexity. Each business situation differs – the people involved, how they interact, and the dynamics of the technologies.

So what kind of guide might we need to understand such a world? Would it be a picture from the sky, of a green carpet? Such a 'top-down' overview might take you to the forest by air, but will be of no help within it. Will the guide have a picture of a mahogany tree, as a single idealized type of forest tree? It is possible that we may find a mahogany tree, but there are hundreds of other types of tree as well. Even mahogany trees grow in different ways. What of the land that the trees grow in, the hills and the earth, the climate and the rainfall that feeds in? And what also of the animals that live in the trees, that both feed off them and which pollinate them and allow them to breed and spread? And what of the trees that die, that decompose and feed both different types and of animals and ultimately future generations of trees?

Like the tropical forest, the world of high-tech entrepreneurship is a rich, vibrant and exiting world full of variety and uncertainty. A simple guide will not only not do, it will mislead. Instead, we need a rich feeling for our world, and the diverse contributions within this book will begin to give just that.

Part I

Uncertainty and innovation in entrepreneurship

Mette Moensted

The first section of this book is concerned with uncertainty as the basis for entrepreneurship, innovation and advanced high-tech. Innovation processes, and how innovation is organized under conditions both of environmental uncertainty and high complexity, is analysed with an organization and competence perspective. The starting point is that if there were certainty, the market mechanism would leave no opportunities for entrepreneurship to exploit. The fluidity and uncertainty of innovation processes pose special problems. These include methodological problems, for example in measuring fluid and chaotic processes. They also include communication problems, between the entrepreneurs on the one hand, and the experts, customers, and investors who are likely to be outside the narrow field of expertise of the high-tech firm's advanced technology on the other hand.

Most economic development and marketing models are based on the evaluation of known factors and the stochastic evaluation of risks. Radical innovations may question these basic conditions that underlie most business development models. For firms that thrive in and on chaos or uncertainty, new ways of iterative decision processes in project management are needed. Experts in large stable customer firms or in venture capital organizations think in terms of the classical models of business development, which is linearly, and which relies on experience. The problem, however, is that in radical innovations, we cannot expect history to repeat itself. Chapters 2, 3 and 5 discuss these conditions for high-tech entrepreneurial processes.

Understanding high-tech entrepreneurs in complex and uncertain environments is quite fundamental for communicating with and persuading customers and investors. This chapter tries to get closer to the radical innovation and early technological development that is an embedded part of the innovation process.

In Chapter 2 Mette Moensted analyses the uncertainty concept as an embedded part of innovation. The search for new knowledge at the boundaries of the organization may be the foundation for creativity, but it also creates vulnerability and risk in entrepreneurial young high-tech firms. The whole process of innovation opens new fields unknown before, intrinsic aspects of radical innovation and of new advanced high-technologies. Creating and enacting a new industry happens before we have knowledge, not after. Young high-tech firms without an established record have to develop projects beyond the resources of their own firm, and they have to create mechanisms to act and decide.

The rhetoric and communication within the scientific communities of practice can form platforms of understanding the differences that matter. The difficulty is in effectively communicating the entrepreneurial growth potential to other groups outside those scientific or technological communities of practice, to groups of experts, customers and investors who are likely to have different mindsets. One of the issues then is how entrepreneurs can create credibility and trust among those outside their own communities of practice, and how at least some of those outside those communities of practice are able to understand the innovation process sufficiently to allow high-tech firms to be created.

In Chapter 3 Ludovic Dibiaggio discusses why Schumpeter's statement of 'small is beautiful' is still valid, but only for high-tech firms in complex environments. The innovation is not considered a homogeneous and uniform process, but is based on various dynamics of learning and knowledge creation. The size and organizational structure of firms has a strong effect on the efficiency of the firm's innovation process.

In environments of radical uncertainty, normal cause and effect relationships do not work. Here, because complex uncertain situations do not succumb to standardization, the standardization procedures that large firms rely on for competitive advantage do not work either. Large firms have lots of other advantages in terms of resources, capacities, and control, but they have less autonomy for flexibility and radical change. Small firms show greater abilities in creating new organizations of more variety of form, within networks, and may do this in very flexible ways, as they are unencumbered by there being established organizations which need to be turned-around first. So here is a niche capability in which small entrepreneurial firms can excel, for handling dynamic, complex, and unpredictable problems, through new forms of absorptive capacity, also examined further in Chapter 5. A case study illustrates some of these features in an illuminating way.

In Chapter 4 Alain Fayolle raises interesting issues as to whether engineers are really high-tech entrepreneurs. As high-tech innovation demands insight in advanced technology by scientists and engineers, these are potentially the high-tech entrepreneurs and interesting partners in the field, and their career patterns are important for recruitment of high-tech entrepreneurs.

The French engineer-entrepreneurs are engineers who follow a special career path. French engineers are graduating from elite institutes of higher learning, and seem to identify with the technical culture. Very few become entrepreneurs. They are compared with German and Dutch engineers, showing different patterns and other identities in management. These engineers should be the foremost basis for recruitment for high-tech entrepreneurs, as they have the technical expertise and the ideas for high-tech innovation. The analysis of the identity of engineers both before and after the creation of these firms shows interesting surprising patterns through a longitudinal study of their careers.

In Chapter 5, Valérie-Inès de La Ville analyses innovation as a collective learning process. The barriers and resistance to radical innovation is analysed within a longitudinal case study of a software company. Innovation is analysed as a social process, which develops in an unplannable and unknowable way, as it is based on both uncertainty and high level of complexity. By looking at dramatic and radical innovation as a collective process of interaction and sense making, technological innovation is seen to be related to the skills and competence of the firm. The social processes involved show the dependency on sharing the ways of understanding between those involved, for improvization to occur. The interaction between people builds up a fragile dynamic capability that is related to the organization and to the competing tasks of the developers.

A continual process of improvization is an essential element of technological innovation, and of entrepreneurship. It is akin to the perception of the process of development as a journey, discussed in Chapter 2. To understand the improvization that lies at the heart of high-tech entrepreneurship, it is necessary to identify the specific social characteristics within the technological 'field' involved, and also to distinguish the 'technique' from the 'technological development' that is required. Here, Alain Fayolle's engineering identity in Chapter 4, and his distinction of 'technique', is particularly relevant.

The first part of this book creates a framework for understanding the specific nature of high-tech entrepreneurship, in its organization, its innovation processes, its skills and its people. Opening up the uncertainty and complexity develops a foundation for understanding the processes of building high-tech firms.

Chapter 2

High-tech, uncertainty and innovation

The opportunity for high-tech entrepreneurship

Mette Moensted

> Reasonable men adapt themselves to their environment; unreasonable men try to adapt their environment to themselves. Thus, all progress is the result of the efforts of unreasonable men.
>
> (George Bernard Shaw)

Why should we look at uncertainty as a framework for understanding high-tech entrepreneurs and innovation? If there was transparency and certainty, the market mechanism would be perfect and no opportunities would be left un-exploited. Uncertainty is a basis for new ideas, allowing new knowledge to be generated, but also combats and controls in the process of establishing and driving innovation. This in itself is a paradox, but some of uncertainty's characteristics are tied to different understandings of the concept of uncertainty.

Innovation and high-tech are both based on new ideas and new technology, which in the early stages are characterized by opportunities to be developed and by knowledge 'not-yet-known'. Specifically, high-tech and innovation in small firms could be characterized as exploring and exploiting opportunities under a high level of uncertainty. The innovation perspective is tied to what will knowledge be and how markets will develop in the future. The further ahead in the future, the higher the level of uncertainty, as we cannot foresee the future. Managers' ability to handle uncertainty and manage the process of innovation in an uncertain environment is the basis for creating and developing growth potential.

Creativity and entrepreneurship are tied to action and exploitation of opportunities, and a perspective of embedded uncertainty creates a framework for understanding the concepts. Malecki (1991) takes the argument beyond the firm to the region, arguing that the instability and uncertainty that together improve entrepreneurship are created by unexpected events and inter-firm rivalry, as well as by fluidity and diversification. This may easily be transferred to a regional ability to create new organizations, products and firms, depending on high-tech entrepreneurs' ability to handle and thrive on uncertainty (Leonard and Sensiper 1998).

Innovation processes are not only based on uncertainty; they also create uncertainty. Leavitt (1986) develops his ideas of pathfinders in the organization as a perspective of understanding some of the paradoxes of managing innovations. The need for the pathfinder to be creative disturbs balances and creates uncertainty in the organization, and can threaten current efficiency. But if innovations are necessary in the long run, then this process is important, and others in organizations have to manage the implementations of the projects that result.

UNCERTAINTY AS A BASIS FOR INNOVATION

It is tempting to distinguish risk from uncertainty. The distinction could actually go further, to perceive uncertainty as a contextual condition that is part of chance and opportunity on the one hand, and risks involving estimable probabilities of failures in the operation on the other hand. In economic considerations it is often assumed that maximization of efficiency cannot be achieved under a high level of uncertainty, i.e. when 'agents cannot anticipate the outcome of a decision and cannot assign probabilities to the outcome' (Beckert 1996: 804). Making this distinction between risk and uncertainty is not new; Knight (1921) distinguished between changes in the economy to which probabilities can be assigned and situations where the individual has no information on which to base calculation of probabilities. The first type Knight calls 'situations of risk', and the latter, 'uncertainty' (Beckert 1996: 807).

Many researchers' concern is for uncertainty as the condition for entrepreneurship and innovation. Julien and Marchesnay (1996) interestingly distinguish between uncertainty as conditions for entrepreneurship, and various kinds of risks as the improbable or unlikely. Like Knight, they tie the concept of risk to variables with low probabilities, a perception also shared by Perrow in *Normal Accidents* (1984). In Perrow's interpretation, high-tech in the chemical and nuclear industries works with an evaluation of risk and probabilities of a combination of errors, within a framework of limiting the probabilities of risk.

Daft and Lengel (1992) change the concept, and distinguish uncertainty from equivocality. Uncertainty refers to clearly formulated questions with right or wrong answers, and equivocality refers to situations where not only the answers are missing, but the questions themselves are unclear. Equivocality thus becomes more like the ambiguity and the embedded uncertainty of innovation tied to communication media and communication richness, discussed extensively here. Daft and Lengel (1992) claim that written communication may reduce uncertainty, but only face-to-face communication, with the richness that it implies, may be used to reduce equivocality (ibid). The complexity, and thus the dependency, of communicating in dialogue rather than in serial monologue communication – such as in writing, including in emails – creates a dependency on local networks or communities of practice where signs and forms of tacit knowledge may be shared to some extent. ICT people, for example, do not only use electronic connections, but also use face-to-face communications and local networks (Jensen *et al.* 2004).

In order to understand entrepreneurial action and the perception of opportunity, the concepts of uncertainty, persuasion, and the creation of trust will have to be linked to other concepts of influence and dependency. A 'quantitatively' high level of uncertainty and low inertia seems to change not only the qualitative conditions for action, but also changes the decision structures, communication and organizational forms. As a manager in a firm working with artificial intelligence declared:

> This firm may disappear from one day to another, as it is based on trust and references. There is no inertia as in production firms.

This is one of the specific characteristics of high-tech entrepreneurship, here seen especially in ICT, and is one of the reasons for questioning the limitations of models of development taken from firms in more stable environments.

These arguments do not imply that everything is based on serendipity, and that we have to wait for opportunities to show up by chance. Atherton (1997) links uncertainty directly and indirectly to the context of entrepreneurs, and to possibilities of manoeuvring and influencing through a variety of channels and mechanisms. Entrepreneurship is action, and the exploring and exploiting of opportunities. The next step for the entrepreneur is to persuade others, and uncertainty has to be communicated as opportunity with low uncertainty – in itself, a paradox.

One small Danish firm had problems persuading a large customer that they had an exceptional innovation, and that, though small, they had solved a problem that large American companies could not. One condition for establishing expectations and confidence is the number of inventors and charlatans promising 'rose gardens'. These promise-making 'crazy inventors' raise suspicion and make it difficult for serious small innovative firms to be heard. They are reminiscent of fourteenth century alchemists, where the hope of finding gold caused royal investors – the 'venture capitalists' of those days – to continue their investments for a long time. The alchemist's image maintained promise for some time, but their lack of results eventually replaced earlier expectations with a loss of credibility: in the long run, trust cannot be maintained without results. The balance between trust and documentation is a problem faced by most innovative units in the early stages. The question is, how long will customers and investors wait for results?

INNOVATION MANAGEMENT AND UNCERTAINTY

The innovation literature mostly examines large organizations and projects that have proven successful (Teece *et al.* 1987; Kanter 1983; Dosi and Fagiolo 1997). They reveal a method, well-known in most growth models, which is a kind of

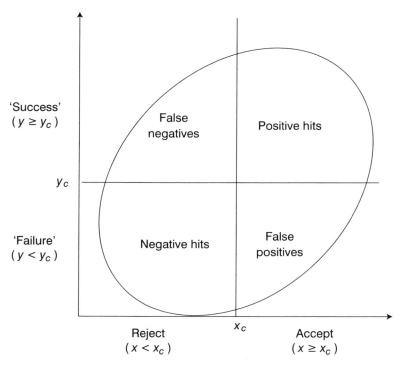

Figure 2.1 *Project selection, decision and outcomes*
Source: Garud et al. (1997), p. 25.

're-engineering of the successes' (e.g. Greiner 1972). The re-engineering perspective presume predictability, and a 'pick-the-winner' strategy, assuming an ability to define clear criteria based on experience, even though expecting history to repeat itself in conditions of radical innovation would be a paradox. The embedded uncertainty of innovation questions the usual cause and effect relationships; innovations are neither re-engineered nor imitations. Uncertainty implies that decisions often have to be taken without what could be considered a rational analytical basis. A normal problem for managers is to decide on potential innovation growth projects at an early stage of development. Here, they often face pressure both to avoid failures of investments in 'false positives' – type I errors – and also projects later proven successful in other contexts, i.e. 'false negatives' or type II errors (Garud *et al.* 1997: 25). This is shown in Figure 2.1.

The general idea of sorting negatives from positives is fundamental to the whole study of innovation and the management of knowledge. It is tied to decisions of managers, and to decision of investors, both trying to find recognisable clues to development. The high level of uncertainty means many errors, and 'war-stories' of both failures and successes are abundant in ex-post interpretations.

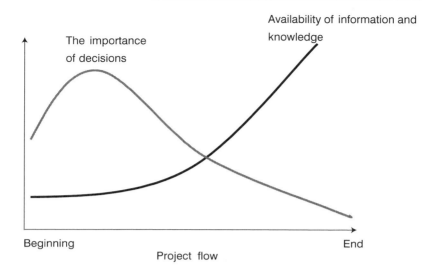

Figure 2.2 *The importance of decisions and the knowledge basis for decisions*
Source: Mikkelsen and Riis (1998), p. 62

The serendipity element is based on the fact that decisions are taken before we have knowledge and not after. This presumes that empirical experience from development projects is the basis for visions and strategy models, reacting as if information is more predictable (Stacey 1992). Ex-post fallacies may create the assumption that we could have predicted and found the knowledge. In most of these innovations, however, there is no chance of finding the unknowable except after the event.

Figure 2.2 shows a model is built on the experience that the most important decisions, with the greatest implications, are made in the early stages, before relevant knowledge is available. Early decisions are based on a high level of uncertainty, but still have to be taken and cannot wait for the necessary knowledge to be generated. The timing of decisions in innovation projects is a challenging and stressful factor for innovation management. The task is to create meaning and to enact a platform for decisions that is based on the not-yet-known, or on some kind of intuition.

Most innovations are not radical, but represent small increments of 'normal change' that refine and improve projects. These are easier to understand and to invest in, since they do not make large changes, and usually allow for a proper technology and market analysis to be undertaken. In some cases, though, it may generate real innovative processes, in what Raghu Garud, based on a study in 3M, calls 'mindful replications' (Garud 2004).

In the early stages of development, high level of uncertainty makes the distinction between 'facts' and 'virtual facts' very difficult. It is very unclear what the 'real' facts are, which arguments are based on facts or tests, and which are based on 'daydreams' or 'virtual facts'. Fundamental innovations are set in motion in a sequence of events that can change the need for competences; 'these innovations have a transilient ... capacity to transform established systems of technology as well as markets' (Van de Ven and Garud, 1989: 196). In microelectronics, for example, instruments for testing have to be developed while the products themselves are developed (Larsen 2001). The secrecy necessary at an early stage makes it even more difficult to create credible scientific arguments for legitimacy and, in these circumstances, it is difficult also to find experts to legitimize them. This is part of a fundamental paradox that sets the scene for most innovation decisions.

The anxiety arising from the high level of uncertainty within radical innovations has been found in a number of other studies (Oakey *et al.* 1990; Herlau and Tetzschner 1999; Elfring and Foss 1997). A tendency towards a preference for small incremental adaptations is further supported by impatience in evaluation, and the need for predictability on the part of investors and managers. The evaluation systems and economic rationality used may use efficiency criteria from another context based on 'weapons from the last war'. This creates a barrier against experimentation, which limits long-run effectiveness. A tendency towards incremental changes arises from the constraints on and the fear of the exploration of fundamental innovations.

The problem is how to perceive radical innovations? Some are like a series of actions where a number of incremental innovations together gradually constitute a radical change, rather than a planned breakthrough. In an analysis of biotech firms in Europe, Rip and Velde (1997) provide a narrative depicting the early innovation processes as 'a journey', where new product experiences and changes in perception arise on the journey. It is not a linear, programmed process to find specified solutions to a very specific problem. Instead, problems, questions and solutions appear during the journey, which may easily end up going somewhere other than originally intended. This perspective is akin to the 'garbage can' model (March and Olsen 1976), focusing on a competent expert team working in a promising innovative field, which assumes that the team has the competence to create innovative solutions.

The whole question of what is high-tech or biotech is not always clear. Oakey *et al.* (1990) characterize biotechnology production 'with high levels of research and intellectual inputs to value added and high value per unit of weight' (Oakey *et al.* 1990: 69). This feature covers both the innovation, the growth potential and the intellectual input and forms the basis of the kind of relationships that the biotech people develop within the industry and with universities. Arie Rip and Robbin te Velde (1997), in their analysis of biotechnological innovation projects, perceive 'product creation processes as innovation journeys with several setbacks along the road'. This means that 'innovation success might be more usefully viewed as "by-products along the journey" than as end results' (Rip and Velde 1997: 12). See Table 2.1.

Table 2.1 *Comparing conventional wisdom with a modern biotechnology study*

Element	Conventional wisdom	Modern biotechnology study
Ideas:	One invention, operationalzed	Reinvention, proliferation, re-implementation, discarding and termination
People:	An entrepreneur with fixed set of full-time people over time	Many entrepreneurs, distracted, fluidly engaging and disengaging over time in a variety of organizational roles
Transactions:	Fixed network of people/firms working out details of an idea	Expanding and contracting network of partisan stakeholders diverging and converging on ideas
Context:	Environment provides opportunities and constraints on innovation process	Innovation process is constrained by and creates multiple enacted environments
Outcomes:	Final result orientation; a stable new order comes into being	Final result may be indeterminate; multiple in-process assessments and spin-offs; integration of new orders with old
Process:	Simple, cumulative sequence of stages or phases	From single to multiple progressions of divergent, parallel, and convergent paths, some of which are related and cumulative, others not

Source: Rip and Velde 1997: 13.

Rip and Velde's study, undertaken for the European Commission, raises a lot of questions, as it is difficult to communicate beyond the 'community of practice'. That group already has joint experience and expertise in the fundamental research development and in the selections made. The 'opening up' of perspectives, and the unwillingness to 'close', as the journey continues, makes it difficult to persuade complementary important groups, such as venture capitalists. If creativity and the generation of knowledge from within communities of practice is an embedded part of the research and development (R&D) culture, then it can also act as a barrier for commercialization. The process perspective, with its changing targets, makes the investment process very difficult, as it is uncertain what, at each stage, is being invested in. Development and trust form another kind of problem in sectors of ICT, where getting access to the data of the customers, without which solutions are impossible, is difficult.

Some case samples

A Danish ICT firm

A small Danish ICT firm specialized on transferring data to new mainframe platforms:

> When transferring data from one platform to another, we, as a firm, have to prove that the technology is working for the customer. When

systems are revised or downsized, most would like to renew the platform. Downsizing is very important in the large systems. When different systems are combined existing errors may multiply. We have to create consistency in data and applications, and then we can transfer automatically.

When conversions of the data go wrong, it is really serious. The development of the expertise in doing these transformations, which runs at night automatically, are highly secret, and the packaging of this is fundamental for the knowledge and competitive status of the firm. I make demonstrations on small data to prove to customers that it is possible, even if everybody admits that up- and downsizing is not a simple matter. But it helps customers to understand, and also to negotiate conditions and price of hardware. We now have a good reference list of customers as a part of our legitimacy.

A Danish AI firm

This artificial intelligence based datamining firm finds it difficult to communicate issues of uncertainty to customers. First, they have to create a pilot project on a small section of data, as a kind of prototype in order to create a basis for the decision. But the time lapse between the first positive acceptance and the pilot project may well be one year. Then another year is easily gone for the real project, and other changes may have to be included as the technology is changing. It is a new project in many ways.

Intermediaries are necessary to create a framework for credibility. The board and a board member, who has the personal credibility of institutional investors, may translate the perspectives to applicability and usefulness:

> We work hard to create credibility. There is no uncertainty on the implementation, in terms of technical uncertainty, and we are very concerned about time schedules. We can create engagement, but have to have customers as a reference. It is a very reference-dependent technology. References have to be large customers, as customers see university references as a negative signal that the technology is not 'proven technology', but experimentation. We do not feel we lack credibility because we are small. But our board of directors stresses that the capital behind us is an important part of the credibility image.

The development of technology in the field of artificial intelligence is so rapid that the demand for proven technology means old and often poorer solutions, than the newer, which has not been tested on a number of firms. Some of these developments are new and, with large datasets, it is unsurprising that customers may be worried. The level of uncertainty, mostly as 'not knowing' and 'not proven', is high and this creates difficult decision conditions for customers. The rhetoric on uncertainty among ICT people is also likely to create uncertainty outside their own community of practice, in whom the concept of newer versions of technology itself is translated to 'risk' rather than 'opportunity':

> Within multimedia, technology is changing rapidly, new tools emerge on the Internet every third week, and while planning the project, and deciding together with the customer, new tools pop up and change conditions. Customers are slow in deciding and cannot evaluate the quality of the offers at very different prices. A CD-ROM project could be offered at 25,000 € or for 140,000 €. The lack of transparency and rapid technology changes creates a high level of uncertainty for small high tech firms as well as for the customers. Thus, customers may have difficulties in formulating what they want, and it is certain that they do not know what they get.

Many innovators present an image of themselves as geniuses and others – such as customers and collaborators – as idiots who do not understand their genius. This may block information exchange and serious dialogue, making it hard to break the ice and to create legitimacy in the innovation. In service firms, innovators cannot document or test their products for customers (Normann 1984), so some serious innovation firms are classified as 'alchemists' and are rejected at this very early stage by possible customers, investors or partners. Without documentation, innovation may easily be perceived as unrealistic or, at least, far from market.

Legitimacy has to be created through collaboration in order to establish practical use of the invention. According to Gibbons *et al.* (1994), knowledge is also created in practice, where customers are involved in the process of development, as was noted in the firm:

> Within artificial intelligence, technology is difficult to understand, and communication with customers about the methods and tools may be problematic. The early theoretical developments were very advanced, and there were problems applying them to large data sets. Customers often considered artificial intelligence as a concept and method too uncertain, and all references to complicated methods or to universities only seemed to increase uncertainty. Projects had to be re-labelled. It was necessary to change some of the concepts, as was necessary in other parts of Europe. In order to signal that this is proven technology, the concepts have changed, because of the poor reputation associated with artificial intelligence and datamining as too many firms cannot really deliver the content. It is difficult to communicate our knowledge to customers. How can we explain the difference that makes a difference?

In this case, these problems of communication still exist, but in the early phases, projects were developed by applying theoretical tools. The identification of hand-written figures on postal orders was not just an application, but also a development project, but one that had to be sold as 'proven technology' to persuade customers.

KNOWLEDGE CREATION DILEMMAS

The perception of knowledge generation seems to have changed, and in a number of research fields it is related to context and to inter-organizational alliances, rather than to the centralized production of knowledge in laboratories. Gibbons *et al.* (1994) analyse the traditional structure of knowledge production, emphasizing the wider implications for firms and for research institutions. Universities and private large firms' research centres concentrate on their own scientific knowledge, and emphasize the importance of R&D as vehicles. They see small firms as receivers of innovative knowledge and as applicants of new knowledge, in a linear process of knowledge production.

They then analyse the change from this linear 'Mode 1' disciplinary based knowledge creation process, to a 'Mode 2' trans-disciplinary applied development and knowledge generation process. This perspective changes the importance not only of universities and traditional centres of knowledge generation, but also of small firms, which may be partners and actors in their own and in joint projects of innovation. In other words, there is a change from having a dependent role of 'receiving' research results, to being an active player which generates new knowledge, alone or with others. The effect is a transformation of the perception of science, to include knowledge generation within practice contexts and within contextual meaning. This raises fundamental questions concerning when knowledge is scientific and how knowledge may obtain legitimacy as recognized knowledge. Latour (1987), for example, studies the legitimacy of scientific findings via references, and discusses how findings become true, when scientists are convinced, or when the right scientists are convinced that the findings are true (Figure 2.3).

In a study of scientific work and uncertainty, it is stressed that the problems of absorbing anomalies, and of transforming local uncertainties to global certainty by convincing the scientific world of the validity of a model or finding. In a mode 2 perspective, the uncertainty tied to taxonomy and diagnostics may reveal some of the limitations of existing explanations, and contribute to the local uncertainty. The outcome and acceptance of new ideas depends on the technical and political uncertainty or on the frameworks used.

The linear thinking in innovation and technology, however, is quite widespread. It has managed to create the models used in evaluating radical innovations in entrepreneurial firms, and creating greater difficulties of credibility for these projects. Callon (1991) makes a discrepancy between 'the technical pole', a scientific pole with certified knowledge, that develops prototypes, and 'the market pole' in the

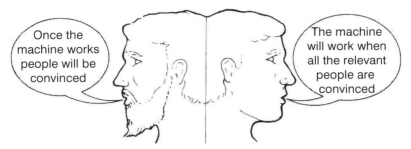

Figure 2.3 *Latour's Janus dictum*

Source: Latour (1987), p.10.

user-consumer relations, which is where many scientific projects reside – e.g. in military R&D or nuclear technology, in biotech and ICT.

When requested knowledge is not known and cannot be foreseen, communication is challenging. As Hastings beautifully notes: 'The trouble is I don't know whom I don't know and I don't know what I need to know that I don't already know' (Hastings 1993: 130). This calls for dialogues, and the gradual sense making of projects from a vague vision. The relations between people in dialogue, exchanging what they do not know, seem to form the basis for the questioning and for development of innovative knowledge (Katzenbach and Smith 1993; Gibbons *et al.* 1994). The lack of predictability makes communication and persuasion of other experts difficult, who often have to lean on other experts' recommendation.

In early stages of innovation, when uncertainty is high, classical 'Taylorist' divisions of labour are inappropriate and classic hierarchies and management control seem impossible when knowledge is created in dialogue, or when 'the game is created while playing'(Garud and Lant 1997), with knowledge being created in horizontal interactions:

> One of the reasons that knowledge is too costly to be generated in-house is that firms are unsure about the particular knowledge they need and another is that, even if they can identify this knowledge, it is often difficult to gain access to it.
>
> (Gibbons *et al.* 1994: 115)

This fundamental issue of the lack of specified knowledge has implications for managing towards other forms of horizontal co-ordination. Problems and solutions cannot be defined in advance, because they grow out of frequent informal communications between the people involved (Daft and Lengel 1992). Organizing not only implies action rationality, but also commitment, as teams cannot proceed if participants are not committed, challenged and motivated by exploring and experimentation (Grant and Baden-Fuller 2000; Coase 1988).

The needs for organizing and for creativity are considered further by Leonard and Sensiper (1998), who stress heterogeneity as a factor for opening the space of opportunities and thus for entrepreneurship and innovation. The knowledge creation system in small biotechnology and computing firms seems to contextually applied knowledge generation rather than to a revision involving receivers and consumers of knowledge (Cook and Brown 1999).

A case of a small biotech company illustrates this well. An expert in extraction from plants in the pharmaceutical industry in a small firm initiates a dialogue with medical doctors and biochemical researchers on the valerian plant as a tranquillizer. This opens new possibilities as the team includes other competencies and options outside the biochemical field. Several groups of researchers have tried, but failed. The young biotech researcher in the dialogue with the existing team has the intuition of a few possibilities of solving the precise extraction part of the problem. He does not describe this as trial-and-error, 'as this would take too long', but rather a sense or intuition of a few possibilities, which may extract only the active matter, but leave those with the side effects.

This is a project which could easily be perceived as chance or serendipity, rather than any kind of organized effort to create innovations. As Pasteur said 'chance favours only the prepared minds'. The various experts in medicine and pharmaceutical research lacked the joint understanding of the active ingredients, plant medicine and plant extraction as a 'space' for generating new alternatives where an openness to share 'the not-yet-known and uncertainty' actually created the innovation. Chance and serendipity are essential for innovations to perceive the difference that makes sense out of fragments or distinguishes sense from non-sense. Serendipity, the luck necessary for the creation of new inventions within science, does not occur for everyone, but only occurs if expertise for the creation of meaning is present. This perspective on uncertainty directly differs from that in economics, where uncertainty is perceived not as serendipity and opportunity, but as risk and anxiety of the unknown, so fundamental innovations are avoided and incremental changes dominate (Moensted 2003).

The problem with these types of development is the perception of the loosening ties between cause and effect (Stacey 1996). The linearity and the meaning of linear cause and effect disappear – which opens the question of how these projects can be evaluated. Most evaluation systems cling to well-defined cause-effect relations, acting 'as-if-certainty' prevails, even if they know uncertainty prevails. Models are used to create at least a feeling of certainty, and systems that were developed to and which reflect 'the last war' change uncertainty to confusion.

SKILLS AND COMPETENCES

A small firm project manager's ability to lead the process of innovation in an uncertain environment is the basis here for understanding the conditions and development of small high-tech firms. It does not relate clearly to a well defined skill. What do skills, expertise and competence mean for small firms and for understanding technology in this context? It is not always clear what kind of expertise is needed, and how it can play in with other skills and competences. The social context and the role of third parties outside the firm, who can legitimize knowledge, are important for understanding the action required and the application of knowledge. As an ICT firm manager in Sophia Antipolis remarked:

> This firm is a commercial business. There is much more than technology in this. It is the combination of different skills and networks, which forms the firm. In this field you cannot develop a prototype and then try to sell it. This is not possible. You have to be close to the market and know the needs and the possible prices. I have never seen a project develop from start to finish without considerable changes. The technology changes and the customers do not really know what is possible or what they want. Insight and dialogue are part of our profession. But it is nearly impossible to explain to finance/banking people.

This ICT specialist is an expert on the technology, but works in a team with people who have insight into the profession and the market. This customer expertise is necessary both to translate technological ideas to implementation, and to create trust.

One problem is: Who is the expert, if you are the first inventor? This issue of expertise at the forefront of technology is a problem in most of the advanced ICT world. It is embedded in the knowledge creation process. With the rapidity of technological change, expertise gets obsolete very quickly. There are many experts whose credibility is tied to the inability to evaluate solutions. Once we leave the linear scientific model – where knowledge is generated at universities, stamped as scientific, and then disseminated – then there is a problem in distinguishing science, knowledge, contextual meaning and professional insight (Gibbons *et al.* 1994). Neither access to new technology, nor professional insight alone creates the necessary expertise. It is their combination that is both the basis of expertise and applied knowledge, and is the basis for developing opportunities for the commercial use of technology. Innovations may challenge existing scientific paradigms and accepted knowledge and experimental break-outs are needed if inertia is to be overcome (Fischoff *et al.* 1997: 309). What creates new knowledge is the questioning and the change in meaning which make it possible to make new choices. A meaningless message does not allow for decision and action, but ambiguous messages do enable more interpretations, and thus enable more possible actions (Langlois 1997: 72; Garud 1997).

If information is not embedded and applicable to be related to other forms of knowledge, information overflow results, which creates neither action nor better decisions. Oakey *et al.* (1990) argue that the quality of information of full-time researchers in very tight collaborations is much better than external information. The experimental nature of research processes and joint experiences are part of this tacit knowledge in the generation of knowledge. Such processes may reveal the nature of knowledge generation in science, where it is not a 'thing', but a process and interaction, where meaning is constructed with other researchers (see also Stacey 2001; Daft and Lengel 1992).

The criteria for what is knowledge also differ in different disciplines. While knowledge is 'what works' within a number of ICT projects, this would not be enough in the biotech industry. As an entrepreneur in a small firm specializing in transfers of mainframe systems with data to a new platform, where credibility to touch data is important, noted:

> New corporations are suspicious and doubt it is possible, what we claim we can do, namely protect data, and then do the last automatic transfer overnight. The initial demonstration is important. But without references we would not get access to data. The process is complex, but when we tried in a large case with large data, we found it worked. I really do not know why. The most important thing is that we do not have any failures. This is important, because if there are errors in the system, a lot of other things may go wrong. It creates chaos when new elements and products are added to a complex programme. In this trade of ICT, it is only reputation and rumours, and this decides whether customers will use you.

Concepts and models are tied to stability and repetition/inertia. But in fundamental innovations and much high-tech, change and dynamics are dominating features, and the driving force for development. Innovation and implicit or tacit knowledge generate a high level of uncertainty, which makes it difficult to create meaning in context. This does not, however, mean chaos. The uncertainty may impede action with analysts, or may result in work by planners and consultants. In interviews, founders of small high-tech firms confirm that their uncertainty keeps them alert, listening to options in the environment, and making quick decisions based on sense-making from fragments or knowledge and information. Karl Weick (2002) emphasizes how time and timing help decision makers, as many dilemmas and paradoxes are only constructed in ex-post analysis. Dilemmas do not block decisions, as these are not obvious at the time. The dilemma between creativity and control is always present in the management of knowledge, for the opening up of opportunities, but also for the implementation of projects and the finishing of products.

What are the skills and competences required to create creativity? Do they allow intuition and present conditions for playfulness? There seems to be an epistemological dance between knowledge and knowing (Cook and Brown 1999) or a vague defined journey (Rip and van de Velde 1997), where goals and milestones are unclear as if driving through fog (Brown 1997). Pathfinders practise innovative and forward iterative thinking, whereas analytical backward thinkers rely on expertise and legitimacy (Leavitt 1986). The two types are not necessarily easy to handle on the same projects or at the same time. The competences for creativity and entrepreneurship are not easily developed in large firms. Various cases and projects within ICT and biomedicine show the need for pathfinders in project management and for holistic perspectives, even if these entrepreneurs also create uncertainty and stress in the organization (ibid., see also Quinn 1988; Van de Ven and Garud 1989).

The complexity of high-tech projects makes them extremely difficult to understand. From the outside, it could appear to be a series of coincidences, even with an element of 'chaos' or trial and error, often described as serendipity and chance, but this element of chance, combined with high-tech knowledge and insight represents some of the complexity of the 'tacit knowledge' of scientific work. Complexity is easily lost, and simple indicators may provide a biased picture of the process.

UNCERTAINTY AND TRUST

In the process of early innovation and when there are high levels of uncertainty, trust surfaces as an important concept for understanding decisions and for the creation of meaning. The systemic vulnerability dominates, and trust-creation becomes an important part of the development of social relations (Luhmann 1979). Trust is linked to technological uncertainty, to reliability to produce, to collaboration and especially to network relations. Uncertainty in technology is linked to the credibility of the people recommending the technological potential.

Trust is also related to both institutional credibility and to social and business relations. Calculated trust (Williamson 1993) is limited to certain transactions such as projects, time and space. Collaboration around the development of a new pharmaceutical product requires trust to involve human resources and investments for the first step, in moving to the first milestone, and in allowing for delays and errors. Trust does not necessarily imply a naïve confidence or full commitment without analysis or reservations. An engineer in Silicon Valley notes:

> The risk in sharing information and recommending others in networks is a kind of support, which is possible for peers and large firms in the first steps, until the small young firm itself may achieve the credibility in handling problems and project development. This may be perceived as a mentor model of building network support

Trust is closely linked to communication about the uncertainty that is the ideas that are not yet documented but are still ideas. The lack of transparency and predictability in a technology is the platform upon which to evaluate competence, capability, legitimacy, credibility and trust.

Granovetter and Swedberg (1992) note 'the necessity of trust for normal functioning of economic action and institutions', especially in complex transactions. The trust element and the conditions for building trust relations are embedded in the network approach because any kind of returns or 'payments' are delayed. Without trust relations there would be no networks (see also Chapters 7 and 16).

Trust relations may compensate for other deficiencies – such as size, power, knowledge or experience – but they cannot replace knowledge per se, they do not exclude the search for new knowledge, and they do not in any way legitimize the uncertainty. Trust in people may be important to help distinguish innovative knowledge from what are 'unrealistic dreams by alchemists', a distinction that is hard, when the experts are also the developers – since the third party experts are not readily available in advanced innovations. The issue of trust is less complicated to handle, especially since business economics seems to tie the concept either to an economically calculated rationale or to a naïve romantic, nearly religious, perspective. From the former, references in a network are used to transfer trust or credibility, among persons to recommend projects, and from institutions to yield credibility. This confidence or legitimacy may well be a condition for trust, but is not sufficient to create trust in the first place (Blomqvist 2002; Krieger 1996).

When looking at the conditions for generating trust and the situations in which you need trust to reduce costs and get access to resources, problems become evident. On the one hand, good, reputable firms are sought as partners in alliances and are trusted because of their good records. Trust is built and based on experience of being trustworthy, and is a result of success, rather than a strategy to get success. Table 2.2 shows some of the contradictions, as trust is easier if you are well established, with a good reputation, but mostly needed if you are not.

Table 2.2 Conditions for, and the need for trust

Factors favouring trust:	Need for trust, when:
Credibility of project	High uncertainty/ambiguity
Trustworthy person	No documented history
Good record of experience	Early innovation no documentation
Competence of team/people	No relevant people contacts
Good reputation	New area of work
Predictability	Rapid change
Certainty	Uncertain market
Similarity – homogeneity	Complementarity

It is primarily at the boundary of the unknown that trust is important, when small new firms and new projects have to rely on their personal credibility from earlier project work to be considered trustworthy and to be recommended by the well reputed. The trust variable thereby becomes important for persuading partners and customers, especially with projects at the early, unstable and unproven level. Trust may also be perceived as a way of limiting costs and creating commitment (Fukuyama 1995). Small young firms have to build up this trust in a step-by-step process, gradually persuading customers, partners and investors, and perhaps using other researchers in this process, just as scientists have to do when new findings are coming up (Latour 1987).

Exercising social control of peers is one way to create confidence, by enlisting people with good reputations. Financing institutions try to get peers into steering groups, boards or teams in order to form the social control groups. The peer groups are people to whom the entrepreneur wants to prove he is trustworthy. Early phases of innovation are often financed by secure investors, who have to rely heavily on people and personal recommendations. Some technical innovators do not feel the same kind of responsibility towards investors as they do to their peers. Further, peers remain important after project completion, if involvement in other projects will take place. Consequently, people and institutions belonging to different communities or social groupings may use the social control within a group as bridges to communicate between communities of practice. In this way, to create trust strategically, they use the recommendations of reputed experts.

The discrepancy between rude economic competition and naïve social trust can be described both as a dilemma and as a dimension to balance out. It may also be seen as a paradox between two paradigms. On the one hand, there is the economic power and risk evaluation, and on the other hand, there is a necessity to build on personal relations with other firms or colleagues for innovative processes in the world of the unknown. This is a contradiction, a duality, which has to be balanced; it is not a choice between two opposite poles, but a decision on which paradigm to pertain to; a puzzle, where the two paradigms cannot be seen at the same time.

CONCLUSION

The chapter opens up understanding of the foundations of innovation and entrepreneurship, based on uncertainty. The uncertainty is perceived as an embedded part of innovation, tied both to uncertainty in technology, market, expertise and the future as the setting for the innovations to come. The not-yet-known is just one embedded aspect of innovation, but the perception of influence and control becomes increasingly important for understanding the conditions for high-tech entrepreneurship growth and development. The uncertainty concept is not only part of the environment, but a part of the process, action, and interaction perspectives to communicate and persuade both customers and other experts. The ability to persuade becomes imperative to change uncertainty and risk into meaning and opportunity.

The uncertain and unpredictable innovations and the need to document results and experience represent a paradox by themselves. Young, small firms may be seen as uncertain and more risky ventures, and require new ways of looking at them. Here, the trust and the legitimacy offered by networks can be invaluable. The analysis of innovation and high-tech through the lenses of uncertainty creates a framework for understanding the limitations of using linear and static models for handling and interpreting processes of innovation. 'Uncertainty' is not 'the unknown' per se, but are the opportunities, which may represent ideas and new meanings, which become tangible innovation possibilities within appropriately knowledgeable contexts. For understanding the management process in high-tech and innovation contexts, the relationship between the known and the not-yet-known is very important.

Chapter 3

For high-tech small is beautiful

Why small firms can handle complexity better

Ludovic Dibiaggio

Research based on construct quantitative correlations between company size and the efficiency of research and development – R&D – tends to highlight the advantages of large companies with regard to innovation. The objective of this chapter is to show that innovation cannot be considered as a homogenous and uniform process. Rather, we should distinguish between the different forms of innovation, and the efficiency in a firm in each depends on specific capabilities, which we will specify. By examining different dynamic processes of learning and knowledge creation, we demonstrate that the choice of organizational structure has a major effect on the efficiency of the company's innovation process. We then demonstrate that an intrinsic organizational advantage can exist for small firms when the environment is a complex one, and is characterized by high levels of uncertainty and unstable technological choices.

Since Schumpeter (1950), the literature has traditionally considered that technological innovation, in the long run, is the preserve of large companies, because of their capacities to wield power over the market, to achieve economies of scale in R&D, and to mobilize the necessary capital. In particular, these companies also capture quasi-rents which are guaranteed by their dominant position. These quasi-rents enable these larger companies to compensate for the risks involved in innovation, which supposedly explains why only large companies are in a position to exploit new technologies. Microsoft is often cited as an example of a company which can, more or less at will, reallocate its investments and become a leader in areas which it had previously neglected, as it has done this, for example, in markets linked to the internet and in video-games. Many empirical studies have apparently confirmed this as a general finding, by identifying a link between firm size, economies of scale, and economies of scope (for example Cohen and Levin 1987; Sherer 1991).

This perspective, however, raises a major question. How are we to explain the survival of smaller firms and the regular entry of new entrepreneurial firms into a game where there said to be only room for course players with specific and persistent advantages? How are we to explain the recent growth in the importance of SMEs in various branches of industry – for example, as found by the Groupe de Recherche et Economie en Gestion des PME in 1993? How are we to justify the survival of small companies – at least marginally – in all situations and in all sectors? If we take a closer look at the above-mentioned studies, we notice that the quantitative criteria they use to measure innovation are at the very least, questionable. In fact, the only indicators used are the volume or percentage of turnover devoted to R&D, and the number of patents applied for.

This approach, however, does not take account of phenomena such as spin-offs or spill-overs, which are known characteristics of start-ups. Spin-offs are companies created as a result of projects which started off in big companies. They are often created by entrepreneurs frustrated by the lack of support for their project from the management of larger firms (Dibiaggio 1998). The contribution of these start-ups is often based on a continuous innovation process in which companies within a network are stakeholders in an innovative project. This interaction produces spill-overs, where the sources of the innovation are various, and cannot be determined. Finally, the number of patent applications does not represent the success of small innovating firms, because the cost of making these applications is so high that they do not do so.

Research shows that the link between the firm size and the intensity of R&D depends strongly on the sector under consideration (Cohen *et al.* 1987). Small firms play an important role in the innovation process (for example Acs and Audrestch 1993), particularly in industries where there are few economies of scale in R&D. There are many explanations for the survival of small firms, but an important one concerns the personal motivation of the involved, and this is based on ownership rights. Berle and Means (1932) emphasized how owner-entrepreneurs can be much more motivated to complete a project over which he or she has complete control, compared with an employee who may not benefit from the resulting profits. However, over and above psychological explanations, the main argument lies in the drawbacks inherent in the bureaucratization of decision-making in large companies. A project requiring investment in R&D has to satisfy a greater number of criteria and hierarchical levels in large companies compared with smaller ones (Sherer 1988, 1991).

This is particularly relevant for small high-tech firms. Many engineers or researchers prefer to work in a convivial atmosphere, within a close-knit team, rather than within structures which are hierarchical and which suffer from bureaucratic inertia (Link and Bozeman 1991). The organizational flexibility of small firms can encourage relationships with universities, which in turn are more inclined to learn and to integrate new knowledge from their relationships with industry. Acs *et al.* (1993a) show that spill-overs from university laboratories contribute more to innovation in small than in large companies. More recently, from studying learning processes in start-ups, Almeida *et al.* (2003) show that while opportunities for learning from other companies are greater in large start-ups compared with smaller ones, the process of effective learning is lower. In other words, when start-ups get bigger, they have more opportunities to exploit their partners' knowledge base, but their effective exploitation of these opportunities diminishes.

Finally, by studying all forms of innovation – innovations as cited in official statistics or in specialized journals – Acs and Audretsch (1993) show that the nature of the relationship between the intensity of innovation and company size changes depending on whether the context is that of high-tech or low-tech industries. The innovation capacities of large firms seem to yield decreasing returns as soon as the context is no longer a traditional one, such as the agro-food industry.

This chpater explores why small firms attain better organizational performances in high-tech activities. First, we specify different forms of innovation related to the complexity of the technological environment in question. We then outline the factors inherent to these specific forms that speed up or slow down technological innovation. This helps to show a link between the size of the firm, its organizational structure, and its performance in terms of innovation, and enables us to demonstrate the organizational advantage of the small firm in especially dynamic innovating activities. We conclude by illustrating our argument with a case study of a Sophia Antipolis start-up specialized in the area of emulators and semi-conductors.

UNCERTAINTY, LEARNING AND INNOVATION

Innovation is always a step into the unknown, where serendipity plays a significant role. Uncertainty, like a question to which one is never certain of getting the right answer, is the motor behind the whole process. There are two forms of uncertainty. One is strategic uncertainty which is seen when actors or decision-makers are not able to predict others' reactions; in this case, co-ordinating plans of action becomes fraught with uncertainty. Here, for example, task distribution cannot be decided in advance because doing so is likely to be ineffective. The other involves the evolution of the environment. Environmental uncertainty exists when it is impossible to predict future events accurately. Both these forms of uncertainty are particularly important in the case of innovation processes, in as much as they both have a significant effect on the type of co-ordination that the firms require.

The amount of uncertainty also differs with the nature of the innovation process concerned. Thinking of innovation as a path towards an adequate response to a particular question, this process may be more or less complex. One may be faced with a simple question, which one can answer immediately. A question may also turn out to be more complex, requiring research to find an answer. In this case, we must develop a method or research strategy which will reflect our expertise in the area concerned. The most extreme example is where we have what we call radical uncertainty: when not only do we not have an answer to the question, but we do not even know what research method is most likely to lead to an answer. We do not know if an answer can be found, and innovation represents finding the best way of asking the question, or even of raising new questions.

Here, we propose an analytical framework for situations characteristic of technological evolution that reflects the type of uncertainty concerned. We assimilate the process of innovation within a learning process: the process of attempting to answer a question, or to find a solution to a problem, which has been more or less defined at the outset. This enables us to recognize different types of situations, each depending both on the nature of the problem to be resolved, and on the state of knowledge about the situation in question. We distinguish three levels of complexity, as situations are more complex the more they involve significant uncertainty.

First, a simple situation is where there is a question which admits no uncertainty as to the expected answer: the answer is known by all concerned – in this case, all those involved with the innovation process – so the individual or collective response is akin to a reflex action. Likely contexts for these simple situations are assembly line work, and ordering a product from a catalogue of references, where procedures can be automated by artificial systems – such as computers, and robots. In these simple situations, innovation does not take place. Competitiveness is achieved by attention to costs. The objective is to minimize lead times – such as production, and delivery – and production errors by setting up rigid and repetitive procedures, as in the Taylorian company. The classic strategy in this situation is to seek economies of scale, and in this case, the size of the company becomes an important criterion for survival.

Second, in problem-solving situations, the attempt is to solve problems which are incompletely defined. The question is clear. Everyone knows that the solution exists, but it is not within immediate reach so a research process has to be set in motion. The problem is broken down into a set of less complex sub-problems, which are in turn broken down into further sub-problems, until the problem to be solved can be decomposed no further. Here we find Simon's traditional framework of nearly decomposable systems which involve the actors in a procedural rationale (Simon 1976, 1981). This type of situation can be found in most R&D departments, where the objective is to improve an existing product, or to adapt a generic product to a specific demand. We tend to find general working procedures, but since the goal is a specific and not a standardized result, while research protocols are routinized, the operations are not. Unlike the simple situation, here we have risks linked to uncertainty as to the solutions. The questions do not demand singular closed answers: the degree of openness depends on the number of variables, the number of links between these variables, and constraints in terms of the time and cost that it will take for a solution to be found.

Third, the complex situation results from an open question: the problem is incompletely defined, there is no predefined solution, there is no procedure guaranteeing a solution, and the outcome is itself largely uncertain. This situation requires a different level of competence: the problem solving method must itself be constructed since the protocol is at least partially undefined. These complex situations are usually close to fundamental research, such as is undertaken in universities or in a private laboratories. While relatively marginal compared to the bulk of industrial activity, it can have a significant impact on the evolution of technologies. From these, complex situations emerge, new technological fields, or significant derivations from existing technological trajectories.

Moore's Law

In the semi-conductor industry, the technological trajectory is directed by Moore's Law. This gives surprisingly accurate prediction of the evolution of the storage capacity ratio of micro-electronic chips. This technology is directed inexorably towards the physical limit of a silicon support: the minimum physical thickness is said to be 0.1 microns. The innovation is therefore rooted in problem-solving situations: we know that a reduction in size is possible, but we need to develop research to find how to do it. Further, we have to find technologies that can fundamentally transform production techniques. Among other potential solutions, introducing conductors of biological origin has been suggested, which modify production methods at every stage. The technological outcome, however, remains largely uncertain, and if several solutions appear, no one can predict which technique will be adopted by the industry; it is a complex research situation.

THE CHARACTERISITICS OF INNOVATION PROCESSES

Dosi (1984) recognizes a number of criteria that characterize the nature of technological processes. These include the cumulative and localized – geographically, culturally, socially, etc. – character of technical progress, the capacity to exploit technological opportunities, and the ability to appropriate an innovation. In this chapter we will try to distinguish the organizational elements that encourage innovation from those that hamper it.

Localized and cumulative learning

Atkinson and Stiglitz (1969) show how technology tends to evolve from already existing technologies, that this has a cumulative effect, and so innovation is specific to the company or to the team which developed it. Teece *et al*. (1994) have since shown that specific innovations are more likely to be diffused towards related domains – for example, from pharmaceuticals towards pesticides rather than towards aeronautics. This is due to the importance of implicit knowledge in the transfer of technology (Dibiaggio 1999). The capacity to use certain types of knowledge depends on already having other knowledge that is not necessarily of direct use in the learning process in hand, and implicit knowledge which is often only partially shared, or not made explicit.

Mastering implicit knowledge gives rise to learning capacities or absorptive capacities (Cohen and Levinthal 1990) in the area of expertise in question. This implicit knowledge is even more difficult to acquire: it may even be tacit knowledge inexpressible through any language or code. This is where we find 'savoir-faire', which can only be transmitted through imitation and experiment. The faster the pace of innovation, the less that knowledge is codified (David and Foray 1996), usually because it becomes too costly and inefficient to do so. New knowledge is largely acquired through practice, through habit and through learning (Stiglitz 1987), none of which is codified. Only when this knowledge has been stabilized can it be codified for diffusion. The choice of technological trajectories is not a random process. The effectiveness of innovation processes is directly linked to how far new technologies can be related to those which a company has already mastered. This usually happens either because the new and the mastered technologies are based on the same type of knowledge, or on complementary knowledge with the scope for beneficial synergies (Nesta and Dibiaggio 2003).

So R&D is constrained by the phenomena of path dependency (David 1985) and irreversibility (Arthur 1989), which condition the processes of technical systems. Innovations are constrained by previous technological choices in such a way that any technical choice reduces the range of subsequent choices. One of the most common examples of this is that of standardization: the normalization of technical choices. Whether formal or informal, standardization sets a common direction for all actors, favouring continuous improvement of technical systems, but imposing strict limits on possible avenues of future exploration, ruling out many potentially fruitful areas of research.

Finally, the faster the rate of innovation, the more localized it becomes, and the more the stabilization of solutions and the ability to diffuse innovation are inhibited. For this reason, technological trajectories tend to be developed where they were initiated. On the other hand the accumulation of innovation is inversely related to its pace of development, because the absence of standards incentivizes the adoption of new technical solutions, solutions that may well be incompatible with those already in place.

Exploiting opportunities and entrepreneurship

The capacity to exploit an innovation is based partly on access to technical and market information, and partly on the decision-making process which leads to investment in R&D projects. The difficulty arises from the interaction between these elements: Is the firm capable of both being informed and being able to select the most promising opportunities? We shall see that, depending on the complexity of the technology concerned, progress may be hindered by a communications gap between decision-making and exploitation. The ability to recognize a technological opportunity requires both mastery of existing technology and intuition concerning future innovations. This difficulty is caused by heterogeneity within the knowledge necessary for mastering technologies which are sometimes completely different. For example, in order to anticipate the convergence of two different technologies, and to foresee the potential opportunities they present, some mastery of both technologies is required.

This is why entrepreneurial skills have more to do with teamwork than with either individual genius or appropriate hierarchical structure. Learning results from the conjunction of several elements, in order to give coherence to observed events and to develop an effective method of solving new problems which may arise. However, another element, often the most challenging, is an ability to question the current coherence even if it is based on tried and tested methods, and being able to envisage new development if the current system becomes fossilized (Dibiaggio 1998). This faculty to question both operational and organizational routines requires a particular attitude. Organizational coherence is enabled by sharing the same code or language (Arrow 1976). This shared culture contributes to a collective learning experience and to the co-ordination of research procedures (Teece *et al.* 1997).

If current knowledge remains unquestioned, current procedures become reinforced and refined, the knowledge system becomes more rigid, the firm is no longer able to admit new ideas, and opportunities concerning alternative technologies are less likely to be recognized, the 'rigidity trap' (Dibiaggio and Musso 1998) is why effective learning must be based both on research for complementary knowledge – coherence – and on research for knowledge which is, or could become, a potential substitute. This is achieved by reinforcing relationships with both actors further upstream – suppliers or fundamental research – and with those further downstream – the market – or with competition.

The exploitation of opportunities may also be limited by the amount of past investment. It is harder to establish research for technical solutions if this questions previous investments in capital or in R&D. The rigidity trap and the size of current investments are the two major sources of hindrances to the exploitation of technological opportunities.

Appropriation of knowledge

Firms tend to reduce their investments in R&D when they think that it will be difficult for them to protect their innovations sufficiently to guarantee a minimum return on investment (Arrow 1962; Spence 1984). Appropriation possibilities are limited, for example, when innovations cannot be patented, or when the characteristics of the product render the patent system ineffective. The extent that appropriation is possible is therefore an important element in determining investment choice in innovation. As Arrow (1996) notes, technical information offers only limited ownership rights, so investment in innovating activities carries a higher risk than simply the risk of failing to cover the outlay, owing to the limited knowledge codification involved. The appropriation factor, however, is a double-edged sword. On one hand it bestows 'private ownership' on the knowledge created, yielding market opportunities. On the other, diffusing an innovation can offer advantage when it sets a market standard, from where profits can be engendered by its adoption and use. This is itself linked to network effects, whereby the more users there are of an innovation, the greater the value that can be obtained by using a network.

The ability to appropriate innovation largely depends on the extent of codification of the knowledge involved, because codified knowledge can more easily be protected by legal systems such as patents, licences or copyright. This type of knowledge is, however, easily imitated and diffused. While uncodified knowledge cannot be patented, it does benefit from some natural protection, according to the complexity of the new technical solutions involved, and its advance on the competition (Mansfield 1985). Tacit knowledge is often difficult to transmit, its acquisition relying on imitation and experiment – learning through practice and habit. Beyond codification, therefore, the importance of implicit knowledge must be acknowledged. Some types of knowledge can be codified, but its acquisition relies on more fundamental knowledge which requires long experience or heavy cost to gain. Beyond legal systems of knowledge protection, therefore, appropriation of knowledge depends essentially on its reproducibility or on the ease with which it can be reused, in other words, the extent to which it is standardized and immediately accessible.

INNOVATIVE CAPACITY, ORGANIZATIONAL STRUCTURE AND FIRM SIZE

We will now examine whether firm size affects capacity for innovation. We first ask which competencies should be developed inside the firm – rather than be sub-contracted – and then ask how the internal and external competencies can best be co-ordinated. For example, despite the strong synergies between electronics competences and those required for software development, both are more efficient if carried out within the same entity. In other cases, it might be best for firms to concentrate on what they do best, and sub-contracting what they do not know how to do. This has been seen as a question of evaluating the respective advantages of developing innovating projects internally, and having recourse to specialized outside companies. The balance is struck on the basis of a comparison between the costs of the transaction and governance costs (Coase 1937; Williamson 1985).

The decision to externalize innovation is based on the gains from using existing specialist knowledge. The cost of sub-contracting, however, is often higher than the simple cost of the service involved: adjacent and non-negligible costs have to be taken into account. These may be incurred both before the transaction – for example in seeking partners, and negotiating – and after it – such as in loss of control, and in possible renegotiating and legal costs. From this transaction cost perspective, choosing between doing an activity internally or sub-contracting it is based only on calculating the difference between the costs and benefits of each option, once all the actual or potential costs have been considered. Besides the static nature of this perspective – the nature of transaction costs or internal management can change rapidly and even radically from one period to another – it must be noticed that it rests entirely on the hypothesis of finding a perfect substitution between 'doing' and 'having done' (Cassiman and Veugeleurs 1998). Research and development results are assumed to be independent of the research method chosen, in which knowledge is assumed to be a homogenous input and how it is dealt with is assumed to have no impact.

Company structure and innovation performance

To address this analytical difficulty, Teece (1996) takes into consideration how the nature of innovation affects organizational choice. Recourse to external competence partly depends on the dependence on a resource over which one has no control: the need is to assess how much externalization will constrain future technological choices. Two criteria determine the degree of dependence. First, the firm will need to rely on external competencies if it does not have them internally. Second, the effectiveness of its technological innovations may depend on them being developed by other companies, over which it will have no control. An innovation is therefore said to be 'autonomous' if it is independent of technical evolution developed outside the firm's field of competence, and is 'systemic' if it relies at least partly on an expertise that the firm does not possess.

With these two criteria, organizational forms which depend on strategic choices in innovation can be described. Vertically integrated, hierarchical firms, perhaps with multiple products, can control the whole set of competences required for technological development when the innovation is systemic. These firms capitalize on one competence – such as technology – and develop a series of products – benefiting from economies of scope. They therefore benefit from effects of size – such as through economies of scale, and access to funding – and illustrate the Schumpeter model: the quasi-rents earned in some areas finance innovation in others. They are also better able to appropriate rents, and to protect from risks arising from environmental and strategic uncertainty. Their weakness lies in a greater propensity to fall into the 'rigidity trap', from the hierarchical organization of their decision-making, and from organizational short-sightedness towards technological opportunities. These are organizational forms well suited to problem-solving situations, having developed reliable routines of problem solving, but they find it difficult to escape from these when confronted by complex situations.

Flexibility requires weaker hierarchy and greater local autonomy. Small high-tech companies tend to resist functional specialization by basing their activities on diversified competencies. In this way, these companies can possess great adaptability and a capacity to create knowledge, generating new technological paradigms by introducing radical innovations which initiate life cycles for products, or even for industries. Teece calls these 'Silicon Valley companies', with examples such as Motorola, Intel, and Hewlett-Packard. These companies, however, with little capacity to protect innovation, put their greatest strategic efforts into technological advances, yielding an advantage when knowledge has to be created, whether the innovation be systemic or autonomous. They have a strong grasp of environmental and strategic uncertainty, because they are proactive in creating their own environment. They are organized project by project, in such a way that the forms of co-ordination are developed concurrently with the innovation process. Their weak hierarchy, however, and lack of operational routine, deprive them of advantages such as economies of scale in processes of information handling and decision-making that is needed in simple problem-solving situations. They are therefore particularly well-suited to complex situations, but not to simple areas.

Another form of flexibility is found in 'virtual companies'. These are entities which externalize 'everything and nothing' with very weak hierarchies, they are highly capable of innovation through their links with competent producers. Their strength lies in their speed of access to markets, but because they cannot develop technological competencies internally, they are exposed to competition from their suppliers. They have no capacity to protect innovation, so they only play a role when the innovations are autonomous and the required knowledge exists externally.

Alliances are another type of organization, being virtual entities which are sometimes ephemeral, but which have developed strong competencies in common. These include consortia such as SEMATECH and Airbus, as well as inter-company research agreements. Alliances unite heterogeneous and complementary competencies without constraining established hierarchies. Absence of knowledge protection however, prevents them from working on projects which create new knowledge, for fear of potential opportunist behaviour on the part of their partners. Alliances are therefore often a way of limiting the financial risks involved in projects which require the use of already established complementary competences. When knowledge must be created, as we will see later, it may turn out to be less risky to have control of the fundamental competencies within the same company.

This way of looking at organizational forms has the advantage of going beyond the traditional borders of the company by examining the nature of the activities undertaken, rather than the way that they are organized. This parallels divisions of labour, to that expounded by Adam Smith. In order that tasks be distributed, technical systems must be decomposed. In order to be efficient, this decomposition must be lasting. If the innovation modifies the nature of the division of labour, the sought after effects of the experiment diminish. Recent research takes this modularization into account at the level of conception activities (Langlois and Robertson 1995; Sanchez and Mahoney 1996), and shows that the speed of technical progress depends largely on the ability to decompose systems into autonomous modules, and to standardize the interfaces, – i.e. the relationships between modules – a prerequisite for maintaining compatibility between modules. This decomposition maintains a division of labour, and facilitates a capability to specialize in the development of parts of the technical system. Autonomy in each innovation ensures that different parts are not obliged to advance at the same rate, and do not have to be co-ordinated in advance.

We therefore find an adaptation between organizational form, size, structure of the technical system and method of innovation that is specific to each firm. We will find more vertically integrated large firms where knowledge can be appropriated and the process is cumulative, with a weak rate of knowledge obsolescence. Vertical integration is more important with systemic innovation. Silicon Valley type companies are better adapted to forms of innovation which are autonomous, rapid and localized in the parts of the system where they specialize. Here, appropriation is linked more to speed of innovation, namely to the rate of obsolescence of products, processes and competencies, than to the legal systems in which they operate. Practice and experience are the only sources of competitive advantage. Virtual companies seem better adapted to highly flexible systems which can respond rapidly to opportunities, thanks to their capacity to mobilize a network of external experts or specialized firms.

This framework, however, is incomplete. Any specialization is limited to a large extent by an inability to foresee the specific characteristics of an innovation in advance; for example, in how far it will be systemic or autonomous, and in how far the various modules will remain compatible, particularly when the pace of innovations is intense. The systems architecture – managed by systems integrators – is then complex. The company needs the competencies necessary for mastering and controlling the overall system. A team from Sussex University has found, for example, that technical systems can never be totally decentralized: system integrators need to integrate more competencies than appear necessary, simply to ensure that the technological knowledge essential to the production of future goods and services dedicated to their market is co-ordinated (Brusoni *et al.* 2001). To do this, they need to possess all the competences internally, at least to allocate tasks efficiently and, if necessary, to redistribute them when interfaces between modules or components need modification. Here, system integration can be thought of, potentially at least, as systemic innovation, as so much of the added value is concentrated within companies holding a wide range of competencies, rather than within specialist companies.

The trend towards decentralizing innovation activity, however, is even stronger where knowledge creation is intense, such as in semi-conductors (Macher and Mowery 2003). Two complementary processes explain this phenomenon. First, micro-electronic chips integrate ever more modules developed by small specialized firms that only deliver either design solutions – chipless – or products whose manufacture is systematically outsourced – fabless. They sell or licence systems, or parts of systems dedicated to specific electronic chips at the conception stage. Second, the commercial objective, the quest for a better product or service, has given way to an objective which seeks to add value: the objective is to adhere as closely as possible to client needs by offering a complete service. This quest for added value means that different products and services have to be integrated, though these are often produced by different actors (Wise and Baumgartner 1999).

Although system architecture has up until now always been handled by integrators such as IBM, Lucent, Motorola, or Philips, the processs has since evolved and system integration can be shared (Dibiaggio 2004). Similarly, for integrators such as IBM, Cable and Wireless, or Ericsson to ensure a high level of added value (Davies *et al.*, 2004), the thinking behind their offer is not always the fruit of a unilateral and centralized decision. Rather, it is the result of complementary industrial partnerships based on long-term relationships.

One reason for this decentralization is organizational constraints arising from the increasing number of designers in project teams. While 25 years ago, an engineer could complete five innovation projects per year, today it would take over 25 engineers to complete one project each year. The reduced time devoted to each project, and the arrival of new methodologies, limits the ability to maintain the pace of productivity gains demanded by industry, and encourages a search for specialized firms and sub-contractors. This raises issues of governance: outsourcing part of a systemic innovation increases the risk of failure in carrying projects through, and requires the engagement and transparency of all those involved. This had led to the emergence of hybrid organizational forms that integrate teams from different companies, but whose relationships rely on trust (Dibiaggio 2004). The challenge is therefore to build relationship networks which are solid, complementary and rapidly mobile, depending on the nature of the project in hand. Strategically, the competitive advantage is no longer determined by the size of the company, but by its positioning within a network of competencies and knowledge.

The specific characteristics of small high-tech firms

The general conclusion that big companies possess greater innovation capacities than small ones must now be tempered according to the specific types of innovation involved. We can now specify the particular conditions where small firms have advantages. The comparative advantages are measured in terms of how far these firms control the innovations – the process itself and the competencies created in the process – and their capacity to absorb new knowledge. We have seen how well adapted organizational structures depend on the nature of the situation-types

– simple, problem-solving or complex – most often encountered, and the speed of innovation.

In simple situations, typically found in mature and fragmented sectors of activity not necessitating a high level of technological competence, the organization is static and based on task repetition. Operational procedures are clear and explicit – codified – in such a way that the creation of new knowledge disrupts the stability of the system. The criterion of efficiency is in minimizing costs, so economies of scale are often the essential factor for success. Innovation is systematically imported in the form of purchasing patents or licences – codified knowledge.

In problem-solving situations, the knowledge exists, but it is often implicit and hard to appropriate. This gives an advantage in the process of integration. Co-ordination is decided ex-ante using stable routines. Uncertainty essentially involves environmental uncertainty – concerning, for example, the demand, the time and cost of the innovation process – so the organization's goal is to adapt to unpredicted variations within an established technological trajectory. Problem-solving situations are advantageous to big multi-product firms which can simultaneously exploit economies of scale and economies of scope. Their flexibility consists of reproducing routines able to guarantee the production of diversified products or services capable of satisfying different demands. The firm ensures incremental innovation based on internally existing knowledge, because this is a question of improving existing routines in order to satisfy specific demands. Recourse to external competencies is mainly to seek competencies complementary to those developed internally, this externalization usually going hand-in-hand with co-operation between the company and the sub-contractor.

Stable regimes also have room for small companies which are either 'dominated' – their strategies depend on the behaviour of large firms in the sector – or 'imitative' – they maintain incremental innovation by acquiring patents. These companies are usually specialized firms whose innovation is relevant at a specific level of the functional chain, and so they rely on a particular distinctive competence. Their advantage comes from mastering a specific competence, and being able to capitalize on economies of scale on a process or product whose demand may be limited by either geographical or market constraints.

In complex situations, technological regimes are rapid and unstable – owing to high rates of knowledge obsolescence. Demand is not standardized. Innovation procedures are not completely scheduled, and work on the basis of seeking systematically for opportunities. Innovation processes are based on mastery of scientific knowledge and deal with ambiguous problems whose solution is uncertain. There is great environmental uncertainty: complementarities between areas are undefined, and the knowledge is still to be created. Success depends on the ability to create new knowledge, usually requiring asking new pertinent questions and finding efficient research strategies which fit the problems faced. This knowledge creation mostly stems from connecting heterogeneous and independent types of knowledge, in order to construct new complementarities (Dibiaggio 1998). The organizational problem is multidimensional: heterogeneous competences need to be mobilized in setting up teams who can develop effective research strategies. The organization needs a dynamic flexibility in an ability to create new basic competencies. Appropriation of this uncodified knowledge is difficult, so diffusion is slow and difficult to organize, and the protection of any subsequent innovation is based on the exclusiveness of the knowledge necessary for it to be made useful.

This shows the systemic advantage of small firms, arising from the flexibility it derives from an ability to mobilize necessary competences while retaining control of the innovation process. The firm can position itself within a knowledge network by sharing its capacities for systems integration and service with partners. Its mastery lies in learning capacities enhanced by active participation in knowledge creation within a network that covers the entire functional chain, from conception to production – and sometimes also distribution if this requires advanced technical skills. So its competitive advantage comes from mastering the co-ordination of complementary – mainly knowledge – assets in contexts of high uncertainty; it masters the added value in complex production processes.

This advantage is often attributed to the small company's greater entrepreneurial abilities. Mastering the relationships between the different functional levels in the innovation process enables the small high-tech firm to anticipate both the evolution of demand and the potential technological evolution. This is more than just privileged information; it is what allows the firm to grasp the challenges inherent in each project. We shall now illustrate how this process works with a case study.

THE EUROPEAN TECHNOLOGIES CASE

European Technologies (ET) was created in 1996 by four people from Texas Instruments, and by 2003 was achieving annual sales of €3.2 million. Its main business is developing integrated circuits dedicated to specific needs.

The firm is not, however, technologically or even strategically – product-market for example – specialized; it does not occupy a niche in which it capitalizes on a distinctive competence. The competitive advantage of the company is based on its organizational 'savoir-faire' and its knowledge of management processes, and not on particular technical expertise. It innovates to address specific needs by mobilizing and managing internal and external competencies to create new complementarities between various partners. We will try to show two dimensions of specific organizational and strategic characteristics which lie behind its success. The first is its mastery of previous implicit knowledge to control the process of innovation in the core of the technical system. This implicit knowledge is mastered by acquiring expertise in development tools, in emulating and managing libraries of dedicated algorithms. The second is its management of networks of specific competencies.

Mastery of previous implicit knowledge

The electronics industry is evolving rapidly. After a period of integration around systems linked to a specific microprocessor, the trend has now shifted towards embedded systems or systems-on-a-chip. The reduced size of imprints and increased complexity of the inherent architecture results in all functions being grouped together on the same chip. Demand also now comes from customers who have no direct competence in electronics, such as assemblers, retailers or users. The service supplied is for 'solutions', which reduces the complexity involved in using the products, but makes the innovation process and the development of the products much more complex (*Electronics Times* 1998). This complexity leads to both more technical possibilities and more constraints, since solutions must make several technologies compatible with each other. In general, more elements – or sub-systems – grouped together within a technical system causes the number of potential solutions to grow exponentially, and this makes it more difficult to control. The specialists of the various sub-systems need to learn to work together to find an effective solution: it is a complex situation.

Expressed differently, software has made it possible to standardize knowledge in the innovation, but this knowledge is implicit and does not need to be mastered. Standardization makes division of labour more possible, with each party specializing on a specific function. In Teece's terminology, the innovation becomes autonomous. Seeking to group all the functions as the same chip has led to a complete overhaul of the system's organization. Innovation becomes systemic once more; innovation knowledge, previously implicit, now has to be mobilized and modified so that the different sub-systems can be made compatible.

Achieving compatibility requires effective co-ordination of horizontal and vertical complementarities. Co-ordinating horizontal complementarities means ensuring an effective design of the different sub-systems without breaking down each module specification into too many independent technical specifications.

Changes in one of the sub-systems can affect all the others. Managing vertical complementarities means co-ordinating the different phases of the functional chain, from conception through to production. In theory, this should justify integration: the innovation is systemic; the priority is to master all the competencies to ensure their co-ordination, as we find in many vertically integrated firms – such as Motorola, Texas Instruments, VLSI Technologies, and IBM. Integration, however, implies a loss of flexibility, through having to adopt a particular technology. If Texas Instruments conceives and produces microcontrollers, it is probable that it will use its own products at the conception phase, even if a competing product is better adapted to the solution under consideration.

ET's strategy as knowledge manager has two aspects. First, it accesses software that makes the conception and development of a set of sub-systems possible. To do this, it provides distribution and training for different suppliers of these tools, which yields both access to the software, and expertise in using the tools. In this way, ET controls the core of the process, in the design of the chip which integrates the different sub-functions. Second, ET has developed libraries of technical development solutions – algorithms. The multiplication of potential algorithms makes the choice very complex, and an ability to mobilize suitable tools becomes an important factor.

ET therefore possesses previous knowledge which underpins the functioning of the system. This is usually implicit knowledge which cannot be easily reproduced or acquired through simple access; expertise is required to ensure that knowledge is co-ordinated and integrated. The firm's expertise enables it to understand and to judge the whole set of innovations in each module in the system, and above all, to retain superior faculties in learning and being able to capitalize on knowledge.

Managing networks of competencies

Here again, the strategic positioning of ET does not rely on one particular competence, but on an ability to respond to all specific demands, whatever the technical competence of the customer. This requires rapid mobilization of complementary competencies, and establishing an efficient innovation process. As before, the firm's mastery of previous knowledge enables it to understand the challenges and the technologies at all levels. Further, confidence is enhanced by its ability to involve potential sub-contractors, suppliers and clients in a partnership network. This is not only a matter of sharing resources, but also of pooling strategic orientations.

ET tries, as much as possible, to keep control of the whole process, but may also intervene as expert in projects which it does not control in a reciprocal way. This strategy has helped customers to see it as an efficient and reliable intermediary, seeking global 'solutions' rather than simply being a producer of products, putting it in an ideal position to gather strategic intelligence. Being an intermediary between its customers' demands and the various partners, ET is in touch both with evolving market needs, and with technological evolution. ET's essential capacity is its ability to learn through its permanent interactions.

The particular characteristics of ET's organization enable it to accumulate advantages for which it is not easy for large companies to do. The variety of competencies and the simplicity of its organizational hierarchy give the firm the necessary flexibility to grasp complex situations. ET has a high capacity for knowledge appropriation, with knowledge protection based on speed of innovation and mobilization of competencies rather than on codification and patents. ET is not based on a large innovation platform for guaranteeing a powerful position as technological leader. Instead, it is a stakeholder in networks of systemic innovations which it cannot control alone. In its ability to mobilize external competencies rapidly, it shows some of the characteristics of a virtual company, but is in no way a 'hollow company', being able to capitalize on growing experience and knowledge of the processes. So, the firm also possesses some of the characteristics of alliances, but without facing the risk of 'free riders', in part because of the atmosphere of trust between the partners, but mainly because of its mastery of implicit knowledge and its faculties of learning.

The strength of this small firm can be seen in its having all the advantages of an integrated company – in its capitalization of knowledge, its organizational coherence and its management of systemic innovations – but without the pitfalls of such companies – in the rigidity trap, in limited projects/scope from competing investments, and in diseconomies of scale.

CONCLUSION

By considering the specific characteristics of processes of learning and of knowledge creation, we have shown that organizational efficiency is a prerequisite for the innovation process. Firm size influences the way activities are organized. Large firms are often better placed to manage innovation processes, having easier access to external funding, and being able to use quasi-rents from its dominant positions to reinvest in innovative activities – the Schumpeter hypothesis. Further, the integration of complementary activities enables large firms to co-ordinate systemic innovations, and to better control the knowledge appropriation and protection processes.

Small firms are usually seen as bringing diversity to the industrial change, by introducing radical innovations, and becoming new players gambling on their distinctive competence. If successful, growth will yield size benefits once the technology has stabilized, and the innovation resolves problem situations. The advantage of the small firm is usually seen as being only temporary, or being linked to positions in limited strategic niches.

We have shown something different. There are cases where small size can constitute a lasting competitive advantage. This is particularly true in systemically complex situations where there are possibilities to integrate and recombine technical systems. The organizational advantage then comes from combining abilities to capitalize on knowledge, being able to appropriate knowledge rapidly, and technical flexibility.

So this leads to the question why we cannot find this competitive advantage in large companies. It is because large-scale production is not advantageous in those contexts where an ability to operate economies of scale or economies of scope does not help growth, but increased size usually brings with it increased governance costs, in management and in internal co-ordination. It is by keeping costs under control and by seeking coherence that specific 'core competences' are developed, which enables them to capitalize on their experience.

Chapter 4

Engineers as high-tech entrepreneurs

French engineers' paths to entrepreneurship

Alain Fayolle

Venture creation has become a major social and economic issue. Of all the new firms created every year, those with technological and innovative potential have always been, and are still, appreciated and supported by public authorities. Innovation, especially technological innovation, has become a vital competitive lever for firms and countries alike.

Innovation is the entrepreneur's basic instrument. Schumpeter (1935) pointed out just how far the innovation function, independently of the capital ownership function, positions entrepreneurs as the engines of economic development. Modern economic thinking also ascribes a fundamental role to innovation in the wealth creation process, through the opportunities it generates (Drucker 1985). Entrepreneurs seek sources of innovation and of change, and for relevant information on creative opportunities. They must know, apply and understand the principles that enable innovations to be implemented with the best possible chance of success. They seek out change, act upon change, and exploit change as an opportunity (Stevenson and Gumpert 1985).

Engineers have always been associated with invention and innovation. Verin (1984) points out the connections between the words engineer, genius and invention. Engineers are bearers of innovation, in that their scientific and technical training and their practical experience makes them able to innovate and prepares them to be pivotal elements in the technological innovation process (Gaudin 1984). Economic history also shows the innovative nature of many French engineers, some of whom were or are still entrepreneurs. This includes, for example, Gustave Eiffel, the Schlumberger brothers, Jean Bertin, Francis Bouyghes, Yvon Gattaz and Truong Trong Thi – who developed the first French micro-computer.

It is therefore natural to wonder whether developed countries might benefit from increasing this particular form of entrepreneurship, in the way that engineers exploit scientific and technical knowledge within society. This raises two further questions. First, are engineers – and here we will look at French engineers – really entrepreneurs? Second, what do we really know about engineer-entrepreneurs?

Data provided by the French National Council of Engineers and Scientists (CNISF) show that few French engineers choose entrepreneurship as a career path (Fayolle 1994). That few engineers create or buy businesses has been observed repeatedly over 30 years (Gattaz 1970; Ribeill 1984; Fayolle 1994). Moreover, little information is available on the venture creation or business buyouts by French engineers, where virtually no research has been undertaken. Some older publications were written by sociologists or historians.

It was a paradox between social demand for more engineer-entrepreneurs on the one hand, and the lack of knowledge and marginality of the phenomenon on the other hand that led us to research the subject in more detail. This chapter is intended to contribute new knowledge on the entrepreneurial behaviours of qualified French engineers. (Here, the term 'entrepreneurial behaviour' is used to refer to a set of actions that lead an engineer into an irreversible venture creation or venture purchase process involving a significant personal and financial investment.) Among other things, this chapter will attempt to clarify a how engineers become entrepreneurs, the paths available to them, and whether they have separate engineer-entrepreneur profiles that affect their behaviour and the types of firms that they create or purchase, especially in the high-tech sector. 'Entrepreneur-like behaviour' may be the result of an engineer's preferences, orientations, decisions or actions relating to innovation or other issues of business management. This is clearly not the same as 'entrepreneurial behaviour'. It will be necessary to identify the factors that have a positive or negative impact on the entrepreneurial propensities of engineers, by examining the identity and characteristics of engineer-entrepreneurs.

To try to understand the behaviour of French engineers, we will look at their personal, educational and career-related paths. Only some of these paths lead to high-tech venture creation and/or development. We assume that engineers will be influenced by their interactions with their environments, which lead them towards certain career paths, and towards certain personal or career-related crises. Thus, these interactions and their consequences form the basis of the engineers' career progressions, helping shape their professional trajectory, and lead them towards entrepreneurial decisions and behaviours. We begin by reviewing the literature on engineers and engineer-entrepreneurs, before setting out the theoretical framework and methodology of the research, and presenting our results.

ENGINEERS AND ENTREPRENEURSHIP

We will now examine the different facets of qualified French engineers and their social and vocational characteristics, before, despite a paucity of data, defining and describing engineer-entrepreneurs and the phenomenon of venture creation and buyouts by engineers. We conclude with a synthesis of the particular nature of French engineers and a comparison with other European engineers.

The social position of French engineers

It is important to understand the discriminatory nature of an engineering degree in France. This qualification is often viewed as a means of obtaining social status and privilege (Bourdieu 1989). Like other prestigious schools, the major engineering schools play a major social function in the transmission of and access to privilege (Magliulo 1982; Bourdieu 1989). An engineering degree also separates engineers from other technical executives, some of whom may practise as engineers without actually being qualified (Lasserre 1989; Bouffartigue 1995).

In the French educational system, there are many different ways of obtaining an engineering degree (Maurice *et al.* 1982). From the outside, the engineering training system appears to be multi-faceted, probably as a result of a lack of internal logic in the way it was structured and developed (Broder 1990). As a training system, it is both hierarchical and stratified (Maurice *et al.* 1982; Broder 1990), with the École Polytechnique forming the summit and a large number of engineering schools in various technical and production-related fields forming the base. This hierarchical structure makes the system somewhat rigid (Broder 1990). As a result, the system has a strong impact on both the trajectories and the careers of French engineers (Maurice, *et al.* 1982). As Broder (1990) notes:

> The hierarchical and highly specialized system in France raises the problem
> of career dynamics, flexibility and the ability to adapt to change.
> > (Broder 1990: 93, free translation from the French)

French engineers also now appear to have entered a period of profound doubt as to their professional identity following upheavals between 1930 and 1945. Until about the mid-nineteenth century, engineers were civil servants working for the State (Verin 1993; Grelon and Ternier 1986; Gille 1964; Ternier 1984). From 1850–1930, they became architects at the service of national industrialization, forming a strong alliance with management (Ternier 1984; Moutet 1985; Lanthier 1979; Lasserre 1989; Saglio 1984). Since 1930, engineers have been in a deep-seated identity crisis, and are still questioning the basis of their social status (Lasserre 1989; Boltanski 1982; Ternier 1984). Are engineers recognized socially for their technical expertise and professionalism – i.e. for their scientific and technical legitimacy – or are they recognized as managers and leaders?

The French engineer-entrepreneur in the literature

Venture creation and business buyouts are rare in the engineering community. From a CNISF (the National Association of French Engineers and Scientists) socio-economic survey, it can be estimated that only five to seven per cent of qualified practising French engineers can be described as engineer-entrepreneurs (based on Fayolle 1994).

Some engineers are attracted to entrepreneurial behaviour while others are not. For example, entrepreneurship is of marginal interest to engineering students and young graduates (Gattaz 1970), but is seen by others as a solution to unemployment, and can be a way for older engineers to overcome the age barrier (Lange 1993; Raveyre and Saglio 1992). Situational and social factors specific to the engineering community lie behind this:

> structural and lasting – perhaps even strengthened – role of the recruitment and training system in the oldest schools on the system's limited ability to encourage and shape entrepreneurial careers.
>
> (Ribeill 1984: 89, translation from French)

Veblin (1971) notes the potential offered by the technical capital of engineers, and the social capital associated with that. Engineers must therefore choose between the routine and comfort of a salaried position as a 'mercenary' manager, or the adventure and risk of a entrepreneurial position.

Increasingly, engineers are being called upon to fill powerful positions in industry and finance, where the key resource is time spent in a large state sector (Cohen 1988). The use of engineers to fill top industrial positions is by no means a recent phenomenon. Thépot (1979) described the beginning of the movement, which was examined by Lanthier (1979) in the electrical sector. The process developed significantly after the Second World War (Cohen 1988), and today it has become widespread.

Bauer and Bertin-Mourot (1987) found that nearly half of all mining sector engineers work in routine positions in the public and private industrial sectors, or in management positions. One top business manager in every four is from a major state engineering organization. The mining sector alone accounted for 17 company presidencies in 1986, and the bridges sector for 13 (Bauer and Bertin-Mourot 1987). Out of 196 managers of the largest turnover French businesses, 48 are from state sectors (Bauer and Bertin-Mourot 1987). Levy-Leboyer (1979), in a study of France's top managers from 1912–73, confirmed that the engineers leading France's major corporations tended to be alumni of the schools with the best reputations in the French educational system.

In smaller firms, educational capital does not necessarily go hand-in-hand with industrial capital (Bunel and Saglio 1979). To achieve leadership positions in small and medium-sized enterprises (SMEs), engineers tend to take different paths and use different assets than those used by their counterparts in larger organizations. Those who head SMEs have usually inherited or purchased the firm; only rarely have they created it (Bunel and Saglio 1979; Raveyre and Saglio 1990; Saglio 1984).

Clearly, then, engineers are well represented in business management positions. This does not necessarily mean, however, that the engineers concerned are entrepreneurs as such – they may not be willing to take the risk of creating or buying a firm of their own. It is evident to us that engineer-entrepreneurs are more than engineers who have risen to management positions; they also need to take initiative, foster change, and accept and assume personal risk, sometimes to a significant level.

Ribeill (1984) argues that the role of schools and the social status of the engineering degree in the nineteenth century explain the power of engineers today. Based on detailed estimates and analyses of two types of causal variables – social origin and type of training – he suggests that:

> The entrepreneurial propensity of an engineer will increase proportionally to the decrease in the social status – the value of the label – obtained from a technical school qualification.
>
> (Ribeill 1984: 84, free translation from the French)

The entrepreneurial propensity of engineers appears to be inversely proportional to the reputation of the schools from which they graduate. However, engineering schools have shown more interest in venture creation and small business in recent years, and have attempted to reposition themselves somewhat in its regard.

In some ways, the entrepreneurial situation of engineers can be summarized as the opposing pulls of routine and the – relative – comfort of a salaried position on one side, versus the risk of an entrepreneurial career on the other. This pull, which varies in strength over time, depending on the context, is the result of a number of past and present factors that influence the vocational choices made by engineers.

Understanding and comparing the French engineer

The professional positions of French engineers, in their technological and market orientation levels, are very diverse. The French national culture shapes their professional positions in terms of social status and does not strongly consider technological ability. The French system selects the best individuals and offers them the opportunity to enter a 'Grande Ecole'. Highly ranked French engineering

'Grandes Ecoles' then prepare their students for general management and not for specialized engineering studies. These engineering schools are the 'generalists', those who cannot enter this very selective system go to more specialized engineering schools. The former have a managerial orientation, the latter have a stronger technological orientation, and sometimes only a technological one. This initial position can then change, depending on the state of the professional culture. If a professional identity is strongly rooted in the technological dimension, any position change will be difficult, otherwise change is possible, and particularly a change to a more market orientated position.

We will now to compare the French engineer with other European engineers, using research into the behaviours towards entrepreneurship and innovation of French, Dutch and German engineers (Fayolle *et al.* 2005).

In Germany, there is a consistent pattern of business-related practices built around 'competence first', on which the professional culture of the German engineer is based. The German apprentice system leads to an exceptionally well-trained work force: about two-thirds of German supervisors hold a Master certificate. German managers are selected on the basis of their expert knowledge, and this knowledge is the most important basis of their authority. The shop floor workers respect their managers, and this leads to a satisfying working relationship. German engineers find it self-evident that they teach subordinates with their knowledge and experience. When a supervisor leaves a preferred subordinate will normally take over his job.

In the Netherlands, a consistent pattern of business-related practices is built around a 'consensus' principle. It is important that decisions are made after everyone has been listened to and if there are disagreements, then there will be searched for a solution that is agreed on by everyone. In connection with this, a Dutch manager also wants freedom to adopt his own approach to the job and for creating own ideas. A Dutch manager takes his tasks seriously, reflected in the expressions 'business is business' and 'business before pleasure'. The orientation of Dutch managers is towards short-term planning: they want to see results quickly. When the results do not come quickly, they also have perseverance; some might call it stubbornness. Dutch engineers are less specialized in a technical area than their German counterparts; they get technical knowledge by buying it or by developing it themselves; not from internal education programs. Dutch managers' authority is also, however, based on knowledge. The Dutch are more impressed by actions than by words. A positive point mentioned by Kympers (1992) is the efficient and economic way of managing, but a negative side is an urge towards perfection, which leads to rigidness.

Comparing French with Dutch and German engineers, it is probably easiest to compare the French engineers coming from the specialized engineering schools. Those who have a technological orientation are quite similar to the German engineers but they are probably more influenced by the intellectual dimension in relation to their education in the French system. Those who have moved towards a market orientation show some similarities with the Dutch engineers. The French engineers coming from the generalist 'Grandes Ecoles' are not easily compared, because their focus is on specific professional situations for which management, as an intellectual activity, is playing an essential role. These engineers often work in the French administration, and the public and private large companies.

In relation to entrepreneurship and innovation, should French engineers design the technical innovation, their German colleagues implement it into a well-controlled manufacturing process and the Dutch, for instance, sell to the market, as they are often stereotyped? We suggest that such kind of diversity might already be built in systematically in a cross-border innovation team as a competitive asset, and not as something which happens to us as a handicap on the European and global scene.

THEORETICAL AND METHODOLOGICAL FRAMEWORK

Venture creation and business buyouts can be examined from at least four standpoints, namely the individual – actor – the firm – emerging organization – the environment – milieu – and the process (Gartner 1985; Bruyat 1993). Research tends to concentrate on one or more of these aspects, depending on the researcher's source discipline. For example, psychologists will focus on the individual, economists on the firm and the environment, and managers on the firm and the process. In this chapter, we have elected to include all four aspects, with emphasis on the time factor within the notion of process. Next, we begin by describing the theoretical framework used for the research, and go on to present the sample and methodological approach.

The theoretical approach

The research described here is an exploratory empirical study. Its purpose is to provide new information on venture creation and business buyouts by members of a specific social group, namely qualified French engineers. We are seeking to describe and explain the individual behaviours of engineers who opt for venture creation or buyout as their personal and/or career path. To establish our framework, we drew on models and determinants of the engineering career and the entrepreneurial process.

Engineers form a specific social group defined by their personal history, social status and professional identity. There are several different research approaches that can be used to describe engineering careers. For example, the engineering career can be viewed as being dependent on individual factors such as values, needs, preferences, motivation and social origin. Here, the works of McClelland (1961, 1979) on the 'need for achievement', Holland (1973, 1992) on the links between working environment and worker personality, Schein (1978) on career anchors and Fayolle (1994) on the importance of host environments are all relevant. It can equally well be viewed as a series of phases corresponding to specific trajectories and social constructs (for example Riverin-Simard 1984; Grossetti 1986; Lojkine 1992; Bouffartigue 1994 and Robin 1994). A more compartmentalized approach can also be taken, based on the strategies required to obtain the technical skills and resources needed for an entrepreneurial career – this is similar to the theoretical approach we used to examine the entrepreneurial process.

The models studied clearly illustrate a major conceptual development. The earlier explanatory frameworks consider psychological characteristics to be important in the entrepreneurial act, while more recent models tend to use the notion of process to understand the wealth and diversity of entrepreneurial situations and behaviours. Within the concept of 'process' is the idea of movement, development, dynamics and time, and many different, complex individual paths can be taken to progress from intention to idea and from idea to action. Yet, in all these paths, it is possible to identify certain constants or common elements around which decisions are made and actions are structured. Some authors look at the venture creation process through the concept of action system (for example Le Marois 1985; Arocena *et al.* 1983; Bruyat 1993, Shapero 1975; Shapero and Sokol 1982; or Pleitner 1985). This allows them to place the would-be entrepreneur – the actor – in a central position within a specific, structured action system that is formed, develops and changes throughout the process (Bruyat 1993).

The theoretical reference framework we used for our fieldwork, is based on the interactionist model. We are not referring solely to the sociological approach developed by Goffman (1973 and 1974), who uses social interaction as the focal point of his analyses. The approach suggested by this model does not exclude individual or general determinisms – socio-political structures, standards and means imposed by society – and mainly emphasizes the fact that behaviours are as much the result of the actor's strategic intentions as of determinisms. It is based on renewed strategic analysis (Bernoux 1990; Amblard *et al.* 1996) and uses the 'interactionist' concept, a sociological theory that ascribes a central role to the interactions between the individual, the resources, the environments and the surrounding socio-political and professional structures. Engineers can be regarded as 'actors' who reason, calculate and estimate the means required to achieve a goal. It is this conscious process that explains their subsequent action, and in particular their professional behaviours.

From this reductionist standpoint, the contexts and situations in which individuals evolve are often underestimated or ignored, while the logic of the actor is over-valued (Bernoux 1990; Amblard *et al.* 1996). However, the actor does not exist alone, independently of the situation with which he or she is faced. Logics can change according to the actions envisaged, as opposed to being defined solely from the actors themselves (Bernoux 1990). The action logic then replaces the logic of the actor, and can be defined simply as a meeting between an actor, with all their social facets, and a situation structured by the weight of institutions, standards, structures, power plays and environmental characteristics (Amblard *et al.* 1996). We feel we will be better able to provide new information on the entrepreneurial behaviours of engineers if we concentrate on their goals, strategies and career choices, paths and action logic within a given professional trajectory. We will also be considering factors related to the individual, the environment and the social structures and standards, an approach we feel is entirely compatible with the 'interactionist' model.

Research methodology

We used the questionnaire technique as the principal means of gathering information. In 1994, we sent a 24-page, 178-question questionnaire to 6,447 engineers from the Rhône-Alpes region of France. The main themes of the survey were based on the reference framework elements, and included individual and educational factors: career choice determinants, current and desired career paths, perceptions of the engineering profession and career advancement criteria, and finally, for engineer-entrepreneurs, factors related to venture creation or business buyouts. It allowed us to explore all aspects of the entrepreneurial process, including the schools from which the engineers graduated and their prior professional experience. The firm itself was also studied – sector, level of innovation, how it was created or purchased, and how it was developed.

We received 681 usable questionnaires – for a return rate of approximately 11 per cent – 182 of which were from engineer-entrepreneurs – 27.6 per cent. The respondents – 95 per cent men and 5 per cent women – were from 116 different schools or institutions. The data was processed and analysed using a statistical application – Modalisa – running on Macintosh. The 178 questions produced 252 variables.

In line with our research focus, we segmented our respondents into homogeneous subgroups. Then, to identify the factors having a positive or negative impact on their entrepreneurial propensities, we selected four sub-groups based on the questions relating to the respondent's entrepreneurial situation at the time of the survey. Type A were engineers who had never been and had never intended to become entrepreneurs – 157 in total. Type B were engineers who had never been and no longer intended to become entrepreneurs – 135 in total. Type C were engineers who had never been entrepreneurs but hoped to become entrepreneurs one day – 186 in total. Type D were engineer-entrepreneurs who had created or purchased at least one firm – 187 in total, of which 143 were still entrepreneurs at the time of the survey, with 21 not being classifiable into any of these four types.

To understand the paths that had led certain engineers to their entrepreneurial careers, we worked exclusively with the type D group. Using the reciprocal averaging (RA) method, we sought to identify different types of engineer-entrepreneurs and entrepreneurial trajectories. We were ultimately able to identify three types of engineer-entrepreneurs who had taken different trajectories and exhibited specific entrepreneur-like behaviours. There were 71 'managerial' engineer-entrepreneurs – type X – 87 'technical' engineer-entrepreneurs – type Y – and 24 'super-technical' engineer-entrepreneurs – type Z. We now present our results and interpretations, and attempt to reconstruct the paths taken by the engineer-entrepreneurs in our sample.

FRENCH ENGINEER-ENTREPRENEURS AND WHERE THEY COME FROM

Based on the engineer types used in our typology of engineer-entrepreneurs, we now attempt to situate the engineers' entrepreneurial positions within their professional trajectories and over time. This involves drawing links between our observations and results, by means of hypothetical relationships that we will explain and develop in the next few pages. Figure 4.1 shows the professional trajectories and entrepreneurial paths taken by the engineers in our sample.

Two main trajectories emerge. On the first trajectory, young graduates (YGs) develop their careers with no entrepreneurial intention or motivation – path 1 – and perhaps without ever being made aware of entrepreneurship (Fayolle 1994). Second, YGs, usually after a few years of professional experience, embrace entrepreneurship as a possible career choice – path 2. These two trajectories will be examined in more detail in the following sections. The age reflects the age of engineers when the study was made, but not necessarily the age when they created or bought their own company.

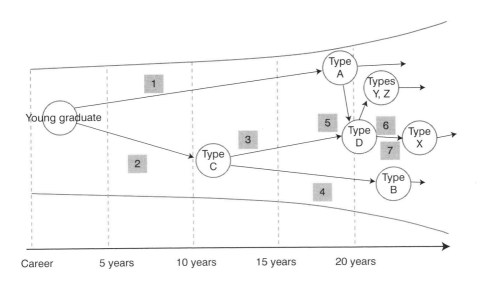

Figure 4.1 Trajectories and entrepreneurial paths of engineers

Engineers not intending to become entrepreneurs, but do so nonetheless

The first trajectory represents engineers who had never been and never intended to become entrepreneurs – type A engineers. Type A engineers are typically around 45 years of age with nearly 20 years of professional experience. They have few dependent children, often have fathers who were engineers, and have a sound scientific and technical education. They exhibit little professional or geographical mobility – some type A engineers have only ever worked for one firm – and their preferences and career orientations are technical in nature. They tend to seek job security, stability and a certain balance between their professional and personal lives. Their professional identity is derived from their expertise, values and scientific and technical reference points.

Type A engineers do not want to become entrepreneurs and had never envisaged entrepreneurial careers, but career 'accidents' or triggers in their professional lives have caused them to engage in entrepreneurship, sometimes in spite of themselves – path 5. These actions or events could include virtual or actual job losses, professional dissatisfaction or the need to complete a technical task that could not be completed for a variety of reasons – strategic, operational, relational, etc. – in the firms for which they worked. Type A engineers embark on the entrepreneurial path as a result of a discontinuity or displacement, with a form of motivation that some authors have described as negative (Shapero 1975; Shapero and Sokol 1982). When they become entrepreneurs, type A engineers tend to apply knowledge capital, skills capital and scientific and technical relationships in their projects.

Engineers wishing to be entrepreneurs who do so within managerial structures

The second major trajectory in Figure 4.1 is taken by engineers who quickly develop the desire and intention to become entrepreneurs – path 2. They have never been entrepreneurs, but would like to become so. These type C engineers are potential entrepreneurs. They are aged around 35 and have slightly over 10 years of professional experience. Their non-engineering training is mainly in the field of management, which means they are open to the various aspects and relative complexity of business. They exhibit a high level of professional and geographical mobility, and hold a variety of positions in their early careers, including non-technical positions. Their professional identity is based on command and hierarchical principles. Managerial values appear to predominate.

Type C engineers want to become entrepreneurs, but they also ascribe importance to management as a career path. In the future, they may either become entrepreneurs, or remain in satisfying positions as employees with large or small firms. In the latter case, their professional orientation is hierarchical and focused on management. These potential trajectories can be found in path 3 of Figure 4.1, which lead type C entrepreneurs to become engineer-entrepreneurs – type D engineers – and in path 4, which leads them to become engineers who have never been and no longer intend to become entrepreneurs – type B engineers. Such people are usually satisfied with their current positions. They used to have entrepreneurial goals, but have set them aside for personal, family or professional reasons.

Type C engineers who do not become entrepreneurs therefore find themselves in the situation of Type B engineers. Type B entrepreneurs have the oldest average age of our sample – 48 years old – and the longest professional experience – 23 years. They have significant family responsibilities, and their additional training means that they have excellent managerial skills. Their careers have tended to focus on upward mobility and management, in a range of positions, usually in large corporations. Type B entrepreneurs exhibit considerable professional and geographical mobility. They seek security and stability in their career choices, and ascribe a lot of importance to the prestige of their jobs, status and profile. They are extremely attached to their profession, and express a high level of job satisfaction.

Trajectories and features of engineer-entrepreneurs

The engineer-entrepreneurs – type D entrepreneurs, see Figure 4.3 (below) – in our sample are slightly over 47 years old on average, and have roughly 22 years of professional experience. They also have a broad variety of additional training. They exhibit considerable professional mobility, along with a range of professional experience in terms of both positions and situations.

When engineers become entrepreneurs, they can be positioned anywhere along a continuum between technical focus and management focus. Where they are on the continuum depends on their career development process (Robin 1994; Bouffartigue 1994; Riverin-Simard 1984; and Lojkine 1992) among others. Engineers can become entrepreneurs at any time in their lives, when they are still at the technical stage of their career or when they have moved on to positions requiring more managerial skills. Within our sample, we found three separate types of engineer-entrepreneurs – types X, Y and Z – and their placement on the continuum is shown in Figure 4.2.

Engineer-entrepreneurs may be highly technically-oriented in their positioning. This would make then 'technical engineer-entrepreneurs', a status we would ascribe to types Y and Z from Figure 4.2, presented in Figures 4.5 and 4.6. They may also be highly management-oriented, in which case they would be 'managerial engineer-entrepreneurs', a status we would ascribe to type X from Figure 4.2, presented in Figure 4.4. We believe managerial engineer-entrepreneurs are mostly the product of paths 2 and 3 from Figure 4.1, while technical engineer-entrepreneurs are a product of path 1.

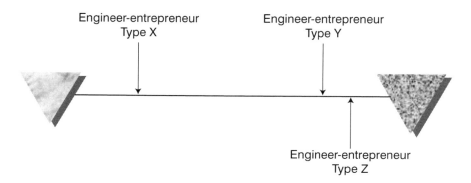

Figure 4.2 *Positioning the engineer-entrepreneur types*

The profile and characteristics of type A engineers are close to those of technical engineer-entrepreneurs, while managerial engineer-entrepreneurs tend to resemble type B and type C engineers. Managerial engineer-entrepreneurs are innovative entrepreneurs within the meaning of Schumpeter's (1935) definition, in that they regularly develop innovations, in the broad sense of the term, and continually challenge the market. The technical capital of managerial engineer-entrepreneurs is less utilized than that of technical engineer-entrepreneurs, and their technical speciality does not necessarily influence the choice of field for their new firm. The professional identity of managerial engineer-entrepreneurs is focused on command and hierarchy, unlike that of technical engineer-entrepreneurs, which is focused on technical skill. Technical engineer-entrepreneurs exhibit a high level of reproductive behaviour, and are best able to use their technical capital on opportunities closely tied to their past experience and engineering specialty area. Their entrepreneurial behaviour is based to a large extent on the notion of technical and professional continuity.

The firms created by the two types of engineer-entrepreneurs are very different. Technical engineer-entrepreneurs tend to create or purchase industrial firms with a strong technological focus, whereas managerial engineer-entrepreneurs opt for consulting, trading and distribution activities instead.

In short, an engineer's position on the technical-managerial continuum has an impact on his or her business activities and entrepreneur-like behaviour. The further they are from the technical end of the continuum, the more likely they are to launch firms in tertiary sectors unrelated to their prior professional experience. Their behaviours are based less on the reproduction of past activities, and their innovations tend to be more service-related and product-related than technological. (By contrast, a position located close to the technical end of the continuum will tend to generate intensely technological innovations.) Type X engineers – managerial engineer-entrepreneurs – on the other hand, make more use of resources and relations and less use of their technical capital. They also tend to have access to

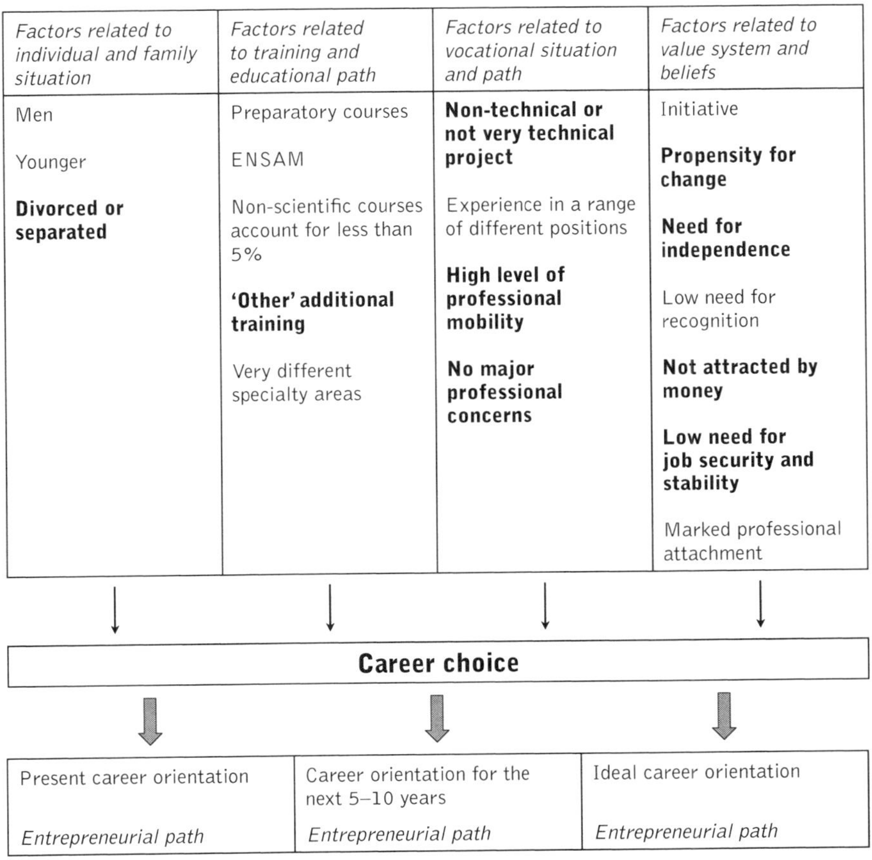

Factors related to individual and family situation	Factors related to training and educational path	Factors related to vocational situation and path	Factors related to value system and beliefs
Men Younger **Divorced or separated**	Preparatory courses ENSAM Non-scientific courses account for less than 5% **'Other' additional training** Very different specialty areas	**Non-technical or not very technical project** Experience in a range of different positions **High level of professional mobility** **No major professional concerns**	Initiative **Propensity for change** **Need for independence** Low need for recognition **Not attracted by money** **Low need for job security and stability** Marked professional attachment

↓ ↓ ↓ ↓

Career choice

⇓ ⇓ ⇓

Present career orientation *Entrepreneurial path*	Career orientation for the next 5–10 years *Entrepreneurial path*	Ideal career orientation *Entrepreneurial path*

Figure 4.3 *Characteristics of engineer-entrepreneurs (factors in bold exhibit the highest characteristics)*

more open opportunities, since they are less dependent on technical specialties. Type Y and Z engineers – technical engineer-entrepreneurs – are much more bound by their technical expertise when selecting opportunities. Table 4.1 highlights the main differences between these types of engineer-entrepreneurs.

CONCLUSION

Researching engineer-entrepreneurs is a way of researching engineers and their career problems. Engineer-entrepreneurs as they appear in our results are still engineers – in other words, the fact of becoming an entrepreneur does not necessarily entail breaking away from their professional identity as engineers. Engineers as a group are fairly homogenous in terms of social position and scientific or technical resources. On the other hand, they are extremely heterogeneous in terms of training and

Table 4.1 *Key features about the three types of engineer-entrepreneurs*

Characteristics of engineer-entrepreneurs	'Manager'	'Technical'	'Super-technical'
Statistical similarities with	Types C and B engineers	Types A and C engineers	Type A engineer
Entrepreneurial behaviors based on	Opportunity orientation Innovation	Resource control orientation/ Opportunity orientation Reproduction	Resource control orientation Reproduction
Innovation orientation	Services Products	Technologies	Technologies Technology development orientation
Types of business	Commerce Retailing Services Consulting	Industry Building industry Civil engineering Consulting	Industry High-technology Building industry Civil engineering

employment access. As a result, their careers are vastly divergent, although basically they tend to be employees.

Variety and difference generate wealth, and every one of these different entrepreneurial types, paths and behaviours is both legitimate, and of interest in a developed economy and society.

Our results show that in the engineering career, and consequently in the paths taken by engineer-entrepreneurs, there is a boundary of technical specialism that separates potential professional paths and identities. A path may be basically technical, in which case the professional identity of the engineer is founded on technical expertise and professionalism, or it may be more open, in which case the engineer moves away from the technical function towards more commercial, administrative financial or other types of functions. In such a case, the professional identity of the engineer will tend to be related more to management and hierarchy.

In attempting to understand the entrepreneurial behaviours of engineers, we rejected the deterministic model (Ribeill 1984) in favour of a more complex model based on the concept of 'interaction'. In our opinion, the entrepreneurial behaviours of French engineers take place within professional trajectories that begin at university and continue throughout their careers. These trajectories are influenced by a number of different factors, including the individual, the personal and family environment, education and educational path, and professional experience. Entrepreneurial behaviours among engineers are the result of forms of logic that depend on the choices made by the individual and his or her educational, personal and professional trajectories. The professional trajectories of engineers are social constructs developed through interactions between different elements – actor, professional opportunities, resources – within each engineer's action system.

Who they are	What they do	What is important for them	Position on the technical-managerial continuum
Average age: 46 yrs Father an engineer Relatives are entrepreneurs Initially trained as engineer Also trained in management Possible MBA Association creator Joins groups	Professional experience: 20 yrs Open to positions with non-scientific and non-technical content 3.5 different firms 5.5 different positions Professional paths related to management	Money Power Qualification Security and stability Technical aspect Professional association	Current specialty very different from that studied at university Projects tend to be less technical Level of proximity to tasks with less technical content (2.73)

Path to entrepreneurship	Entrepreneur-like behaviours
More shaded sense of the role played by the engineering school Earlier awareness of entrepreneurship First entrepreneurial behaviour: 11.7 years after graduating Weaker link between sector of activity and prior professional experience Sector of activity not related to engineering specialty Very different products Different customers Different suppliers	Creator Commercial and distribution activities Main customers: SMEs Innovative, non-technological products and services Partners are managers, not engineers External funding methods Firm's growth rate faster than average for the sector Firm's development: Launching new products. Creation of subsidiaries and franchises

Figure 4.4 'Managerial' engineer-entrepreneurs (Type X)

Who they are	What they do	What is important for them	Position on technical-managerial continuum
Average age: 48.5 yrs Close relatives in business Small family circle Preparatory courses Additional training with high level of scientific and technical content Initially trained as engineer Weight of continuous training	Professional experience: 24 yrs 4 different firms 5.3 different positions Technical functions dominate Technically-oriented professional path Marked entrepreneurial trend in career orientation	Reputation of their qualification Education Technical factors decisive in career choice Power decisive in career choice Attached to the status enjoyed by engineers Professional associations	Current specialty area very close to the area studied at university Projects tend to be technical in nature Level of proximity to tasks with strong technical content (4.4)

Path to entrepreneurship	Entrepreneur-like behaviours
Marked sense of the role played by the engineering school Became aware of entrepreneurship later in life First entrepreneurial behaviour: 12 years after graduating Strong link between sector of activity and past professional experience Sector of activity related to engineering specialty Close products Shared customers Shared suppliers Source of motivation: Independence, autonomy, use of knowledge Job loss or threatened job loss	Creator Buyer Industrial activities Large private firms: main customers New technology development Technological innovation, not related to products or services Partners are engineers, not managers Funded by personal savings Growth rate average for the sector Firm developed through better business opportunities

Figure 4.5 'Technical' engineer-entrepreneurs (Type Y)

Who they are	What they do	What is important for them	Position on technical-managerial continuum
Average age: 51 yrs Not many children Not married Preparatory courses Weight of continuous training Double engineering degree Additional training with strong scientific and technical content Not inclined towards associations	Professional experience: 26.5 yrs 3.54 different firms 4.95 different positions Technical functions dominate Not open to other functions Technically-oriented professional paths	Reputation of qualification Hierarchical relations Technical factors decisive in career choice Need for professional stability and security Recognition of status Attached to the status enjoyed by engineers Marked professional attachment	Current specialty area identical to that studied at university Highly technical projects Level of proximity to tasks with strong technical content (4.3)

Path to entrepreneurship	Entrepreneur-like behaviours
More shaded sense of the role played by the engineering school Early awareness of entrepreneurship, but First entrepreneurial behaviour: 13.25 years after graduating Strong link between sector of activity and past professional experience Close products Shared customers Shared suppliers Low level of motivation Employed by a firm, eventually became a partner Took over family business	Creator Taking over family business Industrial activities Public authorities and agencies: main customers Technological innovation and services New technology development Partners are engineers, not managers Funded by personal savings and by money from family or friends Firm developed through greater business opportunities Growth rate slightly more sustained than average for the sector

Figure 4.6 'Super-technical' engineer-entrepreneurs (Type Z)

As a result, numerous options are possible. The one taken will depend on the choices and non-choices made by the individual at different points in his or her career. In an engineer's professional life, such points emerge regularly as a result of changes in situations or contexts, or following meetings, innovations and personal training.

Some of the early choices made by engineers are of key importance – for example, the choice of school (university) and specialty area – because they will impact upon the future sector of activity and hence upon the type of opportunities available. It is because of these early choices that some engineers remain 'shut into' narrow specialty areas offering little opportunity for development, and others who would like to become entrepreneurs are unable to do so because of the nature of the sector for which they have been trained.

Chapter 5

Collective learning processes in high-tech firms

Enablers and barriers to the innovation process

Valérie-Inès de La Ville

The perspective suggested in this chapter was developed within the framework of longitudinal research undertaken over four years, in interaction with COM One, a young French telecommunications company created in 1987 (de La Ville 1996). Both the historical development of the firm since its foundation and its main evolutions during the time of the study have been retrieved and reconstructed through a qualitative research process (Hindle 2004). In 2004, COM One remained a leading French company specializing in the design, manufacture, sales and marketing of telecom products. For 15 years, the company has been designing products for major PC manufacturers and telecom operators, as well as selling telecommunication devices to the growing market of mobile professionals. COM One has designed stylish, simple, user-friendly and intuitive range of products for major companies operating in the professional markets. Certified ISO9001, the company is headquartered in Bordeaux and employs 55 people, including 25 engineers.

Within a nascent company, the development of the technical knowledge – in individual and collective terms – results from the inevitable involvement of the entrepreneurial team in social relations of various natures (Hite 2005). The strategic skills of COM One were gradually constituted to the processes, the study of which put forward the crucial importance of the discussions and the experiments which crystallized around various technical stakes. To better understand how collective know-how emerges – which found the distinctive skills of the young high-tech firm – supposes that we look further into the bond between individual learning and organizational learning. This chapter proposes to replace the collective learning processes at the very heart of the entrepreneurial practice.

The French philosopher Jacques Ellul (1990) usefully reminds us of the etymological distinction between 'technique' and 'technology', which is a discourse developed about a technique – whether the latter is already established or under development – in different social settings. This fine distinction helps us to consider the social dimension which makes it possible to achieve technical innovations within an entrepreneurial setting and implies determining more accurately the concept of context of communication, an integral part of any process of creative collective undertaking. Within a nascent company, the conversational interactions thus constitute the privileged means by which individual and collective know-how are worked out and co-ordinated in order to face the ambiguity caused by the technological explorations carried out by the entrepreneurial team. Indeed, the techniques are not in themselves meaningful; their significance depends on the social contexts of communication which give form to the interpretations that the individuals forge and retain – individually and collectively – about them.

TECHNOLOGICAL ENTREPRENEURSHIP: AS A COLLECTIVE CREATION

Schumpeterian modelling of economic development describes the processes of innovation like a deviation compared to routine behaviour, a deviation which causes a permanent renewal of the economic system through a sequence of cycles of 'creative destruction'. The interpretation of the writings of Joseph Schumpeter concerning the role of the entrepreneurial process in economic change constitutes a delicate task because successful innovation requires simultaneously a process of breaking-off and the generation of a series of routines.

Beyond the heroic high-tech entrepreneur

Seminal work by Joseph Schumpeter (1934) contributed in spite of itself to define a kind of ideal-type of entrepreneur, the creator of a technological company, a creative and isolated rebel, eager to fight against all odds to prove to the others the superiority of his ideas, and the only one able to introduce successfully an innovation – product or new process – on the market. But the simplification process through which the ideas of Joseph Schumpeter were popularized directly led to an incarnation of this ideal type. For Andrew Van de Ven, this phenomenon:

> is likely to explain why, until recently, the search for features, elements of personality and individual characteristics specific to entrepreneurs constituted the quasi-exclusive orientation of the investigations and the theories worked out in the field of entrepreneurship.
>
> (Van de Ven 1992: 215)

Generally, the theme of the profile of the entrepreneur remains central in all works which examine the phenomenon of the creation of innovating companies, and continues being widely spread by technocratic literature on the competitiveness of small and medium-sized companies. Many stereotypes are still associated with this 'thesis of the heroic entrepreneur' which hinder the comprehension of the processes of technical innovation (Mustar 1994). To establish such a striking short cut between the personal characteristics of the entrepreneur and the success or failure of the young high-tech company appears a specious step to us because the technical innovation does not constitute a purely individual realization, but supposes a process comprising a dimension of collective creation likely to develop over time. Bruno Latour (1987) demonstrates that active social networks and political struggles constitute an essential part of scientific innovation. In the same vein, Michel Callon (1994) notes that the question of the individual origin of the technical innovation is needlessly put forward, since each study devoted to a brilliant inventor leads, not only to a network linking the actors of the innovation, but also to the intersection of many individual trajectories which give consistency in certain moments and places to a collective project that takes shape and manages to last. Beyond the too often heroic role devoted to the entrepreneur, many studies have stressed the importance of team and organization building in the process of founding a new venture (Vesper 1980; Gartner 1985; Stewart 1989; Guth and Ginsberg 1990; Slevin and Covin 1992; Cooper and Daily 1997). This perspective has recently led us to consider that a major topic of entrepreneurship is the enhancement of the intellectual and creative capital of the nascent or established firm (Ahuja and Lampert 2001).

High-tech entrepreneurship as a collective creative process

Two neo-Schumpeterian approaches highlight the capital role of the organization of collective creative actions for achieving success in the process of innovation. Some put forward the discontinuities caused by the technical innovation, and consider that the entrepreneurial structures behave in an abnormal way, their role being to initiate the cycle of 'creative destruction'. From this point of view, the 'Minnesota Innovation Research Program' (MIRP), led by Andrew Van de Ven (1992) (Poole *et al.* 2000), builds a process theory aimed at explaining the origin and operation of several processes of innovation. The role allotted to the entrepreneurs takes into account their aptitude to manage, according to perceived opportunities, a group of complex processes such as the creation of an organization, and the mobilization of rare resources. Another interpretation of the Schumpeterian model is proposed by Richard Nelson and Sidney Winter who examine in greater detail what appears to them:

> to constitute key aspects of the competition in a Schumpeterian meaning – the diversity of the companies, both with regard to their particular characteristics and their experience as well as the cumulated interaction between this variety and the structure of industry.
>
> (Nelson and Winter 1982: 30)

They explain the development of technological innovation by using the concept of progressive evolution: for a given technology, the innovation occurs as the companies explore, and little by little identify new possibilities that are learnt gradually through a process of modification by trial and error, and sometimes of reinvention.

Technology is no longer conceived as an exogenous element, but rather as a variable which firms manage according to their particular social characteristics and the knowledge capital they have accumulated throughout their existence. These economists regard companies as a set of organizational routines treated on a hierarchical basis, which includes, on a lower level, organizational know-how and the way in which it is co-ordinated, and on a higher level, decision-making procedures aimed at determining what must be carried out at the lower levels.

Thus, at a given moment, the routinized practices which are assembled within an organization define a set of activities which the company is able to realize with assurance, i.e. its repertory of skills. Richard Nelson (1991) regrets, however, that the majority of modelling relating to technological innovation has not yet managed to capture the essence of the innovative process, namely its fundamental uncertainty, the differences in opinions, the divergences with regard to identifying practicable paths of development, which appear in any meticulous study of particular technical advances.

In order to better understand the emergence process of distinctive skills within the young high-tech company, it seems essential to try to situate the entrepreneur in relation to the multiple networks he is involved in, and to explore the various bonds which he is able to tie with other individuals or organizations during the process of technical innovation. In order to explore the social dimension which is a constituent part of the high-tech entrepreneurial process, we carried out an in-depth case study of COM One, a young telecommunications company founded in 1987. Over a period of four years we interviewed, on several occasions, 14 people who took part in the creation of the company and who directly contributed to its first years of existence. This investigation gathered 400 pages of accounts and resulted in an extensive monograph of 100 pages which reconstructs both the history of the firm since its foundation, the main orientations taken for technical development – and their correlated discussions – that took place during the time of the study. As the format of this chapter prevents reproducing extensive parts of this monograph and situating precisely every actor, small parts of the accounts given by the actors are used to illustrate their collective ability to set up meaningful technical innovations.

THE SOCIAL FOUNDATIONS OF TECHNOLOGICAL ENTREPRENEURSHIP

Organizational life within high-tech companies, young or older, is often depicted as a disordered, complex and polymorphic reality: individual attributions are not clearly defined and permanently change in order to closely follow the collective dynamics of the creative process; the judgement of peers constitutes a crucial process of co-ordination which results in reinforcing individual commitment and in developing practices of self-checking and shared authority. In this perspective, technical innovation is then mainly described as an informal process of communication which connects the individualities present within the incipient company, and contributes to reinforce individual learning capacities.

This is why, in order to explain the appearance of learning processes at a collective or organizational level, it is necessary to call upon 'leaders', 'champions', 'boundary spanning individuals' and other neo-Schumpeterian inspired conceptualizations of individualities who face the indifference of management or sceptical venture-capitalists (Waldman and Bass 1991; Bouchikhi and Kimberly 1994). However, it seems more difficult to unearth frameworks which deal explicitly with the thorny problem of the nature of the bond between individual learning processes and organizational types of learning processes (Kim 1993). It appeared to us that the constitution of such a link – which cannot rest only on individualities – had to be explored in a more systematic manner. Indeed, considering the way in which the entrepreneurial team manages to be collectively innovative over time, leads to interpreting the social phenomena which contribute to giving shape to the progressive development of distinctive skills and long-term dynamic capabilities within the young high-tech company (Newbert 2005).

The question is no longer then to limit the study of the technological process of entrepreneurship solely to the transfer of knowledge from an individual – the entrepreneur – towards an emerging social group – the nascent organization. It leads to attempts to understand how some technical knowledge is developed in a collective way and referred to as a meaningful innovation, worth being promoted on the market by the entrepreneurial team.

The inter-subjective foundations of individual learning

The Russian psychologist Lev Vygotsky has brilliantly defended the idea of the social genesis of individual knowledge by showing how the children work out individual cognitive schemes during activities shared with adults or other children, in a specific social context (Bronckardt and Mounoud 1985). The concept of 'activity' that he forged has the merit of integrating at the same time the social conditions – interactive – and the individual characteristics – cognitive – of the learning process. By engaging in a shared activity and by exploring the inter-subjective space that it creates, the individual is led to open up to an alter ego and gradually to work out his own interpretations of the situation (Levine et al. 1993; Crossley 1996). In the field of organizations, H.A. Simon makes a similar observation:

> What an individual learns within an organization depends directly on what the other members know (or believe) already and on the type of information available in the organizational environment.
>
> (Simon 1991: 125)

Serge Moscovici also reminds us that the notion of 'social representation' was conceived to express the social dimension of knowledge forged by the individual (Moscovici 1994). Indeed, the social representations objectified by an individual during a joint activity, direct the practices to come: the social representations held by an individual take into account the possible reactions of others to their own ideas or actions. It is the performative character of this concept which appears particularly interesting to us: a social representation is not simply a cognitive representation of the joint activity it takes into account the social imperatives for the continuation of the joint activity. As a result, it directly focuses the individual action according to normative implications aimed at defining the framework for the reciprocal commitment of the participants to a meaningful relationship which makes it possible to pursue the joint activity.

Nevertheless, it is unrealistic to believe that the individuals involved in a joint technical project would see the situations in the same way, and allow the natural emergence of strong social cohesion and a harmonious community of practice. The individual learning experiences are not only unequally distributed within the young company, but are founded on contrasting social representations according both to the technical activities to which the individuals have taken part and to the personal history of each participant. For example, the sudden breakdown of the relationships between the designers and the technical director, cofounder of COM One, concerning the development of a new product, offers a good illustration of the complexity of an interaction.

Learning at COM One

The accounts of the engineers at COM One bring many illustrations of their participation in a wide rage of activities shared with other engineers, sub-contractors, prospective customers, managers, end-users, competitors or administrations. By being involved in projects and relationships as varied as the design of the products, the production possibilities offered by sub-contractors, the continuous adaptation to regulatory modifications or the satisfaction of the end-user, each engineer had the opportunity to explore a broad and rich inter-subjective space and thus, to objectify a certain quantity of information crucial for the development of new products.

The developers of COM One recall that during the early days, when the engineering department operated in a very rudimentary fashion, the technical director trained them in the development of new products and was directly involved in the projects by working very closely with his team to overcome the difficulties which were emerging. But when a few months later, the technical director suggested exploring the possibility of producing a completely revolutionary product – a modem able to function with a very low level of electricity consumption – the team of the developers collectively refused to participate in this process of investigation.

Indeed, COM One's designers had gradually become aware of the need for better organization and for partially safeguarding the stages of technical development processes within COM One, in order to increase its efficiency and to improve the reliability of the prices and delivery times announced to powerful customers. Confronted with the suggestion to explore a new avenue on the technical level, but which, a priori, presented little chance of success, the pressure felt by the engineers in the design team became suddenly too strong, carrying their level of anxiety to an unbearable level and leading them to call into question the confidence which they had expressed thus far in the technical director. The definition of the normative imperatives necessary for the continuation of the joint activity of development under good conditions diverged too much between the design engineers and the technical director, making continued collaboration impossible and leading ineluctably to the calling into question of the relationship.

COM One's rapid growth as well as the multiplication of projects under development within the design department, constituted factors which brought to light such different social representations that they led to a sudden breakdown of the interaction between the developers and the technical director. He had to give up the management of the team of developers and shut himself away in a company office in order to continue his exploratory work. In order to finish his project, he recruited a young developer and signed an agreement with a university laboratory. His work, removed from the daily operation of the design team, made it possible to create a truly innovative product – the 'light modem', which represented 50 per cent of the sales of COM One over three years.

This illustration makes it possible to underline the interest of the concept of 'joint activity': it is profoundly linked to the idea of ambiguity of interpretation and presupposes active participation in the interaction in order to forge both inter-subjective and autonomous knowledge. The perceived quality of the relationship between the participants directly determines the richness of the inter-subjective space explored through reciprocal involvement in a joint activity, as James March and Johan Olsen point out:

> Moreover, we seldom found our interpretations on our personal observations alone; they rest amply on interpretations that others offer to us. Our degree of confidence in the latter clearly depends on the confidence which we grant to their interpreters.
>
> (March and Olsen 1975: 155)

Thus, a distant or recalcitrant participation by one of the participants in a joint technical activity is likely to impoverish the collective exploration process of a restricted inter-subjective space and as a result, directly limits the interaction's learning potential for the participants.

The reframing of technical activities as a collective learning process

This second level of our framework tackles the link between individual and collective knowledge forged during conversational interactions intended to interpret the plausible meaning of the various technical activities carried out by the members of the young high-tech company.

The permanent conversational effort undertaken in order to share problems, collectively to seek acceptable solutions, and to encourage a thorough exchange of opinions in the course of action is often described as a major characteristic of the behaviour of managers within young innovative companies:

> by taking part continuously with the others in the resolution of the problems which the company faces and by bringing about a language of requirements and activities which is meaningful for all.
>
> (Burns and Stalker 1961: 125)

Indeed, the root of the word communication clearly contains a social dimension which directly conveys the idea of sharing, participating and pooling, and even sometimes of communion. By allotting an interpretative framework to a joint activity, the participants in the interaction evaluate the degree of their own commitment to allow the pursuit of the interaction. Erving Goffman (1986) shows that each interpretative frame includes a set of normative requirements which define the acceptable behaviour allowing the deepening of the joint activity and thus, directing the learning potential brought about by the interaction. The frame mobilized to interpret the joint activity acts as a 'cognitive pilot' by directly guiding the learning capacities of the participants in the interaction. If the framework used by one of the participants proves to be erroneous, his learning attempts are likely to be misleading and his behaviour could in some cases appear as socially unacceptable for the other members of the interaction.

The process of technical innovation requires a continuous inter-subjective exploration of the interpretative frames likely to be applied to the joint design activity in order to reduce the ambiguity produced by the multiplicity of potentially sense-bearing settings. Karl Weick (1993b) points out that the design activity often consists of modifying the framework of attention and significance applied to a flow of ongoing social practices, rather than to impose an a priori stable model of intentions of actions undertaken to achieve a pre-defined goal. Thus, during the process of high-tech entrepreneurship, it is through conversational interactions that the ambiguous significance of the techniques under development are collectively explored, and that the commercial possibilities of a technical innovation are discussed, or that endeavours are made to find an acceptable technical solution to meet the requirements defined by a customer.

However, to choose the relevant interpretative frame is not an easy task and very often, the individuals hesitate as to the frame which they must use to interpret correctly the direction of the technical joint activity and to anticipate its possible evolutions. Under these conditions, any information, no matter how small, can result in discrediting certain frames and in confirming others; the interpretative frames are indeed very vulnerable and are the subject of misunderstandings in practice. Erving Goffman shows with meticulousness how the frames are constantly manipulated during daily conversations and can be, in certain cases, voluntarily transformed in order to induce a desired behaviour on part of the participants in the interaction.

Case example: differences in interpretive framing within COM One

It was possible for us to observe at COM One how the technical director and the design engineers had proposed two antagonist frames – that we label 'originality' versus 'safety' – which, having functioned as cognitive pilots supporting the divergent interpretative processes, led to a sudden breakdown in the social relationships between the design team and the technical director. At COM One, various frames gave shape to the research and new product design processes, for example, to ensure that the prototypes could be correctly reproduced in order to guarantee a smooth passage to a large sale production, or to lower the costs in order to be able to access foreign markets, and directed the definition of the priorities to be considered by the engineers in their ordinary design practice.

By handling various interpretative frames, managers find themselves in a situation where they can influence the collective process of exploration of the various interpretations which can be called upon for a technical problem, with the aim of supporting and of accelerating the innovative efforts within the young company. It seems interesting to decipher which types of frames are used in various situations such as, for instance, when a prototype – an incomplete version of the desired product – is presented to a customer, or when the innovative efforts are directed towards the realization of an 'incremental innovation' versus a 'radical innovation'.

To activate a relevant frame is not always easy. Putting forward a frame of 'emergency' can result in privileging reflexes rather than reflection in the exploration of technical difficulties, leading to priority being given to well-mastered techniques within the company in order to ease and accelerate the outcome of the design process. Nevertheless, such a choice contributes in the long run to exhausting the creative potential of the young high-tech company. On projects presented using frames which do not place the emphasis on urgency, the engineers are more likely to explore techniques with which they are less familiar, an investigation stage which makes it possible to enrich the technical repertoire as well as the collective learning capacities within the company.

In order to channel ambiguous joint technical activities going on within the young high-tech company, the processes of collective setting and redefining relevant interpretative frames continuously take place mainly through conversational interactions. As they cannot be stored in files or precise written procedures, these interpretative frames are maintained thanks to their constant re-use in practice, in the pursuit of joint activities and of conversations and, quite simply, through the constitution of managerial, behavioural and interpretative routines (Weick 1995).

The institutionalization of routines enables the formation of dynamic capabilities

The permanence of these interpretative frames is directly related to their continuous use in practice and conversations within the young high-tech company. Thus, the concept of 'frame' can only be understood in a relation of co-presence of the participants in the interaction. Conversely, the emergence of some distinctive skills within the young high-tech company presupposes the permanence of such interpretative frames beyond the initial protagonists involved in a joint activity, and must consequently be connected to the concept of 'organizational memory' (Walsh and Ungson 1991). Anthony Giddens (1987) explicitly deals with this problem in his theory of structuring. The interpretative frames used during the process of investigation and product design are created and maintained during joint technical activities even though they simultaneously contribute to directing and channelling these same joint activities. The structuring process refers to the production and the reproduction of relations of interdependence – social systems – through the use of rules and resources – structures – during joint technical activities. This concept of 'duality of structure' expresses the idea that the rules which control the social systems are at the same time the conditions and the results of the activities undertaken by the participants in the interaction. This idea is directly applicable to the discourses dealing with technical dynamics of which Karl Weick has given a fine analysis:

> Technology is both a posterior product of lessons learned while implementing a specific technical system and an a priori source of options that can be realized in a specific technical system.
>
> (Weick 1990: 5)

The stabilization of these practices also presupposes the capacity to use the information in a systematic way in an attempt to influence and to control the process of reproduction or transposition of the interpretative frames used to give a direction to the joint technical activities. Thus, the processes of memorization reinforce the reproduction of ordinary practices and make it possible to perpetuate the social imperatives needed to pursue relevant technical joint activities within the company. It is through ordinary conversations that the process of collective memorization organizes individual perceptions and gives a coherent texture to the community of exploration that constitutes young high-tech companies. And when the structures — rules and resources — are accepted, used and placed in a daily context, they are stabilized and end up being institutionalized. Nevertheless, unintentional consequences are likely to appear since the participants in the interactions have only a partial understanding of the social system in which they are involved (Giddens 1987).

Case example: routines and dynamic capabilities at COM One

For example, within COM One, the progressive routinization of collective practices of investigation and development caused the institutionalization of certain skills at the expense of others being formed.

Through the product design process for its customers, and the development of a very specific know-how relating to the different regulatory standards operating on the European telecommunications markets — before 1998 — COM One collectively forged a series of routinized practices which reinforced the perceived originality of its competitive position as a specialized sub-contractor.

But in parallel, the efforts made by COM One to develop its own products and to set up a distribution network on the European market remained sporadic, with little co-ordination and did not give rise to collective practices routinized within the company. Thus, the marketing of COM One's own products was postponed on several occasions, reinforcing the mistrust of the distributors who were tired of waiting for the promised products and who finally decided to give priority to other competitors to constitute their own range.

This decision of course increased the natural tendency within COM One to regard the design projects on behalf of powerful industrial customers as a priority, and also further convinced the commercial team charged with creating a European distribution network that the routinized operation of the design team would not make it possible to take into account the requirements related to the launching of COM One's own line of products.

Given the series of routinized practices which are gradually set up within the young high-tech company, a multiplicity of institutionalized orders emerges and gives form to a complex series of distinctive capacities. The main stake facing the entrepreneurial team then consists in controlling a dynamic balance between the various institutionalized technological routines in order to reinforce the individual and collective learning capacities and to ensure that distinctive skills can emerge, take shape, evolve, and become more and more complex in the long term.

For Richard Nelson and Sydney Winter, 'the idea of "organizational genetics" raises a major challenge: to manage to understand how the continuity of a routinized behaviour acts to channel organizational change' (Nelson and Winter 1982). The process of reframing, partly triggered in an intentional way by the managers, or simply emerging from the joint technical activities in which the members of the young company are involved, achieves this dynamic balance by allowing the social representations and strategic discourses to evolve and to work out a series of ambiguous plausible worlds which call for increased collective investigations. Thus, within the young high-tech company, the significance granted to the techniques and the potential uses which result from them, depend on the interpretations enshrined in the social practices which are regarded as acceptable and enriching within the entrepreneurial team.

MANAGING TECHNICAL UNCERTAINTY THROUGH RHETORICAL INTERVENTIONS

This chapter logically leads to the proposal of studying the rhetorical devices (Simons 1989; Potter 1996) used within the teams of research and design to convince their participants to increase their efforts of exploration in a direction and thus, to make them accept collectively that certain technical possibilities be thoroughly examined whereas others remain unexplored. Ellul's (1990) distinction between 'techniques' and 'technologies' suggests another way of conceiving technology as the collective rhetorical ability to frame a technical activity.

According to Michel Meyer, rhetorical dynamics are the means through which people negotiate the distance among their interpretations about a specific matter, a precise problem (Meyer 1993). This definition reminds us that this concept integrates the contextual social conditions in which the discourses are enshrined. This perspective makes it possible to better understand the various rhetorical dynamics present in the inter-subjective dialogical spaces created by the joint technical activities in the young high-tech company.

This definition of technology opens tracks of research to look further into the concept of 'technological idiosyncrasy' sketched by Richard Nelson and Sydney Winter:

> It does imply that it is quite inappropriate to conceive of firm behaviour in terms of deliberate choice from a broad menu of alternatives that some external observer considers to be 'available' opportunities for the organization. The menu is not broad, but narrow and idiosyncratic.
>
> (Nelson and Winter 1982: 134)

80

This notion embraces the specific way in which technical advances are collectively explored and interpreted within the entrepreneurial firm, confirming the importance of the entrepreneurial team as an original social community which evolves and perpetuates itself, by addressing a series of normative requirements. This governs the technical exploration that is allowed and developed within the young high-tech company (de La Ville 2000).

Coping with contrasting technological idiosyncrasies

Under which conditions does a plurality of 'technological idiosyncrasies' reinforce the design of competitive techniques and when is it likely to constitute an obstacle for the development of distinctive dynamic capabilities within the young high-tech company? The answer should not be sought in a hypothetical logic of intrinsic development of the techniques, but rather in the comprehension of the possibilities of exploration offered by the social contexts or the interpretative frameworks to which the engineers refer when they make irreversible technical decisions.

Through our in-depth study of COM One, we have been able to identify various forms of technological idiosyncrasies that are likely to coexist during the process of high-tech entrepreneurship which aim at establishing differentiated innovative paths and contributing to producing communication contexts with quite contrasting normative implications.

First, a defensive technology. In this case, collective innovative efforts aim at preventing that certain technical know how developed within the young high-tech company, which is easily imitated by other competitors.

Second, an imitative technology. This is the collective innovative efforts that are intended to supplement certain technical know-how developed within the young high-tech company, in order to integrate new sources of valorization within the framework of interactions where the young company lets itself be guided by some of its influential partners.

Third, a submissive technology. This involves pushing the young high-tech company to follow frantically the rhythm of innovation and the requirements imposed by the technical evolution specific to the activities of certain external stakeholders, who are mainly customers (Reuber and Fisher 2005). In this case, the young high-tech company is likely to exhaust its resources – which are inevitably very limited – in following the requirements of certain customers without being able to develop really original technical know-how likely to be appreciated by other potential customers.

Fourth, an insular technology. This allows the young high-tech company to develop its own range of techniques which it can enhance in an autonomous way. The risk of this approach is to privilege too narrow a frame in the course of the collective action which reduces the scope of the innovative efforts, limiting the future possibilities of enhancing the innovation carried out as a result.

Fifth, an influential technology. This aims at promoting certain standards in the environment through different lobbying attempts. This type of framing mobilizes the know-how of institutionalization that the young company develops during the first years of its existence. It leads to the imposition of a technical standard that the company developed and under which certain circumstances might become a world standard.

These different types of innovative behaviours develop simultaneously according to the personality and tacit knowledge held by the participants as well as their involvement in several relational networks (Hite 2005). They structure very distinct interpretative frames, whose normative requirements produce very contrasting visions as to the human or financial, or technical choices to be made as a priority. These technological idiosyncrasies also contribute to define what is at stake for the pursuit of collective innovative efforts.

Partially directing collective technological improvizations

To wonder about the dominant technological idiosyncrasies during the entrepreneurial process results in conceiving the rhetorical dynamic which connects individual cognitive schemes and collective interpretative frames. This prospect brings an explanation as to the various modes of structuring distinctive skills which can appear during the young high-tech company's development. A difficult task for strategic management then consists in locating, proportioning, influencing and balancing these multiple technological idiosyncrasies which develop simultaneously, because each one of them structures a stage open to certain forms of collective improvization.

The collective improvization indeed confirms the ambiguous bond of interdependence which links the actors and allows the active exploration of a common ground of action. Karl Weick points out that in the theatre and in music, improvization, i.e. the simultaneity of co-ordination and individual expression, is possible only because the various actors have an equivalent understanding of what is occurring and of what that could mean (Weick 1993a, 1998; Miner et al. 2001). Thus, if an innovation is to see the light of day, it seems necessary to operate on the socio-cultural frame of interpretation in order to support the emergence of new collective improvizations in practice. But, at the same time, it is advisable to control the evolution of the level of ambiguity and anguish caused by such a reframing process. The entrepreneurial team must take care to set up dialogical devices intended to encourage communication, leading collective investigations and confronting interpretative frames.

The dialogical or staging devices can be either of formal or abstract nature: fictitious boards of directors, scenarios of a business plan, presentation of various prototypes, training sessions, working on new contractual proposals, seminars to explore the axes of development which appear accessible to the company, think tanks on the installation of means of co-ordination between departments, etc. The acceptance of ambiguity is a factor of innovation because when interpretative frames are multiple or partially ambiguous, individuals feel free to experiment, to test possibilities likely to be erroneous and to try several types of collective improvization. The entrepreneurial team must take care that the socio-cultural framework which guides the innovative efforts does not drastically reduce the level of ambiguity in the precise fields where it seems necessary to support the emergence of new forms of collective improvization.

In the light of the multiplicity of potentially significant interpretative frames and the feeling of anguish which accompanies it, non-verbal communication and chit-chat constitute invaluable sources of co-ordination; they make it possible to maintain a certain social order which guarantees the direction of the efforts carried out by the participants to continue their collaboration. This perspective also takes into account the emotions and the emotional ties which give rise to multiple collective improvizations and which directly contribute to the collective definition of the potential value of a new technique.

Preventing interpretative blockages to enhance on-going improvization

Is the entrepreneurial team not in a situation of permanent improvization with regard to customers or partners with whom it wishes to maintain and develop lasting bonds in order to promote its innovative potential? During the high-tech entrepreneurial process, the members of the young company are confronted with a great complexity of meanings, in particular with regard to the potential value of the technical innovations accomplished during collective improvizations.

However, the process of retrospective sense-making is extremely vulnerable: it is about a collective attempt, always precarious, to order the flood of actions in progress (Weick 1995). The collective exploration of certain interpretative frames is thus likely to worsen or to be blocked, causing a brutal halt in the capacity for collective improvization. In particular, when conflicting interpretative frames emerge from the participation in joint technical activities, two interdependent phenomena result (March 1991).

The first is an unbearable increase in anguish within the initial team, which is no longer sufficiently able collectively to interpret for the common exploration to continue. The second is an inability successfully to conclude collective improvizations, since the methods at the origin of conflicting interpretative frames limit the possibilities of experimentation of new behaviours, with the result that a possible failure will not be assumed in a collective way, but will be used to call into question the finality of the interaction itself. This can lead the manager to support the breaking away of technical teams having developed interpretative frameworks which are too conflicting, in order to allow the re-creation of differentiated socio-cultural contexts, fully ambiguous and more propitious for the appearance of new forms of technological improvization.

The main contribution of this approach is to explain why the entrepreneurial team cannot claim to control the substance of the collectively built entrepreneurial project: its contents will always be partly beyond its control, because it is not possible for it to control completely the framing and reframing processes carried out collectively in practice (Shotter 1990). Moreover, the entrepreneur does not intervene without risks, in a rhetorical register with the hope of reducing the vulnerability of the young high-tech company. The additional costs that are likely to appear in various forms such as difficulties in developing large-scale production batches based on a new technique; opening of the market at a slower rate than expected; under-estimation of the commercial investments necessary to promote the products to the target concerned; and insufficient capitalization can be, in particular, due to an inefficient or badly controlled reframing process by the entrepreneurial team. The reframing, a rhetorical process by nature, is based on the handling of an infinity of criteria such as urgency, need, complementarity, contradiction, competitiveness, and the assertion of the paradoxes, in order to trigger the collective search for new interpretative frameworks making it possible at the same time to maintain ambiguity at an acceptable level and to pursue a collective undertaking through improvization.

We have suggested various lines of reflection aimed at considering the rhetorical dimension which characterizes the strategic management in high-tech entrepreneurial settings. These openings constitute a heuristic framework likely to help the entrepreneur and the research and design teams to become aware of their priorities to lead to the development of the high-tech company.

CONCLUSION

As a very provisional conclusion, stress must be placed on the dialogical nature of the technical skills which enable the young high-tech company to emerge in a lasting and justifiable way in a competitive field whose contours are also built through a multiplicity of interactions between various actors or stakeholders, both internal or external (Barhami and Evans 1989; Klofsten 1997; Johannisson and Moensted 1997; Reuber and Fischer 2005; Hite 2005). Thus, the gradually instituted entrepreneurial process always remains a fragile, singular and provisional order, but also evolutionary because it is constantly being constructed within the particular social community formed by the entrepreneurial team.

Rhetorical dynamics appear then as a central part of the activity of the entrepreneurial team because they open more or less rich inter-subjective spaces allowing the development of collective capacities of exploration within the young high-tech company (de La Ville and Mounoud 2003). These same rhetorical dynamics – by achieving a collective legitimization of some interpretative frames at the expenses of others – lead to a progressive reduction in the range of techniques being explored, a process which is absolutely necessary to support the collective exploratory capacity of the nascent high-tech firm. This social phenomenon of collective sense-making contributes directly to the emergence and the institutionalization of some distinctive capacity held by the young high-tech company: it constitutes a singular process of technological actualization among many other possibilities (de Coninck 1994).

Different entrepreneurial ways of facing uncertainty

Simon Harris

This second part of the book now explores variety and complexity in the high-tech entrepreneurship context, and the variety in the ways that the intrinsic uncertainties explored in the first part are managed in different contexts. In particular, it looks at the different social domains – networks etc. – and examines the different 'milieu' in which high-tech entrepreneurship operates.

In this, we see how we are not dealing with a 'global' concept. Our various contributors, from different European countries and with different scholarly and professional backgrounds, help us to see that there is not one standardized global approach. Rather, there is a diversity of approach and, in the following chapters, we gain a flavour of that diversity. We will see different approaches, different cultural contexts, and different resources that are essential in the high-tech entrepreneurship process.

In Chapter 6, Michel Bernasconi, Ludovic Dibiaggio and Michel Ferrary look at similarities and differences in the environments or 'milieu' for high-tech entrepreneurship, by examining and comparing two regions in the world that have strong high-tech clusters, Sophia Antipolis and Silicon Valley. By linking ideas from network research to the notion of 'development poles', it focuses on the issues of network richness.

There are strong similarities. Within a theme of the importance of networks that reoccur throughout this part and the next, both Silicon Valley and Sophia Antipolis are geographically focused centres of expertise in which there are communities of common practice, rich environments within which knowledge can be shared, resources can become accessible, and linkages made. Here, highly valuable weak ties can most readily be formed, and once formed, used in the process of business development.

In Sophia Antipolis, however, some aspects seem to be more important. First, weakness is also found in weak ties. Although weak ties give access to resources, transferring them needs stronger ties. Second, the role of institutions is found to be greater; it is these that provide many of the necessary additional resources. Above all, emphasis in Sophia Antipolis appears to be not so much in the extent of the networks, the communities of practice, and the institutions, but in their richness.

Different national environments and different institutional environments are examined by Simon Harris in Chapter 7. He examines network formation of high-tech entrepreneurs, within closely matched international entrepreneurs in the worldwide electronics industry, in the different contexts of France – around Sophia Antipolis – in Scotland, and in the Netherlands. In such a globalized high-tech industry, where standards and processes are set on a global stage, we might expect firms to pursue their network relationships in a more or less similar way. While all these entrepreneurs fully own and control their businesses, comparisons are also made within the UK with another group who are institutionally different, in that they are financed by venture capital firms.

He finds that network formation and use, even in such a globalized high-tech industry, is a localized phenomenon, localized to different national cultures, and localized to different institutional cultures. In all, there was a need for a 'milieu', enabling networks of relationships of different types, in all its richness. One aspect of culture is the way relationships form, develop and affect the social world. The necessary strong ties of high-tech entrepreneurships are culture phenomena, in which there is considerable variety.

Taking a normative perspective based on long practitioner experience in the field, rather than an analytical approach, Philippe Albert and Lynda Gaynor look at incubators as support structures in Chapter 8, and give a flavour of the complex and diverse ways in which incubators help the development of their incubatee businesses. They present the different and subtle range of resources that are required for successful high-tech entrepreneurship. They argue that good incubators and good incubatee–incubator relationships are important for high-tech businesses and for economic development, evidenced by the rapid expansion in the number of incubators. The different services that incubators can offer are described.

A number of roles are presented for incubators. The 'cluster' role highlights the benefit for high-tech young companies of close proximity to others in the neighbourhood, and how the incubator can maximize the advantage that can be taken of this proximity. Another is the role is the provider of a 'milieu' through an infrastructure that helps to link the incubate companies with people and recourses inside and outside the incubator. Another is the role that can be played by different institutions around the incubator that are associated or linked in some way with it. Incubators provide a 'learning place' setting where the incubatee businesses learn how to develop their businesses, learning from specialist advisers inside and outside the incubator, as well as from their neighbours. In a similar way, they can be seen as a resource repository, where essential resources, which include knowledge and access to knowledge and skills reside.

While there is no analysis as to which is the most effective, the authors indicate best practices with respect to the different services on the basis of extensive experience. It is evident that all the roles are closely linked with one another: they are not isolated. Overall, they present the variety and complexity of the work that incubators do, and argue that the sponsors of incubators, which include universities and local governments, do not understand that variety and complexity.

Chapter 9 looks at strategy development processes, and in it Franck Moreau considers the considerable complexities involved in the ways in which the strategies of young high-tech firms are themselves developed and managed. He distinguishes two separate domains of concern in the strategy development process. The first is its 'temporality', its dynamics. Sequential development takes place stage by stage. Although commonly advocated in entrepreneurship texts, this is naïve; it is and should be much more complex. Simultaneous development involves different elements of firms developed in parallel; with developments taking place in one time period anticipating the expected or desired future requirements.

The second is the extent to which the different aspects of management, e.g. marketing or finance, and processes of development within the firm are integrated together, the 'interprocessural integration'. This can be weak or strong. Combining these two dimensions gives us four characterizations of the ways in which firms can develop. The 'classical' process, typically recommended for entrepreneurial firms, involves sequential development with strong processural integration. Without the strong integration, we see the 'simple' development process that typifies many young firms' strategy development, or lack of it. A 'chaotic' process, predictably, results from combining weak integration with sequential temporality, since developments occur for no coherent purpose.

High-tech entrepreneurial firms involve complex resources, complex environments, and advanced resource integration requirements. It also involves high levels of uncertainty. In these, the strategy development process needs to be 'complex' as well; involving sequentially developed strategies that exhibit strong integration. As time passes, the need for ever-more sequential temporality and ever more integration in processes also increases. The patterns of development are complex, and dynamic, and the capabilities for managing the strategy development process involved in this are both sophisticated and complex as well. Multifaceted developments take place simultaneously and need to be integrated with one another in sophisticated ways. Simple or sequential conceptualizations of small firm development will not do. Once again we see that there are no unique rules, and no set patterns.

Knowledge-rich university spin-out firms are a particular context examined in Chapter 10 by Céline Druilhe and Elizabeth Garnsey, and the dynamic processes of development in this particular type of firm. By using the Penrosian resource-based view in a dynamic perspective, outwith its normal home within comparative statics, they create a model that sees five stages of firm development. The first involves opportunity recognition, where the potential spin-out company has highly limited resources for establishing a business. The most that a group of inspirationally commercial academics can do, without gaining access to a range of other resources that are not normally familiar to them, is to do what they already do. This is to provide knowledge services, in the form of contract research and development (R&D), technical services, and consultancy. Even a move to stage two, the licensing of intellectual property for other parties to use, or information service provision, requires not only new skills and financial resources, but also the knowledge and perception that these resources are actually needed. In universities, even the capabilities to undertake the opportunity recognition, basic primary requirement in spin-outs, are not present.

Firms in stage three are going beyond supplying knowledge, the stock-in-trade of the academic, and are supplying a product, though in this case software products, which though they do not require complex manufacturing and service operations, do require a commercial organization, a commercial mindset, and a commercial inclination. Here we are managements, in a Penrosian way, mobilizing and combining new resources, in this case commercial knowledge and abilities, with their original technical knowledge abilities.

This process continues in stages four and five, where we see the beginnings of a venture base, with the mobilization and combination of an increasingly full range of production and commercial capabilities. Stage four involves manufacture, beginning with niche products being outsourced, and developing towards mass products, with more in-house involvement, such as in product design and development. Stage five, where a venture base becomes complete, involves full in-house manufacture. The resource requirements are progressively greater in each stage, and the requirements for relevant knowledge demanded of the managers also becomes progressively greater.

The route to development depends on the resources that are resident, the resources that are needed, and the resources that become available. Each route to development and each pattern of development is unique; there are no 'general' patterns. The dynamics of development depend on how the resources are assimilated, which can differ according to the responses to feedback and the way that learning and change takes place.

The learning patterns and the ways that resources are adapted and adopted are unique in each situation. For example, these types of firms usually face such extensive resource constraints that new partnerships and collaborations are normally required. In each of these, the balance between the parties in terms of power and knowledge is unique. The choices that are made, and the abilities of the management involved to learn and to acquire other knowledge and resources in such a way as to change the balance of power and knowledge, are also unique. Entrepreneurs can be flexible, and can add capabilities, but their abilities to do so will vary.

Concluding this part, in Chapter 11, Michel Bernasconi looks at the creation process that lies at the heart of high-tech entrepreneurship. By adopting a systemic approach to understanding the process in a more fine-grained way, he shows the different systems that are required to manage the complexity inherent in the process of development, to manage the process of strategy formulation and implementation – including strategy emergence as well as planning – and to manage the immense uncertainties involved in the development of activities. This helps us to envision the whole process including its complexity and uncertainty in a useful way, which embraces both strategy formulation and strategy implementation.

A starting conceptualization involves three familiar phases in the company creation process: opportunity recognition, then business creation. In this framework, it is important to recall that the purpose is not to build a company as a legal form, although doing so may well be an outcome of the process. Rather, it is the activity, the resource base that is involved, and how it is organized that is important. In other words, it is the project and the projects. Five dimensions of these resources are considered.

These dimensions are the entrepreneur as a person, the environment of the firm that is itself highly complex, embracing the competitive environment, the local 'milieu', the social capital, the organization of the firm, the activities undertaken, and the financial resources involved. These dimensions are all closely and dynamically interlinked, in complex ways. The systemic approach adopted in this analysis shows how these dimensions, and the complex relationships between them, evolve over time as the firm develops from one phase of development to another. In this respect, we are engaged with an evolving project, and the entrepreneurial job is to manage this process. The relationships between the dimensions become stronger and stronger as the firms progress from one stage to another, and a major role of the entrepreneur is to strengthen the relationships between the dimensions. The way that this is done and the way the firm develops as a result is unique.

Further, it is not a linear or even a singularly progressive process. Businesses may well be created from the identification of single opportunities, and then companies can be developed from these, but the projects involved in this process are not singular, and their development is not staged. The issues within the different dimensions change as the business develops, and there are aspects of all the stages involved at the same time. Businesses may well be going through the business creation phase but, by then, new opportunities are being recognized. Once developed as a company, new businesses will continue to be created, and within these, new opportunities created again.

This final chapter of Part II shows very clearly that seeing the creation process as a linear and singular process is an unrealistic simplification. The pattern of development of each firm is special and unique, and the environment in which it can be fostered and developed is also highly diverse.

Chapter 6

High-tech clusters
Network richness in Sophia Antipolis and Silicon Valley

Michel Bernasconi,
Ludovic Dibiaggio and Michel Ferrary

Entrepreneurship has become one of the pillars of economic development. Since Marshall (1920) we have seen how vital is the milieu and the local environment for the success of new companies, which is why entrepreneurs tend to gather in geographical clusters. The emergence of new high-tech based industries – such as semi-conductors, computers, biotechnology, etc. – in certain well-determined geographical areas has incited dreams beyond the sphere of economics. With these exceptional cases being held up as models, repeated attempts have been made to reproduce these successes in regions designated as future Silicon Valleys.

Recent studies on social networks highlight the importance of the processes of innovation within clusters (Nohria and Eccles 1992). In highly competitive environments where the speed and pertinence of information is crucial, social networks appear as alternative – or supplementary – modes of co-ordination to market co-ordination (Saxenian 1994). The seminal work of Granovetter (1973, 1985) on the strength of links between agents provides a powerful analytical tool for describing the structure of social networks. While strong links are sources of confidence, procure a certain amount of security, and facilitate the adaptability of network members during crisis periods, weak links give access to information which is available outside familiar social circles (Granovetter 1982; Krachardt and Stern 1988).

The structuring of these networks is not a matter of chance, and is often influenced by agents at the heart of the territory. The objective of this chapter is to put into perspective certain structural characteristics of the networks central to technological clusters, through a comparison between Silicon Valley and Sophia Antipolis. Specifically, we test two hypotheses concerning the conditions of development of a high-tech cluster.

There are a range of complementary and interdependent centres of expertise to ensure the continuity of the life cycle of newly created companies. To express this phenomenon, we will use the concept of community of practice (Brown and Duguid 1991; Wenger 1998), meaning a collection of individuals, experts in the same domain, who are linked by strong ties. If we accept that all learning necessarily involves a practical dimension which can not be codified, a large part of the processes of knowledge creation and diffusion is relayed through the practice of a common activity. More generally, members of a community of practice tend to share the same language and the same schemas because they regularly face the same types of environments and have to solve the same problems. The result is that communication between them is facilitated. If the production of knowledge results from social interaction (Nonaka and Takeuchi 1995), then the frequent interaction enabled by strong links encourages knowledge accumulation and the emergence of expertise. Following the works of Coser (1975) and Perry-Smith and Shalley (2003), we shall define strong links as those which produce knowledge.

Social networks can ensure that these centres of expertise are co-ordinated informally, through weak links. Weak links function to diffuse information within an industrial district, and co-ordinate individuals/communities of practice who possess complementary and interdependent expertise. Following Granovetter (1973), we hypothesize that weak links are links for the diffusion of knowledge, since they have been found to be a powerful force in the diffusion of information, notably in the field of research (Reagans and Zuckerman 2001).

If both these conditions exist, the development dynamic of a cluster may be handicapped by the absence of a community of practice. This is a necessary element for ensuring the continuity of the life cycle of companies in their creation or development phase. Added to this could be the lack of co-ordination between communities of practice. The morphogenesis of socio-economic networks in high-tech clusters will be determined by two partially overlapping dynamics. First, there is the transformation of strictly social links into socio-economic links. Second, there is the activation of potential social links related to membership of a social network. A challenge lies in defining an exhaustive list of communities of practice necessary for the development dynamic of a high-tech cluster.

Our methodology is based on a comparative study between two high-tech clusters: Silicon Valley in California and Sophia Antipolis in the Provence Alpes Côte-d'Azur region. Silicon Valley is often described as the archetypal industrial cluster (Miller 1995). It serves as a reference model in our comparative study, not as a functional norm to be copied but as a structural norm − a point of reference to identify the relative weights of different communities of practice and to estimate the efficiency of information circulation.

Our line of research arises from Granovetter's (1973) seminal work. The first section comprises a review of the literature concerning the function of industrial clusters, which will point out its limitations in analysing social networks. The second defines a theoretical framework to explain the morphogenesis and the dynamic functioning of networks in a high-tech cluster. The third and final sections test this explanatory model through a comparative study between Silicon Valley, which is presented as the reference in terms of high-tech clusters, and Sophia Antipolis, which was explicitly inspired by the Californian model. The measurement of their divergences aims to identify factors which help to explain the nature of endogenous growth within clusters.

A THEORETICAL MODEL OF INDUSTRIAL DISTRICTS

The economic viewpoint tends to understand relations between individuals as transactions in which the market becomes the main mediator of all forms of relationship or social structuring. From this point of view, regional clusters are regarded as geographical groupings of companies which often hold complementary resources, and whose co-ordination is based on market relationships. Since Marshall (1920), it is customary to expect that the clustering of companies increases their productivity, their rate of innovation, and their rate of creation (Porter 1998; Becattini 1990; Piore and Sabel 1989; Salais and Storper 1993). Traditionally, the geographical localization of industrial companies can be explained either by material reasons such as reduction of transport and communication costs, or by privileged access to specific resources. There are also external economies related to, for example, shared use of infrastructures (Krugman 1991). Arthur (1990) also points out the cumulative process resulting from 'accidents' such as the setting up of Shockley, Packards, Varian and Terman all in Silicon Valley during the 1940s and 1950s (Arthur 1994).

The concept of cluster used by geographers and sociologists goes further than that used by economists. Beyond mere closeness in terms of geography or industrial sector, they are also interested in the synergy between actors which this closeness allows (Nachum and Keeble 2000). A complementary study on the externalities of knowledge (Jaffe *et al.* 1993; Audretsch and Feldman 1996) shows that geographical and cognitive proximity contribute to improved productivity of activities with a high intensity of research and development (R&D). These externalities prove to be effective if the companies are in relationship networks with clients, suppliers, competitors, universities and research centres, and public institutions which offer potential support (Kline and Rosenberg 1986; Lundvall 1988; Nelson 1993). These networks have to be localized, in order to promote the informal relationships that result in the emergence of common codes, shared social norms and improved flows of information and knowledge (Storper 1995). This process builds up capacities of collective learning (Storper 1995, 1997; Keeble *et al.* 1999) whose content is hard to explain and codify. The tacit character of the knowledge mobilized in high-tech activities makes social networks into important vectors of knowledge circulation (Nohria 1992; Nonaka 1994) and encourages the type of creativity which leads to innovation (Perry-Smith and Shalley 2003). So the circulation of information does indeed depend on the quality of social interaction.

Beyond the questions of externalities or the imperfect codification of knowledge, work rooted in sociology has emphasized the importance of both the nature and the structure of social relationships in ensuring the co-ordination of complementary activities. Here, the sociology of economics has highlighted the intricacy of company networks and the organizational role of the social structure in which economic activity is embedded (Granovetter and Sweberg 1992). Many studies illustrate these ideas, with cases of innovative and entrepreneurial environments; usually Silicon Valley (Saxenian 1994; Castilla *et al.* 2000; Kenney 2000; Ferrary 2001). These studies show that networks are based on ethnic communities – Jewish for the diamond merchants described by Coleman (1988) – Chinese for import/export (Granovetter 1985), Indian in the networks of East African traders (Marris and Sommerset 1971), and French for the Parisian restaurants analysed by Ferrary (1999).

Social communities (Tönnies 1955) allow the build up of the trusting relationships and mutual knowledge important in the creation process. Within a social community strong links are forged between agents, relationships which are solid, reciprocal and based on trust (Granovetter 1973), which strengthen the economic efficiency of community members. The set of social links maintained by an individual constitutes his or her social capital (Bourdieu 1980), and this conditions his or her economic efficiency.

This increased efficiency mainly arises from improved sharing of information and knowledge about others and about the environment. More refined and reliable information about strategies or capabilities are transferred through social links, which act as catalysts to learning (Larson 1992). Granovetter (1973) explored further into the intensity of links between agents in relationships, and the efficiency of information transfer. He finds that, contrary to intuition, informational efficiency – the speed and richness of information diffused over a network – is in fact greater in networks with weak links. Castilla *et al.* (2000) note how other individuals with weak links are held are more likely to frequent different circles from which they gain access to different, and different types of, information (Castilla *et al.* 2000: 62).

From this synthesis, we can recognize three essential functions for the socialization of economic actors. First, informal relationships improve information diffusion. Second, socialization improves anticipation of individual behaviour. Third, since individuals do not only optimize their economic interests but also pursue social objectives – such as recognition, and status – their behaviour is modified. Interpersonal relationships based on mutual confidence encourage contractual relationships, and act as discriminating factors when selecting co-contactors or industrial partners.

Three conditions enable exchange relationships of to emerge within social networks: the geographical proximity of co-contractors, the time value of the social relationship of the exchange, and the modification of the nature of professional relationships.

The geographical proximity of co-contractors is the prime condition necessary for building up interpersonal links based on trust (Ghosal and Nehapiet 1998) because it encourages the quality of individual relationships. For example, when banks carry out financing activities, their risk evaluation is based on a mixture of account information, with more subtle information acquired through the proximity of the borrower and subjective opinion. Californian venture capitalists have the advantage of being familiar with the local market compared to outside competition (Ferrary 2001). Their healthy and trusting relationships with the community leaders – local businessmen, real estate agents, lawyers, accountants and others – enables them to acquire the information necessary for risk evaluation. The geographical proximity resulting from their local implantation encourages an acquaintanceship between individuals upon which trusting relationships can be founded.

The time value of the social relationship of the exchange reduces both the cost and the time of accessing information because contractors can learn from each other. The regularity of the relationship, however, also generates information which is a source of competitive advantage. In other words, repetition results in trust and thus reduces transaction costs.

The modification of the nature of professional relationships is a more intricate condition. Proximity and temporality in professional relations are necessary but insufficient conditions for the establishment of ties of trust. The nature of the relationship must also evolve if a personal relationship is to be created between contractors. The professional relationship becomes the precursor to an informal relationship which leads to information exchanges that, a priori, are not professional. This friendliness is not only the result of the natural sociability of individuals, but is also to do with the strategy of rational actors wishing to embed economic exchanges in the social context in order to consolidate them. For example, it is in a banker's interest to get to know the entrepreneur he is financing, whose personal plans may have a bearing on his professional projects. Discovering the entrepreneur's personality will enable the banker to evaluate his management style, as well as his capacity to deal with the unexpected. He may also find out how couples get on in the case of a husband and wife teams (Ferrary 2002). These non-professional encounters permit exchanges of information which influence the evaluation of risk and which contribute to a relationship of trust.

The studies in Silicon Valley show that the proximity of relationships between economic actors, as well as their complementary and multiplex nature encourages the circulation of information, particularly of the tacit knowledge which is favourable to innovation and high-tech company creation. However, these studies were more concerned with the effects of social networks on economic activity than on the conditions which cause these networks to break into the economic sphere. This justifies an analysis of the morphogenesis of socio-economic networks.

AN ANALYTICAL FRAMEWORK FOR HIGH-TECH CLUSTER NETWORKS

In order to connect micro-social interactions and macro-social phenomena, Granovetter (1973) showed that through social networks, interactions between individuals become macro-social phenomena, which then retroact symmetrically on individuals and small groups. As he later noted at the heart of his analysis is the notion of interpersonal ties which are strengthened through time, emotional intensity, intimateness – or mutual confidence – and reciprocal services between those involved (Castilla *et al.* 2000: 46). Depending on the intensity of the relationship, the link is assessed to be strong, weak or absent. An individual's strong links form a dense network, and weak links form a loose network.

Basing ourselves on this theoretical framework, we define a high-tech industrial district as being a geographical cluster of communities of practice in which the individuals are united by strong links to produce and accumulate knowledge in a given area. It is through the existence of weak links that these complementary and interdependent communities of practice are co-ordinated, and that information is diffused among them.

We make a distinction between social relations whose end is economic – work relationships, relations between industrial partners, etc. – which may be linked strongly or weakly, and social relationships with no economic end – family relationships, friendly relationships, associative or ethnic relationships, etc. – which may also be strongly or weakly linked. Like Grossetti and Bès (2002), we consider that the nature of the links in one dimension may affect the dynamic of the links in the other dimension. For example, strong links between social relations in a non-economic sphere will encourage the creation of links in the economic sphere.

Expertise generating communities of practice from social links with economic ends

The intensity of their relationships can have an impact on the cognitive structure and performance of individuals. Thus, team work encourages experimentation through a commonly elaborated language. Work is thereby organized in communities of practice (Lave and Wenger 1990; Brown and Duguid 1991), that is to say around a stable and coherent group which shares the same objective or at least the same interest in their professional practice. Belonging to the community considerably reduces the amount of time spent on collective learning to solve a problem. Research has shown that beyond communities of practice, agents sharing common problems communicate intensively about them, for example by meeting outside work, and electronically. These interpretation networks (Brown and Duguid 1991) or practices networks (Brown and Duguid 2000), however, are informal and naturally emerging (Lave and Wenger 1990), develop rapidly and become institutionalized in the form of professional associations or specialized journals (Constant 1987).

Even if the organization remains the principal means of diffusing knowledge (Kogut and Zander 1992), communities of practice – as well as the local job market – are able to reach beyond the boundaries of the company to diffuse knowledge throughout a particular geographical area (Saxenian 1999).

Centres of expertise co-ordinated by weak social links

A high-tech cluster, whose performance is measured by endogenous growth, will be constituted by several different communities of practice. These can include research laboratories, universities, large companies, legal practices, venture-capital companies, consultancies, recruitment agencies, and newspapers, which together contain the various domains of expertise necessary for the cycle of company creation and development. Non-redundant information between the members of these communities circulates through the weak links between communities, which are in themselves bound by strong links. The absence or destruction of these weak links between centres of excellence also destroys the circulation of information necessary for the co-ordination of the economic actors.

In terms of the morphogenesis of networks within clusters, it is necessary to distinguish between social and economic networks. Social networks are those whose end is a priori non-economic – such as family relationships, friendly relationships, associative or ethnic relationships. It is the permeability between these purely social activities and the economic activity of individuals in the same geographical location that transforms social networks into the socio-economic networks, and these determine how a cluster functions. Clusters are also distinguished by the places where socialization occurs – for example conferences, company boards, and associations. These areas, prone to the interpenetration of communities of practice, enable weak links to be forged on a regular basis.

A dynamic approach to networks and the activation of virtual social links

Granovetter (1973) insists on the transformability of social links, in particular where strong links are concerned. (The transitivity of social links is explored further in Chapter 16.) A social actor has virtual social capital which will materialize depending on the interests of the actor himself and those of other network members.

The nature of the link – strong, weak of virtual – is not fixed, and its density evolves over time depending on professional mobility and centres of interest. Creating new links is not merely a matter of chance, as has been suggested by small world models. There are simple mechanisms which create and transform the nature of social links. Institutions such as universities, churches, companies, associations, political parties, etc. play an important part in this process. Membership of the same organization is a spur to multiple social interactions, and makes it possible to create strong links between individuals. Companies contain highly favourable organizational conditions for strong links to be forged between individuals who are members of the same professional practice, and this enables expertise to be produced and accumulated. The professional mobility of individuals between these organizations encourages the creation of weak links. This, as we have seen, encourages the diffusion of information and the co-ordination of centres of expertise. The pattern of shifting relationships plays an essential role in the dynamic of high-tech industrial clusters.

The social embeddedness of economic actors is not the result of a strict social determinism, but may result from individual strategies (in the sense of Crozier and Friedberg 1977), that is to say the strategy of actors of limited rationality who optimize their interests by accumulating social capital. From this point of view, becoming a member of a professional association or participating in a conference appear as the behaviour of an actor aiming to embed himself into networks relevant to his economic activity.

COMPARING SILICON VALLEY AND SOPHIA ANTIPOLIS CLUSTERS

Neither Silicon Valley (SV) nor Sophia Antipolis (SA) are areas with clearly defined geographical boundaries. (Here, we follow most previous studies, and consider the area of Santa Clara County as giving the relevant data for Silicon Valley.) SV is estimated to have a surface area of 2,400 km^2 for 2.5 million inhabitants and 1.35 million jobs of which over four per cent are in activities linked to high-tech. SA has a surface area of about 3,000 km^2 but fewer than 1,000,000 inhabitants and about 350,000 jobs, under 10 per cent of which are in activities linked to the technology cluster. The difference in scale is a large one, because SV has two and a half times as many inhabitants as SA, almost three times as many jobs and 18 times as many jobs involved with activities linked to the technologies of the industrial district. However, the area of specialization of the two clusters is comparable – computer technology/communications, semi-conductors, software, biotechnology, and the air-space industry – even if obviously, in each area of specialization, a wider range of activities and more diversified employment is found in SV.

The objective of a comparative study between the two technology parks is to identify the differences both in terms of communities of practice and in terms of the weak links which are vectors of information circulation. We wish to explain how these differences affect the dynamics of the development of the high-tech clusters concerned. The interest and pertinence of carrying out this comparative study between SA and SV lie in the fact that SV constitutes the worldwide reference in the field of high-tech clusters, both in academic terms and in terms of practices in industrial policy. As far as SA is concerned, its creation was directly inspired by SV (Longhi and Masboungi 1998) and this justifies comparing it with the American model. Apart from obvious differences of scale, the two sites have different histories and development cycles. The first success stories in SV occurred during the 1950s, while the first companies only set up in SA during the 1970s as the result of an explicit political choice. Nevertheless, the growth of SA has been relatively limited and that the threshold necessary for positive feedback remains to be reached. See Table 6.1.

If we compare efficiency in innovation, SA appears to be relatively productive because only 14 times fewer patents were applied for in SA than in SV – with 18 times fewer employees related to cluster activities. Furthermore, SA has always managed to have a positive balance of employment and company creation each year. Even if SV has seen a 3.9 per cent growth in employment per year over the last ten years – in spite of the loss of 29,000 jobs in 2001 – SA has created over 9,500 jobs in cluster linked activities, 7,168 of which were created during the past six years, in other words, an average increase of four per cent per year.

The largest performance gap, however, is found in the ability to reach critical thresholds in terms of financing and company growth, characteristic criteria of the intensity of endogenous development. For example, risk capital funds raised in SV amounted to $21 billion in 2000 and $6 billion in 2001 – $0.5 billion in 1990 – compared with €101 million in 2000 and €46 million in 2001 in SA. Fifty-four companies of over 500 employees have their headquarters in SV, but there are only two in SA, where there is no company with more than 1,000 employees. Over the last 10 years, SV has seen between 40 and 75 companies with turnovers of over $1 million and a 20 per cent per year growth rate. In the early 1990s, not a single strong growth company existed in SA, but by 2000 there were five, increasing to six in 2001. More than 20 SV companies are listed on the stock exchange, but there are none in SA.

Finally, the vitality of SV can be seen in its capacity to ride the successive waves of technological innovation because of a permanent process of destruction and reconstruction of skills. SA has not seen any real endogenous dynamic since the wave of telecommunications which encouraged clusters of semi-conductors, software and multimedia. See Tables 6.2 and 6.3.

EXPERTISE ACCUMULATION WITHIN COMMUNITIES OF PRACTICE

Our analytical framework indicates that high-tech industrial clusters are characterized by communities of practice producing complementary and interdependent fields of expertise. These in turn ensure the continuity of company life cycles from creation to maturity. Such communities of practice take shape within companies which ensure the creation and development of strong social links with economic ends, between experts in a given practice. This expertise is improved by the high frequency of professional interactions.

Table 6.1 Comparison Silicon Valley – Sophia Antipolis

	SV	SA	SV/SA		SV	SA	SV/SA
Surface area	2400	3000	0.80	Headhunters	987	52	18.98
Population	2.5m	1m	2.50	Heads of public relations	622	174	3.57
Employment	1.35m	0.35m	3.85	Consultants	14065	745	18.88
Techno employment	540000	29000	18.62	Investment bankers	470	0	–
Students	324568	22191	14.63	Merchant bankers	2796	1564	1.79
Public or quasi-public researchers	9207	1397	6.59	Chartered accountants	19130	1714	11.16
Employees of large companies	632667	17322	36.52	Journalists	490	148	3.31
Venture capitalists	1660	9	184.44	Patent applications 2001	6500	470	13.80
Company lawyers	47280	414	114.20				

Table 6.2 Silicon Valley

		Students	Researchers	Large company employees	Venture capitalists	Company lawyers	Headhunters	Public relations	Consultants	Investment bankers	Merchant bankers	Company accountants	Journalists
		324568	9207	632667	1660	47280	987	622	14065	470	2796	19130	490
Students	324568	1											
Researchers	9207	35.25	1										
Large company employees	632667	0.51	0.01	1									
Venture capitalists	1660	195.52	5.55	381.12	1								
Company lawyers	47280	6.86	0.19	13.38	0.04	1							
Headhunters	987	328.84	9.33	641.00	1.68	47.90	1						
Public relations	622	521.81	14.80	1017.15	2.67	76.01	1.59	1					
Consultants	14065	23.08	0.65	44.98	0.12	3.36	0.07	0.04	1				
Investment bankers	470	690.57	19.59	1346.10	3.53	100.60	2.10	1.32	29.93	1			
Merchant bankers	2796	116.08	3.29	226.28	0.59	16.91	0.35	0.22	5.03	0.17	1		
Chartered accountants	19130	16.97	0.48	33.07	0.09	2.47	0.05	0.03	0.74	0.02	0.15	1	
Journalists	490	662.38	18.79	1291.16	3.39	96.49	2.01	1.27	28.70	0.96	5.71	39.04	1

Table 6.3 Sophia Antipolis

		Students	Researchers	Large company employees	Venture capitalists	Company lawyers	Headhunters	Public relations	Consultants	Investment bankers	Merchant bankers	Company accountants	Journalists
		22191	1397	17322	9	414	52	174	745	0	1564	1714	148
Students	22191	1											
Researchers	1397	15.88	1										
Large company employees.	17322	1.28	0.08	1									
Venture capitalists	9	2465.67	155.22	1924.67	1								
Company lawyers	414	53.60	3.37	41.84	0.02	1							
Headhunters	52	426.75	26.87	333.12	0.17	7.96	1						
Public relations	174	127.53	8.03	99.55	0.05	2.38	0.30	1					
Consultants	745	29.79	1.88	23.25	0.01	0.56	0.07	0.23	1				
Investment bankers	0	ns	ns	ns	ns	ns	ns	ns	ns				
Merchant bankers	1564	14.19	0.89	11.08	0.01	0.26	0.03	0.11	0.48	0.00	1		
Chartered accountants	1714	12.95	0.82	10.11	0.01	0.24	0.03	0.10	0.43	0.00	0.91	1	
Journalists	148	149.94	9.44	117.04	0.06	2.80	0.35	1.18	5.03	0.00	10.57	11.58	1

Analysing an industrial cluster from the standpoint of communities of practice enables us to enquire as to the continuity of the chain of domains of expertise necessary for company creation and development. We can also wonder about the probability that domains of expertise establish contact and interact with each other through weak links. The interest of analysing a high-tech cluster is that it allows us to understand the factors leading to innovation and company creation. It also enables us to understand other actors in the innovative milieu, notably lawyers, financiers, consultants, journalists or training institutes. We may see how they modify systems of representation and produce common frameworks related to their expertise, which are adopted by others in the cluster. The market development of technological innovation depends on full understanding by those directly or indirectly concerned with the company creation.

DEFINING THE COMMUNITIES OF PRACTICE

Defining an exhaustive list of communities of practice is an essential component of research methodology, since for an analysis based only on one or on a limited number of actors cannot hope to grasp the dynamic of a cluster that is defined by systemic interaction of all its component members. We define 12 communities of practice that are partly institutionalized in the organizations that are located within the cluster. These communities, besides their official functions, have informal functions which contribute to the dynamic processes of the cluster. Using a functionalist approach (Parsons 1964), we define the economic actor by the function he fulfils within the cluster.

University institutions are centres of pedagogical expertise to prepare human capital and potential entrepreneurs. Informally, the university also serves as an entrepreneurial 'passageway' where future entrepreneurs can define their project while continuing their studies – for example, Yahoo and Google were created by Stanford University students while they were studying. Finally, university training programmes give rise to relationships where social capital is accumulated

Public or private research centres are centres of expertise which generate innovation whose function in the productive sphere of the cluster is formed through the transfer of technologies allowing the development of the activity. Informally, these research centres also function as entrepreneurial 'passageways'. (Xerox/Parc is a private research centre which has given rise to researchers creating companies, for example Juniper Network.)

Large companies housing several communities of practice generating expertise: they develop centres of technological and managerial competence for products corresponding to markets, and ensure their distribution. They also carry out several informal functions – entrepreneurial 'passageways', human resources reserves for SMEs, networkers and association members. Finally, by acquiring companies in their technology management portfolios, they are a factor of financial incitation for creators – for example, Cisco Sytem bought up 39 Californian start-ups between 1993 and 2002 (Ferrary 2003).

Venture capital companies' official function is to ensure the financing of start-ups during the creation and development phase. More informally, venture-capital companies encourage industrial partnerships between the companies they finance and clients and suppliers (Kenney and Florida 2000). Their central role in socio-economic networks puts them in a strategic position for bringing actors into contact with one another. They provide consultancy for entrepreneurs through getting them to share experiences with other start-ups. They are also pro-active in inciting researchers to create companies. Finally, their investment decisions constitute a signal for the cluster community as to a company's economic viability.

Lawyers firms develop legal expertise in the fields of company creation and protection of innovations. This expertise is particularly complex because it is difficult to use legal tools and concepts on innovations which modify the reality under which such tools and concepts were defined. This expertise is particularly important in the high-tech sector because the quality of protection afforded to an innovation may well condition its ability to keep its competitive advantage. Legal firms also function informally as catalysts for contacts between actors in the cluster.

Recruitment agencies' function is to foster the activity of the job market in highly qualified human capital. Their membership of social networks enables them to identify and recruit human capital with exceptional scientific and managerial skills. Consulting companies' function is to develop and diffuse managerial expertise in various domains – project management, marketing, logistics, information systems, etc. Indirectly, through their consulting role, they encourage the transfer between companies of best management practice. Chartered accountants firms' function is to develop expertise in accounts management for small high-tech companies. Frequent innovations being characteristic of the sector, such firms will have creative accounting in valuation of assets. Public relations companies' function is to ensure media coverage of companies and publicity for the company's products in markets linked to its activity.

Merchant banks develop financial skills in dealing with means of payment – sometimes these are specific, such as internet payments – and means of financing adapted to the particular characteristics of the high-tech sector. Investment banks develop expertise in initial public offering (IPO) and sales of SMEs to large groups. This stage is a fundamental one for financing the further development and marketing of the technology developed by small companies. Newspapers give media coverage to high-tech companies and their products. They contribute to the creation of an entrepreneurial culture within the cluster and the value of this in the public eye.

COMPARING THE PREPONDERANCE OF COMMUNITIES OF PRACTICE

Here, we undertook systematic research on telephone directories to list institutions, companies and establishments constituting a community of practice. We carried out internet searches to find out the number of employees. Finally, we corroborated our results through a series of qualitative interviews. The SA figures only concern companies linked to the technological activities of the industrial cluster, whose decision-making centres are local. The figures relative to SA companies – employment, size of companies etc. – are taken from the Dynamis database (cf. Bernasconi and Moreau 2003) and the SIRIUS database of the CCI Nice Côte d'Azur.

The first interesting dimension in this comparative analysis concerns the relative presence of communities of practice within the cluster relative to the objective proportions mentioned above – a ratio of 1:8 for example in terms of active employees in the high-tech sector. Even if certain ratios (see Table 6.1) are not that big – Silicon Valley has only six times as many researchers, 14 times more students, 18 times more consultants and only 3.5 times as many heads of public relations and 1.5 times as many merchant banks – other ratios point towards gaps between the clusters – absence of investment banks in SA, and quasi absence, compared to SV, of company lawyers, venture capitalists and employees of large companies. Once again, the threshold effect is important. For example, although there are 14 times fewer students in SA than in SV, it is however necessary to compare 320,000 to 20,000 to have an idea of the differences in the number of potential young project creators.

This comparison highlights the absence of certain communities of practice which are essential for company creation and for the dynamic of endogenous development of a high-tech cluster. (There are 1,662 professional associations in SV, for 10 in SA. There are 10 universities, about 40 private or public research centres, 8,718 large companies with over 100 employees – 20 in SA – 330 venture capital companies, 3,152 legal firms specialized in company law and legal areas related to company activity, 329 recruitment companies employing 2,813 consultancy firms, 1,913 chartered accounting firms, 311 public relations companies, nearly 700 merchant banks employing about 3000 people in financial services, 47 investment banks and about one hundred newspapers employing approximately 500 journalists devoted to the high-tech environment of SV.)

As well as the communities of practice themselves, the dynamic of industrial clusters depends on the quality of interactions between the members of these complementary and interdependent communities of practice. The first requirement for the interaction of representatives of communities of practice is that their respective proportions make contact probable. Thus, if a cluster contains only one venture capitalist per 10,000 researchers – potential company creators – there is a very low probability that each researcher will encounter a financer.

From this point of view, analysing of the ratios of SV is doubly interesting. First, the ratios allow the proportions between the communities of practice to be identified. Second, they enable a basis of comparison which shows up not only differences in size, but also the differences in the actual communities of practice represented. If students, researchers and employees of large companies are potential creators of companies, we have to analyse the ratios of individuals belonging to each community of practice relative to the potential creators of companies. These ratios highlight the potential mobilization of the resources necessary for the creation and development of start-ups.

SA is distinguished by a relative lack of venture capitalists relative to the potential number of company creators – one per 2,465 students, one per 155 researchers and one per 1,924 employees of large companies. The weakness of these ratios considerably reduces the financing opportunities for innovative projects. We find similar gaps for investment banks, company lawyers and to a slightly lesser extent for head-hunters. On the other hand, we find a favourable ratio in SA – or similar communities – when we relate the number of researchers, consultants and merchant bankers to the number of students and employees of large companies.

These ratios demonstrate that the weakness of endogenous growth in the high-tech cluster of SA is not due to the lack of communities of practice generating innovations, but rather to the lack of communities of practice which might support and accompany company creation and development.

WEAK AND VIRTUAL LINKS IN INFORMATION FLOW

As well as the presence of communities of practice creating the expertise necessary for development dynamic of a high-tech cluster, endogenous growth also depends on the presence of weak social links between interdependent communities of practice so that these can put their complementary competences to use and bring about the circulation of information.

We have followed the works of Portes (1995) on the role of ethnic social networks in the determination of sectors of economic activity, and those of Saxenian and Li (2003) on the Chinese and Indian networks in Silicon Valley. To illustrate the role of weak links which are understood to operate within ethnic communities, we will explore the economic role of the French community in Silicon Valley more closely. This community is made up of about 4,500 people (from data kindly provided by the San Francisco French Consulate during 2000). Community members are found in the various organizations which ensure the continuity of the life cycle of newly created companies. Thus Stanford University has several French professors in its various departments, about 10 French people work in venture capital companies, a few in lawyers firms and others have become figureheads of the French community because of their economic success – Jean-Louis Gassée, Eric Benhamou, etc. (Bernasconi 1995).

Silicon Valley's French community has its non-economic institutions of socialization – the French school of Palo Alto, la Maison Française, the ciné-club, French restaurants etc. – national celebrations, Bastille day on 14 July, Beaujolais nouveau days and newspapers and associations with a more economic aim – Doing Business in French, Eurotrash, SiliconFrench, etc. Finally, the French spend time together in informal social gatherings, dinner parties, travelling, sports, etc. All these social gatherings enable the French to meet and potentially to envisage joint economic activities.

Silicon Valley's French community is noteworthy for its gregariousness. This leads members to share cultural and social activities aimed at reproducing characteristics of French culture and practising their native language. These gatherings are therefore not motivated by economic reasons. Their social nature is seen by the diversity of professions present: there are engineers and executives from Silicon Valley's large French and American companies, French entrepreneurs and French lawyers or venture capitalists. However, there are also French teachers from the region's French Lycée, university professors, restaurant owners, journalists, painters, students, and non-working wives or husbands. The weak and strong – non-economic – social links built up through community activities gives rise to social links which are potentially economic. A French national in Silicon Valley wanting to create a company naturally talks about it within the ethnic – French – community in social gatherings, in order to obtain advice and information. In the same way, once the project has been formalized, the entrepreneur will talk to French venture capitalists in Silicon Valley, to obtain finance. It is this real or potential socio-economic link which enables an entrepreneur to find financing. The importance of social networks is reinforced by the way that venture capitalists work (Ferrary 2001): they do not consider financing a project unless the entrepreneurs in question have been recommended by a reliable member of their own social network.

Our own enquiries indicated 439 French created companies in Silicon Valley, of which around thirty were high-tech companies created by French immigrants (from San Francisco French Consulate data). Of all these firms, 43 were financed by one or more of the 12 French venture capitalists operating in Silicon Valley. Most French entrepreneurs in Silicon Valley are financed by French venture capitalists operating in the region – out of the total number of 1,500 venture capitalists in the area. This can be explained by the importance of the purely social networks that preceded the existence of economic exchange. A Frenchman who sets up in Silicon Valley has little chance of an encounter with potential investors, but his nationality, through activation of weak links, automatically gives access to French investors, who will themselves be able to activate a chain of strong or weak links in order to mobilize the necessary complementary resources. The capacity to find an investor is directly determined by membership of an ethnic community, and by the density of non-economic links.

Although weak links play an important role in information circulation, and help to mobilize complementary resources rapidly, the activation of potential links increases this process and enables new complementarities to be created. A priori membership of networks ensures the multiplication of skills and diversities of origin within clusters. Networks intervene naturally as a system of selection after the fact, and validate new members — or not — as potential resources. In other words, potential links constitute the creation of variety within the complex system that Garnsey (1998b) describes.

Networks of social links, like those of weak links, emerge naturally thanks to shared interests or common characteristics. The effectiveness of these links for informal co-ordination is directly related to the number of members and their competences or economic functions. An absence of communities of practice will therefore immediately affect the efficiency of this mode of co-ordination. SA has no shortage of institutions or places where socializing can take place, whether this be socio-economic — Jeunes Chambres Economiques (an association of young executives), Sophia Start up, Sophia Professional Women's Network, etc. — or purely social — expatriates' clubs (since 12 per cent of the local population is foreign), international schools, sports clubs, etc. It is not easy, however, to study the presence of communities of practice in informal networks, but it seems clear that in clubs with economic objectives, all communities of practice must be represented in order to facilitate the creation of activities.

One instructive example is the Sophia Start Up club. The club gathers those with a project in mind — essentially researchers, students and company employees — start-up directors and representatives of various communities of practice. The objective of the club is to improve the diffusion of information concerning company creation and to promote projects in Sophia Antipolis. Almost 100 members meet every month, most of whom joined after participating in a project, for example as creator, financer or consultant, and most are local. All the venture capitalists and investment bank representatives, however, are from Paris or from abroad, and attend to keep in touch with the communities of practice involved in the projects that they are financing. They themselves admit that their remoteness is a hindrance, and does not allow close and effective relationships to be developed.

CONCLUSION

We have considered the dynamic functioning of high-tech clusters and found that it depends on the nature and structure of the social networks underlying those clusters. We have been lead to question the morphogenesis of these socio-economic networks. We have defined two conditions necessary for a process of endogenous growth to appear. First, there must be a set of communities of practice whose actors are united by strong links in order to constitute centres of expertise necessary for company creation and development. Second, there must be weak links between these complementary and interdependent communities of practice to encourage the circulation of information.

It follows that the weakness of endogenous growth within a high-tech cluster may be due to two non-exclusive factors. The first is the lack of one or more centres of expertise constituted around communities of practice to ensure the continuity of the life cycle of companies from creation to maturity. The second is the lack of interaction between the communities of practice due to the absence of weak links between the members of the communities of expertise.

The comparison between the high-tech clusters of Silicon Valley and Sophia Antipolis shows that the relative weakness of endogenous growth in Sophia Antipolis is related to the lack of certain communities of practice, in particular, venture capitalists, company lawyers and merchant banks. Because of the systemic interdependence of the efficiency of communities of practice, the fact that not all of these are represented in Sophia Antipolis hinders the efficiency of those which are present, for example the research laboratories and the universities. This, more globally, handicaps the endogenous growth which the cluster might otherwise engender.

Concerning the role of weak links in information circulation between communities of practice, the analysis of both clusters shows that situations for inter-professional socializing emerge spontaneously. These constitute communities of interest within which weak links are built up between complementary and interdependent economic actors. This convergence between the two clusters suggests that the interdependence of communities of practice leads to the spontaneous emergence of weak link networks.

In conclusion, the weakness of endogenous growth in Sophia Antipolis seems related to the absence of certain communities of practice which are essential for company creation, rather than to the lack of social links between those communities of practice which are present within the cluster.

Chapter 7

Network relationships in different cultures

High-tech globalization
meets local cultures

Simon Harris

The importance of networks to the development and growth of high-technology entrepreneurial businesses has been highlighted both in Chapters 6 and 16, and elsewhere (Moensted 2003; Yli-Renko *et al.* 2001). These networks can be with customers, suppliers, supporters or information providers. Often we discuss them as 'ties' between 'firms', but what are they, and what do they mean for high-technology entrepreneurial businesses? At the root of our businesses are people – the entrepreneurs themselves – and the 'ties' are their relationships with others: we are dealing with the messy, complicated, infinitely varied world of inter-personal relationships.

In Chapters 8 and 11, authors discuss the different milieu that foster or hinder the development of high-tech firms. Key elements of this milieu is the way in which the development of relationships of different types are encouraged to occur; indeed, one of the most important resources that help firms to foster is a 'milieu' that helps new important inter-personal relationships to develop (Harris and Bovaird 1996). We know that the ability of the entrepreneurs who developing young firms to develop network relationships with those who will be key suppliers of tangible resources – such as finance, personnel, raw materials – and intangible resources – such as access to other networks, key skills, new customer relationships – is critical for their development. In high-tech environments, two factors lead to the need for additional, special types of relationships.

First, technology is a borderless phenomenon, and high-tech enterprises tend to look to international markets – and to international suppliers (of knowledge as well as of inputs) – from the outset (Harris and Ghauri 2000). Important relationships for high-tech entrepreneurs can be with individuals in other countries to the new territories and new cultures that will, very often, be associated with the firm's success. International business development for high-tech firms tends to rely on co-operative strategies developed with through linkages with mangers from different national and institutional cultures (Axelsson and Easton 1992). This requires shared language, beliefs and understandings, to enable processes of interaction and discussion and the generation of appropriate levels of trust (Ghauri and Usunier 1996).

Second, high-tech entrepreneurs need relationships that may bridge the chasm of complexity, and enable communication to, for example, those who are providing finance who may not have technical understanding of the technologies that underpin the venture. In both cases, we are seeing the need for high-tech entrepreneurs to extend themselves beyond their 'home' culture of their nation, and of their technological domain. Network relationships are a critical part of that process. The nature of relationships, however, is itself an important element of culture. In different national cultures, the people with whom relationships are formed differ, as do the way in which those relationships are formed. In different types of institutions, whether government, financial or entrepreneurial, the 'means of relationship formation' also differs. It is a complex world that the growth high-tech entrepreneur has to deal with.

Here we will explore some of that complexity in the two areas of culture difference that we have now highlighted. First, we will compare the network relationships formed by high-tech entrepreneurs from different national cultures. We will explore reasons why, on the basis of research into different national cultures, we might expect them to be different, and we will then examine the network relationships of matched, successful electronics firms in three countries to see if these differences are seen in practice. Second, we will carry out the same process in comparing the relationship formation of entrepreneurs in different institutional culture settings: entrepreneurs who own their own firms, and entrepreneurs who depend on venture capital finance to maintain their positions.

THE GLOBAL NATURE OF HIGH-TECH BUSINESSES

There is nothing new about the existence of the smaller international firm. Until recent decades, international trade had been dominated by traders and merchants profiting from the exchange of goods from one country or region to another. Small businesses, often with unique and difficult to imitate craft skills, have profited from the sale of their production on a global scale. In their days, Bavarian swords, French herbal medicines, English woollens, and Venetian glass have been examples of world-dominating high-tech industries pioneered and developed by entrepreneurs. It is only during the last century that international trade has become to be dominated by trade within and among large and multinational firms. History may well see this as an aberration.

New technology is beginning to make further, and perhaps more rapid changes. New methods of communication and transport give greater access to smaller manufacturing and service firms to actual and potential customers worldwide. The rapid transfer of new technology worldwide, and the associated global standardization of products, from motor cars to electronic products, yields not only competitive advantage but also a potential ability to supply to businesses the knowledge and capability to master and innovate with new technologies for the benefit of customers worldwide (Levitt 1983; Ohmae 1983).

The standardization of many high-tech products, the customer needs they are seeking to meet, and the technical processes employed used mean that nearly all manufacturers of these products are facing an international customer marketplace. High-tech businesses, even though they operate out of different countries, share technological and technical languages, enabling, on a technical level at least, communication between participants in the industry worldwide. The national contexts will inevitably be different, but are all mainly technologically and globally determined. Communication in high-tech industries invariably involves the English language, though usually of a technological type, even in circumstances when all the interlocutors share a different first language (Harris 2000).

In many high-tech industries global changes have resulted in the emergence and growth of new smaller firms created for, and supplying to, international markets. Examples of these are in component supply, industrial electronics, industrial consulting, computer software, research, product design and development, transport, travel and information technology. Firms in these industries mainly meet the needs of specialist industrial sectors with tailored industrial electronic hardware and/or software, or supply components to other manufacturers of electronics products.

The kinds of product they make are diverse, each manufacturer supplying specialized products for particular uses. For example, young entrepreneurial electronics firms – using diverse technologies embracing software, optics, and new material science – supply specialist components to the worldwide electronics industry. Their creative dynamism can present competitive advantages in comparison to larger firms. But they face the challenge of addressing customers who may well be located in different countries. How do such entrepreneurs address international market places? Scholars in international business have been paying attention to this for many years, and one thing emerges time and time again: they do it through network relationships internationally.

THE IMPORTANCE OF NETWORK RELATIONSHIPS

The importance of interpersonal relationships to firms' development has long been recognized (Coase 1937; Penrose 1959). Relationships within networks help firms to develop (Hite and Hesterly 2001; Moensted 2003). Interpersonal relationships tie entrepreneurs with others within social networks outside their firms, and enable them to generate value from their external networks (Adler and Kwon 2002; Gulati et al. 2000).

For entrepreneurs, personal relationships have been found to be critical in the foreign market entry process (Ellis 2000), helping them to identify international partners (Wong and Ellis 2002). The clearest strategic value of these network relationships is in facilitating innovation through the acquisition of knowledge and information (Kogut 2000; Yli-Renko *et al.* 2001), and this requires social interaction between people, and strong trust (Tsai 2000). Strong relationships, however, may also carry pitfalls and costs: in obligations (Adler and Kwon 2002), in restricted freedom of action (Powell and Smith-Doer 1994), and in limits to speed of action (Jeffries and Reed 2000).

What, however, is a relationship? Relationships with others are probably the most complex and difficult things that most humans have to deal with in their lives; certainly more difficult than scholarship in management. It is evident to us all that relationships are not all the same.

DIFFERENT QUALITIES OF NETWORK RELATIONSHIPS

We need to distinguish important relationships, and we need to identify quality relationships. Important relationships enable strategically important exchanges, of tangible goods and services or of intangible knowledge and understanding, to take place (Blyer and Coff 2003; Koka and Prescott 2002). Entrepreneurs can be involved in many different types of networks, and have many different relationships, but many of these will not be not be intended to be economically important for their firms. A small number of strong network ties can be a far greater asset than a large number of weak ones (Shankar and Bayus 2003).

Trust between the parties involved seems to be the key discriminator between the high quality ties that contribute most to network relationships from the weak ties that do not, and is a useful means for distinguishing those that meaningfully contribute to the firm (Adler and Kwon 2002). Inter-personal trust develops over time as knowledge of the other person grows. The strongest and highest level network relationships take time to develop, but are much more important than the simple ordinary technical exchanges which may not develop very much (Kotabe *et al.* 2003).

Barney and Hanson (1994) distinguish different levels of trust in network relationships. Weak ties occur when partners have no significant vulnerabilities to exploit, semi-strong ties when contractual safeguards mutually protect the two parties, and the strong ties when there partners maintain a high level of confidence that opportunistic behaviour will be avoided even without the assurance provided with formal contractual safeguards. We may take this strong form of trust that results when partners share a common vision, objectives and standards, as indicating a relationship that contributes real strategic value for a high-tech entrepreneur. Now we will turn to some difficulties that may be faced when this is done internationally.

INTERNATIONAL DIFFERENCES IN THE NATURE OF BUSINESS RELATIONSHIPS

While there are clear benefits from building network relationships within and between firms, there are particular challenges when this is done internationally. In the context of building relationships across countries, Kostova and Roth (2003) note

> Geographical distance, cultural differences, and language barriers limit the possibilities for extensive personal interaction between organisational members. … Furthermore, institutional and cultural differences … often result in a lack of shared norms and values …
>
> (Kostova and Roth 2003: 304)

The strongest empirical evidence is for different processes of relationship development between countries in international alliances and joint ventures. While network relationships are very important to both US and Japanese steel manufacturers, firms in those countries develop them in very different ways (Kotabe *et al.* 2003). Distributor relationship development processes differ markedly between Canada and Mexico on the one hand, and Chile and Mexico on the other hand (Griffith *et al.* 2000). In the development of trust and commitment, significant differences in the patterns of interpersonal trust building have been found between US and Peruvian export managers (Marshall and Bouch 2001).

Chinese culture, for example, leads their firms to pay relatively greater attention to the development of relationships between the people involved in comparison to US culture, which leads to relatively greater attention to intellectual property or technological knowledge (Li *et al.* 2001). We also know, for example, that the way that co-operative strategies are built, in the processes used to make international co-operative decisions differ between countries (Steensma *et al.* 2000; Marshall and Boush 2001).

All this points to managers in different countries having different expectations about relationships with others. These differences, mainly researched within large multinational enterprises, appear to be equally important when we are considering the development of relationships between firms in the networks of entrepreneurial firms. Specifically, we have two aspects to consider: the cultural differences between nations that can occasion differences in the types of relationships that may be formed, and differences in the kind of institutional backgrounds of firms that may result in different types of relationships. We will now examine each of these in turn.

HOW DIFFERENT NATIONAL CULTURES CAN AFFECT RELATIONSHIPS

We have strong grounds for believing that network relationships may be culture dependent. The purpose and nature of relationships are value laden, and we know that these values vary from country to country (Schein 1985). Schein noted how managers of different national backgrounds can be expected to hold different underpinning values, different assumptions regarding the environment, and different expectations about relationships among people. Different values about what is of value in life will influence the motivations for the development of relationships with others within networks. Different assumptions regarding the environment will result in differences in the bases for trust behind relationships, and differences in willingness to co-operate. Different expectations about relationships among people may influence both with whom these relationships will be sought, and the processes which will and will not lead to its formation.

We also have specific grounds for supposing that the nature of relationships and the way in which they are developed may be culture dependent. First, a great deal of evidence has accumulated that national values have a significant effect on management preferences and processes (Tayeb 1988). Second, the phenomenon of network relationships lies at the heart of the cultural concept; the notion of kinship lies at the heart of culture, and network relationships is itself a kinship phenomenon. We can neither presume the purpose nor the nature of relationships: they may be associated with cultural values concerning, for example, what businesses and relationships are for (Schein 1985; Hofstede 2001). Entrepreneurs from countries associated with some cultural values appear to have a greater regard for network relationships in having shared objectives and values with their partners, and of the strategic importance of cooperative strategies, than their counterparts in countries associated with other values (Steensma *et al.* 2000). Third, we know that the foundations of relationship trust (Dyer and Chuh 2000) and the relationship development processes firms pursue (Griffith *et al.* 2000) differ between cultures.

Management researchers have examined the influence of national values and cultural background on management practices and preferences in different countries. A number of researchers have employed the methods associated with social psychology, and have quantitatively explored the consequences on social and work organizations and relationships (Hofstede 2001; Laurent 1983, Trompenaars and Hampden-Turner 1997), based on the previous work of social anthropologists (e.g. Douglas 1978; Kluckholn and Strotdbeck 1961). This quantitative research has employed structured, quantitative questionnaire techniques to explore similarities and differences in values and attitudes according to pre-determined categories between individuals in different countries.

One value orientation that has been given great attention is the notion of uncertainty avoidance: a person's predisposition to accepting and welcoming the novel, unknown and strange on the one hand, or their predisposition to reject or avoid the uncertainty presented by new circumstances, challenges or relationships on the other hand (Hofstede 2001). In low uncertainty avoiding countries, people relish the chance of meeting new people and new types of people, of forming new ties outside their normal circles. In high uncertainty avoiding countries, new relationships may not be developed so readily, and the focus may well be on deep loyal relationships within narrower social groups.

One distinction as to the way that people relate to one another is in the notion of hierarchy. In some cultures, it is very difficult for people who have high levels of power and/or responsibility within a social or work group to form close relationships with those that do not: there is a strong sense of hierarchy and, as Hofstede, phrases it, the 'power distance' is great. In these societies, we might find that it is difficult for people at different power levels within society to form quality relationships of the type that we have been discussing. In less hierarchical countries, the 'power distance' is less, and trust-building relationships can be built between people of different status more easily.

Gert Hofstede has combined a number of aspects of interpersonal and human orientations into a composite concept of 'masculinity-femininity'. In 'feminine' societies, great store is placed on the quality of working life, and, harmony in work relationships is very important, and a business is a social family with duties and obligations that go beyond the material. In masculine societies, it is achievement of material accomplishments that matters; winning the competitive battle. In this environment, relationships are developed as the means to the business end: and may be judged and valued on that basis. In feminine societies, by contrast, they are an end in themselves.

Another notion of contrast between cultures is different orientations towards time: long-termism and short-termism. Quality relationships based on knowledge and trust, can take time to develop, time which short-term focused societies may not allow to develop. In long-term societies we might expect a focus on a few deep relationships, rather than the shallower relationships that we might expect in more short-term focused societies.

HOW DIFFERENT INSTITUTIONAL CULTURES CAN AFFECT RELATIONSHIP NETWORKS

It would be naïve to think, however, that it might only be national cultures that can result in different approaches to relationship ties. Clearly, every human has his or her own unique approach to the business of relationships. Many of us have spent entertaining hours discussing the different orientations of men and women on this subject; and to no concrete conclusion. Within business circles, however, attention has focused on differences between institutional cultures that reside within firms and organizations.

New institutionalism has developed over recent decades to become a broad, complex body of theory, with separate but parallel developments within sociological, economic, and political research (Ben-Ner and Putterman 2000). Notwithstanding their discipline roots, all have argued that differences in underlying institutional structures lead to differences in firms. Three 'pillars' of the institutional environment are recognized (Scott and Meyer 1994). The regulatory pillar includes the laws and rules that promote some behaviour and discourage others. The cognitive pillar includes cognitive structures and social knowledge, which are the frames and schemas within which information is interpreted. The normative pillar includes the socially shared norms, values, beliefs and assumptions that are socially shared but carried by individuals, in other words, the cultural values that we discussed earlier. From an entirely different perspective, Nobel prize-winning economist Douglass North has used historical analysis of the evolution of firms, economies, and economic systems to understand differences in business and political organizations and economies (North 1991):

> Institutions are ... the humanly-devised constraints that structure interaction. They are composed of formal rules (statute law, common law, regulations), informal constraints (conventions, norms of behaviour, and self imposed codes of conduct), and the enforcement characteristics of both.
>
> (North 1994: 1)

A wide range of 'institutional' contextual factors have been empirically noted to contribute to differences in practices between countries (Carr and Tomkins 1998; Hickson and Pugh 1995). These differences can be broad, including different ownership structures and systems, different corporate governance and legal frameworks, and different education, capital, and social systems (Whitly 1999). The importance of some of these has been empirically demonstrated (Pedersen and Thomsen 2003; Thomsen and Pedersen 2000).

This is clearly very important for the high-tech entrepreneur exploring network ties. The ways that different entrepreneurs will form relationships will differ: some are domineering characters who inspire followers, others are consensual team builders. The way that they form relationships and their expectations of those relationships will clearly be very different. Relationship formation by large industrial corporations will be different to that of entrepreneurs: there are corporate rules, corporate traditions, corporate histories, in short, corporate cultures. Yet these corporations may well be partners, suppliers or customers.

Overall, we can expect differences in the way that entrepreneurs may seek network relationships, who they seek them with, and what they hope to gain from them to result from different institutional factors. These can include the traditions of the industry concerned, and the ownership and governance structures of the firms in those industries. We will now turn to examining the way that relationships vary between similar high-tech entrepreneurs in different national cultures, and in different institutional frameworks.

OUR STUDY

To examine and separate any differences that may have been occasioned by differences in national culture from those that may have been occasioned by differences in institutional setting, we have adopted a 'quasi-experimental' approach. This requires close attention to close matching of the entrepreneurs being studied in all aspects except for the influence being examined.

They were all part owners of their firms, and we considered them all to be the prime architects of business relationships, and the prime holders and coordinators of the network relationships involved. The firms were all young, growing, and profitable. They were all electronics engineers, and their businesses were all in a sub-segment within Standard Industrial Code 33.20/1, and developed and combined electronic hardware and software technologies to address the needs of industrial customers worldwide. In this segment of the electronics industry, customers, manufacturing issues, and standards are determined on a global scale (Harris 2000) so we might expect few differences between the nations, but the potential influence of institutional factors will also be less. These entrepreneurs were not samples but were almost the whole populations within regions of those countries of a very specific, matched, type: in similar industrial settings, with similar – preferably the same – markets, organizationally and institutionally similar, and with similar backgrounds. Forty-one entrepreneurs with well established firms were studied, 14 in the Netherlands, 15 in Scotland, and 12 in the Alpes-Maritimes department of France.

To examine the possible affect of different institutional structures on network relationship formation, the entrepreneurs and their firms were in similar industrial settings, in the same country, with similar – preferably the same – markets, and with similar backgrounds. Twenty-three entrepreneurs with well-established firms were studied in Scotland, 15 being the owner managers noted previously who all held a dominant shareholding in their firms, and eight who were similar in every respect except in that they had a dominant external institutional shareholder, in the form of a merchant bank, or venture capital company.

Observing the entrepreneurs' network relationships

Questionnaires would not access the quality of data that we were seeking; this required the use of interviews, and for this we followed a highly structured 'native category' interview protocol (Harris 2000), that attempted to access the interviewees' own 'native categories' of data. Interviews of 100–240 minutes in length involved in-depth conversations around non-directive questions that enabled the entrepreneurs to express their own underlying considerations and beliefs (Buckley and Chapman 1997; Strauss and Corbin 1991). We conducted all the interviews at the interviewees' own business premises.

The interviews started with the question 'What do you think about when you consider the future of your business?'. After the explanation of each issue raised by the entrepreneur himself, we asked 'Who do you discuss [this issue] with, or consult with?'. This yielded a list of people who had the most important relationships with the entrepreneur. To maintain equivalence, we asked interviewees the same questions in the same order, deviating from this only to obtain clarification. To assess the value that the entrepreneurs found in those relationships in dealing with strategic issues, and to elicit their underlying beliefs about the role of the relationships in that process, we then asked, for each issue: 'What do you seek when you discuss [the issue raised] with these people?'. This was a difficult question for most interviewees to address. It yielded, however, deep views about each other party, and sufficient data to be able to assess whether they were based on knowledge and trust.

It was necessary, however, to gain some finer grained data concerning the origins, background, nature, function and outcomes of each relationship with which to triangulate and confirm the data that would be used in analysis. Later in the interview, the following set of questions were posed for each relationship that the entrepreneur had highlighted: 'When and how did you meet?', 'How would you describe your relationship with them?', 'When and how do you discuss things?', 'How do you regard his/her views and opinions?', 'How have they affected the business?'. To ensure that no important relationships were missed, the entrepreneurs were asked 'Are there, or have there been other people important to you in the development of your business?'.

Measuring network relationships

We used verbal protocol analysis (Ericsson and Simon 1985) to analyse transcripts and notes from the interviews, to yield a list of network relationships relationships for each entrepreneur. First, each relationship described was designated as being a locus of network relationships or not, by having evidence of being strategically important: we were only interested in the former. The quality of the relationship had also to be sufficient: so high trust based relationships were identified.

Each entrepreneur's source of network relationships then had to be determined from this data, according to the codes representing the type of people involved, developed above. The coding process was binary, the entrepreneurs either formed network relationships with people of different types, or they did not. This is the most robust form of coded data, and least open to coding bias (Ericsson and Simon 1985), confirmed by a high correlation between code sheets that were completed by nationals from the three countries involved. This coding was undertaken in four categories of network relationships. The first category involved none at all. The second is with network ties based on personal friends – for example from school or social life – and family relationships.

The third category was specific business associates, defined to be named individuals who were named and described as being important in the strategic development of the entrepreneurs' firms in their own right. These were often close friends as well, working as entrepreneurs in similar, sometimes competing or collaborating firms. The fourth category involved generic groups of people who were regarded as being collectively important for the development of the firms, but who were not specifically named individuals. Examples included well informed distributors, customers, and suppliers who were used regularly and trusted.

Text segments from interview transcripts and notes were explicitly attributed to codes to enable replicability. We analysed the data in detail using non-parametric methods to test the statistical significance of the differences between the groups. This started with the chi-squared test for two independent samples, which is highly robust and appropriate for this type of data set (Pett 1997), but also used the robust and highly conservative Fisher exact test not only because the minimum expected count in any cell was often less than five, but also because it provided a reliable crosscheck (Conover 1999). Pearson's phi (Φ) was used to measure the strength of differences between the nation groups, which can be interpreted in the same way as the more commonplace Pearson's R (Hinkle *et al.* 1994).

DIFFERENT NETWORK TIES IN DIFFERENT COUNTRY CULTURES

The values research, summarized in Table 7.1, yields clear pictures concerning how network relationships would be developed in the Netherlands and the United Kingdom. Both countries share a range of orientations: analytical and universalist ways of thinking; low uncertainty avoidance, highly egalitarian orientations, and achievement orientations. Dutch and British entrepreneurs are likely form network relationships with specific groups who can be seen to be useful for the firms' development.

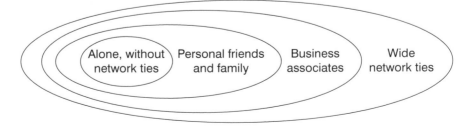

Figure 7.1 *Four different categories of network ties*

Table 7.1 *Values orientations in France, the Netherlands and Great Britain*

Author	Dimension of Values	France	Netherlands	Britain
Hofstede	Individualism (vs collectivism)	High	High	High
Trompenaars	Individualism (vs communitarianism)	Low	High	High
Hofstede	Power distance	High	Low	Low
Laurent	Organizations as hierarchical-relationship systems	High	Low	Low
Laurent	Organizations as authority systems	High	Medium	Medium
Hofstede	Long-term (vs short-term)	–	High	Low
Trompenaars	Sequential (vs synchronic) time	Low	High	High
Trompenaars	Short (vs long) time horizon	Medium	Low	High
Trompenaars	Short (vs long) past horizon	Low	High	High
Trompenaars	Short (vs long) future horizon	Low	High	High
Hofstede	Masculinity (vs femininity)	Medium	Low	High
Trompenaars	Task (vs person) orientation	High	Low	-
Trompenaars	Neutral (vs sffective) relationships	Low	High	High
Laurent	Organisations as role formation systems	High	Low	High
Trompenaars	Achieved (vs ascribed) status	Low	Medium	High
Trompenaars	Specific (vs diffuse) involvement	Medium	Low	High
Trompenaars	Inner (vs outer) directed	High	High	High
Laurent	Managers holding a social role	High	Low	Low
Laurent	Organizations as political systems	High	Low	Low
Hofstede	Uncertainty avoidance	High	Low	Low
Trompenaars	Uncertainty avoidance	High	Low	Low
Trompenaars	Analytical (vs integrational) thinking	Low	Medium	High
Trompenaars	Universalism (vs particularism)	Low	High	High

Nearly all the values data for the Netherlands indicate a strong focus on network relationships as an asset. Femininity will establish an expectation that strong network relationships will be developed to maintain harmony inside and outside the firm, and to resolve conflicts before they get serious. Long-termism indicates a need for thoroughness, which when combined with the feminine orientation, suggests development of strong trust based network relationships, developed over time, with a wide range of people, inside and outside the firm. So while relationships with diverse new partners would be sought, network relationships will be needed, which would take time. Network relationships will be seen as very important and will be in well-trusted long-standing relationships.

The cultural values research gives a different pattern of expectations for British entrepreneurs: they would be likely to develop their businesses with relatively little emphasis on trust-based network relationships. The masculine orientation implies decisive, forthright leadership, and bold actions without the need for involvement of other people. At the most, some close associates may be involved if necessary. Like the Dutch entrepreneurs, they may form many new relationships with diverse partners, but short-termism and masculinity means that they will not develop these into strong network relationships based on trust. So masculinity and short-termism, attenuated by low uncertainty avoidance, indicate strong trust-based network relationships to be less important in Britain. Forming deals and contracts is important, but these do not require depth of knowledge of the other parties. While some relationships may well deepen, based on performance achievement against agreements, and over time, this may not be sought actively: the contrasts in our expectations between the Netherlands and Britain are clear.

The national values research gives a more mixed pattern of expectations concerning the nature and role of network relationships in France. Further confusing the picture, France's particularist orientation implies that consistent patterns are less likely than in universalistic countries such as the Netherlands and Britain. French entrepreneurs will develop network relationships according to their own views and needs, in the context of their firm and their industry. The other values orientations provide conflicting indications. On one hand, French task orientation implies a practical willingness to engage with anyone that can be useful. Its long-termism and its high uncertainty avoidance suggest an unwillingness to risk error, which may manifest itself as a desire to consult with all those with a relevant interest or knowledge, whether these are inside or outside the firm. France's integrational orientation, not shared by the Netherlands or Britain, also implies an inclination to consult widely to seek, accept and integrate different ideas and notions. So French entrepreneurs may develop network relationships with people widely, like Dutch entrepreneurs and unlike British entrepreneurs; one would expect that French entrepreneurs would make greater use of network relationships in the management of their businesses than British entrepreneurs.

THE DIFFERENCES FOUND IN THE THREE COUNTRIES

Table 7.2 shows the network relationships in use by the entrepreneurs in the three countries very clearly. In ways entirely consistent with our expectations from the cultural research outlined before, the British entrepreneurs made much less use of network relationships, almost half of them making major developmental initiatives for their firms without the use of network relationships. By contrast, only seven per cent of the Dutch and 17 per cent of the French entrepreneurs did this.

Table 7.2 *Entrepreneurs' network ties in the three countries*

Developments involve:	%			$\Phi(p)$		
	French	Dutch	British	French v Dutch	French v British	Dutch v British
Alone?	17	7	47	_	−.316*	−.422****
Personal friends and family?	33	79	40	−.456****	_	.39***
Business associates?	67	86	53	_	_	.350**
Wide network ties?	50	50	20	_	.316*	.315**

Significance levels: **** ≥ 2½%   2½% > *** ≥ 5%   5% > ** ≥ 10% 10%   * ≥ 15%

Matching this pattern, half of the French and Dutch used wide external networks of supplier or customer companies in major developmental initiatives, whereas only one-fifth of the British entrepreneurs did this. So we see a distinct pattern with French and Dutch entrepreneurs using network relationships far more in the building of their businesses than British entrepreneurs, a pattern entirely consistent with what we would expect from the cultural traits in those countries. We might have expected the Dutch to network relationships more than the French. We found this, but the difference was not significant.

A similar overall pattern was found in the use of network relationships of specific business associates who were known well to, and are important to, the entrepreneurs. All the national groups used these far more than the 'wide' networks, and once again, the Dutch used them the most (86 per cent), the British the least (53 per cent), with the French in between (67 per cent). One pattern was, however, a surprise, in no way predicted by the cultural values research. Perhaps surprisingly in firms in highly sophisticated, technological environments, all these entrepreneur groups made use of their old personal friends and family relatives – siblings, uncles, etc. The Dutch, however, did this far more than did the British and the French. The main role of these relationships was as a source of 'wise counsel' for individuals facing the lonely task of pioneers in a new technological landscape. These most highly trusted individuals were typically also entrepreneurs, and were able to share the common feelings and experiences facing humans who have embarked on ventures with perilous and uncertain futures.

While Table 7.2 shows the differences in statistical terms, some quotations from three entrepreneurs, one from each country, perhaps illustrates the different types of network ties more vibrantly:

> British entrepreneur: Iain, [Chairman] made introductions to a number of people, and I spent a few weeks living out of a suitcase travelling around, meeting them. I hated it, but it worked. Nothing came of most of the meetings, but from two, [this] led to other meetings, other people. One

thing led to another, and eventually I met with someone in the labs of (large US multinational). The contract with them set us up.

Dutch entrepreneur: We hold long meetings, which last for several days where people get to know each other better. This is for our distributors, our larger customers, some of our suppliers, and, of course, all our people here ... these meetings are to get to know them better, and to enable them to get to know us, When we understand the problems that each other have, then we will know what we can do and what we cannot do, what we will do and what we may not do.

... I will not do business with people I do not know well, do not trust. That is bad business.

French entrepreneur: I have learned a lot from some of the customers I have been working with. These American companies are very good, they get a lot out of their people and we are able to learn. I now, for one year, hold meetings with all the product development managers and the commercials every week and we discuss everything. They are not used to this mostly. I now do not hide anything, they must share this adventure. Of course, we cannot involve the junior staff in this, but all the managers are there, and this is a lot of us because we are not making or selling anything ourselves. It is not like this in [large electronics firms]. There you only know what you must and not more.

DIFFERENT NETWORK TIES IN DIFFERENT INSTITUTIONAL CULTURES

High-tech entrepreneurs can often find that it is government departments or agencies that are their customers, partners, and occasionally their suppliers – organizations in whom it is essential to build network ties to survive in many sectors. Research has highlighted how different institutional frameworks can lead to very different approaches to doing things, and especially towards the formation of business relationships.

Interaction between agency pressures on managers and the formal structures of the organizations involved has been highlighted as being an important factor behind the choices and actions of individual actors (Scott and Meyer 1994). Pedersen and Thomsen's work especially highlights the importance of governance and institutional ownership to management practice, and this has become a recent focus of research. Research in the US has shown agency effects leading firms mainly owned by their managers – private companies – to take greater risks than those with mainly external shareholders – public companies (Eisenmann 2002; Tihani *et al.* 2003; Schulze *et al.* 2003; Wright *et al.* 2002). Research in France (Durand and

Varas 2003), Germany (Tuschke and Sanders 2003) and India (Ramsaswamy *et al*. 2002) has found similar but more complex relationships, with institutional factors including, for example, different unique resources and evolutionary trajectories, different conceptualizations of industrial success recipes, and different corporate cultures and histories.

Here we are going to consider the network relationships of entrepreneurs that are similar in most respects, but with one major institutional difference. Some will be owner managers who do not have an agency relationship with any outside owners or shareholders; these are the entrepreneurs that we considered before in our international comparison. These entrepreneurs have financed the development of their firms with debt finance, provided by banks, friends, relatives and partners, business and personal. In some cases, they shared ownership, most usually with business or family partners, and sometimes with providers of venture capital. In all these firms, however, full ownership control remained with the entrepreneurs themselves. We will call these people owner–entrepreneurs.

The other group we will call venture-capital entrepreneurs. This group did not have ownership control of their firms; on average, they held 15 per cent of the shares of 'their' businesses, this ranging from five to 35 per cent. In all these firms, the majority ownership resided in one financial institution, or in a consortium of financial institutions. It would, of course, have been interesting and useful to have been able to examine the network relationships of venture-capital entrepreneurs in France – Alpes-Maritimes – and in the Netherlands. They did not exist in quantity: just one was found in the Netherlands, and one in Alpes-Maritimes. Venture capital backing of entrepreneurs has reputably been building in these countries, but it remains, predominantly, an Anglo-Saxon phenomenon.

These venture-capital entrepreneurs were invariably trained managers, usually with MBAs and with large company experience, as well as having technical backgrounds. Their tenure at the companies was short – between two and five years, in comparison with the eight to 15 years of the owner-entrepreneurs. They viewed their firms as stages in an entrepreneurial-management career, in comparison with the owner-entrepreneurs who saw their firms as fundamental parts of their lives. They saw their roles as being professional managers, with some risk and with major financial rewards in prospect. They were, for institutional reasons, a culturally very different group.

In comparison with the owner-entrepreneurs, we would expect venture capital entrepreneurs, because they are in a hurry, to develop wide networks much faster, but there will be insufficient time to develop such deep relationships. Their more varied career backgrounds within large and other entrepreneurial firms, and their having ties with financial backers, however, will have enabled them to form more business-associate relationships who might help them to achieve not only the rapid success they crave, but also their subsequent venture capital financed business opportunity. Involving family and personal friends would not, of course,

127

be regarded as professional management behaviour; it does not have a place on any MBA programmes. Nevertheless, modern management training extols the virtues of networking, so we would not expect important issues to be considered alone. Overall, we would expect this group to do a lot more networking, except with personal friends and family.

Examining Table 7.3, that is exactly what we find. Developments are more rarely undertaken without using network ties, though the difference here with the owner-entrepreneurs is not statistically significant. The most significant difference is in the use of personal friends and family ties. The venture capital entrepreneur never used these, whereas 40 per cent of the owner-entrepreneurs used these linkages for dealing with at least one important issue. They also networked a lot more, and the relationships they formed here were used more widely. Nearly all discussed their business issues with their business associates, who were usually the directors of the venture capital firms that were financing them, senior managers that they had recruited to help them manage their firms – who were often former colleagues from their periods of employment at large firms – and other former colleagues who had remained friends.

This analysis helps to conceptualize the comparisons of the three owner-groups and to offer some valuable insights. Most evidently, while the differences between the national groups are statistically significant and meaningful, they are substantially lower in scale than the differences seen between the different institutional contexts. This highlights how it is easy to interpret differences as being the outcome of national values differences, where they may not be. It seems to be important, therefore, when researching difference in these aspects, to take care not to attribute differences to national values, when these might more appropriately be attributable to institutional differences.

Table 7.3 Network ties of institutionally different types of entrepreneurs

Developments involve	Owner entrepreneurs	Venture capital entrepreneurs	Owner vs Venture capital entrepreneurs (Φ (p))
Alone?	47%	38%	–
Personal friends and family?	40%	0%	.434***
Business associates?	53%	88%	–.342*
Wide network ties?	20%	50%	–.315*

Significance levels: **** $\geq 2\frac{1}{2}$% $2\frac{1}{2}$% > *** ≥ 5%   5% > ** ≥ 10% 10% * ≥ 15%

National differences can interact with institutional differences to cause greater differences between groups. They can, in some areas, interact to counteract each other. Making generalized statements concerning network tie formation in particular countries is clearly a dangerous activity. It is not appropriate to attribute behaviour to singular factors, whether national values, institutional frameworks, or other reasons.

CONCLUSION

The comparisons that we have made between the network relationships of closely matched but all successful, high-tech entrepreneurs in three national cultures and in two different institutional cultures give some important messages for our understanding of high-tech entrepreneurship, for high-tech entrepreneurs themselves, and for policy to encourage high-tech entrepreneurship.

Our understanding of high-tech entrepreneurship is enhanced by the observation that cultural factors – whether from different nations or from different institutional environments – profoundly influence the network relationships which high-tech entrepreneurs use to help the development of their businesses. This is despite massive globalization in the industries themselves, and the technologies that they are using. All the entrepreneurs found network relationships to be crucial – this corroborates the discussions in Chapters 6 and 15. But the way that network relationships work varies from culture to culture – indeed, most social anthropologists would argue that network relationships are themselves an important defining aspect of culture. They are a cultural phenomenon. That makes the patterns and pictures that we are trying to discuss in developing our understanding of high-tech entrepreneurship more complicated, more multi-dimensional, rather complex. Simple one-dimensional models of network relationships will not do – our world is too rich for that.

High-tech entrepreneurs should appreciate that making linkages is essential for them to make the ventures that they will have to make into new cultures. The venture to resource financial capital will involve a venture into a new cultural landscape. Customers can reside in very different types of organizations – such as large companies or government departments. With the globalization in the high-tech world, increasingly, customers and suppliers of inputs are within different national resources. In these different cultural environments, the ways that relationships are formed are very different.

So entrepreneurs should not believe that there is only one way to form network relationships. The way that is right for any entrepreneur will reflect their own orientation towards relationship formation, which will be, to some extent, a personal characteristic. But it must also reflect the 'way of relationship formation' in the environment towards which they are hoping to venture. In this process, learning from experience and from observation, both of oneself and from others, is important. So is the role of 'bridge-builders', who can help to take entrepreneurs

129

into the cultural environments where they will be foreign. Networking to find these 'bridge-builders' is an important process.

Our policies for fostering high-tech entrepreneurship can nevertheless begin from the starting point that network relationships are essential for firm development. We cannot, however, necessarily give general rules to our entrepreneurs as to who they should develop network relationships with, or how they should do it. But we can try to ensure that there is a 'milieu' or environment that can enable appropriate network relationships to blossom in a sensitive way: thereafter, it is up to the entrepreneurs. The institutional structure, of course, can help, by providing meetings and events which may enable people to get to know each other. Small things, however, can be important as well, as the following quotation from the managing director of a highly successful city-centre incubator organization in England illustrates:

> Our most important asset here is not our on-site venture capital, our team of advisers, our flexible property facilities, our flexible administrative support. All that helps, but the most important, from looking at the development of our high-technology enterprises, is our coffee machine. And the coffee is lousy! That machine has been responsible for the creation of three firms, all of which are thriving, for saving two, and for powering the development of another three.
>
> Why? Well, it's situated very visibly, so everyone knows it's there, it's central, so it's easy to get to, yet it's comfortable and quiet to sit near. That is how it works. People keep meeting there by chance, they discuss their problems, their worries, their ideas. These can be other entrepreneurs or they can be people from very different places, from universities, from government offices, from support offices. They get to know each other, and then to trust each other. Out of many such chance meetings, real development can take place.

This milieu suits the kinds of firms in that incubator unit; that culture. Policy may best develop appropriate milieu for the many and diverse types of high-tech entrepreneurs that are discussed in this book, milieu that helps people from different institutional cultures and different national cultures, or people with experience in those cultures, who may be bridge builders, to interact.

Chapter 8

Technology business incubation management
Lessons of experience

Philippe Albert and Lynda Gaynor

New companies are presented with multiple difficulties when facing established competitors. Support systems have been created to help the fledgling enterprises by tilting the competitive environment in their favour. These support systems for enterprise creation use a myriad of approaches, including tax advantages, training, and exemption from statutory obligations.

Among these tools, incubation has appeared as one useful process for encouraging, counselling, and networking young companies, and appears to have developed into an efficient way to focus and integrate the different mechanisms devoted to start-ups.

Incubators appeared over 30 years ago as a novel support structure for companies. They have proven to be more rounded, more malleable and more adaptable to the needs of start-up companies experiencing rapid metamorphoses than previous approaches. Over the years, incubators have proven their worth, have spread worldwide, and have engaged a growing range of economic players, including local authorities, universities, and large corporations.

While a large majority of incubators and nurseries for business projects deal with all types of enterprise, from arts and crafts to household service providers and small manufacturers, a number specialize in high-tech projects and companies. There has been significant growth in the number of these technology business incubators. While the number of technology business incubators increased dramatically between 1999 and 2001, the origin of this type of incubator may be traced back to 1980. Of 310 university business incubators worldwide surveyed by Lendner (2002), and from a response rate of 44 per cent – 130 incubators – it was established that the majority of university business incubators were technology business incubators.

Technology business incubators have a number of specific characteristics which are determined by the salient features of high-tech start-ups, and particularly their high level of risk and their complexity. As Albert and Mougenot (1988) and Bernasconi (2004) identify, high-tech companies face instability in their sector;

they have a close relationship with their scientific environment, they have particular financial needs from the high levels of investment they have to make, and they face difficulties in identifying and capturing their initial markets. Incubators have been developed in order to assist entrepreneurs in high-tech start up companies to adapt to and manage, as far as possible, the risks and the complexities they face.

The main role of the incubator management as regards the fledging firm is not only to reduce some of the risks the entrepreneurs face, it is also to sharpen the entrepreneurial team's ability to cope with the various risks involved, and to bring about the incubator 'friendly' resources and competences that will help the entrepreneurial team when making decisions on human resources, technology, marketing, and sales and finance.

Technology business incubators are of particular interest because of their role in innovation and technology transfer which can be regarded as a cornerstone of sustained national economic success, and because of the singular way in which they have been able to cope with the very specific characteristics and needs of high-tech start-ups.

Their growth has been driven by three forces. First, nation-states have sought to develop their own technology innovation, particularly by encouraging the development of high-tech companies. Second, developing science parks around research centres and universities has been a popular way for regional, city and local development agencies to boost the value of their research and development (R&D) centres and universities through growth in local economic activity. Third, universities and research centres themselves have sought to capitalize on their patents and know-how in order to generate new revenue streams.

In general, and over the long term, incubation has been seen – although this has not been statistically proven – to be not only effective, but also a low cost tool for fostering entrepreneurship, economic wealth and growth. In this chapter, we attempt to synthesize key components of technology business incubation in the contemporary context, and examine the trends and best practices of such incubation. Next, we review the evolving literature on business incubation, and follow this with an overview of the objectives and contribution of the different types of sponsors usually involved in incubation, since the main sponsor(s) have a critical effect on the overall incubator profile.

We then look at the profile and practices of technology business incubators based on a number of key differentiating factors. We believe that a managerial approach is particularly appropriate to the study of high-tech incubation and the special incubator–incubatee relationship that this involves. We conclude with an examination of some key issues and best practices in technology business incubators from this managerial perspective.

DEFINING INCUBATION AND INCUBATORS

The literature on incubators has moved through a life-cycle, as incubators themselves have became more popular and been established widely over the last 20 years. Early work simply describes incubators, and then proposed successful practices and configurations. More recently, studies here addressed more complex issues, such as assessing incubators effects, based on the combined impact on multiple stakeholders – sponsors, local economy and tenant firms (see reviews by Albert and Gaynor 2001; Hackett and Dilts 2004). Hackett and Dilts (2004) classified this evolution in incubator research under five different research themes: incubator development studies, incubator configuration studies, incubatee development studies, incubator–incubation impact studies, and studies that theorize about incubators–incubation.

In relation to high-tech business incubation, a particular obstacle in reviewing this literature is that much of the theory is embedded in research classified under entrepreneurship, networks, organizational learning and SME growth rather than under incubation per se. From its hey day in the 1980s when many studies focused exclusively on incubation – 17 of the 39 articles considered by Hacket and Dilts relate to the five-year period 1984–8 – the knowledge base has become widely diffused, and has only started to become re-centred in an incubation context (see for example the recent study by Peters *et al.* 2004).

This phenomenon is amply illustrated in the review by Hackett and Dilts who focussed on incubator-incubation academic literature between 1984 and 2002. Of 26 research perspectives identified, 17 were only cited once, and of these, 14 originated since 1992. This indicates that relevant research from a similar perspective is located in the body of work generated in other domains which has not been considered specifically in relation to the incubation process.

Hackett and Dilts also found that the articles were mainly published in journals with an economic development perspective, and concluded that while there has been a lot of description of incubator facilities, there has been relatively little on the incubatees and their innovations. They particularly noted the lack of a business incubation process model, and proposed a moratorium on incubator facility configuration studies in order to facilitate a focus on incubation process studies.

It is widely recognized that incubators are highly embedded in their social, cultural and economic environments, and that these influence their focus and their configuration. This characteristic has presented significant challenges in reaching common definitions for research purposes. Hackett and Dilts note the ambiguity in definitions of 'business incubator' and 'business incubation' within the literature. Most definitions of incubation refer to the post-company creation phase and define incubators in terms of their outputs, such as in new enterprises.

Incubators have traditionally been described in terms of what they do – help, support, accelerate or enhance – what they are trying to achieve – incubatee

133

development, incubatee growth rate or incubatee success in general undefined terms – and who they work with – entrepreneurs, new enterprises, entrepreneurial companies or start-ups.

More useful definitions are those which incorporate the combined impact of the interdependence between both tangible features – accommodation, support services – and intangible features – knowledge, confidence, credibility, companionship – of incubators, as well as the position in the life-cycle of the incubatee. Examples include those of Allen and McCluskey (1990), Tornatzky *et al.* (1996), and Hackett and Dilts (2004). Following this school of thinking, we define incubators as 'a place where specific professional resources are organized to help the emergence and first development of new companies'.

We now consider the interlinked incubator–incubatee relationship in greater detail (e.g. Peters *et al.* 2004). Our particular interest is in the iterative process of how the structures, activities and philosophy of incubators affect, and are affected by, the specific characteristics of high-tech companies.

Taking a managerial perspective, we try to identify both the conditions required for an incubator to be successful, and the conditions required for start-ups to be successful during the incubation process – say, between two years before to five years after their creation. We believe that these two sets of conditions are interlinked, and cannot be separated artificially for individual analysis. Next, we summarize of the objectives and contributions of technology business incubator sponsors, and follow this with an outline of the profiles and practices of technology business incubators.

OBJECTIVES AND CONTRIBUTIONS OF THE SPONSORS

Albert *et al.* (2004) analysed incubators according to their objectives and the contribution of their primary sponsors. The primary sponsor was found to be the factor which had the largest influence on incubator's objectives, priorities and configurations. There are various types of sponsors who are involved in technology business incubators. Academic sponsors include universities or university departments, and there are also public research centres. In the area of local development, sponsors include local government – town or local councils – regional governments, and development agencies. In the corporate world, there are corporate entities, large and small, as well as venture capitalists and other financiers.

Other stakeholders that are often involved, but which are rarely primary sponsors, are the state – through a ministry or department – local chambers of commerce, and local successful entrepreneurs. These different actors often play different but complementary roles in the creation, management and policy creation activities of a technology business incubator. A summary of the ways in which the contribution and objectives of incubators differ depending on the identity of the primary sponsor is set out in Table 8.1.

Table 8.1 *Sponsors of business technology incubation: objectives and contribution*

	Public – national, regional and local economic development agencies	University and public research centres	Corporate entities
Objectives (Why involved?)	Job creation Economic development Support to particular target groups or industries Development of SMEs and clusters	Commercialization of research investment Development of entrepreneurial spirit Civic responsibility Image New sources of finance	To monitor and have access to new technologies and to new markets Profits To develop entrepreneurial spirit among employees – keep talents
Contribution (Potential value-added they offer incubatees)	Credibility Seed capital Maintenance and management of the physical buildings and adjoining area Linkages to national and international programmes	Credibilty Access to research facilities and equipment Access to national and international research programmes and funding Access to scientific knowledge and highly skilled human resources	Concept testing technical advice and support Intellectual property advice Financial resources Prototype and market testing Access to commercial markets Access to multiple competencies

Where many parties are involved, the profile, focus and priorities of a technology business incubator vary according to the relative influence of the different parties. Ideally, all three types of promoter contribute in equal measure, to create a well-rounded support environment for ventures within the incubator. In reality, one or two promoters may dominate and this influences the nature of the overall offering.

Table 8.1 shows that the primary objectives of the sponsors may be slightly different, and that the resources provided by the sponsors will depend on the nature of these institutions. For start-ups joining a technology business incubator, the type of sponsor acting behind it will determine the type of environment in which they will evolve.

PROFILE AND PRACTICES OF TECHNOLOGY BUSINESS INCUBATORS

The key determining factors in the profile and practices of technology business incubators are the degree of specialization, the relative strength of the infrastructure, the strategic services provided, and the effectiveness of the service delivery. Each of these is now discussed in more detail.

Degree of specialization

Technology business incubators can be divided into two main camps: those which focus on the phase before company creation – known as incubators in France, and sometimes called nurseries or innovation centres elsewhere – and those focusing on the phase after company creation – known widely as incubators, or in the terminology of the Commission of the European Union, Business Innovation Centres (BICs).

Some incubators, however, straddle the two phases, as the incubation process is an on-going one which, particularly for high-tech start-up, begins before the effective creation of the company, and follows on through the first years after the creation. Technology incubators, by definition, specialize to a greater or lesser degree on technology-based companies. Table 8.2 presents some salient examples of the different types of technology on which technology centred incubators focus.

Infrastructural services

The services that are most frequently provided by technology business incubators to companies can loosely be divided into infrastructural services which include accommodation, shared services and technical support and strategic services, which includes strategic and technical advice, access to networks, training, individual coaching, and the break from isolation and membership of a community of peers.

Accommodation

High-tech start-ups have a more demanding requirement than other start-ups for accommodation that allows them to expand or to downsize rapidly in response to changes in the market. This includes large spaces available outside the incubator

Table 8.2 Examples of incubators specializing in different technologies

Technology	Example
Information Technology (IT)	*University of Central Florida Technology Incubator.* NBIA 2004 incubator of the year in technology category
Software	*jvp Studio*, Jerusalem, Israel. Formerly the Jerusalem Software Incubator and recently privatized and purchased by a venture capital company
Biotechnology	*Eclosion*, Geneva, Switzerland. A new venture financed by the Canton of Geneva to incubate life-sciences companies
Medical devices	*Medical Device Development Centre*, Vancouver, Canada
Nanotechnology	*Minatec Centre for Innovation in Micro and Nano Technology*, Grenoble, France
Energy and environment	*Environmental Business Cluster*, San Jose, California

but within the same commercial and scientific milieu for a post-incubation period of exceptional expansion. The difference in accommodation needs in technology business incubators is most acutely evident in the bio-tech sector, where companies often require laboratories, clean rooms and specialized equipment to be available within the incubator for controlled tests to be carried out.

Shared services

These mainly involve logistical support and administrative services. Technology companies operating in an international market dominated by multinationals need a first class support structure to give them the appropriate image of seriousness and effectiveness. Cocooning them too much, however, can have a negative impact. The management may not develop the resource-seeking skills that they need to grow the company. So, while insufficient resources create complications and pressures, excessive resources can also have a detrimental effect if not managed appropriately.

Technical support

High-tech incubators are, by their nature, filled with specialized IT and laboratory equipment which the start-ups use to develop or implement their market offerings. The more specialized the incubator is within a particular sector, the higher the degree of sophistication of equipment it can provide. One of the key advantages for small companies is to have access to the necessary hardware and software, but without the responsibility for maintaining it, or for keeping licenses up to date. Conversely, this is a specialist expertise which can be provided by the management of the incubator, either through outsourcing or in-house technicians.

Strategic services

Strategic services are the most critical for fledgling companies. It is the presence of strategic services which distinguishes incubators from real-estate providers, and it is the depth and quality of the strategic services which differentiates incubators from each other. The quality and effectiveness of strategic services is much more difficult to measure. Unlike infrastructural services, they are not generic but rather defined by the technological specialization and the stage of development of the companies within the incubator.

Strategic and technical advice

It is vital that incubators draw the entrepreneurs' attention to the need to match one of many possible target markets to one of the many different applications of the start-up's primary technologies. Most often, this involves an iterative process of trial and error. Unfortunately, this makes it extremely difficult to calculate the length of time to market entry, and as a result, also makes it difficult to predict the financial needs of the company during the incubation period, before the start-up can achieve a regular income flow.

Access to networks

An incubator can, through its network, be in a position to provide pertinent advice in relation to a number of services. One is in the area of technological developments and intellectual property. Another is in the commercial environment, and it can do this principally by putting companies in contact with large corporates which are at the coal-face of marketing technology, who are in a position to validate the options available to a start-up, and who can aid them in the commercialization of their project. There is also a need to achieve complementarity of skills within a start-up team through effective recruitment. Finally, it is necessary to secure finance appropriate to the stage and pace of growth of the venture.

In order to achieve all this, an incubator should be well embedded in the local environment and connected to the specific business networks and external resources. The successful developmental process of an incubator lies in its combining of the synergies within it, as well as synergies between it and the external environment. Incubators therefore tend to be more effective if they are part of a wider programme and organization which have their own established networks.

Access to networks, particularly providers of finance and seed capital, and experts with specific knowledge on the market structure and dynamics, is therefore critical.

Training

For start-ups to be able to make the most of opportunities that may be available within networks, their management teams need to have well-honed skills in a wide range of areas including finance, communications, marketing and recruitment. Formal training allows the entrepreneurial team to develop these skills through a group process of learning from the experience of peers and experts.

Training opportunities are offered through a large set of tools, which include coaching, counselling, networking, training, and peer influence. As in every other educational process, it is very difficult to know when and how it is that the entrepreneurs are developing new skills. If however, the incubator environment and networks are rich, relevant, skilled and friendly and are dedicated to new ventures, the entrepreneurs have a greater likelihood of progressing quickly in building a successful company.

Individual coaching

The initial breadth and depth of different skills required by entrepreneurs varies from person to person, depending on their previous background and their future role in the start-up. In order to address this effectively, individual coaching is a highly effective way of supplementing formal training, by filling in expertise gaps and honing critical skills.

The break from isolation and membership of a community of peers

Entrepreneurs such as academics, researchers and corporate managers can find the transition from their previous environment in large, resourced entities to the unique setting of a small start-up in a cut-throat commercial world personally difficult to navigate. Technology business incubators allow their small companies to exist within a larger campus, and provide informal, continuous access to fellow entrepreneurs in similar situations.

The management of technology business incubators must look for ways of delivering these services from within their own resources or through links with the external environment. The profile of their internal resources is strongly influenced by the identity of the primary sponsor, as they tend to propose the use of their own resources and expertise.

Incubation services delivery

From a client's viewpoint, the different accommodation and logistical services can be clearly identified, but the 'soft' services – counselling, coaching, training, networking, etc. – may be seen as one package of resources that they can use upon request.

The entrepreneur's objective is to make his or her way efficiently through the process of development from a company concept, to company building, and then to the company take-off and first developments. This complex process of inter-related activities is iterative, non-linear, and always involves a painful trial and error process. The incubator's effectiveness lies in its ability to help the entrepreneur in this process, by delivering its infrastructure and its strategic services in a stage-appropriate manner. This requires the incubator management to evaluate, on an ongoing basis, the current state of flux of the entrepreneurs' resources and their company building objectives. We view the strategic tasks of the incubator management as first evaluating the trilogy, and second, maintaining progress against milestones.

Evaluating the trilogy

The initial evaluation is made during the selection process and should be reassessed regularly. The objective of the evaluation is to check the coherence of the three fundamental elements involved. One element is the entrepreneur's – or the entrepreneurial team's – profile. This depends on factors that include their age, personality, experience, and personal objectives. Another element is the entrepreneur's resources, in other words, the entrepreneur's skills, personal networks, social capital, and financial resources. The third element is the business concept. This involves the business size, the business model and the type of development of the company that is sketched out by the entrepreneur (Figure 8.1).

The entrepreneurial process and the incubation process are both learning processes. The way that entrepreneurs – or the entrepreneurial teams – learn from their various activities, and are able to manoeuvre and adapt strategies and tactics, is extremely important. A vital service in incubators is in diagnosing capacities of the entrepreneurial team, and to help them to know their strong and their weak points.

Regularly monitor the progress of the company building against milestones

Entrepreneurs work simultaneously on different tasks, and it is not usually possible to equate the company creation process with a traditional project management. Uncertainty and complexity force the entrepreneur continually to reassess and reconcile the various dimensions of their project. This uncertainty makes the time programming of the various stages extremely difficult.

The incubator coach, however, can help entrepreneurs to navigate their way ahead, and can try to help them find new solutions when they reach impasse. This is very often the case where technological solutions or market targets are concerned. In addition, the time allocation of the entrepreneur's efforts may be disproportionate in some tasks. Here, an incubator coach can be important in helping them to redirect their efforts by, for example, sub-contracting some tasks.

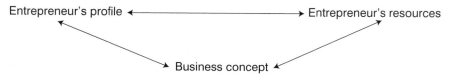

Figure 8.1 *Evaluating the trilogy*

EFFECTIVE MANAGEMENT OF TECHNOLOGY BUSINESS INCUBATORS

Our research work as well as our experience working with high-tech start-ups in Sophia Antipolis (France) and Lyon (France) gives us an insight into the conditions which can help best to support and to work with start-ups, from the point of view both of the incubators themselves and the companies within them. We will look at the effective management of technology business incubators under two headings, the incubator institutional conditions, and the incubator management team role.

The incubator institutional conditions

By nature, technology incubators are finely balanced entities, because they deal with new high-tech companies which are characterized by fragility and uncertainty. Two European studies (European Commission 2001, 2002) have shown that technology incubators are much more secure when they are supported by strong institutions which can afford ups and downs in some marginal activities.

Specifically, technology incubators tend to be better off when strongly linked with organizations such as universities and research centres, which can give easy access to technology, talents and resources. This means that they have secure, open and balanced relationships with various parts of the university, and do not compete heavily with them. Technology incubators are also in a better position when they do not stand alone but are part of wider programmes, such as business economic development programmes or technology programmes. Incubators located within multi-faceted milieu such as science parks, where corporations, research institutions, SMEs and state support agencies are closely knitted together, may benefit hugely from the close proximity of personnel, knowledge and training resources which these offer and which can be harnessed.

Generally, multi-stakeholder governance including universities, large firms, local entrepreneurs and local government can yield better acceptance in the community if the usual conflicts of interest that can arise within these structures can be properly managed. The acceptance by the community is very important, as the value perceived even in the best incubator is no more than the use that the community makes of it. (The reference here to community does not mean necessarily 'local' community, but the relevant business and social environment of the technology business incubators. This means that very often their natural partners may be outside the local community.) The governance norms should allow room for flexibility and adaptability, and should certainly not impede the incubator activity by heavy reporting requirements and control systems. It should look not only at short term outcomes, but also at long-term objectives.

While some technology incubators are private (Lendner 2002, found that in Europe, 15 per cent of universities incubators were private), most need public or private sponsorship. Long-term sustainability for the incubator can be achieved if recognition and proof of success are regularly communicated to the various stakeholders. This includes regularly demonstrating how efficiently the incubator is managed, how well its resources are used, and the degree to which it delivers added value to incubatees.

The incubator management team role

Managing incubators is a difficult challenge, and one which is widely underestimated. Why? Managing technology start-ups is a risky business, which is replete with uncertainty, so coaching and counselling high-tech entrepreneurs – or entrepreneurial teams – requires advanced competences and knowledge of the business process, applied technology, finance, and many other aspects. Not only is knowledge required in these areas, but also the support of a large set of relevant networks. Moreover, the job requires talented psychological and social skills and high moral values in order for the incubator management to be recognized by entrepreneurs as a trustworthy partner. Furthermore, the incubator manager needs to have the appropriate skills for managing his small team in a complex institutional environment. Sponsors seldom understand the complexity of this multi-faceted task – high-tech is high touch. New incubator managers often have little experience of incubation management, and often have received, at best, scant training. Even the most competent and experienced managers, however, are faced with managing the divergent expectations of stakeholders, unrealistic objectives regarding potential markets, as well as short term expectations which fluctuate with changes in politics.

The management team needs properly to understand and manage a range of interlinked but complex processes. First, there is the recruitment of projects – or start-ups. This requires proper marketing and PR programmes linked with efficient selection methods. Second, there is the delivery of the incubation services, which has already been discussed. Third, there is the generation of resources. The key to sustainable success is to get good, flexible resources at low cost. Effective managers try to gain access to external resources, particularly knowledge and networks, which can be placed at the disposal of the start-ups. In tandem with this, it is important to find a sufficiently high level of stable revenue sources. This can be either through an anchor tenant, who rents equipment and space on a long-term basis to external third parties, or through long-term financial commitments from sponsors. The critical factor is to ensure that the optimal balance is achieved between stability and flexibility. If too much of the revenue is fixed, the incubator loses its entrepreneurial edge and the ability to react to changing circumstances. If too little is fixed, the management spend far too much time on raising finance and managing the pressurized resources of the incubator rather than assisting the entrepreneurs within it.

Fourth, there is the management of the start-up portfolio. The start-up portfolio of an incubator is made up of its tenants and of its graduates. The gradual development of a successful portfolio depends on the coherence of the process: the selection of an adequate quality and quantity of start-ups relative to the relevant market target, and the incubation resources available. The quality of the portfolio and the degree of satisfaction of the entrepreneurs with incubator services create the incubator's image, and this may generate a virtuous circle of success. Graduates should be seen as a key asset of the incubator and should be used, where possible, as resources, mentors, coaches and business angels.

So this means that the incubator management team should be proactive with the start-up firms, and work closely with the entrepreneurs. Studies have shown that real added value is given when managers of the incubator are personally strongly involved with sound relationships with the incubatees. In this, they are aware that entrepreneurship is first of all a human venture, that every project development process is different and specific, and this means that each business deserves its own 'tailor-made' coaching.

In order to achieve all of this, it is clear that the management team of an incubator needs to be properly recruited so that it has the depth, diversity, stability and flexibility necessary to meet the needs of entrepreneurs. As this is rarely achievable in a single individual, in Europe at least, successful incubators tend to have teams of five or six people.

CONCLUSION

The focus of this chapter has been the main dimensions and key factors of the management of technology business incubators. The extensive diffusion of technology business incubators worldwide shows that it is a powerful concept which has been widely accepted.

The term 'technology business incubator', however, remains a generic concept, which needs to be adapted to specific objectives and to local conditions. The profile of entrepreneurs and their background, the type of firms, the objectives of the incubator sponsors, and the nature of the local environment all shape very different types of incubators. There is great variety in technology business incubators worldwide, and this makes it a very interesting phenomenon to examine, and explains why it is so difficult to compare technology business incubators with each other.

Furthermore, technology business incubation remains a relatively young phenomenon which is in a state of continuing evolution, reacting to economic cycles and new waves of technology. However, it seems highly likely that incubators will continue to develop in the future; that the efficient ones will become a great asset for their partners, and that international networks of incubators will help them to improve their efficiency and effectiveness.

Chapter 9

Strategy development processes

The importance of considering integration and timing

Franck Moreau

What do we know about the development of high-tech start-ups? In spite of the many contributions on this subject, both descriptive and prescriptive models have been widely criticized. Without rejecting the possibility of a global model that explains and predicts the development of high-tech start-ups (Tzokas *et al.* 2001), it is widely acknowledged that these models share some common disadvantages.

Being limited and oversimplified, they are not representative (McCann 1991; Albert *et al.* 1994; Sammut 1998); they are inadequate and imprecise (Saporta 1994; Slevin and Covin 1995; Levie and Hay 1998); they either wrongly define company development as a unified, linear, sequential process (Stanworth and Curran 1976; Storey 1994) or argue a stochastic – non-sequential – development (Reynolds and Miller 1992; Hansen and Bird 1997). Other models have been criticized as impractical because of the diversity of definitions used and the difficulty in identifying company development phases (O'Farrell and Hitchens 1988; Hanks *et al.* 1993; Chell 2001). These models have also been criticized for being under conceptualized due to a lack of underlying theoretical analysis (Garnsey and Hefferman 2001; Bhidé 2000).

Even if certain authors have revised and rectified their initial models, confirming their significance (Eggers *et al.* 1994; Adizes 1999), such models still have real limitations.

This is even truer when we consider that most of these descriptive and normative works have dealt with the development, evolution, trajectories or paths of growth of young companies in general (Steinmetz 1969; Greiner, 1972; Stanworth and Curran 1976; Galbraith 1982; Churchill and Lewis 1983; Quinn and Cameron 1983; Miller and Friesen 1984; Flamholtz 1986). Only rarely do works specifically deal with start-ups (McCann 1991; Hansen and Bird 1997; Blais and Toulouse 1992) or companies exhibiting strong growth (Delmar and Davidsson 1998; Julien 2002). It is even rarer for them to deal both with start-ups and with start-ups having a strong potential for growth (Carter *et al.* 1996; Garnsey and Hefferman 2001; Mustar 2001; Julien 2002).

The difficulty in constructing a model in the uncertain universe of innovation means that there no development model is specifically dedicated to high-tech start-ups. This absence has inspired complementary empirical works which aim better to define the development modes and processes in such companies (e.g. Bernasconi and Moensted 2000; Garnsey 1998a). In this chapter we begin by proposing a new approach to understanding the modes of development of high-tech start-ups. We then present four modes of development which we have observed. We conclude by examining the internal and external variables likely to influence entrepreneurs' choice of development mode.

A NEW APPROACH TO UNDERSTANDING HIGH-TECH START-UP DEVELOPMENT

This research originated in three exploratory case studies of start-ups (Moreau and Bernasconi 2002), undertaken using a process-based approach (Albert *et al.* 1994; Fayolle 2000; Hernandez 2001). The development of the companies concerned is mainly defined in terms of technological development – from the invention or discovery of the technology to the final offer – business development – from the first client to diversification – and financial development – from the initial investment to the point of being self financing. The company is also considered as a dynamic combination of resources and competencies (Sanchez *et al.* 1996; Marchesnay 2002).

The company directors conceived and carried out the companies' development differently according to their technological, market and financial development, as well as their skills management. Two of the companies had followed a 'sequential' development process, in which progression was traditional, going 'from idea to market'. One company had adopted a 'simultaneous' process, the three processes mentioned above being enmeshed and interdependent, and progressed simultaneously. These case studies indicated that 'time' and 'integration' might differentiate the modes of start-up development. To examine whether companies might follow differing modes of development according to 'temporal' and 'integration' criteria, we will first define these terms more precisely.

The temporal criteria

The concept of 'temporal criteria' comes from the managerial literature concerning the conception and launching of new industrial products (Wheelwright and Clark 1994; Tarondeau 1998). It expresses the wish of entrepreneurs to conform to either a sequential or a simultaneous operational development of these processes and the activities they involve. These activities might include processes of technological development, technology acquisition, commercial development, segmentation, financial development, and fund seeking. While traditional models clearly come down on the side of sequential development, this does not happen with start-ups.

Many start-ups wait for the product to be fully finalized before embarking on the marketing and sales phases, while the different phases of technological development are staggered with financing and refinancing. However, other companies prefer to launch certain products – such as 'bread and butter' activities, or intermediary products – rapidly. Sometimes they will sell half finished or imperfect products in order to better develop their offer in the light of improved knowledge of client expectations, and in order to finance further technological development. Finally, the temporal criterion corresponds to how the sequence of the company's development process is organized over time: companies can be positioned at any point along a continuum from sequential to simultaneous development.

The integration criteria

The way we consider the sequencing of development processes involves how the three development processes – technological, market and financial – are co-ordinated. We distinguish between modes of company development according to how far these three processes are integrated. Our criterion is based on various definitions of integration (Miller and Friesen 1983; Divry 2000). In high-tech start-ups, integration is the capacity to take into account information and make decisions for a development process – for example, technological development – in the light of information and decisions to be taken concerning other development processes – for example, market development. Inter-process integration corresponds to the interdependence – in terms of convergence and coherence – of the rationale specific to each development process.

Integration occurs when, for example, the choice of using a particular technology takes into account the effect that choice has on the type of product, and vice-versa. An 'integrated' choice also takes account of other factors such as the type of customer, customer needs, the market, the business model, and the company's organization.

The weakest level of integration corresponds to independent processes which may be termed 'free' or 'autonomous'. One director of a European company, for example, when giving feedback as to the reasons for the failure of his project, mentioned the absence of any real interaction between the choices concerning marketing and sales and the process of technological development. The strongest level of integration corresponds to integrated processes, which may be termed 'interdependent'. This occurs when all aspects of each development process are fully taken into account in decision-making and subsequent actions. For example, technological development not only conditions, but is conditioned by market development, and this in turn, conditions and is conditioned by, for example, financial development.

The degree of integration between development processes depends on how far the directing team is willing and able to bring about the coherence and convergence of all the activities included in the different development processes. This requires an intense level of information exchange and a recognition that these efforts will pay off for the good of the company. To be effective, information exchange between those responsible for the different processes must be of sufficient frequency and of high quality. Success also supposes that the directors are capable of managing and acting on such complex information flows. (In this, the level of integration can be increased by setting up a market intelligence process through which those responsible for different development processes receive information relative to the market from real or potential clients, as described in Chapter 13.)

AN OPERATIONAL MODEL OF HIGH-TECH START UP DEVELOPMENT

Having defined the criteria of temporality and integration, and explained their relevance, we will now present the typology which resulted from a study of 20 start-ups (Moreau 2003). This study firstly brought to light a distinction between different types of development (see Figure 9.1): among the 20 companies studied, five had opted for a sequential-independent development (type 1), five for a sequential-integrated development (type 2), seven for a simultaneous-integrated development (type 3), and three for a simultaneous-independent development (type 4).

Each type of development was then defined using the traditional terms of strategic analysis – planned or incremental strategy, and technology-driven or market-driven rationale. Type 1 companies – termed simple – tended to have planned development and be technology-driven. Type 2 companies – termed traditional – tended to have planned development and be real or virtual market-driven. Type 3 companies – termed complex – tended to have incremental development and be real market-driven. Type 4 companies – termed chaotic – tended to have incremental development and be technology-driven.

Having identified them with their principal characteristics, we now propose an operational model of these four types of development.

The simple model – type 1

This operational model is completely coherent with existing models (Galbraith 1982; Gordon Bell and McNamara 1991; André 2000). Most of the operational models define several stages of development: conception, launching, development of technology, prototypes, product launch then market development. Underlying the rationale behind these models is the idea that the different stages call for an increase in financing and the necessity of funding, first from the founders, and then by third

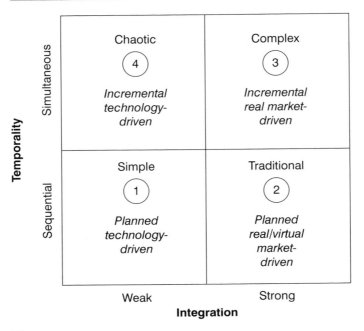

Figure 9.1 *A typology of start-up development modes*

parties – relatives, private organizations, banks, public funding, risk-capital, etc. The contribution of each of these parties depends on the stage of development.

The founders successively work on the concept, 'define' the business model, ensure technological development, and carry out prototyping. They segment and test the market, launch their offer, then market it and develop their market, all the while building up customer loyalty. The 'activities' follow each other, each stage only beginning when the preceding one has been accomplished. The principal characteristics of this development process lie in the need to finish each stage before beginning the next. For example, the company waits until the development phase is completed before testing and making a prototype. These actions require prior funding in the form of personal or private resources, bank loans, public subsidies or external capital – marginally, risk capital – while awaiting the moment when, if it is successful, the project will become self-financing.

In this situation, any failure in the phases of product launching or market development means going back to reconsider the earlier stage when technological choices were made. This implies a high risk of global failure, given that the very philosophy of these companies is based around technological choice. To put it bluntly, one could say that such companies 'sell whatever they develop'. See Figure 9.2.

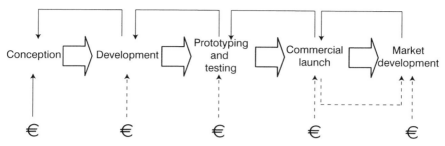

Figure 9.2 *Operational model of 'simple' company development*

The traditional model – type 2

The traditional model is similar to the simple model. In the traditional model, activities succeed one another in a logical chronological progression. However, the activities may overlap, and development is strongly planned and anticipated. This implies that market, technological and organizational choices are pre-conditioned by the business model and the pre-creation phase where strategy is defined – such as choice of activity, positioning. So despite apparent similarities, there is a real contrast with the simple model, because in the traditional model the company develops what it is going to – or at least what it should – sell.

Apart from these two points, the principal difference between the traditional and simple models has to do with financing. Besides personal and private capital, the financing of the traditional model rests notably on risk capital, which conforms to the companies' high level of ambition.

If the project's launch fails, it is also possible to return to the conception, research and development phases. However, this can only happen if the investors consider this to be financially justified, and if they are willing to reinvest the necessary sums. The formalization of the initial idea means that any change may be interpreted as a questioning of the original analysis, or even of the expertise of the creator-director. Those doubts might have repercussions on the relationship of trust linking the creator-director to his or her investors, employees or partners.

The traditional model was first developed in Silicon Valley, and is probably one of the most common start-up models. It is close to the simple model but the distinction between the two is an important one. Independent of the economic climate, many start-ups have failed because they fell somewhere between the two models. Take, for example, a non-finalized company project which is still in the 'construction' phase – and which is not yet fully emerged – seeking recourse to risk capital. This incongruity probably arises from a lack of experience on the part of many entrepreneurs which leads them to unrealistic appreciation of the realities of risk capital, and to unrealistic ambitions – possibly raised by the publicity given in

149

the early 2000s to individual examples of stunning success stories. See Figure 9.3. We will now look at a real case example.

Case example: Alpha

Alpha is a company that produces image creation and transformation software. It was created in 1998, following a transfer of technology from a research institute. The company grew rapidly, employing 80 people by the end of 2001. The project's aim was to provide a link between the different products in image processing, and to exchange data common in different uses. The technology developed appeared to have a competitive advantage because of the advances it offered, because of its many potential applications, because it could be used both by professionals and by the general public.

As is usual with the traditional mode of development, the market's acceptance of the innovation was more difficult than had been foreseen at the outset. Some of the products, and their sequence of deployment, had to be adjusted or even withdrawn, contrary to initial forecasts. A product for composing panoramic images, for example, did not meet the expectations of the professional market. They reacted by repositioning this product both for a very precise target – virtual visits for estate agents – and for the general public.

Above all, the company shifted from exclusively producing image processing software, to providing other editing activities, selling OEM licences, and e-business. Alpha thus adopted a market pull approach, by developing new products that responded to needs which had not been identified at the outset. One example was introducing a product that slowed down the speed of images. Adopting this mode of development shows the firm's fundamental wish to render interdependent, the

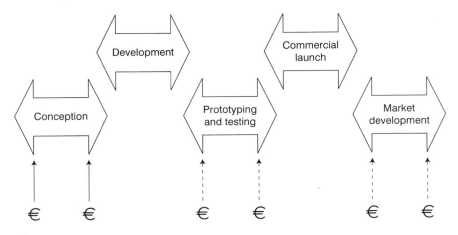

Figure 9.3 *Operational model of traditional development*

rationales concerning the marketing and sales, the technology, and the financial development. The integration of these rationales was effected retro-actively: the need for financing was defined by the development of technology, which is itself was defined according to the needs and expectations of the market, this in turn having been defined by the business model and by the expectations of financial partners.

This sequential management of development did not raise any major difficulties. The directing team managed to set up, in successive phases, an organization which was capable of reacting rapidly and modifying its initial choices. However, this sequential development, and above all the company's choice to exploit all of its potential, meant taking time to obtain new financial resources from external sources to enable expansion of its competencies.

The complex model – type 3

Companies opting for a complex model have a very different approach. These companies have opted to develop their technological, marketing and financial activities in parallel. In this model, the ideas of conception, development of technology, construction of prototypes, marketing the product, and financing are inter-related. Unlike the previous project types, the business model in this case involves obtaining financial flows rapidly, in order to enable the company to be self-financing after the initial funding. We could say that 'the company develops, or will develop what it sells'.

Even if these companies have ambition and vision anyway, it is the dynamic interaction between the various components of the project – the founder's ambition, the market needs, the technological choices – which enables the project itself to emerge and take shape. This does not preclude taking definite decisions relative to only one component, but the way in which such decisions are carried out remains undefined and subject to evolution. This leads to wide differences between the original – loosely formalized –concept of the project, and the project which eventually results. This difference, however, does not detract from the satisfaction of the founding team, nor diminish the project's performance.

The strong integration of the processes we have mentioned is sure to generate a certain level of complexity. It is clear that managing the process of company creation and development bears some resemblance to the notion of simultaneous engineering when launching a new product. We can imagine that creating and developing a start-up is even more complex because there may be a lack of predefined initial objectives – a common situation at the outset of an innovating project – as well as the need to recruit and weld together a team of people who do not know each other; we may also add the absence of financial support in the early stages. See Figure 9.4.

In the complex model, the company simultaneously defines both the form of the jigsaw pieces, and the picture which will result when the jigsaw is completed. This goes further than traditional incremental strategy, or 'making things up as one

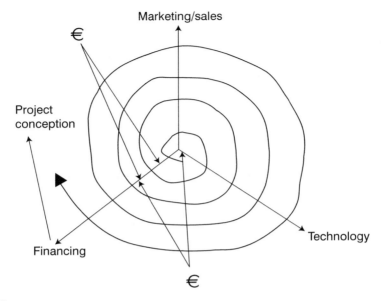

Figure 9.4 *Operational model of complex development*

goes along', because it involves not only defining strategy in terms of the company's outputs, but also defining both the company and its outputs in parallel. In order to do this, these companies rely on three practices: the development of a 'bread and butter' activity – which may or may not be linked to its strategy – the development of an intermediate activity, and/or a response to specific market demands which can finance and nourish the base of the company's overall competencies.

The complex model therefore comprises of carrying out the same activities described in the traditional model, but managing them simultaneously. The company manages at the same time, the development of technology, its resulting output and access to the market, as well as an organization corresponding to its business model. Paradoxically, despite being labelled 'complex', this model rests on a desire for balance. This balance is clearly visible both through the financing plan and the rhythm of growth.

Case example: Omega

Omega, created in 1996 by four former experts from a large electronics company, specialize in embedded systems on electronic chips. Omega set up a development platform for embedded systems which enabled considerable gains to be made both in time and conception costs. The company developed rapidly and employed 40 people by the end of 2001. Omega, unlike Alpha, did not opt for a traditional sequential mode of development. With real market needs as a starting point, the company chose to combine the activities of development, production, and marketing and sales, while relying solely on available financial resources.

Omega's initial growth was supported by a 'bread and butter' activity of training for CAO software whose licence had been obtained by the company, and which it used to develop its technological platform. The company also managed to avoid devoting time and resources to an over-abundance of projects, concentrating instead on the construction of the technological platform.

From an operational standpoint, the originality in the way the company was developed was characterized by the interdependence and parallel processes of financing, technological competence building, and marketing. This interdependence took the form of technical, financial or commercial partnerships being involved beyond their initial contribution. For example, customers contributed to the development of the platform and/or to funding; the financial partners also brought in managerial and other competences.

Even if the level of complexity that had to be managed might have done some harm and resulted in lengthening development times beyond those forecast, the directing team estimates that use of internal resources was improved, which avoided a resource deficit which would have much more damaging. The team was also able to manage the technology-market-organization interfaces very well, which ensured the continuation of the company's development by keeping it in touch with the market.

The chaotic model – type 4

The chaotic company also carries out the various development activities, but unlike the complex model, there is no real integration between the rationales behind each activity. The absence of co-ordination reasons, whether for human, technical, organizational, managerial, or political, makes each development process independent. It is evidently impossible, without a lot of 'luck', for these projects to achieve a high level of performance, at least not for any length of time. We may even wonder if these are truly 'projects'. They have no vision or intention, no finalized project to speak of, no definite goal, no clearly thought out organization, and no control – even at an emerging level – over the development process. In such a situation, it is difficult to consider that we are truly dealing with a company and an entrepreneurial project. To return to our earlier phraseology, this company 'develops without knowing what the clients want, or what it will sell'.

In terms of financing, the chaotic project model is based on its capacity for self-financing, but as we have seen, it also manifests the wish to seek external funding. This is hard to justify and seems to have more to do with the wish to make up for the project's lack of true economic basis than with a predefined choice relevant to its development needs. See Figure 9.5.

This mode of development may well exist because of a lack of real integration between the different development procedures. If this is the case, the 'chaotic'

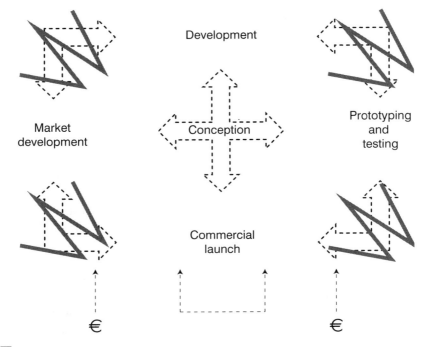

Figure 9.5 *Operational model of chaotic development*

company is the unsought-for consequence of a lack of knowledge, an inability to co-ordinate, communicate, or take joint decisions. However, to follow this mode of development deliberately, with no effort at co-ordination, would mean relying on luck alone to achieve coherence between the project's various components. Even if entrepreneurship can be considered as a process of creating new activities involving constant re-adaptation and gradually shaping an emerging project, the absence of integration in the chaotic model has more to do with 'bad management' than deliberate and hardly justifiable decisions. In other words, the chaotic model looks like a complex model which has been 'mismanaged', or which has 'gone wrong'. It could also be likened to a simple model which has been made more complex because of a wish to manage everything at once without establishing priorities or even really defining what the company project is.

DEVELOPMENT MODES, TYPES OF PROJECT AND UNCERTAINTY

As well as looking at the types of development modes pertaining to high-tech start-ups, it is worth examining the variables liable to affect the model chosen. In order to do this, we have tried to demonstrate possible relationships between the four modes of development and three other variables, namely the entrepreneur – the creator's origin – the project itself – its time scale, ambition and the precision of definition at the outset – and the competitive environment – the intensity of competition, intensity of the innovation, extent of opportunity, estimated duration of technological advance. We cannot, with the cases used here, prove the scientific validity of these relationships, but we can put forward some suggestions.

For variables linked to the entrepreneur, due to the small sample, we were unable to identify entrepreneurs' origins with respect to qualifications or experience. We were equally unable to identify the context of their creation – spin-offs – which would appear to be linked to each of the modes of development adopted. In full accordance with the literature on the subject, however, we see the entrepreneur playing a key role in the choice and implementation of the project's development, or, to quote Bernasconi: 'each configuration of entrepreneurs is a special case which … influences the form and dynamic of the project' (Bernasconi and Moensted 2000: 62).

The development mode and the initial vision

The initial vision of the creation project can be defined by the objectives and terms defined by the entrepreneur. It is useful to ask whether this initial vision might have an influence on the development mode that is finally adopted.

The creator-directors of 'simple' type companies recognize that they had defined their objectives and their projects' 'raison d'être' precisely. They also defined their technological, commercial and financial objectives very precisely right from the outset. The same entrepreneurs show far less anticipation regarding development procedures.

In 'chaotic' model companies, the commercial and financial objectives seem relatively undefined. On the other hand, there is a clear definition of the technological objectives, indicating that science or technology lies at the root of the project. There appears to be weak anticipation concerning development procedures.

In complex model companies, the initial objectives tend to be less precise than for the other types of company. This is true whether we take the development process as a whole or consider just one aspect, for example, technological development. We do notice, however, a strong anticipation as to how the company is to be developed, expressed as incremental process of the development.

The creator-directors of the traditional company define both the commercial and financial objectives with great precision, as well as anticipating the procedures precisely. The technological objectives, however, are less specific. It can be supposed that these companies anticipate more and proceed 'retroactively'. They start with very precise market and financial objectives, and then plan their development and their technological choices in accordance with these.

To summarize, we notice that this mode of development – sequential and integrated – initially devotes a lot of thought to the 'why' and 'how' of the company which probably indicates considerable anticipation whose aim is to forecast and integrate the different components of development.

The development mode and the business environment

Elements of the competitive environment may influence the choice of one mode of development over another. We can observe a number of relevant phenomena when we refer to the ways in which this competitive environment is perceived by creator-directors.

It appears that entrepreneurs who adopt the 'simple' development model estimate their environment to be less competitive and less innovating than that perceived by creators of the other types of company. They perceive the time frame for the opportunity to be more restricted than those who choose the chaotic or complex models. These companies do seem however – at least in the eyes of their directors – to possess a real technological advance over their competitors. Chaotic type companies appear to evolve within environments judged to be highly competitive and innovating. According to their directors, this environment undergoes radical innovations and the rhythm of innovation is rather slow. The time frame for the opportunities seem less restricted than those open to the 'simple ' and 'traditional' types of development, and the creators of such companies feel they have a technological advance of at least two years.

Directors of the 'complex' type of company appear to judge their environment as highly competitive and innovating with a rapid and seemingly incremental rhythm of innovation. The creator-directors of these companies estimate that they have fairly wide windows of opportunity, although paradoxically, they feel their technological advance to be relatively short – less than six months.

Finally, directors of the traditional type of company declare their environments to be only slightly competitive and 'highly' innovative. Their windows of opportunity appear narrower than those pertaining to chaotic or complex modes of development, and again according to the directors, their technological advance is negligible – less than one year.

From this analysis, one can examine the relationship between modes of development and uncertainty. If we consider uncertainty to be stronger when innovation is strong and the competitive environment highly competitive, we can hypothesize that the 'chaotic' and 'complex' modes of development will be the best adapted to face uncertainty. On the contrary, 'simple' and 'traditional' modes of development seem more adapted to less uncertain situations.

CONCLUSION

In this chapter we have tried to show that different modes of development exist in high-tech start-ups. To demonstrate these differences, we have used criteria of temporality and integration. We have described four distinct modes of operational development: simple, traditional, complex and chaotic.

We are fully aware that here we are interpreting 'perceived realities'. The aim of this interpretation has been to carry out an exploratory study and verify the intuition that different modes of development do exist. Under these conditions, 'precision' is not and cannot be guaranteed. It will be necessary to evaluate temporality and integration more fully, and set up measurements which are less subjective than those provided by the directors own perceptions of these variables.

This being said, we are relatively confident about the global 'coherence' of our description of these modes of development. However, we wish neither to limit nor to simplify reality. In practice, the creation and development of a start-up is obviously a difficult task, and as such, cannot be reduced to only one effort to construct a model. For example, it is perfectly possible that a company such as those we have described, may evolve from one model of development to another as it grows. Nevertheless, our proposition should enable entrepreneurs to envisage other development models than those which have traditionally been suggested, and provide them with new frames of reference and reflection.

Chapter 10

University spin-out firms

Patterns of development
based on expertise

Céline Druilhe and Elizabeth Garnsey

Academics who wish to commercialize university research are often presented with two choices: either license their technology to an existing company or start their own. Yet this dichotomy conceals the great diversity found among companies spinning out from universities, despite their common origin. Differences include their knowledge base, the activities they undertake, the development of their business models and the nature of their development experience. In the literature on spin-outs, typologies nevertheless often focus on generalized sequences of development and are underpinned by a linear conception of the creation and development of new companies. In contrast, the process of innovation is now widely accepted to be an iterative, non-linear process in which feedback loops modify developments. The same applies to entrepreneurial new firm creation. This chapter analyses university spin-outs as diverse undertakings involving a non-linear development process.

The definition of spin-out has changed over time. The term was used until recently to refer to a company founded by members of a university department or originating in another company. In response to universities' increasing interest in the commercialization of research and changes in the availability of start-up capital, the term is increasingly used to refer to a start-up with a technology in which a university department has claim to the intellectual property, so making venture capital a possible source of funding. Shane (2004) has examined spin-outs in which MIT had intellectual property rights in order to ascertain the type of technologies exploited by academic spin-outs. These were found to be technologies that established firms were unlikely to license for a variety of reasons.

Accordingly, the assumption is made that a technology-based idea is generated from research, protected by patents, and transferred to a firm newly established to commercialize the idea. Venture capital has not been a significant source of finance for academic spin-outs because it does not provide seed capital of the kind early stage ventures need. Some research and development companies are unusual in that they have been able to obtain venture capital on the prospects offered by outstanding new technologies with a large eventual market, e.g. in biotechnology.

Our definition of spin-outs is closer to the original sense of the term: in this chapter they are firms whose products or services stem from knowledge generated in a university setting by a member of the university who founds or co-founds the firm. The founders may or may not leave university employment, but have gained relevant knowledge at the university and made use of its resources in founding the company; there may or may not be university intellectual property and investment in the venture. Wider definitions also include indirect spin-outs – started by former members of the university – but here we are concerned with direct spin-outs, i.e. those whose founders were members of the university at the time when they started their firms.

In this chapter we show that academic spin-outs, in this wider sense, are diverse and do not follow a linear development process. We develop a typology of business activities in university-based spin-outs which is grounded in a dynamic view of the entrepreneurial process and in the concept of the business model. We argue that the selection of a business model is not a discrete stage; instead a business model evolves in the course of entrepreneurial firm formation. Business models develop and change as companies evolve, as the entrepreneurs refine or shift opportunities and as the marketplace becomes better known to them.

This chapter draws on evidence from spin-outs stemming from Cambridge University in the UK, presented here to illustrate the range of entrepreneurial activities originating from the science base in a single organizational setting. Cambridge University is an interesting case for the scope and history of local entrepreneurial activities. In the last 20–30 years although high-tech activity was not confined to spin-outs from the university, these have had significant influence. In 1985 it was found that 25 per cent of the high-tech firms in the Cambridge area had a founder originating from Cambridge University or a research establishment coming from the Cambridge area (Segal Quince & Partners 1985). This percentage fell to 17 per cent among companies founded since 1990, as the high-tech complex grew (Segal Quince Wicksteed 2000): an increasing number of ventures spun out of existing companies while others were attracted to the region. As a whole, between 1979 and 2002, over 100 spin-outs – following our definition – were formed in Cambridge, of which nearly two-thirds were started between 1997 and 2002 (Druilhe and Garnsey 2004). During that period, only 19 of these companies were started on the basis of university-owned intellectual property.

After a brief review of the typologies existing in the literature on spin-out companies, a conceptualization of the entrepreneurial process is proposed and serves as a basis for establishing a typology of business activities and for explaining processes of activity selection. We conclude with lessons and implications for entrepreneurs, policy-makers and technology transfer advisers.

SPIN-OUT DIVERSITY IN THE LITERATURE

Despite the significant growth of the literature on academic spin-outs in recent years, largely reflecting increased public and academic interest, the diversity of spin-outs has for a long time remained a neglected issue. It is only currently emerging as a subject of research (Wright *et al*. 2004). Table 10.1 outlines some of the typologies that have been proposed.

While these typologies are useful, dynamic processes may be overlooked when classifications focus on static categories. Bullock (1983) was one of the few to identify a dynamic process, whereby 'soft companies' develop and grow into 'hard companies'. While this transition was effected by a number of early MIT spin-outs, it has been found only in a minority of recent cases in the UK. We suggest that business activity, initial conditions and the detection of distinctive opportunities have an influence on the entrepreneurial process, but these influences are not static and will evolve with, and be specific to, a particular venture.

Our typology of spin-outs draws on the resource-based view of the firm and, more specifically, Penrose's original model, which implied a feedback element allowing for the way in which entrepreneurs adapt and modify their business ideas as they gain experience (Penrose 1995). The framework draws on our earlier work which applied Penrosean thinking to the early growth of companies and the emergence of academic spin-outs (Druilhe 2003; Garnsey 1998a). The relevance of resource-based approaches (Barney 1991; Grant 1991; Montgomery 1995; Penrose 1995) to new firm formation has been recognized by Autio (1997) Brush *et al*. (2001) and Heirman *et al*. (2003). Here we draw attention to neglected concepts in Penrose's work.

CONCEPTUALIZATION OF THE ENTREPRENEURIAL PROCESS

Before turning to an examination of business models for academic spin-outs, we present here an account of the entrepreneurial process which we view as comprising the pursuit of an opportunity and the mobilization of resources to deliver value and capture returns. When embodied in new firm formation, this involves the creation of a resource base for business activity. In contrast with recent definitions of enterprise as involving the recognition and exploitation of new opportunities (e.g. Shane 2000; Venkataraman 1997), we see the essence of entrepreneurial activity in the way entrepreneurs match up opportunities and resources. The entrepreneur who aims to start a new business has to develop a business idea of the means to create value and capture returns and, through the entrepreneurial process, translate this into a business model that can be implemented. Unlike other authors (Reynolds and White 1997) who divide the entrepreneurial process into a pre- and a post-venture formation phase, we see the initial period, when the company is not yet

Table 10.1 *Categorization of spin-outs in the literature*

References	Types	Main factor affecting the definition of types
Bullock (1983)	Soft company: company that starts as technical consultancy solving specific problems and requiring low initial funding and management skills. Hard company: company that sells standardized and relatively simplified products to a general market.	Pattern of development
Stankiewicz (1994)	Consultancy and research and development (R&D) contracting mode: this mode includes consultancies which sell product-solving capability, service companies which perform specific technical functions based on its special skills and/or access to unique equipment, customizing vendors who develop new client specific applications of existing equipment and/or software, and R&D contractors. Product-orientated mode: company organized around a well-developed product concept and focus on the advanced development, production and marketing of a product. Technological-asset orientated mode: company concerned with the development of technologies which are subsequently commercialized through spinning out new firms, licensing, joint ventures or other types of alliance.	Companies are distinguished according to their mode of operation, each requiring a different set of technical skills, a different approach to management and financing, different linkages to the academic knowledge base and a different form of infrastructural support.
Mustar (1997)	Companies that have no or few links with R&D, no links with the public sector and no partnerships with other companies. Companies that keep very close links with the research sector, other firms and public authorities and which have succeeded in attracting investment from industry or venture capital at an early stage. Companies that feature midway between these two extremes. Companies that are solely, but strongly, linked to the scientific sector.	Links that spin-out companies maintain with the science base
Autio (1997)	Science-based firms: companies that are relatively more active in transforming scientific knowledge into basic technologies. Engineering-based firms: companies that are relatively more active in transforming basic technologies into application-specific technologies.	Link between the niche markets of new technology-based firms and the transformation of knowledge they undertake

continued ...

Table 10.1 continued...

References	Types	Main factor affecting the definition of types
Nicolaou and Birley (2003)	Orthodox spin-outs: companies that involve both the academic inventor and the technology spinning out from the institution. Hybrid spin-outs: companies that involve the technology spinning out and the academic(s) retaining his or her university position, but holding a directorship, membership of the scientific advisory board or other part-time position within the company. Technology spin-outs: companies that involve the technology spinning out but the academic maintaining no connection with the newly established firm (although the academic may hold an equity stake in the new company or provide advice on a consultancy basis).	Links and involvement that the academic maintains with the newly established firm
Heirman and Clarysse (2004)	Venture capital (VC)-backed start-ups: companies started with external capital usually with a proprietary and innovative technology that can be used for several applications but are far from a market ready product at start. Prospectors: these companies are in an early stage of product development at founding but on average their technology base is more mature than that of VC backed start-ups. Product start-ups: these companies usually have a product that is close to market in a first version. They are less involved with innovative and platform technologies than the VC-backed start-ups but more so than the prospectors. Transitional start-ups: these firms started as technical consultancies without a concrete product idea and later on evolved to a product-oriented company.	Variations in starting resource configuration

formed, as an integral part of entrepreneurial activity, and as a critical period in which entrepreneurs recognize an initial opportunity, initiate the mobilization of resources for their intended business activity.

Thus the following activities are essential to the entrepreneurial process: opportunity recognition, mobilization of new combinations of resources, and organization of the venture's resource base.

Opportunity recognition

The first difficulty facing academic entrepreneurs is to identify and select a viable productive opportunity. Opportunities are objectively identifiable but their recognition is subjective and often depends on access to special knowledge. Penrose refers to productive opportunities as 'the productive possibilities that the firms' "entrepreneurs" see and can take advantage of' (Penrose 1995: 31). Research carried out in the university may result in potential for technologies that are highly generic and require further work to develop applications, with consequent uncertainty. The original patents are often insufficient; further developments, improvements and intellectual property protection are required if these technologies are to be exploited commercially. The 'pre-competitive' status of this knowledge makes the task of identifying a market opportunity difficult (Garnsey and Moore 1993). For scientists engaged in this type of research, the most suitable opportunity may be to provide 'knowledge services' on a consultancy basis to make use of the scarce knowledge they have that is valuable to customers. Prior knowledge can be expected to aid opportunity detection (Druilhe 2003; Nicolaou and Birley 2003; Shane 2000), as will connections and social capital (Aldrich 1999; Druilhe 2003; Nicolaou and Birley 2003). Individual motivations provide incentives to pursue the opportunity. These incentives may be prospects of gain but other factors – such as personal values and commitment to a project, concern to see their project in use, prestige – are also important in the creation of spin-outs (Druilhe 2003; Weatherston 1993).

Mobilization of new combinations of resources

As compared with other business entrepreneurs, scientists can combine new resources through scarce expertise that may give rise to new productive activity based on leading edge technology. But most scientists lack the business background and the investment capital required to cover the expenses incurred in the lengthy development work needed to bring a technology closer to market. Academic research grants do not cover these costs, but academics can often make use of university facilities to reduce the expenditure required on infrastructure while an innovative productive base is being created (Druilhe and Garnsey 2001). Scientist-entrepreneurs tend to minimize early resource outlays to keep open the pursuit of shifting opportunities. They find ways to exert leverage from the resources at their disposal. Resources available in the university and market environments are critical in this respect. The availability of investment finance affects the way new enterprises reach the market with their innovations.

Organization of the venture's resource base

To realize the perceived opportunity it is necessary to organize business activity, the conversion of inputs into revenue-generating outputs. This is supported by the firm's resource base that makes it possible to process resource inputs, produce a given type of output and secure returns from customers. Some resources, financial, physical and human, are mobilized from outside, others are created within the firm, where they are combined to make productive activity possible.

A productive base may be very simple, as in the case of a company providing research services, or very complex, as in the case of a plant or other installation. The term 'productive base' can also be applied to service activities. For example research services require the productive capacity to generate, process, store and retrieve information and convert it into meaningful knowledge communicated to clients. As it grows, the firm's resources may come to support a variety of productive bases, but Penrose pointed out that: '... movement into a new base requires a firm to achieve competence in some significantly different area of technology' (Penrose 1995: 110).

Development is an iterative, non-linear process in which the entrepreneurial venture tends to adapt to unfolding opportunities. Certain developmental processes are common in new firms: these involve the way they mobilize and build resources to form a resource base capable of generating market returns. Companies that face and solve similar developmental problems in sequence will go through similar phases of activity (Garnsey 1998). Intensive sequential activities are to be seen when employees are recruited to man new facilities for example, as found by researchers who have examined computer hardware or other companies producing similar products on the basis of similar business models (e.g. Bell and McNamara 1991) But there are no invariant phases of activity in new firm development because different problems arise in different kinds ventures and are addressed in different ways. The building of different kinds of resource base involves different sequences of activity. Problems may be addressed in parallel, or may recur. Moreover ventures may or may not inherit a resource base from another organization through spin-out. In order to illustrate this variety of experiences, we now turn to different types of business activity.

TYPES OF BUSINESS ACTIVITY AND ENTREPRENEURIAL PROGRESS

If business activity refers to what the company does, the concept of business model refers to how the company's activities are organized to secure returns: how activity is resourced, the way this creates value and how returns are realized. Penrose's concepts of productive base and productive opportunity, which bridge firm and market, provide theoretical grounding for this notion of 'business model'. The concept gained ground with the rise of Internet ventures, when alliances and partnerships were critical to the elaboration of a business model. Hence Zott and Amit's definition (2003): 'a business model elucidates how an enterprise works with those external stakeholders with whom it engages in economic exchanges in order to create value for all involved parties' (Zott and Amit 2003: 5–6). Partnerships are important for new, resource-constrained ventures, whether or not internet based. Business activity can be organized on the basis of a variety of business models. For example product companies can be differentiated by whether they engage in in-house manufacture or outsource production. These are among the features of the business model that affect how the firm creates value and secures returns. Another aspect of a business model is how the company sells the product, whether through direct sale, franchising or partnerships with resellers. Here we restrict our analysis to the types of activity that underlie the new ventures' business models.

A two-dimensional typology

A two-dimensional typology of business activities in spin-outs relates the productive opportunity pursued and the kind of productive base aimed at to realize returns. The nature and intensity of resources academic entrepreneurs require for realizing a business opportunity are likely to vary considerably according to the type of activity undertaken and the amount of resources already possessed, including prior knowledge, contacts and experience. On the whole, the closer the scientist's knowledge and experience to the business activity, and the fewer the resources required, the better placed is the entrepreneur to solve the problems that will arise. We can distinguish between several categories of university spin-outs, along a spectrum shown in Figure 10.1, in which business activities are classed according to the relevance of the academic entrepreneur's prior experience and the resource requirements for the new company.

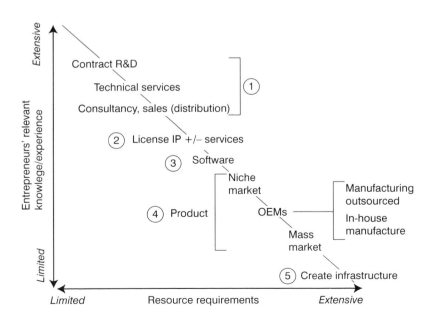

Figure 10.1 Typology of academic spin-outs activities

Each type of business activity requires different sets of resources, whether these are skills, financing, technology or infrastructural support. We also suggest that the relevance of the business and academic experience of the academic entrepreneur will vary with each type of business activity.

Contract research and development (R&D), technical services, consultancy

The most accessible entrepreneurial activity appears to be the provision of research-based consultancy or research services to customers. These activities are closest to the scientist-entrepreneur's academic work and are unlikely to be based on patents or to demand significant technology development. They draw directly on the scientists' expertise. Resource requirements are likely to be limited and the company is better able to develop on a self-financed basis. This is the 'soft start up' par excellence whereby the founder acquires business and market experience through consultancy, generates cash-flow and builds credibility, before in some cases moving on to production.

License intellectual property with or without service provision

Another accessible opportunity for academic founders involves the development of technological resources and their protection with intellectual property rights (IPR) that can be licensed or sold to customers. In this case the productive activity is to develop a technology from 'pre-competitive' on to 'near-market' status and find ways to appropriate returns from the scientists' research findings through licensing or sale. The term 'development company' can be used to refer to a company of this kind that pulls together initial intellectual property rights, on which future IPR are built through research and development (see Company A for an example). As intellectual resources, these are not embodied in a physical production base for making products. Licensing and a variety of research contracts with pharmaceutical corporations is the route chosen by drug discovery ventures which do not aim at integrated drug production because of the extent of production costs.

Case example: A form of licensing by Company A

The scientist and her team conducted research on rapid diagnostic kits for the developing world with a view to commercializing those tests at fair prices to developing countries. The opportunity of fulfilling the needs of these developing countries was perceived early on and became the focus of the group's research. The research conducted in the laboratory led to the development of a platform technology that could be applied to different types of diseases. The decision was taken to start a development company to which the university IP would be licensed and which would work on the development of most-needed diagnostic kits for several diseases prevalent in the developing world. Value would then be added to the IP which could be licensed for production to partners with the appropriate facilities.

Software start-ups

These have certain features in common with IP-based start-ups since their product involves licensing software, but there is also a production process for software production, albeit one with lower scaling-up costs than for the production of physical products.

Product companies

These vary widely, from small instrumentation companies that target niche markets to companies involved in mass production. The creation of a physical production base requires investment capital and is likely to be remote from the scientists' experience. Companies B and C offer two examples of Cambridge spin-outs involved in scientific instrumentation.

Case example: Product-based Company B

The recognition of an opportunity built directly on the scientist's prior knowledge and connections: a focused market was recognized on the basis of scientific instrumentation developed for scientific experiments in the academic laboratory. Commercial and scientific activities were complementary. Development of the technology for own use and the connections formed during research with suppliers and users of the technology resulted in the early identification of a market opportunity. Products could be sold in technical markets alongside a service relying on the expert knowledge of the scientist. He could leverage his links to the academic, governmental, and corporate scientific communities to access customers. Resources required to reach a niche market were accessible. The scientist started a product-oriented company, following an organic development path, relying mostly on self-financing after initial seed funding was provided by friends and family support or public innovation grants. The entrepreneur explained:

> I decided to build up as much capital internally as possible. I followed a much more old-fashioned business model than had been popular during the dot com boom. In my case where I had a scientific start-up, where it was really a spin-out of my lab, protecting that IPR ownership was actually more important to me than spinning out something quickly to do an IPO and get out.

Case example: Product-based Company C

Robotics equipment for the biotechnology research market was developed within a university department. A productive opportunity was recognized by the entrepreneurs through their contacts with geneticists. This enabled them to identify a market for low cost, compact automation equipment for biotechnology labs. Although there were many difficulties in developing the product to a high standard of quality and reliability – as shown by the failure of a different, rival project using the same initial IP to achieve this – the precision engineering and software technology of the newly created productive base was state of the art rather than immature. Early development costs were covered by another university department. The funds available in this customer department resulted from earlier academic enterprise by the customer scientist, who had acted as distributor of equipment for genetic research. His simple retailing 'productive base' had generated revenues which subsidized the development of the more extensive productive base required for scientific instrument production. The entrepreneurs who founded the laboratory equipment company avoided external funding because they wanted to retain control over their company. These entrepreneurs were new to the product and market, but were experienced engineers with business knowledge. Their new product stream and impressive trading performance attracted a US company that acquired the venture in 2000, realizing very high returns to the entrepreneurs.

Creation of infrastructure

The most demanding route would appear to be the creation of a physical infrastructure for the output of a product based on research. This is the case for telecommunication companies needing a new infrastructure, and those environmental companies that require an infrastructure to support their green technologies. However partnerships can make it possible to realize this objective, and the prospect of market diffusion can be used to attract funding.

The two-dimensional representation of business activities does not encompass all the factors that influence the selection of the business model of a new company. Our objective is rather to show that the entrepreneurial process varies depending upon the type of business activity undertaken, for university spin-outs as for other ventures. We suggest that the route to market is likely to be faster in the case of a contract service company than in the case of a production company: resource requirements that have to be met through the entrepreneurial process for the 'softer' type of company are more limited while the entrepreneur is more likely to be able to leverage existing resources and knowledge.

Early progress

Academics who provide research-oriented services benefit from a ready-made productive base from which to operate. They can secure returns more easily than those with generic and far from market technologies. But at the other extreme the robotics equipment case (Company C) shows that academic entrepreneurs who are sufficiently motivated, skilled and market focused can create a productive base in-house that delivers products of high value to customers and secures them very high level of returns. This venture started with a mature business model for growth through retained earnings and was able to avoid time-consuming experiments with alternative funding and activities. The difficulty of selecting a viable opportunity on the basis of limited prior knowledge relating to commercial issues, and of obtaining the resources to set up the necessary productive base, are negative factors in the rate and extent of advance made by projects on the route to market. However, other factors can override these difficulties, in particular the motivation, experience, knowledge and networking activities of the entrepreneurs. These were factors all affecting the robustness of the venture's resource base.

A number of factors, including maturity of the entrepreneurs' initial resources and the business model selected, influence the kinds of phases the venture experiences. In the case of academic spin-outs, the engineering or economic consultancy that engages immediately in earning sustainable revenues from expertise does not experience the same sequence of phases as a venture with mature designs to license out, or one which needs finance to convert scientific knowledge into a marketable output.

Depending on the activity selected, entrepreneurs face a variety of challenges in building a resource base for their venture that is capable of generating sustainable returns. These vary with initial resource endowments, the intensity and availability of the resources required and the market readiness of their technology. The matching process requires continual attention to external factors, notably the specifics of the targeted market, its size, the competitive intensity of the sector and the maturity of rivals' technology. Entrepreneurs who engage in the process of building marketable competencies are able to strengthen the resource base of their venture in relation to realistic market prospects. This improves their chances of enlisting the resources of other organizations through partnering, to remedy some of the limitations of their own resource base.

Evolving business activities: the interplay between internal resource configurations and the external environment

The business models of new ventures are modified as entrepreneurs improve their knowledge of resources and opportunities. Through engagement with others and involvement in entrepreneurial activities, academic entrepreneurs develop relevant knowledge and experience. This allows them to improve their perception of opportunities, while gaining a better understanding of the resource configurations required to pursue the refined or newly perceived opportunities. In the case of development companies, these may initially be set up to commercialize a technology for licensing but may later aim at downstream services and production. A reverse transition may occur as the objectives of the business model change from production to licensing. In the previous section we classed case studies by type of activity, but it is common to find some shift in categories activity as the new business develops (see examples of Companies D and E).

Case example: Evolving business activity in Company D

Company D aimed to develop an anaesthetic technique for laser surgery; a costly resource requirement delayed the creation of value, and hence returns. The scientists had direct industrial experience and industrial contacts, which triggered the recognition of a specific commercial opportunity. But it was clear that the resources required to develop the technology to the point where it could provide a productive base would be considerable. Raising commercial funds was necessary where research grants were unavailable for this purpose.

The technology required heavy patent protection and regulatory approval was needed for medical devices. The scientists subsequently undertook further R&D within the university to develop the technology. Self-funding ensured early development but did not suffice to carry the technology through clinical trials. The team engaged in a lengthy process exploring various routes to market, including licensing, outsourcing development, and starting a VC-backed company.

Resource mobilization was all the more difficult when selection of the route to market was not straightforward. The team eventually opted to set up a development company, incubated within the university by the research groups and associates with relevant technical skills. A development company is created specifically to advance a technology that has commercial potential, and must attract investors or partners by offering them a stake in eventual returns. A seed investment by a university-affiliated fund eventually provided finance needed for R&D and patenting costs. Prior industrial knowledge, useful connections and the market focus of the technology aided initial progress for this type of enterprise. The lengthy development period, the difficulty of creating a productive base and the extent of financial resources required slowed down development. Although the scientists initially aimed at licensing their early-stage technology, they eventually set up a development company to move the technology closer to market while redefining their business model and examining various options including production.

Case example: Evolving business activity in Company E

A productive opportunity was identified on the basis of applied research done in the lab and involved developing a motion capture system and software for the sport and medical markets. Yet the potential for value-creation and returns was soon found to be too low in relation to costs, once further development of the technology had been undertaken. The mobilization of resources was problematic because the technology was in the public domain. Without intellectual property rights the business model had limited capacity to deliver returns to investors:

> We have talked to many, many people and there are lots of things which are – almost – working but not quite. Actually we feel quite depressed about it all. Getting finance is clearly much, much harder than actually getting on and building our product.

Private investors were not prepared to invest enough for the entrepreneurs to scale-up development and commercialization. The opportunity was then refined and it appeared that a niche market existed in the development of the motion capture system for very specific applications, alongside the provision of a service by the company. This business model would have involved custom manufacturing and setting up a product and service company which would assist customers in using the systems. This business model did not satisfy the lead scientist who was not keen to engage in manufacturing and in setting up a service company. Although the scientists decided not to proceed with commercialization, further research was carried out on the technology for which applications were found in various settings. Economic value was therefore created in technology developed for experimental medical and sports applications, but no financial return was generated for the originators. The emphasis shifted from being a purely product-oriented company to supplying a product with a supporting service. Further exploration of the market showed that targeting niche markets for specific applications and providing a customized offer were required to capture returns. But this model did not meet the scientists' preferences and commercialization was abandoned.

LESSONS DRAWN FROM THE CASES AND THE CONCEPTUAL FRAMEWORK

The typology developed points to the diversity of spin-out companies and the need for a focused, case-by-case approach not only from academic entrepreneurs but also from technology transfer advisers.

Practical implications for entrepreneurs

That the innovation process is non-linear has now been widely accepted. Yet the entrepreneurial process is still commonly presented as a linear process undergoing a sequence of phases (Vohora *et al.* 2004). There is a lack of clarity as to the nature of phases: Do they refer to tasks and activities, a sequence of events or the solution of start-up problems? While there are start-up and early growth problems that need to be solved sequentially – resources cannot be mobilized until they are accessible, revenues cannot be generated unless productive resources have been mobilized – these problems are of a generic nature and they recur in new forms as the business develops. Sustaining revenues, for example, is not a juncture that can be overcome, it is an ongoing challenge to young firms. Iterations and feedback effects prevent linear growth but also accompany problem solving that allows new ventures to overcome resource constraints and respond to opportunities ahead of slower competitors. The entrepreneurial process, like the process of innovation more generally, is not linear because responses and feedback effects enable adaptive learning and change.

A resource-constrained academic venture usually needs to set up appropriate partnerships and collaborations to make up for its resource limitations. But the balance of power in these relationships will depend on the leverage the venture can gain from its own resources. The kinds of network and social capital from which the entrepreneur can gain leverage depends on the type of business activity pursued. It is often easier for a R&D company to set up the links it needs – some of which will already be in place – than for an academic spin-out company ultimately targeting mass markets, which requires the building of complex partnerships.

Entrepreneurs who are flexible and adapt to new opportunities should view a change of business model and market focus as part of their learning experience rather than as an admission of inadequacy.

Practical implications for policy makers and technology transfer advisers

Standard metrics used to assess commercialization activities are not sufficiently informative. The number of spin-outs and their employee size does not reveal resource costs in relation to actual and potential returns of academic ventures. Analysis should show how resources were obtained in specific instances and relate commercialization progress to whether initial resources were pre-competitive or near market. What unintended or alternative forms of value were created may be relevant to gauging positive externalities and social returns from spin-out activity.

Technology transfer executives and policy makers need to pay more attention to the diversity of spin-outs. When they are considered as a generic category there is a failure to distinguish new ventures by resource intensity of requirements, by maturity of resources and market potential. Only a small minority of spin-outs will be high-growth and high return for the originating institutions. On the other hand, scientific and economic consultancies earning fees can make a contribution to the economy without recourse to intellectual property.

Inflated expectations were created for the returns academic spin-outs can achieve for originating institutions during the technology boom. A more realistic assessment should not deter universities from supporting the creation of spin-outs, with their proven potential for long term economic returns and contribution to the local economy.

Recognizing the heterogeneity of spin-outs also endorses the provision of support that recognizes the different needs and resource requirements of different types of spin-out, instead of a standardized approach. The benefits of partnering need to be conveyed, but also the advantages of creating value from which leverage can be achieved in building partnerships. Ventures need sector specialists and experts experienced in different kinds of business models. A proactive and focused approach adapts the level and nature of support to the venture's situation.

Chapter 11

Creation processes as evolving projects

High-tech firms as emerging systems

Michel Bernasconi

It is valuable for both researchers and practitioners to understand the processes underlying the creation of high-tech companies. Researchers are interested in the complexity of these processes, their continuous evolution, and linking these to changing technology and the evolving the business model. Investors and those involved with start-ups, are interested in devising general rules to guide their practice. Both groups share an interest in going beyond individual cases to try, in their own way, to extrapolate general approaches or to identify factors which are more or less conducive to success.

Most entrepreneurs, by contrast, approach the creation of a company as an exceptional experience. They lack the necessary knowledge or experience to face the situations which they are likely to meet. Investors and accompanying professionals know, from experience, that the creation project is bound to undergo profound changes, and that the initial business plan has practically no chance of being realized in its original form. As early as 1984, Massacrier and Rigaud highlighted the gap between provisional forecasts and the final outcomes; they thus called for approaches which would enable entrepreneurs to simulate their projects in advance. So it is tempting to try to construct a model of the creation process aimed at enabling entrepreneurs to learn from previous experiences in order to better anticipate their project. Models can, despite being oversimplifications, provide an opportunity to grasp the complexity of the undertaking and to anticipate certain lines of action.

Following Bygrave and Hofer (1991) the entrepreneurial process can be seen as falling into three phases: the identification of a business opportunity, the exploitation of that opportunity and the creation of value. This apparently linear process is, in reality, ongoing and dynamic. In the case of technological start-ups, more or less specific propositions have been contributed (Gordon Bell and McNamara 1991; Tesfaye 1997; Klofsten 1997). Using different language, these authors all define the process as first, opportunity recognition, then action leading to activity creation, and finally, company creation. The uncertainty inherent in technology means that the transition from one phase to another is neither easy nor linear, and frequently results in more or less radical redefinitions of the project. It is common that the initial activity is not the one which will result in the creation of value, and be the basis upon which the company can grow. The creation process has been described as one of 'making it up as you go along' (Avenier 1997); it is an ongoing process with comings and goings (Marchesnay 2002) and back doubling (Garnsey 1996). These descriptions are particularly applicable to start-ups in a context of high uncertainty.

In this chapter we propose an approach to start-up creation which takes account of these characteristics; the company being created is considered as an evolving system. The first part of the chapter reminds us how a systemic approach gives a clearer idea of the processes behind the creation of start-ups: we present the dimensions of this system. We then discuss the dynamics of the system itself, before illustrating the analysis with a case study.

A SYSTEMIC APPROACH TOWARDS COMPANY CREATION

The project's evolution is catered for by traditional entrepreneurial approaches, but these approaches do not sufficiently highlight the fact that evolution is not merely one aspect of company creation; it is the essential element of company creation. So we propose a systemic approach with a model which will more fully describe this situation.

An approach particularly suited to start-ups

The systemic approach is useful for analysing entrepreneurship, since it is, by definition, a holistic and teleological approach. The holistic approach meets our concern to take in to account all the variables which could possibly be considered pertinent in understanding the evolution of a management system. The systemic approach is also a teleological one, since the process of company creation throughout the 'lifetime' of the project, involves successive reorganizations of the relationship between the company's objectives and the means through which these are achieved. This teleological and holistic dimension has been adopted particularly in French works on entrepreneurship (Bruyat 1994; Bréchet 1994; Sammut 2001; Marchesnay 2002; Fayolle 2004).

The systemic approach also allows us to embrace the complexity of start-ups by focusing, in particular, on the evolution of the relationships between the components rather than on the components themselves, since company evolution depends on the interaction of these elements. The systemic approach considers that an organization cannot be examined independently from its environment, that is to say the social forces, culture and institution with which it interacts. It may appear complex and difficult for practitioners to use, but supporters may argue that in fact this approach explains a great deal about what are airily described as 'implementation' problems in the literature (Bhalla *et al*. 2005). It may help us to better grasp a company's evolution, seeing this more as a process of implementation than as a process of decision-making. The entrepreneurial approach involves taking account simultaneously of both the strategy and its implementation.

In this way, our understanding of the evolution of start-ups will be deepened. The approach involves analysing the businesses, not by making comparisons between them, nor by evaluating them relative to existing models, but rather by analysing each company with respect to its own evolution.

The dimensions of the system

Understanding a system means describing its component parts, the relationship between them and the dynamic of the system itself. Bruyat (1994) reminds us of the consensus of the scientific community about the four dimensions necessary for studying company creation, namely: the creator, the creation process, the environment and the new company. Sammut (2001) suggests that we observe the creation process by simultaneously taking account of five key variables, the entrepreneur, the financial resources, the environment, the organization and the activity. We will present these five variables or dimensions, and will present them in order, highlighting their particularities in the context of start-up creation.

The entrepreneurs

Entrepreneurship research has always been concerned with what makes an individual into an entrepreneur, the point discussed in Chapter 4. However, the transformation does not stop there. In the bilateral relationship between the company and the entrepreneur, Bruyat (1994) reminds us that it continues well beyond the actual creation of the company. Fayolle (2004) calls this phenomenon the 'entrepreneurial situation'. While both these authors centre their approach on the individual entrepreneur, start-up creation is often the work of an entrepreneurial team: studies undertaken out in various countries show start-ups usually to be created by two or three people (for example Pleschak 1997, in Germany; APCE 2000, in France; Prevezer 2001, in US biotechnology, and Gasse 2002, in Quebec).

The importance of founding teams in building ambitious projects with rapid growth has been clearly demonstrated (Cooper and Dailey 1997; Cooney 1999). Therefore, if we recognize the existence of entrepreneurial teams in start-up creation, we should extend the entrepreneurial situation from the individual to the team. The emergence of the team itself, changes within the team due to evolution or conflict, and the transformation of the people involved into a true management team, all needs to be taken into account.

With this in mind, Bernasconi (2000) proposed a typology of entrepreneurs observable in the initial stages of the technological project: the one-man band, the team of researchers, the professional team, the group of professionals. These types make no claim to scientific validity, but they do highlight the relationships which exist between creators and projects. In the context of the relationship project/entrepreneur mentioned above, the initial entrepreneurial configuration has consequence for the project as a whole.

The one-man band is an engineer or scientist who is often alone at the beginning. His project consists of creating an activity based on strong technological skills. From his point of view, his technological know-how gives the project validity. This can lead to his under-estimating other relevant variables of management such as marketing or finance. This type of entrepreneur may limit the project's development, unless he is able to become a 'conductor' capable of working with the right people and leading specialists of domains other than his own.

Spin-off of researchers consists of scientists wishing to reap the benefits of studies carried out in their public or private laboratories. These spin-offs are more and more frequently accompanied by incubators which have now been set up in most universities and laboratories, a subject discussed in some depth in Chapter 10. The development of projects founded by researchers is limited by the fact that they tend to behave as they have always done before and thus operate as a research company. As such they often keep up their relationship with their former employer. The main challenge lies in the successful transformation from researcher to entrepreneur, and in the capacity to create a complementary team; as Chapter 10 clearly showed, there can be significant weaknesses of researchers in different projects.

The spin-off of professionals corresponds to company creation by a team having already led a similar project within a different company. It is often an excellent point of departure for a start-up. An existing and competent team which takes the risk of creating a company already disposes of numerous technological, industry sector and management skills. These constitute a real advantage which might hopefully result in an ambitious project. The members of the team already know each other, the initial costs and risks have often been borne by the 'surrogate company'. If this company also fosters the initiative, the chances of success are even greater.

Europe Technologies, a company founded in Sophia Antipolis in 1996 by four people who previously worked at Texas Instruments near Nice is a good example, discussed in Chapter 3. The company was created from a conviction that the embedded systems market would grow significantly, that these systems needed an integrated approach – which other companies in the sector did not offer – and that Texas Instruments would be a major customer. On the strength of their technological vision and these hypotheses, the company raised over €15 million and saw significant market growth with large industrial clients.

The group of professionals is usually made up of a team of professionals who get together to build a project considered to be particularly innovative. The role of scientists and technicians is balanced by those with managerial profiles in line with the project's needs. This team is constituted either at the very beginning, or in the initial phases of the project. On paper, this configuration presents the best chances for development since each individual contributes relevant skills to the project. The risk of this type of situation lies in the quality of human relationships within the team.

These four types of entrepreneur are only archetypes which show the variety of possible situations. Nevertheless, they have the merit of pointing out that teams are important, and that the initial configuration of the team will affect the dynamics of company creation.

The activity

The activity of the young company is difficult to define, because it constantly evolves, shaping itself as time passes. The activity may show characteristics typical of the sector, the type of technology, the type of offer, the product-market link, or even the positioning within the value chain. A good representation of the start-up creation process may also be offered by the business model, which can describe the components of an activity and the interrelated workings of these components as a system (Magretta 2002).

In the initial phases of a technological project, it is often difficult to define the activity precisely because of the large number of choices to be made and validated.

So these projects have often been defined according to simple generic typologies based on the nature of the activity, product or service, and the intensity of the innovation (Albert and Mougenot 1988, Bernasconi 2000). Examples include a product based on improving the offer or a product based on a breakthrough, on a service or on a research activity. To these categories can be added the 'bread and butter' activity which often takes the form of consultancy or sale of services, and which is used in the initial stages to generate revenue.

The organization

The need to characterize organizations according to their stage of development has been the object of much of the literature. For example, many organizational models are based on the life cycle theory, as pioneered by Greiner (1972). Quinn and Cameron (1983) tried to identify the characteristics of organizations over stages in time, and evaluated the performance associated with each stage. For Churchill and Lewis (1983) each stage presents key problems, and the later works of Churchill (1998) shed light on the management needs according to each stage.

For technological companies, Blais and Toulouse (1992) note different degrees of formalization of the principal management skills depending on the stage of evolution – intensity of structuring, size of management systems and planning processes.

These authors all illustrate how organizations build themselves progressively in a non-linear manner during the creation process.

Financial resources

The financial approach to start-ups has shown a number of particular features. To sum these up: there is a large gap between spending and income, rapid decisions impact on the financial structure, immaterial assets are highly important, and there is a permanent need to evaluate the company (Gasiglia *et al.* 2000). These companies are also distinguished by the special characteristics of the stages which require financing, the finance required and the variety of actors participating in the financing. The financial approach of investors consists of using stage by stage models such as that of Gordon Bell and McNamara (1991). These investors tend to identify financing according to the stage in which funds are needed: business plan, prototype, product, initial sales and commercial development. For each of these stages, the types of investors will be different, and the amounts mobilized will rise in line with the company's growth.

This theoretical sequential model of financing is straightforward, but it does not match reality, where the development of start-ups is usually, as we have already seen, anything but sequential. The unpredictability of a company's life obviously affects how resources are consumed and the need to find new funds. In particular, when the young company does not find its initial market easily, going back to start again nearly always requires refinancing. So the mobilization of financial resources becomes extremely important in terms of the amounts required and the time spent by the director to find it. The financial is ever present throughout the development of the company, even though the ways of obtaining funding and the actors who seek it change.

The environment

The environment is ever-present in approaches to company creation. Regulations and competition often predominate and present an environment replete with opportunities and threats. Strategic analysis has long considered these environmental elements, with a range of tools to analyse them. The personal environment of the entrepreneur is also an important element before, during and after the company creation. This 'starting' environment is made up of family, friends and more generally by what may be termed social capital (Bourdieu 1981), which provides the entrepreneur with resources, support and credibility.

As well as these two types of environment, one has to add the geographical context, or more specifically, the innovative milieu. This has been proposed by the GREMI (Groupe de Recherche Européen sur les Milieux Innovateurs), a European group for research into innovative milieux. Since Marshall (1920), economists, geographers and sociologists, with different words and approaches, have all explored both the tangible and intangible characteristics of regions and the advantages they offer to companies: external economies, access to resources, innovation, etc. It should be noted, as is noted in Chapter 6, that the relationship between the personal environment and the region is often made through networking.

The role played by territories and their effect on the characteristics of company creation has been particularly well illustrated by Lanciano-Morandat and Nohara (2001) in their comparison between spin-offs in two science parks, INRIA Grenoble and Sophia Antipolis. They show that the effects of the differences in the two 'milieu' exceed the similarities of the company – INRIA – present on both sites. These differences have to do both with the characteristics of the companies themselves and of the nature of the relationships which are created within the respective milieu. The multifaceted nature of the environment means that it needs to be examined in its competitive, personal and regional dimensions.

These five dimensions of the system form the basis of the entrepreneurial process. These dimensions are not, evidently, independent, and their interactions, or the management of their interactions, will play an important part in the project's success. Taking the cue from Sammut (1998) we can show the elements of the system in Figure 11.1.

Success in developing a technological company thus depends on managing the interactions between the dimensions of the system at a given point in time. It also requires guiding the evolution of each dimension dynamically, in line with the evolution of the project. Next, we examine the dynamics of the system.

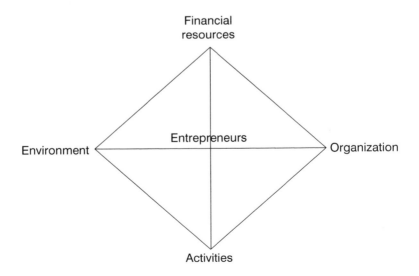

Figure 11.1 The five elements of the system

THE DYNAMICS OF THE EVOLUTIONARY SYSTEM

We saw in the introduction that the three phases commonly recognized in the process of company creation are the opportunity recognition, opportunity exploitation and value creation. We will slightly modify these phases in order better to describe and grasp the challenge of the entrepreneurial situation. We shall change the first phase 'opportunity recognition' to 'opportunity creation'. It is insufficient merely to recognize a business opportunity. The opportunity must be constructed, by exploring all its component parts – which amounts to creating the opportunity. Business opportunities in technology must not only be identified and recognized, they have to be invented!

For the second phase, we prefer the term 'creating activity' to 'exploiting opportunity'. Exploiting an opportunity sounds like a natural progression from the previous phase: first comes the recognition, then the exploitation. All the work and analysis on the subject mentioned above a show that in matters of technology, passing from one phase to another is anything but a linear progression. During the second phase, the entrepreneur has to create an activity, that is to say, establish a technology-product-market segment trio. Studies have shown that the trio in the second phase is not necessarily the one envisaged during the first. The creation of an activity is in itself a key step to embark upon. It could be a step taken all at once, in line with the original project and based on previous formulations, or it may be done in stages and steps. Calling the second phase creation rather than exploitation of the opportunity highlights that it is a matter of actively changing the stakes, and is not simply a continuation of the preceding stage.

Finally, we shall call the third phase 'company creation' rather than 'value creation'. From our standpoint, the term value creation has the disadvantage of being inexplicit; the value concerned may be defined in various ways and therefore remains abstract. Once the activity has been created, the organization which will ensure its development has to be constructed. This organization is specific to the activity concerned, and cannot therefore be imagined, let alone set up, before the activity has been established. Once this has been done the entrepreneurs – or others who have appeared to complement or replace them – can genuinely make a choice about which structure, process and management styles best suit the development of the activity in question. This new phase is itself completely different from the growth phase that follows it. If so few young companies actually undergo strong growth it is because getting to this phase is no easy matter. We are therefore dealing with the creation of a company, not in the legal sense of the term, but in the creation of an economic organization which must be able to support the activity's development.

This process is represented in Figure 11.2. The apparent simplicity and linear nature of this diagram should not hide the complexity and non-linear nature of the reality. The actors involved in creating start-ups, as well as researchers, both know that in reality the road is full of double-backs. In innovative projects, correspondence

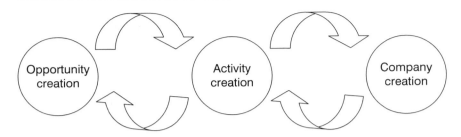

Figure 11.2 *Evolving process of company creation*

to the market is a critical phase which necessitates continuous adjustments and questioning; these are shown in the diagram by the backward loops.

Having introduced the dynamic of the entrepreneurial process, we shall now deal with the evolution of the system's dimensions during the company's own evolution. During this evolution, these systems become more complex, and the interactions between them increase.

The evolution and growing complexity of the dimensions

During the implementation of a project, the entrepreneurial process undergoes a profound transformation. In the transition from opportunity-recognition to activity-creation, we note the transformation of an individual into an entrepreneur, or from a project team into a team of entrepreneurs. Then in the transition from activity-creation to company-creation, the entrepreneurial process has to mutate from being an entrepreneurial team to being a team of company directors. The entrepreneurial dimension evolves significantly in its composition and learning processes.

During the opportunity-recognition phase, the activity will be defined only in outline. It will often undergo considerable modifications during the initial phases of the project. Examples abound of changes in this phase, from one product to another, from one market segment to another, or even from a product to a service, or from an offer for end consumers being changed for one aimed at distributors.

At the business opportunity stage, an organization rarely exists beyond a few working methods between the project creators. When the activity is created, the organization begins to become structured, often fairly informally, according to the first tasks undertaken and the human and financial resources that are mobilized. With company creation comes development in activity and personnel, requiring a more formal organization with structures, modes of co-ordination and management systems.

The environment and its various dimensions will become more complex as the activity develops and the organization is built up. The company interacts more and more with its competitive environment, namely its customers, competitors, partners, regulatory bodies and suppliers. Interaction with the regional environment and the 'milieu' becomes richer, and involves contacts with universities and laboratories, consultants, local funding agencies, incubators, schools and universities. The personal environment of the entrepreneur is also broadens. If the company has international ambitions, the environments with which it – and its management – interacts become even more numerous.

Depending on the phase of development, the financial needs and the financial resources will evolve significantly. The evolution of financial resources is one of the key elements of the project's survival. Fund raising and cash-flow follow each other and condition the speed of development. One of the most important preoccupations of entrepreneurs, and one which takes up much of their time, is to ensure the permanent availability of sufficient finance.

The evolution of interactions between dimensions

The systemic nature of our model encourages consideration of the necessary interaction between the dimensions. Even if these interactions are present from the beginning, they will certainly be reinforced as the entrepreneurial process advances.

In the opportunity-creation phase, the amount of interaction between dimensions is frequently not very strong, since each dimension is regarded as a separate element which has to be optimized or further exploited. The perceived need may be, for example, to improve the technology, do a market study or set up financial forecasts.

In creating the activity, from the time that the first operational decisions are made, the relationships between the dimensions become more important and are reinforced as action is undertaken. For example, first market initiatives need to be coordinated with an embryonic organization, but at the same time, funds need to be found to reinforce the team and meet demands for more resources. To actually create the company, the dimensions need to operate together; any systemic failure to manage their interactions will result in difficulties that will threaten the company's ability to stand the test of time.

When looked at in this way, setting up a project means embarking on a series of 'back-tracking' actions within a system composed of the same elements. At each 'back-track', the elements become better defined and the interrelationships between them grow (see Figure 11.3).

THE 3DVIZU CASE

This case is a real one; it was followed over time by the author who knew the entrepreneur before the start-up, and still follows the project. The names of the company and the entrepreneur, however, have been changed.

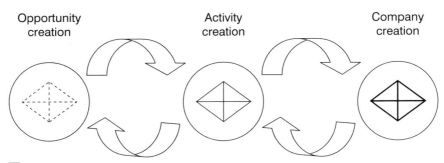

| Opportunity creation | Activity creation | Company creation |

Figure 11.3 *Progression of interactions between the different dimensions of the project*

Mr Leblanc is a serial entrepreneur who has always worked on CAO software. In the mid-1980s he created a company which has become a world leader in CAO for architects. Between 1996 and 1999 he was looking for a business opportunity in the domain of 3D to which he could contribute his knowledge of the sector and his entrepreneurial skills. He chose a 3D modeller which had been developed for a few years using Apple Macintosh computers. He joined up with a developer, who transformed it for use on Microsoft Windows. With the help of some business angels, he created the company 3DVizu in January 2000, headquartered in Montreal, Canada but with the development team in Nice, France.

To avoid competing head on with the powerful editor suppliers who already controlled the market, the product was quickly repositioned as a 3D viewer tool. This had the advantage of being able to compact files from modellers, and manipulate complex 3D objects simply and rapidly, so it was accessible through the Internet. The final product-market decision was 3D viewer software aimed at architects wishing to compose virtual prototypes, distributed through Internet download. A strategy of partnership with specialized platform sites was set up, as well as communication campaigns targeting architects. Funds of Canadian $1.7 million were raised in January 2001, which enabled this strategy to be put into operation.

Unfortunately, the expected results were not attained, because architects were not yet ready to exchange information in 3D. So a repositioning of the product was needed, and a new product was developed using the same technology. This a 3D component viewer for software applications for construction life cycles, which also enables building conception teams or those designing complex installations to exchange 3D images of a project in progress.

This evolution from architects towards engineering companies involved fundamental changes in the characteristics of the project. The limited initial financial resources meant a reduction in personnel, and the management team had to look at itself anew with different priorities in mind. The new product required enormous development if it was to be compatible with the CAO 3D tools on the market, and be integrated into the users' computer environments. The marketing strategy changed from Internet distribution to partnerships with distributors and direct contact with referenced customers.

The re-financing necessary for this new strategy was estimated at Canadian $10 million over time. In March 2002 a second investor provided Canadian $2 million. This sum covered the evolution of the product and the marketing suitable for the new strategy. However, all this took longer than expected, and it was not until early 2004 that the first contracts were signed. Using this case as an illustration, we will now try to show how the model can be applied, and what can be learned from this experience.

Analysis of the emerging system in the case

First, it is clear that the progression of this project was anything but linear. The opportunity-creation took a long time to mature, between two and three years. The activity-creation was not completed at the first attempt, but needed to be done twice, with a significant change in the technology-product-market segment trio. Only at the end of the second attempt did the company look as if it would be able to create the activity. More than five years later, in 2005, the company has still not been created.

If we now examine the progress of the dimensions during the three phases, we can how each of them evolved, and the growing complexity of their interactions.

The opportunity-creation phase was concentrated around an entrepreneur who was highly competent in the sector. That is why he was looking for an activity within his area of competence. Because he was a newcomer to the area, he had no strong network in the local environment but nevertheless disposed of a social capital linked to his previous experience. The financial resources were weak, and the organization was based on a bread and butter activity. The diverse elements of the project were yet to be assembled.

The activity-creation phase was characterized by the choice of setting up the headquarters of the company in Montreal, then a subsidiary in Nice, which called for a double interaction in both environments. The effort of integration to obtain external economies and to become embedded with local networks varied between one place and the other, depending on the project's evolution. Thus even if the first investor was found in France, the second was in Quebec. The activity evolved from a 'mass market' approach – there are several million architects worldwide – to a complex niche product for large industrial companies. The consequences, in terms of the characteristics of the product, its price and marketing methods, are evident. Finance was found first for the architect market, and then for the engineering market. However, despite the effort dedicated to this changeover, and despite the time that it took, the funding found was still not in synchronization with the stage of development in activity.

The entrepreneurial process at the outset comprised a group of people previously known to the entrepreneur. The failure of the first strategy, and the financial limitations, led to a reduction in the size of the team with former members leaving and new ones, more appropriate for the new strategy, took their place. The partnership between the entrepreneur and the initial developer was itself broken, and a different developer was found.

The organization proceeded in a zig-zag fashion, exemplified by the increase in staff to 25 employees, only for this to fall to eight, split between Montreal and Nice. The functions and tasks followed these changes. The costs of the structure and the organization peaked just as the first product failed, and from then on, the company became smaller and smaller.

The analysis of the activity-creation phase shows that each dimension underwent profound modifications, and that the interactions were rarely harmonious. At one time, there was money and a team but no market, at another no money and no team, but a potential market. The entrepreneur's vision had been a good one, but as is often the case, the market emerged more slowly than predicted, and the creation of the activity was difficult.

The company-creation – in the sense of our model – is not complete five years later, despite its 25 employees. Even if the company is created one day, its final form will be very different from the one that the founder originally envisaged.

CONCLUSION

This chapter aimed to examine the dynamic of the creation and development of high-tech start-ups. We chose a systemic approach in order to take account of the evolutionary process of such companies. Five dimensions were defined mentioned – the entrepreneur, the financial resources, the environment, the organization and the activity – and these enabled us to observe the system at each stage of its evolution. By observing the way that each dimension changed and the way that the interactions between the dimensions grew as the entrepreneurial process advanced, this evolution became easier to describe and to understand. Into this systemic approach normative elements, based on research and evidence, can be fitted, which allows more concrete illustrations of the proposed approach. In this way, entrepreneurs may better see where they lie, and have greater control of their development process.

Overall, this approach should help entrepreneurs better to understand the causes and effects of the changes which they are bound to encounter during the first years of their project. Emphasizing the setting up of a company has enabled us to demonstrate the embryonic and emerging nature of strategy in the case of start-ups. If a strategy is necessary, this approach shows how control of a start-up's evolution is strongly linked to the capacity of entrepreneurs to handle the different dimensions coherently.

Managing innovative high-tech firms

Michel Bernasconi

The third part of the book deals with functional and managerial approaches of high-tech start-up business. These companies are special not only because of the global nature of the business environment in which they engage, but also because of the particular management practices they operate. The uncertainty of their businesses, the delicate technological choices that they have to make, and the constant search for financial resources that they need to undertake, all mean that these entrepreneurs need advanced management tools and managerial skills.

The chapters of this third part examine approaches for high-tech start-ups in four key areas. The first three of these are marketing (Paul Millier, in Chapter 12), competitive intelligence (Gil Ayache, in Chapter 13), and in technology development projects (Dominique Jolly, in Chapter 14). Linking all these, in Chapter 16, Mette Moensted stresses how networking management appears to be a critical management practice of young innovative companies, and the ways with which they face uncertainty. The network approach is underlined by nearly every author of the third part as a relevant practice: networking is helpful in building a new market, it is necessary to set up a competitive intelligence system, it is the key to get credibility and an important way to access finance.

In Chapter 12, Paul Millier stresses that 75 per cent of new business failures are attributed to marketing weaknesses. Traditional marketing methods don't work in technological innovations; but the ability of a new company to identify and serve a market is critical. The most radical case is when markets are created for breakthrough innovations. Here, high-tech means high-uncertainty. To face this situation, Paul Millier describes the marketing characteristics of high-tech start-ups, establishing the context in which action takes place. He pinpoints the marketing errors typically inherent within high-tech start-ups. He then proposes an array of principles and marketing rules that permit development of durable growth in a business based on an innovative technology.

In Chapter 13, Gil Ayache stresses that innovation does not necessarily come from existing competitors. Supporting the theme of diversity and complexity that runs through this book, he highlights how competitive innovations can come from anywhere – including from sources that might not expect it. To tackle that challenge Ayache proposes an approach to expand the analysis to competitive intelligence, which involves a network perspective. He then examines the particular characteristics of scanning for high-tech companies, and points out the conditions necessary for setting up a system of competitive intelligence. He describes a minimum system of monitoring and intelligence which remains accessible for young companies.

Young innovative companies need methods to guide how they allocate resources between different investment opportunities or existing technology programs. In Chapter 14, Dominique Jolly proposes an analytical process for auditing research and development (R&D) projects, and for selecting those with higher potential value for the company. His work attempts to adapt an elaborate analytical tool designed for multi-project companies, for the world of the small ones. His model takes into account two sets of criteria, with 16 criteria in each. The controllable criteria are the accumulated competencies and assets that depend on a firm's behaviour and decisions. The non-controllable criteria refer to the intrinsic potential, the appeal or attractiveness of one given technology which does not depend on the firm's action. The framework appears to be a better way of capturing and managing the complexity and uncertainty inherent in those choices, than more simple models such as the financial ones that are then advocated.

In Chapter 16, Mette Moensted stresses the importance of networks in the high-tech environment and in the start-up process. In an uncertain and turbulent environment, networking is an important way for gaining access to resources, for creating legitimacy for the firm and for its ideas, and for organizing for innovation. Networking puts the emphasis on transaction benefits rather than on the transactions costs (Williamson 1979). For entrepreneurs, networking is more than just 'doing networking' and 'using' networks. Being able to understand and manage networks appears as a new critical competence in the leadership and management of young high-tech firms. In networks, leadership and power is developed in a social process, and is based on the ways in which the entrepreneurs act with the others in the network, and the way in which they negotiate with them.

Chapter 12

Marketing technological innovations
The challenges of creating markets

Paul Millier

'Change is the only constant' is a slogan in its own right, but one that sums up a large part of what characterizes technological innovation (Shanklin and Ryans 1984). Turbulence and uncertainty are the daily bread of the adventurers of technology who gobble up each year $20 billion in products that are doomed to failure (Clugston 1995). That three-quarters of these failures are attributable to marketing weakness encourages us to think seriously about how the marketing of high-tech business is tackled. The best high-tech businesses do not get it wrong. Companies such as Compaq consider that in bringing high technologies to the market, there is a greater need for innovation in marketing than in the technology. Marketing is often the missing link in high-tech firms (Canion 1989).

This chapter presents an approach to marketing adapted for high-tech start-ups. The first part describes the marketing characteristics facing high-tech start-ups; it establishes the context in which action takes place. The second pinpoints the marketing errors inherent within high-tech firms, and the errors of reasoning which so often doom these firms to failure. The third suggests a range of principles that may permit the development of durable growth based on an innovative technology.

MARKETING CHARACTERISTICS OF HIGH-TECH START-UPS

High-tech and high uncertainty

Biotech Organ invented a process of extracting and encapsulating active cells (Lysaght and Aebischer 1999) that allowed bio-artificial organs to be made. By allowing bio-artificial pancreas to cure diabetics, insulin injections for diabetics can become a thing of the past. Similar processes can also be applied to at least 30 illnesses, some with no known treatment today. As the list of illnesses ever grows, the market grows, also to be estimated in tens of millions of dollars. We may wonder where the list will finish, but what if all these illnesses are different, in terms of treatment, or do some have common points?

The situation becomes more complex and more uncertain when we realize that each illness may require two to three cells or molecules. In addition, at least three sorts of membranes can be used to make the biocompatible envelope of the organs, and we presently do not know which is the best adapted to each illness and to each active substance. As for the shape of the organ, its form can vary from a long twisted string, or a sausage-shape, to a sphere. If we add to this the fact that the new organ can be implanted near the organ to be treated in order to stimulate it, or just under the skin or deep in the body, we come to already 30 illnesses x three cells x three membranes x three shapes x three localizations = 2430 possible combinations. As yet, Biotech Organ does not know what to sell: the extruded membrane, the extraction of cells, the encapsulation of cells or the organs themselves? Biotech Organ has not yet defined their business model.

As for the in vivo and in vitro trials, who will perform them and how long will this take? What doctors will accept to take the risk of promoting bio-artificial organs with all the technical and sometimes ethical problems that arise? Finally, who are the customers and who decides on the market: doctors, patients, laboratories, surgeons, insurance companies?

The dream, little by little, becomes a nightmare, as Biotech Organ finds itself progressively snowed under this avalanche of questions and doubts. This is so characteristic of the world of high-tech. It is no surprise that in these conditions the results always take three times longer to come to light than forecast. How can innovative firms avoid having to ask their financial partners for budgetary extensions? High-tech adventures typically last three times longer and cost three times more than planned.

Biotech Organ is not alone in this position and tens of other entrepreneurs have also experienced uncertainty on multiple levels. This include the market – limit, segmentation; the customers – who are they? how will they behave?; the competition – what will be the reaction of the insulin manufacturer's lobby?; the regulatory environment – what test? how can an authorization for this non-conventional treatment be obtained for its release on the market? Then we have the product which can take at least 2430 forms; the product implementation; the product price – what mode of calculation should be retained to be comparable to or on the contrary incommensurable with competitive technologies?; and the manufacturing and conservation of products.

This example shows us that the uncertainty surrounding Biotech Organ is such that the marketing models available to us require, at the least, to be adapted. In fact, as Green (1991) concluded, the mainstream in strategic planning relies on rather unrealistic hypotheses such as that the information on the market exists and is reliable; that the market and the competition are identifiable; that demand–supply is stable; and that economic rationality prevails.

A marketing definition of high-tech

The example of Biotech Organ also allows us to approach a definition of high-tech. Commonly, the meaning behind the word high-tech is high-technological content, predominantly scientific and technical personnel, heavy preliminary research, close link with science and the expression of a technological principle pushed to its limit. The high-tech product is, in fact, often assimilated, for example, to higher performance, greater precision, higher integration, or more miniaturization.

From a marketing standpoint, these conditions are insufficient in their own right to justify a specific approach. How does one or 10 years of research change the way a product is sold? If this does not affect the manner in which the customer perceives the product or service, it does not. To clarify the definition of high-tech, let us compare two examples. One is a new football boot key for the base and studs which allow boot studs to be changed in two minutes instead of half an hour; the other is the bio-artificial organs of Biotech Organ.

The first results from repeatedly hearing football players grumbling and complaining that they cannot easily and quickly change their muddy studs during a match. This product originates from the demand, requested and sought after by customers. This 'new product' really only requires a traditional marketing approach based on the knowledge of the competition and its products, on aggressive communication, on a strong promotion in relation to distribution networks and a positioning of the offer which seeks to maximize its value in relation to customers.

The second results from the initiative of the supplier – Biotech Organ – and disrupts the working habits of the profession and the ideas concerning the way patients are treated. It is necessary now to consider a certain incurable illness – diabetes for example – now to be curable. Surgeons will have to learn how to implant bio-artificial organs. This 'new product' upsets the organization of the market by minimizing the role of some – laboratories producing classical remedies like insulin – by introducing certain other players – such as surgeons and laboratories producing organs – and by changing the situation of the competition – with some competitors becoming incomparable.

This type of product, which we call a high-tech product or technological innovation, affects the social body and requires a deconstruction and a reconstruction of the latter around the innovation. It is therefore necessary to carry out fundamental work if the project is to come to terms with where the difference reside. It is necessary to assemble the pieces of the jigsaw puzzle without knowing the final picture, and without having all the pieces. The easy instructive guidelines of the 'marketing mix' can be forgotten.

From a marketing viewpoint, a high-tech product is a product – or a service – which is a breakthrough in the sense that its irruption upsets the market to a point where this market can no longer be described in the same way before and after. It will necessitate suppliers to define or redefine their activity; to segment or

191

re-segment their market so as to describe it as it is found after the introduction of the technological innovation; and to elaborate or revise their offer. Further, they will need to assess or reassess a versatile and multiform competition and to position or reposition themselves in relation to this; understand the new behaviours of customers; to help the market to be constructed by inventing applications to their product and by organizing the network of players who make up this new industry; and sometimes to invent their customer.

Case company: How Science & Mesure invents their customer

This last point is surprising and often difficult to absorb: how can a customer be invented? Science & Mesure develops equipment of unequalled performance to carry out surface analysis. Their equipment allows the composition of all types of material – metal, plastic, rubber, etc. – to be known in record time, and its undesirable components to be diagnosed. Its use does not require any specific skills: it is a high-performance product which corresponds to a real need, which others meet at an exorbitant price. One approach would be to evoke the potential American and Japanese competition, by finding an organization that would help customers buy the analyser – thereby keeping the know-how. Instead, they attracted customers with a 'co-ownership' purchase, so that customers would group together with a set of rules for the use of a shared machine. Science & Mesure invented the customer by uniting conditions favourable for purchasing by customers. We now focus on this second type of marketing, which diverges from the mainstream.

Three components to take into consideration in high-tech start-ups

As soon as we speak about high-tech entrepreneurship, we integrate three factors that influence the definition and the implementation of marketing in this type of firm. One is the strong presence of technology; one is that the firms are in the starting-up phase; and one is the personality of the managers.

First dimension: The marketing of the technology before that of the product

The Biotech Organ case shows how technology exerts a strong pressure on the adaptation of marketing, because neither the product nor the market yet exists. Everything has to be constructed. The principles of active cell encapsulation are still years away from products which will be the artificial pancreas, thyroid, the kidney or 'reliever of cancerous pain'.

So it is necessary to start marketing the technology well before it is a product, so that the idea passes to the market in the right conditions. In high-tech products, there is a life before life, a technological project lifecycle before the product lifecycle. True technological marketing is first carried out by technicians who will address other technicians to prepare the technical, foundations of what will be the future market.

Second dimension: marketing oriented around the customer rather than the market

The second dimension of the global marketing problem is that the firm is starting up. This of course implies a whole string of a priori negatives from customers – and from certain financers – concerning who will supply if the firm disappears, and who will continue the production in future.

This implies a marketing approach that brings confidence to the customers and stakeholders. This will begin by relying heavily on the manager's contact network. Similarly, this marketing will be marked, at least in the early years, by an approach which is much more 'customer' than 'market'. The strategy of will involve 'laying siege' to the customer, and applying methodically the theory of commitment (Joule and Beauvois 1987) on the principle of 'he who has helped will help'. In other words, your customers are more committed by what they do and have done with you than what they think of you. This tactic involves, first, soliciting from your 'prospects' a little inexpensive service, and then bringing them to progressively become more and more committed to you until they buy.

Case example: Soft Method

Soft Method has developed a software program that combines machining method and CAD; which enables a conceptual pilot study of a complex nature to be run in half a day whereas before it required a week. Perceived as being too young by their customers, Soft Method did not manage to pull off a first contract. So the manager approached a leading automobile parts manufacturer in the following way: 'We are currently studying a pilot project development software program. Before going any further, we would like to test with you the feasibility of this concept and take note of your suggestions to continue our development in a direction which conforms to your needs'. Intrigued as well as flattered by, for once, being approached before being sold a catalogue product which does not fit his needs, the client accepts to play the role of expert.

Less than three months later – easy, because the software program was already ready – the approach was 'thanks to your precious advice, we have developed a prototype of the software which gives promising results. Would you test it for us to tell us what you think?'. Enthralled that his suggestions have been so fruitful, the customer accepts this time to play the role of beta tester – guinea-pig – which is more expensive and committing than the first simple request for advice.

The beta test took place correctly and it is agreed to integrate – this time in reality – the results of the test and to further improve the product. The third step: commercial approach and sale at a price fairly negotiated by taking into consideration the help brought by the customer. Advantage? A first sale of course, but also a real sales experience and an unhoped-for and unexpected reference to display and show to the next prospects.

Third dimension: the personality of managers

Without caricaturing, high-tech entrepreneurs are often enthusiastic, even overexcited, by their technical projects. They can often overvalue technical dimensions, and being capable of using complex mathematic models to analyse their scientific and technical data does not always correspond to an ability to analyse market data in more than an approximate and even 'offhand' manner!

Impatience to see projects brought to a successful conclusion can confuse activism with efficiency, 'busyman' with 'businessman', and taking advantage of opportunities, with strategy! For some, marketing strategy means making appointments and visiting customers. 'Marketing strategy', may be in 'the business plan for the bankers two years ago', may be more oral than written, and may be fuzzy and imprecise. Complexity increases when companies grow, and entrepreneurs have to share his/her vision with partners, and put forward a direction in which to channel collaborators' energy.

MARKETING DANGERS INHERENT IN HIGH-TECH

Mixing up technology and product

The key for football boot studs is a targeted product with a specifications document and a definition corresponding to the expectations of identified customers. We often lose this clarity with high-tech products, because innovators often mistake the technology for the product! How does this confusion emerge?

Let us consider reasons the example of ultra-thin glass-wool. This glass-wool is four times thinner than traditional thermal insulating glass-wool. It is also soft, white, silky-smooth like cotton wool and retains water even better than cotton wool. An inventor might think that this innovative product can access both glass-wool and cotton wool applications (see Figure 12.1).

It appears to offer the allure of 'the miracle of loaves and fishes', but contains a paradox: the richness of the innovation encompasses at the same time the main seed of its weakness.

This weakness comes from the comfortable yet menacing dispersion which is established around the project. With the already long list of applications growing every day, the illusion grows that the potential market has no limit. An energetic

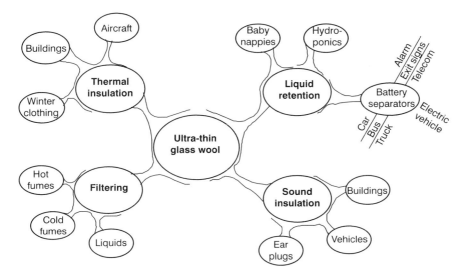

Figure 12.1 *A proliferation of applications*

entrepreneur might multiply the fax-mailing or emailing shots to cast the net wider still, to find yet other customers with other ideas for use of the product. But the fibre creation of glass-wool is a technological principle. Making glass-wool fibrous does not guarantee that it can be used as a support for immunological testing or as glass-wool battery separators. In these situations, entrepreneurs often display two characteristics.

The first is the seeking of the universal product which suits all applications; a consequence of enthusiasm. To do this, they often take their analysis back to the level of the technological principle which will constitute the common denominator to all products. They subsequently hunt to improve optimally while considering that this improvement will have an impact on the complete set of products. But in doing so there is the risk that they remain on the technological level and of never returning to the level of the product. 'Would you ask a king to dine with his servants?'. They feel helpless as they realize that all their life will not be sufficiently long for them to develop enough products to cater for the abundance of application demands which are so different from one to another.

This leads to the second characteristic, which is the most common. Here, they reassure themselves by clutching onto the idea of a particular customer for whom they are developing a specific product which no one else would want. For example, industrialists could become obsessed with manufacturing filters for burning and acid fumes because a customer is crying out loud and strong that he has this need. However, this customer may be the only one with this need. Entrepreneurs tend only to be attentive to cases where there is a problem. Even if 99 per cent of industrial customers do not have any problems with their fumes, they only hear those who do: they only listen to what supports their conviction and turn a deaf ear to what contradicts it. Worse, it is more likely to be the customer who will manage the start-up instead of the entrepreneur, a true strategic error.

Two traps in high-tech: 'the device' and the myth of big market

In the cases of the universal product, and in the too specific product, entrepreneurs are at risk of being the victim of the first trap faced in innovation: that of 'the device'. This is where there is a marvel of technology, but one that is unmarketable. As Davidow (1986) defines, 'the device' is an object which has been developed for self-enjoyment but which does not suit anyone in spite of its incomparable performance. In this way, a pressure gauge accurate to 10-9 bar would be 'a device' in the chemical industry. There, in spite of it having 'the best performance in the market', no manufacturer needs such high performance. The best product is the one that customers buy, and it may not be the most technologically advanced. 'The device' is the fruit of technological work, whereas the product is the fruit of both technological and marketing work in combination. It may at best impress competitors, but not customers.

With a 'second to none' product, however, a second trap of technological innovation may then threaten. This is the myth of the big market. The market for the most accurate pressure sensor on the market, that leaves behind all the others may, for the innovator, be seen as the sensor market in 'the complete market of pressure measurement'.

As soon as the market is expressed in terms of the main function of the product – such as the market of pressure measurement, of water heating, of high-speed machining, of controlling hidden defects, etc. – or in terms of the name of the main competing product – such as the cotton-wool market, iron bars for concrete, milling machines, etc. – we fall into the trap of the myth of the big, homogeneous, quantifiable and sure market.

The first trap is getting the wrong target. The function is not the expectations of customers. The competitive products, refers to the offer, not the demand. The unique expression used to describe, the market is both incorrect and portrays an unreal homogeneity. By saying 'my market is the concrete reinforcement market' – the function of the product – or the iron bar market – the competitive product – expresses neither the diversity of the demand. Nor does it express the real opportunity for a metal fibre reinforcement which is integrated in the concrete during mixing, and which avoids the fastidious operation of placing iron bars prior to pouring concrete into a mould.

The consolidation of cliffs, the repair of sewer pipes, underground works, concrete projection, the restoration of façades, all have reinforcement problems unresolved by classical techniques. The real market for our fibre may be there, but that requires considerable marketing analysis to bring this result to light. It is easier to harbour an illusion that a 10 per cent market share of iron bars on applications is feasible, even if the latter has given entire satisfaction for more than 30 years.

PRINCIPLES OF MARKETING ADAPTED TO HIGH-TECH START-UPS

We have just discovered some traps which threaten innovation, in order to recognize them. But avoiding traps is not a strategy or, at least, is a hollow or negative strategy. To progress and construct something else requires principles and rules.

Marketing responses to problems arising through technological innovation

The marketing responses which we can formulate to avoid the pitfalls of innovation can be seen to reside in three principles: proliferation, segmentation and focus. See Figure 12.2.

Proliferation

Proliferation happens when projects go in many directions – as seen with Biotech Organ or the ultra-thin glass-wool. It arouses great creativity. It is no longer a project of ultra-fine glass-wool which we have to manage, but 100 projects of products based on glass-wool suggested by customers.

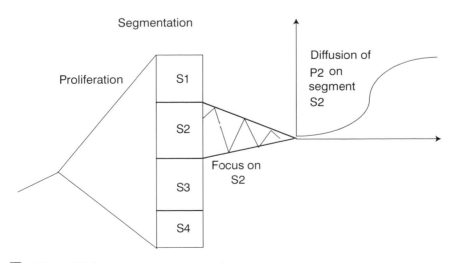

Figure 12.2 Proliferation, segmentation, focus

Each demands specific development; there are 100 possible lines of development, offering a much larger scope of choice than one project path, with the choice of 100 paths, some will be more favourable than others.

The proliferation phase is a turbulent, chaotic phase of challenge for the project and for the firm as it leaves the original intentions of the team which gave birth to the project. It is a phase of possible reversal of the objectives and of seizing the opportunities, characteristic of what we can call an emerging strategy (Blais and Toulouse 1993).

Although it is chaotic and sometimes uncomfortable, this phase is necessary for the success of innovations. Under the influence of customers, suppliers and competitors, the firm starts to evolve by integrating its environment in order to find its place. The majority of firms that continue inflexibility to follow a direction chosen at the onset fail.

Segmentation

Firms usually lack the means to embark on all the possible paths revealed during the proliferation phase: choice is necessary, by ceasing diverging, and by analysing the market through segmentation. Here, a vision is established.

In highly technical firms, one approach is a segmentation matrix, where applications appear in the columns and the behaviour of customers in relation to the technology proposed appear in the rows. At the non-empty cross-overs of the columns and the rows are the market segments which can finally be named and quantified (Millier 1995). See Figure 12.3.

This matrix formally distinguishes the application – the technical problem to resolve – from the market – the segment – which avoids mixing them up. It is this confusion that is one of the most dangerous in the technical world. It leads to the

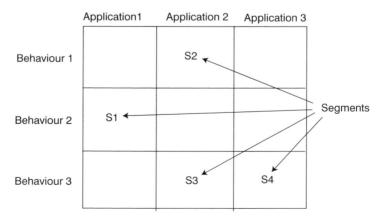

Figure 12.3 Segmentation matrix

illusion that if there is a technical problem to resolve this is sufficient for there to be a market.

It is not enough to say 'automobile bumpers must be ever lighter and ever more resistant. As my material is light and resistant I will sell 40,000 tons within the next two years for automobile bumpers'. It is in fact necessary to know what price the customer is prepared to pay, what risks are perceived by the customer and will hold him back from buying and what are the motivations which will push him to be interested in the offer. It is all this that determines the behaviour customers are going to show in relation to this material. Some customers may be enthusiastic, and others not.

Armed with this vision of the market, firms must then draw up a diagnosis destined to rank the market segments depending on the position they hold in relation to each other, as can be seen in Figure 12.4.

Focus

With this diagnosis, firms may then proceed into the third phase, that of focusing. Focusing means choosing a small number of market segments. It is on these market segments that they will concentrate their energy, to resolve all the problems, one after the other, until ready to 'take the plunge'. Focusing is invariably accompanied by intense, active and balanced collaboration with a partner, usually, a customer. This principle of co-development presents several advantages. First it allows the development costs to be shared. Second, it allows the supplier to adapt to customer demands and the customer to adapt his needs to the possibilities of a technology

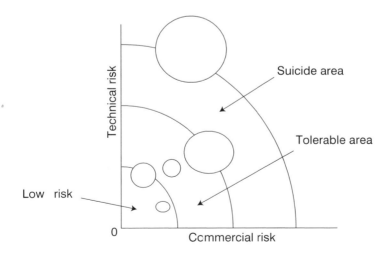

Figure 12.4 *Diagnosis of the marketing situation of the firm (Source: Millier 1989)*

that he is discovering. Third, it commits the customer to the project to the extent that he gives his backing on points which he would in other circumstances have criticized. Fourth, it allows confidence to be progressively built up between the partners. Fifth, the customer can suggest new ideas of applications. Sixth, problems can be resolved quickly.

There are also disadvantages, in terms of confidentiality, of industrial ownership and exclusivity that the customer frequently demands and which must be treated ad hoc. It also requires proselytizing by the entrepreneur who must manage to convince his partners that his project is as important for them as it is for him.

Adjustment of the principle for the entrepreneurs

Even if theoretically valid, the principle of proliferation/segmentation/focus, finishing with co-development, presents an implementation difficulty for entrepreneurs: it takes time. A start-up may not be able to afford the money or time required for stimulating the market – proliferation – for a marketing survey – segmentation – for concentration of development – focus – for a final result which is planned for, say, two years hence. So entrepreneurs must do some of these things simultaneously.

Canvassing and collecting information

Entrepreneurs can collect marketing information when canvassing. Multiple visits, coupled with sales propositions, allow a good first impression of market reaction. Proliferation is encouraged by as much canvassing as possible, to provoke as many reactions, suggestions and good ideas from the customers as possible.

From a first year of canvassing – which may result in some sales, some distancing for carrying out a formal synthesis of the information will help for to describing the market – segmentation – and for diagnosis of the position on the different segments. This will help choice of the segments which to concentrate resources – focus.

Case example: Spymag

Spymag developed a re-inscribable magnetic tracer that enables mobile bodies to be traced – cars, pallets, laundry, people, etc. – during their movement and transportation, which enables processes to be optimized – such as in managing taxis, or following medication within hospitals. After a year running from one potential customer to another, the creators had sufficient information to make a structured segmentation of their market and to determine which segments they were going to target.

Taking advantage of their background experience as management computer scientists, the creators proposed to customers that, with their system of magnetic tracer, they study and install management and operation management software. To not be dispersed, and to find synergies, they offered only their management services to target customers. In this way they built up a body of customers that they knew well, with whom they gained confidence. On this basis of trust, Spymag is now in a better position to sell the magnetic tracing system.

Sales and development

Apparently paradoxical in its implementation synergy is possible between sales and development. There are two essential forms: the sale of services on the basis of the proposed innovation, and the associated sustainable commercial activity.

Case example: Blueskye

An example of the first form is Blueskye, which develops software add-ons; functional computing bricks that 'boost' a core software. The firm is only one year old, so it cannot risk failure. And yet, it is not really known if customers are going to purchase the product, at least until the last minute – even if there is an initial apparent intention to do so, when it is presented to them. As a result, there is risk of developing and packaging the product too early, motivated by a fear of losing the investment: the innovator's dilemma (Latour 1998) of 'When he can he does not know how, when he knows how he no longer can'.

At the beginning everything is possible, nothing is fixed, the conception is still very open, but the innovator does not know what to choose. In the end the innovator has learned through experience and difficulties encountered. The innovator has, however, been obliged to make investment in for example, technical choice, hiring of personnel, patents, distributors, partners, which restrict possible future scope. During the development of add-ons, therefore Blueskye has delayed the taking irreversible choices, by offering its customers a computer engineering service in parallel to its products. Each consultation benefits Bluskye on two levels. First, it generates revenue. Second, it establishes field observations of recurrent customer problems. Having identified and formulated the problems, Bluesky package the solutions worked out during their service interventions in one or several software add-ons. Sure of their products, they can then sell with a much less risk.

Introduction of the notion of transitory state

There is ambiguity in this period of the firm which includes proliferation and focus: it is still of a technical nature, but it is already in commercial contact with the market. Customers are reacting to the idea that is being proposed, which they modify, break down, and question, but meanwhile, they also question their own needs. We see a prototyping of need throughout the elaboration of the product.

This contact with the customer – a marketing activity – comes into play when the product is not yet completely defined: it is a transitory state.

The transitory state is the incubation period during which the product is integrated into its environment. The firm proposes a provisional offer to chosen customers, but does not put the product in a catalogue. This allows the product to be modified at will before final packaging, allowing an entrepreneur to 'play for time' before defining the product.

It is a period of investment, during which all the elements of the offer are discussed with the customer; product, quality, price, service. This is easier said than done. Firms more easily invest in the development of the product, than in the development of price or service. Yet this is indispensable, because in most cases future users of high-tech products cannot themselves determine the advantage they will gain from using the product, neither knowing where adoption will lead him nor the service that will be needed.

In this period, the real advantage of undertaking operations with customers is in the accumulation of know-how. This in turn leads to the creation of a complete product, and not 'a device'. It is learned how to be in command of not only the product but also of the conditions leading it to be adopted by the customer. All the elements accompanying the product such as after sales service, price, service, payment conditions, distribution, storage, lead-times are determined.

This notion of investment is extremely important. Too many young companies fail because of haste, canvassing before the development phase of their product has been finished. While still in its transitory state, the product is already perceived as being '*the* money maker'. The work is rushed, done badly and, moreover, by being unfocused, the firm takes on more than can be handled.

Sometimes the entrepreneurs hire a sales representative in order to generate revenues quickly at this stage, which is usually counter productive. If the product still has teething problems, sales may not result, which discourages the representative, and causes criticisms from the customers not to be heeded by the entrepreneur. A negative spiral is reinforced when the scenario appears again with other customers. The salary of the sales representative nevertheless eats up the resources of the company.

The transitory state must be considered as being much more than an episode in the life of the company. It is a phenomenon called upon to renew itself each time the offer disrupts the market and the customer's values. This is in fact frequent in high-tech, where product life cycles are often short. The transitory state is like a creative breathing of the company, breathing in knowledge, breathing out product innovations.

Guaranteeing growth

Despite all the interest the proliferation/focus principle brings, it has a limit. Very often firms are not satisfied with focus on such a small number of segments. A plan can comprise the complete group of segments that will be penetrated. In what order, by doing what and with what means are important questions in young high-tech companies where technological obsolescence shortens the life of products. To avoid the life span of the company being the same as that of the product, it is necessary to think very early on of the markets and therefore of the future products.

The development of an innovative activity presents some guidelines. First, attack the market by the segments of least importance – the access segments – which are the intermediary marketing objectives. Second, capitalize on what has been acquired on the first segments to attack the biggest segments which are the real development objective. Third, firmly secure positions before attacking new segments. And overall, adjust our growth to our means and ambitions. These will now be considered in turn.

Set intermediary objectives

The first involves fixing the intermediary marketing objectives instead of charging immediately into the big attractive market that is the ultimate target. These are the market access segments or intermediary segments. In an intermediary segment, the commercial issues are relatively modest, but there is little short-term – technical and commercial – risk, and the size is appropriate to a small company. These first segments offer 'lines of least effort and resistance': firms go where success is easier to generate, so the chances of success are relatively high. This presents several advantages. First, an early success is psychologically encouraging. It leads to experiment in real dimensions, to progress with customers, to become more familiar with the market, and to discover the operating rules. It enables market learning without the risk of dramatic failure.

Capitalize on what has been acquired

The second rule is to capitalize on what has been acquired. In the access segments, experience is gained through contact with the first customers. Then the firm capitalizes on this know-how, to access other customers in the same segment. Commercial experience is acquired by testing out arguments and by observing customer reactions. This capital of competencies, experience, and references is built up. These market segments represent higher stakes for the company, and demand additional investment – technical and commercial – for entry. They are less forgiving of errors. Step by step, with the accumulation of experience, bigger and bigger market segments can be entered, and the firm can progressively be developed.

This strategy allows gradual entry of lesser markets by avoiding the worst risks involved: it is a prudent strategy of taking little steps at a time.

Firmly secure our positions

The third rule is firmly securing positions which means 'working' segments until all the problems have been completely resolved before investing in new areas. The more a segment is penetrated, and the better it is known, the better customers can be convinced, and the better margins will be. The aim is to take the highest share of the market segment as possible: gaining at least 30 per cent of a small segment known and in which there are strong capabilities, gives greater control in the long term. Taking two per cent of a large market is no security: it is at the mercy of competitors. The keystone of this strategy resides in the tight definition of the market segments.

The strategy of attacking segments one after the other has a final advantage. It allows better control of our growth, to adjust development to the means available. The greater the technical problems, the larger and wider the markets are, and the more severe the market is, the more substantial the investment must be. As Davidow (1986) notes, taking market share in a market where the competition is already implanted requires an investment equivalent to 70 per cent of the leader's turnover. Moreover, as the need in working capital is proportional to growth, it is in our interest to select segments in such a way as to be able to adjust them to our possibilities. Exponential growth is no better than an unsuccessful take-off if the finance or people to do it cannot be enlisted. On the other hand, growth that is adjusted to means allows self-financing of development. Behind this approach, there is a simple logic. We go first to markets where little is at stake and where there is little investment. Then we climb progressively to markets where there is more at stake and where there is a higher investment. By doing so progressively, as the money comes in, the development can be self-financed.

ESSENTIAL MESSAGES FOR HIGH-TECH ENTRPRENEURS

Overcoming uncertainty

The first message is that the adventure of high-tech is very uncertain, more than risky. A risk is a probability of not being able to overcome identified difficulties. In high-tech, we do not even know what we do not know: the only way to determine the difficulties is to go out to meet them. Managers of high-tech projects are disadvantaged to find that the more they work on them, the higher the risk becomes, whereas intuitively this should be the opposite. The problems should be determined if subsequently they are to be resolved.

Avoiding the two confusions

The second message is to be wary of the two frequent confusions which jeopardize the future of a high number of high-tech companies. The first is taking the technology – the principle – for the product. Customers do not buy the technology, but the product. The second confusion is mistaking the application – the technical problem to be resolved for the customer – for the market – the solvent demand. This leads us to delude ourselves as much on the nature and definition of the market as on its size.

These two types of confusion have a common cause which is the 'approximately', the 'roughly', and the 'it'll do!'. This is a widespread marketing sin whereby we guess rather than analyse what customers want. It is extremely difficult, even impossible, to guess what a customer feels from the point of view only of a supplier. The need is to study and analyse the psychology and the motivations of customers, in order to understand what could inspire them to adopt a high-tech product. Compaq succeeded not by heading off from the standpoint of the technologies that they were going to incorporate in their product, but by asking customers what they needed and what they did not already have (Canion 1989).

Construct the market

The third message is to construct the market. The marketing approach should aim to create the market, which implies two things. The first is to make the customers discover the applications of a product that they do not yet know, and its advantages. This they can only perceive if they change their way of viewing the problem. For example, we can make them become aware of the cost of a piece of equipment in relation to its entire life instead of its purchasing price. The second element of this construction consists in listing the strengths, players and uncertainties present. For example BioTech Organ should make the surgeons, the membrane manufacturers, the patients, the organs, the illnesses, the tests, the distribution circuits, the insurance companies, the hospitals, and competitors all concur.

Adopt the principle of proliferation/segmentation/focus

The first principle called proliferation/segmentation/focus consists of taking inspiration from the creativity of the market to open up the horizon of possibilities, then to concentrate our energy on some segments and to not scatter resources across many without ever reaching sufficient 'critical mass' in any to be successful. One key way is to attack segments is with the help of co-development partners that are most often pioneer customers in the market.

Progressively develop the firm's activities

The second principle is progressively to develop the firm's activities. This means attacking segments one after the other by firmly securing our positions before jumping onto the following segment. This step-by-step strategy allows us, through a judicial choice of the order of segments, to adjust our growth to our means and our experience.

Work in a 'transitional' state as long as possible

The last message calls for working 'transitionally' as long as the activity is not steady, i.e. that there are no regular sales of catalogue products to defined and identified customers. The 'transitory state' is this long period of 'running in' and of investment throughout which the technology and the need to become respectively a product and a market are mutually encountered and defined. This is the period during which the technicians are still in charge of the product to come, while this has already been offered to customers from whom we are waiting for feedback. In the transitory state, the supplier's and the customer's ideas are confused. The main preoccupation is to stabilize the definition of the complete project, of the customer's need and the commercialization conditions. By contrast, the central preoccupation of the permanent regime is to increase the level of sales, the image of leader of the company, and to negotiate the product definition.

In the case of high-tech, marketing – through analysis and though the central tool of segmentation – supports, justifies and formalizes the initial intuition of the inventor by giving him a visual representation of a shared common vision. Through information from the marketing process, the creator is in the position of being more confident in the decisions he takes because he is in full knowledge of the facts and of the consequences. Then, through the developmental marketing approach, the initial dream takes shape and is realized. It involves, however, a process of iteration, with doubts being repeatedly cast on the project.

Chapter 13

Creating competitive intelligence
Competing technologies come from anywhere

Gil Ayache

This chapter contributes a cultural perspective for entrepreneurs in innovative advanced technology sectors. It examines the particular characteristics of environmental scanning for their companies, and points out the conditions necessary for setting up a system of competitive intelligence. It describes an accessible method for setting up a minimum system of monitoring and intelligence. Finally, it proposes a more ambitious project of adopting a true management system of information resources.

Developing an advanced technology activity can be profitable and has the potential for long-term growth, but it also involves risk-taking and uncertainty: young high-tech companies rapidly face the all difficulties described in the preceding chapters. Customers also, are 'disturbed by producers' uncertainty, as well as by the complexity of the products and their rate of change' (Laban 1989). The problem is in focusing on the needs both of clients and users, even as new technologies often alter the customers' perceptions (Von Hippel 1989). It is the intangible factors which are important, but these require 'intimacy' with users (McKenna 1985). So the high-tech sector is as concerned by the uncertainty of the markets as with the technologies themselves (Moriarty and Kosnik 1989): the innovation process is a continuous one.

ENVIROMENTAL SCANNING FOR ADVANCED TECHNOLOGY COMPANIES

Greater openness towards technological scanning

High-tech companies can possess a culture which predisposes them to new information technology, to consulting patents and to scientific and technological scanning. But knowledge of their own markets and competitors often remains superficial. Given the higher uncertainty of their environment, the danger of being unable to anticipate development on all fronts threatens these companies' long-term survival. They need to acquire competitive intelligence.

Technological scanning requires strategic scanning

First, the practice of technological scanning needs to be properly understood, integrating all the necessary dimensions of the technologies, accounting for the continuous process of innovation, and identifying competing technologies. Technological scanning is often reduced to mere scientific and technical scanning, including monitoring norms and patents. This way of looking at things is too simple, and carries the risk of not capturing the true challenges of technological development.

This attitude comes from a lack of understanding of the technological dimension and its implications, as the first case example illustrates.

Case example: The misleading analogies of the development of wind technology

In a study of a strategy to develop wind power in France, the director in charge of renewable energies at EDF was asked why EDF had abandoned research and development of 1960s wind power prototypes. He gave a two-fold answer. First, a choice had been made for nuclear energy. Second, wind power had involved difficulties for the EDF, in that it was not their 'job': 'EDF has no competence in aeronautics'.

However, when one analyses the successes and failures of wind power worldwide, it is noticeable that none of the leading firms in the field – such as Vestas, Enercon, Tacke and Zond – come from the aeronautics sector. Moreover, attempts to develop wind power made by the sector's giants – for example Boeing, NASA-DOE, Aérospatiale and Ratier Figeac – have all ended in either failure or withdrawal. The answer to this apparent paradox is that 'Wind turbines are not airplanes' (Gipe 1995). A helicopter or a propeller airplane must work actively with high rotation speeds and intensive maintenance with high added value. A wind turbine has to turn passively, theoretically all the time – when there is enough wind – with a low rotation speed and minimum maintenance – Zond has four people to maintain the 343 wind turbines on its site at Sky River.

The contexts and objectives of setting up these techniques appear as key elements in defining the technology. So if the context and the objective are different, the technology is different: a technology remained to be developed for wind power. Developing this technology was exactly what a great number of firms were about to do. Their creators came from sectors as different as industrial electronics – Enercon – and metallic frameworks – Vestas. This example serves to guard against over-simplified views of technology. Morin (1985, 1992) views technology as the art of setting up, in a specific context and for a specific aim, all the science, techniques and rules which contribute to the achievement of an economic activity at each stage of this activity. It comprises the conception, industrialization, production, marketing, logistics, invoicing, after-sales service, as well as the associated functions of management and information. There were a number of implications of this view.

What are frequently referred to as a 'transfer of technologies' has only been a 'transport of techniques', which can result in failure when insufficient account is taken of the specific contexts and objectives of the parties involved (Morin 1992).

In the high-tech sector more than elsewhere, it is necessary to be in tune with the customer if we want to understand the context and the objectives of use (Moriarty and Kosnik 1989; Laban 1989). If these are not understood, products will remain mere technical objects (Millier 1989). New technologies, however, can profoundly modify the context of use and the perception of needs. A constant and reactive relationship with customers is needed, associating them with the process of execution (Von Hippel 1989). This interactive relationship is needed if the connection to customers is to make sense, because in innovative products the customers have no idea of what the company is capable of offering before the offer itself is formulated (Laban 1989).

So technological scanning is first and foremost a matter of contextual and strategic scanning.

Dominant design, technological breakthroughs and the survival of start-ups

Technological scanning therefore involves global and context-related scanning. This is truer when the context is one of uncertainty or change; such a context is typical of innovating sectors and advanced technology, as described by Utterback (1994):

> A pioneering firm gets the ball rolling with its initial product, a growing market begins to take shape around that product, and new competitors are inspired to enter and either expand the market further or take a chunk of it with their own product versions. At this embryonic stage, no firm has a 'lock' on the market. No one's product is really perfected. No single firm has mastered the processes of manufacturing, or achieved unassailable control of the distribution channels. Customers have not developed their own sense of the ideal product design or what they want in terms of features or functions. The market and the industry are in a fluid stage of development. Everyone – producers and customers – is learning as they move along. This environment is conducive to market entry by many firms as long as capital and technical barriers are not too high.
>
> (Utterback 1994)

209

As competition and experimentation intensifies, some options dominate and ultimately converge towards a dominant design. Utterback defines this as the design which finally 'wins the allegiance of the marketplace'. It is this design that competitors and innovators will have to adopt if they hope to survive. Few companies get beyond this stage. The competitive environment undergoes a radical transformation from being an environment where a large number of competitors develop original products, to being an environment with few companies which have adopted the same design.

The dominant design depends on several complex factors. First is the possession of assets, such as a distribution circuit, an image, a solid financial basis, or upstream or downstream integration. The IBM PC, for example, was far from being the most efficient product, but it was able to prevail in the market because of the confidence inspired by IBM and its financial and other capabilities.

Second, are the agreements concerning standardization between industrialists and public authorities, as is presently the case with high definition TV, or with the central role of MITI in Japan or with agencies such as NASA in the US.

Third, companies' strategies to capture the markets can mean linking up with the holders of peripheral assets. In the case of VCR recorders, once again, the least efficient standard was able to capture the consumer market because JVC concluded agreements for the reproduction of films in VHS standard, even though Sony's Betamax standard remained the reference for the professional market.

Fourth, communication between producers and users explains the success of the Danish wind power industry through the Danish Owners Association. This relationship contrasts with the difficulties encountered in the US, where the American Wind Energy Association remained dominated by constructers and developers (Gipe 1995).

Case example: EPCGlobal, a standard for radio frequency identification (RFID)

One of the obstacles to the development of RFID lies in the mutual in compatibility of the systems. If two companies do not have the same RFID supplier, their systems will not be able to communicate, which limits the applications to the limited circle of the company itself. Despite a few international standards in some specialized areas like the transport of animals, wider standardization is awaited. This limits the diffusion of these technologies, despite their huge potential.

In order to impose a dominant design with Electronic Production Code (EPC) definition standards, organizations which together make up about 100 companies in the world – EAN International and Uniform Code Council (UCC) – have formed a joint venture, EPC Global.

To accelerate this process, EPC Global have obtained technology from the research consortium which founded RFID – Auto-ID Center – and has taken an active role in founding Auto-ID. This is a federation of laboratories that will follow up the work of Auto-ID Center – MIT, University of Cambridge, University of Adelaide, Keio University, Fudan University, and University of St Gallen. They have set up standards within pilot projects in leading companies such as Wal-Mart, Gillette, Procter & Gamble, Tesco and Marks & Spencer. They are also involved the main software editors, such as SAP which integrated the EPC specifications in the Supply Chain module of its Enterprise Resource Planning (ERP). Similarly, Sun, PeopleSoft and Microsoft have joined EPCGlobal.

Strategies for young high-tech companies

A young company can be supported by superstructures – incubators, knowledge clusters etc. – as the international success of start-ups from Israeli incubators shows (Ayache and Rey 1999). In order to impose design, JC Technology Ltd, which accompanies start-ups in Jerusalem's Patir Research Centre incubator, gives prime importance to connecting with the best marketing, industrial property and industrial design specialists from the moment the innovation comes to light. This incubator actively helps companies to find strategic partners who are leaders in their markets, as did Visionnix with Essilor. As a shareholder in the companies, the incubator plays a central role in seeking financial partners for increasing their capital, and if required, for going public with a stockmarket quotation.

To impose a standard, Dalloz *et al.* (2000) recommend that high-tech start-ups operate through networks: it is the superstructure organization that creates value. A small company can increase its potential ten-fold by having virtual communities of partners.

While some competitors struggle to increase their competitiveness by improving their products and innovating in their manufacturing processes, they sometimes know nothing about the technological revolutions to come. Foster (1986) suggests thinking about technological discontinuities by introducing 'S' curves. He shows that all technology has a limited performance potential – tangible and intangible factors. The winning company can anticipate the moment when the potential progress of the technology has reached saturation. Utterback (1994) cites the principal stages of waves of innovation in the sector of writing: the mechanical typewriter with Remington, the electric typewriter with IBM, and finally the micro-computer. Although IBM managed to impose its design as dominant, the company missed the last transition by failing to invest in the key technologies – the 'brain' of the new product – because it took too long to recognize the potential of the operating system and microprocessor. In 2005, IBM sold its PC business to the Chinese company Lenovo.

Tushman and O'Reilly (1997) take up all these concepts. They show that the more complex the product, the more it can be decomposed into sub-systems, the greater the number of technologies involved. The source of lasting competitive advantage

211

lies in a strategy which covers all the patterns of innovation. Incremental innovation which improves existing technologies, architectural innovation reconfigures existing technologies, and technological discontinuities which reinvent products or the markets. Concurring with Hamel and Prahalad (1990), they recommend investment in key sub-components of products in order to bring about waves of innovation in each of these. Here it is vital for advanced technology companies to master the process of the dominant design, to undertake architectural innovations, initiate product substitutions and develop central components. Without these capacities, they have little chance of long-term survival, but to possess them, they need intelligence about all of the complex mechanisms which together contribute to a state of permanent competitiveness through innovation.

Combining differentiated and integrated scanning in innovative sectors

How can scanning be organized when so many parameters must be dealt with? One option is to investigate particular areas of information deemed priority, another is to look out for all information potentially necessary to the company. These ways are not mutually exclusive. Scanning should be neither enclosed within a strictly utilitarian field, nor be bogged down in information. It needs active interaction between the three key domains of knowledge in the company: the technologies, the markets and the procedures.

This view of scanning comes from one of the key explanations of the capacity to innovate (Dougherty 1997). First, it is necessary to integrate knowledge in marketing, in science and techniques and in operational procedures into projects or products. In this way all the company's resources can be mobilized in the innovation process. The three domains of knowledge must also, however, be differentiated by becoming autonomous. This will endanger the continual enrichment of the most highly specialized knowledge.

So the connections between integration and differentiation of knowledge cannot be established along linear paths; the connections involved are the result of a 'spiral' interconnection. Tatsuno (1990) explained the success of Japanese companies through the 'Mandala of creativity'. An initial spiral of creativity differentiates between each domain of the company. This is organized into five stages (see Figure 13.1). Sairiyo is the recycling of old ideas, tansaku is the exploring of new ideas, ikusei is the nurturing of creative ideas, hassoo is the generating of breakthroughs and kaizen is the refining of ideas.

Integration occurs through operational project management, which associates the different company functions of research and development (R&D), marketing and sales, industrialization and production (see Figure 13.2). This system conforms to the 'complex model' presented by Moreau in Chapter 9, and enables the deepening of knowledge also to involve broadening to include the different

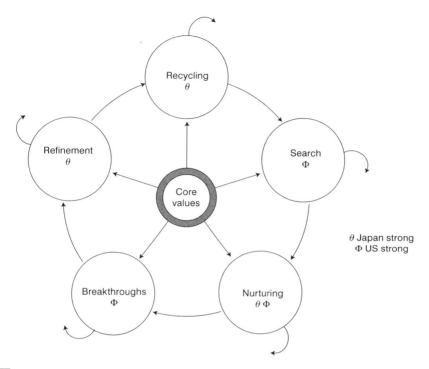

■ **Figure 13.1** *Building up knowledge through the 'Mandala of creativity' (Source: Tatsuno 1990)*

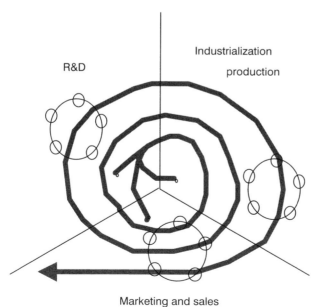

■ **Figure 13.2** *Integrating knowledge through a project (Source: Adapted from Tatsuno 1990)*

company functions. Scanning in innovative sectors must fulfil both of these roles through interaction. Scanning must therefore both organize information search around precise requirements – integrated scanning – and develop the autonomous search for information around each of the domains of knowledge – differentiated scanning. The interconnection of these two approaches avoids the pitfall of compartmentalizing scanning inside the company.

Nonaka and Takeuchi (1995) cite the example of how KAO resituated its business when the company reconsidered its analysis of its technological cores from the viewpoint of scientific knowledge – differentiated scanning – and not only from the viewpoint of products – integrated scanning. President Tokiwa explained that this way of doing things enabled the company to enlarge its field of possibilities. The company was able to give value to its competences on new and apparently unrelated markets – cosmetics, food, polymers, new materials, computer accessories (diskettes, etc.). From their standpoint, these were connected and thus constituted parts of the same business.

This approach results in two ways of conceiving of the organization of a system of search and monitoring for innovating companies. The first is oriented towards responding to precise questions arising from thinking about strategy. It organizes search and monitoring by carrying out projects around each strategic theme. The second aims at systematically treating information as a strategic resource of the company. Information is totally integrated into strategic management: the management of information resources. This is what we will explore in sections three and four, but asking first about the conditions for minimum success in setting up competitive intelligence.

KEY FACTORS FOR SUCCESS IN COMPETITIVE INTELLIGENCE

Broadening the strategic vision

In order to gain vision, we must first of all broaden the field of strategic analysis. Most company information systems focalize on sector leaders – portfolio analysis – or on the best performers in the class – benchmarking. In the long term, these strategies do not work because they are simplistic. It results in following the leader and tagging the best in the class, strategies which limit the company's ambition to merely improving its competitive position. Newcomers, instead, revolutionize the sector and challenge the giants.

Modern strategic thought requires a completely different approach, achieved by changing the ground rules imposed by the leaders (Ohmae 1991). The idea is to rewrite the rules of the sector in order to create a new competitive space. This requires improved integration of breakthroughs, as well as seeking every opportunity to get the most value from central competences (Morin 1985; Hamel and Prahalad

1994). Broadening the company's field of vision is needed, and this can be done in three stages.

Rethinking the company's business

A first stage is to rethink the company's business. Companies often suffer from tunnel vision which reduces the field of future possibilities. Strategic choices may be diametrically opposed depending on whether the field of vision is wide or narrow. For example, in 1984 Sikorsky decided to enlarge its business by integrating the central competence of composites. The company president William F. Paul declared 'We see composites as one of the main strengths of Sikorsky Aircraft. The way to enhance that strength is to sell it' (quoted in *Business Week* 1984). At the same time, Eurocopter decided to concentrate on its core business by externalizing the composite competence to sub-contractors.

The small French company, Zodiac, specialized in the construction of inflatable boats. It became one of the main suppliers of equipment for world aeronautics, and the world leader in inflatable swimming pools and inflatable craft. This was made possible because of the company's open-ended and evolutionary vision of its business. Zodiac 'branched out', enriching its technological capital through a policy of reasoned acquisitions of new activities with affinities to the business.

The key functions approach

Once the business has opened up its horizons, it is necessary to make sure that company personnel are not technologically short-sighted: their specialized culture could also limit the field of possibilities.

The original domain of the German manufacturer of wind turbines, Tacke, was manufacturing mechanical gear boxes, conceived its wind turbines around its core business, the gear box. Its competitor, Enercon, whose background was in electronics and regulation, preferred to get rid of this mechanical core. It was able to do this by introducing an innovation: a gearless turbine made of a variable speed annular generator directly connected to the blades. This increased the added value for the company and improved performance for the customer – for example better productivity, more hard-wearing, and no noisy gearbox.

This example illustrates the risk of being caught in the 'rigidity trap' described by Dibiaggio in Chapter 3. To minimize this risk, it is better to take a functional approach. Ohmae (1991) recommends concentrating on the objective functions of the user. Using this basis, a useful investigative tool is the hierarchical functional decomposition described by Dibiaggio in Chapter 3.

This method focuses on the functions really expected by the user – rather than by key technologies. It implies the active search for and evaluation of the whole set of technologies, as well as their combination, in order to achieve the sought after

215

functionality in the best possible way (Galant *et al.* 1997). In the food industry, for example, the function produced 'supplying consumers with pleasurable taste' can be achieved through regulating by taste, texture, or temperature. This involves combining the technologies of fermentation, of neuronal networks, of taste modelling, all correlated with the parameters of command, which constitutes an innovative breakthrough.

Stimulate the company culture through foresight

The risk of short-sightedness from technical specialization, and the lack of openness to the environment or restricted vision of the business, is even greater for companies in innovating sectors. This is because the choices of technology are numerous and often mutually exclusive, the environment is unstable and the business will certainly change. The short-sighted company might then pass up potentials for growth in un-thought-of fields of application; it will not be able to impose a dominant design on the market.

Now market and value studies reach their limits: the market does not know what it wants, and engineers do not always have a product to optimize. Foresight is required, and mobilization of suitable technological resources onto more traditional methods (Seurat 1994). It combines constants, heavy trends, emerging trends, and potential breakthroughs concerning the evolution of the environment. Watch must be kept on various interdependent factors that may hold the keys to the future, be they technological, economic, sociological, competitive, legal, political, or strategic.

Foresight therefore means constructing possible futures on the basis of these interdependences. These possible futures will give us a better understanding of the environment and its evolution as well as of possible turning points. Foresight is the pedagogical tool of reference for a culture of competitive intelligence in a turbulent environment.

Making connections with signals

Once a company's vision has been broadened, the information must be deciphered and given meaning. The true challenge of successful scanning is to have the words and signs with which to understand what is being looked at, in order that their implications can be seized. The relationship between the environment being scanned, and the company seeking meaning, can only be achieved through the mediation of an expert who has the words and the knowledge necessary to decode the information. Otherwise, signals are just so much 'smoke', like that observed by the lay spectator at a rocket launch, compared to what is seen by a specialist in propulsion only. The latter fully understands the significance of information about the temperature, the kinetics of gas, the shape of the tailpipe outlets, etc. (Morin 1995).

Guilhou (2000) distinguishes strong signals from weak signals in terms of strategic challenge. Strong signals are those which we know nothing about, but whose characteristics and intention may at any moment perturb or compromise our mission. The directors of a company must concentrate all their energy on this type of signal, which should result in strategic decision-making. Weak signals are those about which everything is known, where there is enough control, and there is a permanent capacity to intervene. This type of decision is the responsibility of the conventional company organization, and should result in tactical decision-making.

The earlier that strong signals, and their meaning, are detected, the more a company can anticipate. These signals are often not visible (see Figure 13.3). The challenge of competitive intelligence is to make information and knowledge available so that decisions can be taken at a very early stage in the decision-making process.

Seurat (1994) cites two examples of strong signal convergence to explain two eventful innovations of the past 20 years. These examples are in the watch making industry with Swatch, and in the automobile industry with Matra Automobile's Espace.

For Swatch, the meaningful signals came in the form of the relatively lukewarm attitude of consumers towards watches laden with technological gadgets and increasing numbers of functions, the growing hostility towards digital display, and the possibilities offered by plastics and robotics. For the Espace, the signals were the success of vans in the US, the return of family and convivial values in Europe, an

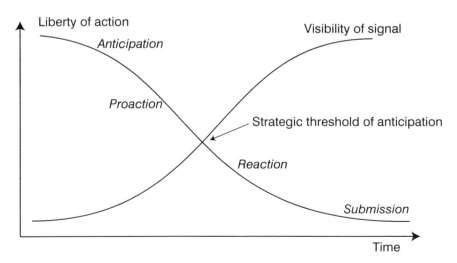

Figure 13.3 The strategic threshold of anticipation (Source: SRI, cited by Morin)

increasing demand for estate cars and increasing possibilities for using composites with manufacture and assembly speed advantages.

In both cases it was a matter of being ready to see and interpret meaningful weak signals (Morin 1995). This requires building up networks of experts in each of the fields of observation, and focusing on the critical factors to monitor. These emerge from the enlarged strategic reflection which defines the most important themes (see Figure 13.4) and incorporates the challenges of scanning. In the final analysis, the process of competitive intelligence is the responsibility of the director in charge of strategy.

Integrating competitive intelligence into the strategic process

De Boisanger (1987) pointed out that if

> Intelligence demonstrates the double necessity of knowing and under-standing, the information must not remain an intellectual exercise, which although certainly gratifying, serves no practical purpose: it is only justified when it leads to action: from knowing to understanding to acting. This sequence takes us from the point of recognizing information, through to its exploitation through action.

If the most is to be made of practising competitive intelligence, whose aim is to transform information into full understanding of its implications, knowledge management and technological resources management complete the strategic process, by leading to decision-making and strategic action, as shown in Figure 13.5.

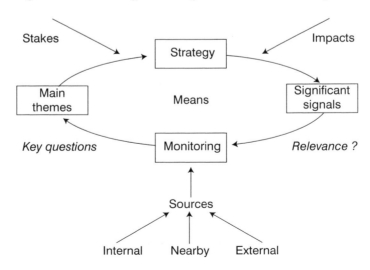

Figure 13.4 A process as part of the strategy (Source: Morin 1993)

The continuum described incorporates the first two dimensions of structuring young companies discussed by Bernasconi in Chapter 11: cognitive knowledge and transition to action. It remains to set up the third dimension which is the structuring of the scanning system.

SETTING UP A MINIMUM SYSTEM OF INTEGRATED SCANNING

A four-phase process of information and surveillance

The system of information and surveillance can be organized around a cyclical process in four phases. The first is planning and management for the targeting of needs. The second is collection for raw information gathering. The third is analysis for processing and analysing the information. The fourth is dissemination for diffusing and using the information. This basic process was presented in a pioneering article by Seurat (1986), then by Seurat and Rougeaux (1990, 1991), then further developed by Kahaner (1996).

Quality experts will recognize Deming's wheel, the 'PDCA' cycle with its four phases (– plan, do, check, act –) applied to product information. Here, the basic economic intelligence process is placed within a quality procedure. The activity is in itself a 'process of learning by doing, by using and by learning' which permits enrichment and collective codification (see Chapter 3). This phase is crucial in the transitory state described by Millier in Chapter 12. The process of continuous learning then becomes a support for company creation seen as an evolving project, as Bernasconi proposes in Chapter 11.

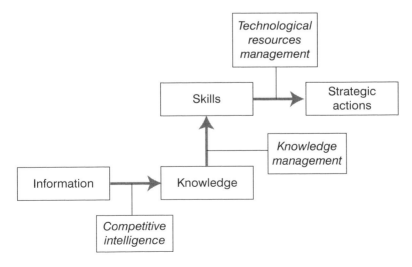

Figure 13.5 *From competitive intelligence to technological resources management*

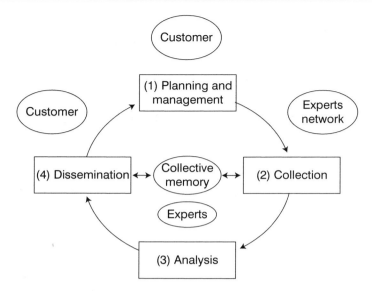

Figure 13.6 *The basic process of competitive intelligence (Source: Derived from Seurat 1987 and Rougeaux 1990)*

The first phase: planning and management

The first 'planning and management' phase is of crucial importance, for this imposes limits on the uncertainty and even the ambiguity highlighted throughout this book. This phase must specify the questions asked by the internal 'client' and the strategic objectives sought, in other words, the use to be made of the information. As Ohmae (1991) notes, 'We cannot overstress the importance of the right formulation of the key questions to be studied'.

A question is only valid if it is relevant to its context and its aim. This implies identifying the critical factors to monitor, those which are meaningful, and those which are pertinent, which will answer the right questions (Dou 1997). In Chapter 14, Jolly develops 32 criteria within technological themes.

The second phase: 'collection'

This organizes the information gathering plan, and structures start up scanners into a network of gate keepers. This phase consists of listing privileged information sources – both internal and external – which will impart knowledge about critical factors, and provide answers to key questions. Here, as Millier suggests in Chapter 12, key early customers can be recruited to help this process. So both internal and external experts situated at the nodes of information flows should be progressively organized into gate keeper networks which must be maintained and consolidated.

The third phase 'analysis'

The third phase, 'Analysis', involves acquiring, validating and processing information to answer the questions asked. This phase represents the cognitive capacity of the start-up, and presents the opportunity to refine or even to reformulate the key questions.

The fourth phase 'dissemination'

'Dissemination' is part of the quality process: it is a question of 'diffusing the information, that is to say, making sure that the entire structure participates in the movement towards openness' (Seurat 1986). In the start-up, dissemination constitutes the completion of its 'nervous system'. The return of information to the gate keeping network must not be forgotten. This ensures that the network is enriched and consolidated according to the formula of 'get information, give information'.

Constructing the collective memory

At the heart of this arrangement is the process of capitalizing on competitive intelligence, through a 'collective memory' established in a document system. However, beyond these traditional surveillance files, it is necessary to decompose information into separate elements to enrich the whole set of memory zones (Besson and Possin 1997). The task of recomposing in order to link the information gathered in this way constitutes the memory of the company. This process is necessarily the work of a team within the company, so undertaking it has the benefit of connecting the company with its environment.

MANAGING INFORMATION RESOURCES

Beyond this organizational process, we suggest that a framework of systematic strategic management of information and of information sources is set up. This will be the construction of a collective memory.

The three logistics functions

Morin (1985) proposed assimilating technological resources management (TRM) to asset management with six key functions, inventory, evaluation, surveillance, enrichment, safeguard and optimization. Similarly, we suggest that the information resources management (IRM) is set up using these same functions, which are needed for organizing access to information.

Inventory

The utility of information for the company depends on the extent to which it questions the strategy which has been followed. This establishes the basis of a first inventory: that of information necessary for the development of the young company. This work should be done in parallel with vital strategic thinking by the directors.

This inventory will try to identify internal or other accessible sources of information which are often ill-known and under-exploited. In order to do this, 'who knows what' needs to be continually reviewed, and targeted on precise questions. This is particularly true for young companies where each associate and partner has a potential network which needs to be activated.

Evaluation

In high-tech sectors, information and its sources can rapidly become over-abundant. This means that care must be taken as to the relevance, interest and quality of information sources, and of the information gathered. Access to strategically valuable information in appropriate time, cost and confidentiality can constitute a considerable competitive advantage, even more for young companies than for mature ones.

Surveillance

The surveillance function is a reminder that competitive intelligence requires a permanent state of alert. As mentioned before, setting up a vigilance network which mobilizes experts to permanently survey critical factors, is a fundamental part of the structuring of a young high-tech company. This network should be lastingly associated with virtual communities of partners.

The three strategic functions

These functions are strategic because they address the issue of allocating resource priorities in the company.

Enrichment function

The young company faces a double imperative. It needs to be sufficiently proactive, being able to respond to the meaningful weak signals. It also needs to be able to use the accumulated information in order to get maximum benefit, by processing the information in the best way. It needs to acquire and then to enrich the capacity to decode the signals. This will lead to the necessary enrichment of intangible capital, to ensure an effective gate keeper function. This function can include: training, partnership with a university, purchase of a service from information brokers that integrate the transfer of know-how, recruitment of personnel with multi-expertise, and internal development. To get the most out of this information, it is necessary to achieve 'intelligence between dispersed elements of information' (Besson and Possin 1998). To do this, the young company team should be qualified in models of strategic information processing. It will then be able to acquire the indispensable capacity of collective codification.

The safeguard function

The safeguard function mainly concerns conserving expertise and making knowledge explicit. In young companies, where expertise remains mobile, the codification of expertise is often only considered to be of secondary importance. This questions the degree of confidentiality necessary at all stages of the economic intelligence process. In young companies, where collaborators have easy access to information vital to the company, a policy of secrecy and suspicion can easily lead to creativity being stifled.

The optimization function

At this stage, a major question remains unanswered. Information obtained through the competitive intelligence process responds to objective demands on the part of the company, a process of information pull.

But there are other sources of information which could hold competitive improvements and development opportunities for the company, and these should be acted on. Over and above the competitive intelligence process, information for its own sake should play a role in the company's development. This is through a system of differentiated scanning, involving information push.

In high-tech companies, personnel should be kept informed of priority themes. This will provoke them to undertake research in their specialized area, and encourage them to give meaning to information flows in order to alert decision-makers inside the company. Besson and Possin (1997) recommend decomposing and fragmenting raw information from integrated information scanning to feed a series of memory files. This, in turn creates new themes for differentiated scanning and new links. Nonaka and Takeuchi (1995), for example, propose a hypertext like structure, which enables relationships to be made between integrated and differentiated knowledge.

CONCLUSION

Mastering information has become a major challenge of strategy. This challenge is even more pronounced for innovating companies, and is vital for high-tech companies. Castells (1985) sees a key characteristic of high-tech companies is that their principal object is information:

> What computers do is process, and finally produce information. What telecoms do is transmit information with growing complexity. What a new media does is diffuse information. What a robot does is use pre-formatted information for another activity. What genetic engineering does is decode the information system of a living being to try to programme it.

For innovating companies in advanced technology, setting up a system of competitive intelligence holds a supplementary advantage. It makes it possible to learn about how to develop an organisational form which is particularly adapted to this type of company. Their turbulent environment is such that as Fréry (1998) notes:

> ... strategies dominated by costs become shorter and shorter term, more and more random and are succeeded by an almost uninterrupted succession of breakthroughs and differentiation ... a hypercompetitive environment. A transactional company – one which rests on a network of partnerships linked by a series of recurrent transactions – is thus a structural configuration which is continually adaptable. In this case, the transactional company, through its inevitable changes, uncertainties and discontinuities, is the best placed to ensure the pertinence of the strategy.
>
> (Fréry: 1998: 61–84)

Finally, a scanning network such as we suggest, which shares a common culture of both foresight and extended vision, can play a central role in the management of permanent transformation (Laszlo and Laugel 1998) which is necessary for high-tech companies throughout their lives. This will also enable us to resolve the paradox for the researcher, who, by definition, knows his problem, but that is all he knows.

The functional approach enables us to think continuously about new outlets, key technologies in competition, substitute products, etc. However, such an approach requires a great effort from companies which are generally fragile financially speaking, and which have to concentrate their efforts on production and clients. Benchmarking and reengineering could be useful to optimize these procedures.

Sub-contracting part of the scanning activity – databases, Internet, and consultancy – to third parties does, however, involve the problem of interpretation and financing. We prefer to organize a 'partnership scan', which is more in keeping with the transactional model which must be developed by high-tech companies.

Chapter 14

Evaluating technology development projects

A multiplexity of controllability and uncontrollability

Dominique Jolly

At its early stages of development, any young innovative company faces a collection of investment opportunities into different technology projects. There is seldom only one track, only one technical solution; choices have to be made. After a few years, once a few projects have started, again the start-up has to make choices. These decisions are sensitive issues because companies face uncertainty in estimating future research avenues as well as future outcomes, and this is especially true for young innovative companies.

From an operational perspective, this means allocating resources – such as capital, people, physical facilities, equipment – through an array of significantly different technology investment opportunities or existing programmes. Questions include: Which programmes should be slowed down, scaled back, or even cut off?, Which should be sustained, expanded, or boosted?, and which new projects should be launched? This is about screening, prioritizing and selecting projects to be funded and determining the level of funding for each project chosen, under the constraints of limited funding, needing to achieve a sound portfolio, and alignment with corporate strategy.

In allocating resources across an array of significantly different investment opportunities or existing technology programs, there is internal competition for limited resources. There may be an intuitive process, depending upon unexpected opportunities. An un-formalized approach to technology management, however, puts the decision-maker under strong pressures from various interest groups. It exacerbates personality based as well as individual and emotional preferences. In order to formalize and to systematize this decision process, technology portfolio models were designed in the 1980s. Seminal approaches to technology portfolio modelling should be attributed to Foster (1981) or Harris *et al.* (1981). Although other approaches were developed during the 1980s and 1990s, managers seem not to use them (Cooper *et al.* 1998; Henriksen and Traynor 1999), perhaps because of their drawbacks. Much has been written on evaluation models, but very little work on the criteria and measures for technology auditing under a high level of uncertainty.

This chapter offers an entrepreneurial business framework for auditing technology development projects. This is it useful for many reasons. First, young innovative companies are often launched by people educated and trained in engineering or science rather than in management techniques. This chapter adopts a practical focus for helping them to implement a technology audit, allowing entrepreneurs of high-tech start-ups to channel their expertise. Second, the method presented here takes into account the unstable and unpredictable conditions and environmental uncertainty faced by high-tech start-ups. This is done by distinguishing different external dimensions: market, competition, techniques and other aspects of their environment, each captured with a set of criteria encompassing several aspects. The method also pays attention as well to uncertainty related to internal resources, skills and competences, by distinguishing technological and complementary resources. It tries to track several indeterminate dimensions such as the market reaction to the company design.

The first section defines technology and casts a light on the existing models for auditing technology. This shows the limited interest devoted in the literature to the design of auditing criteria and proper measurement techniques. The second section suggests that there are two distinct sets of criteria for auditing technology: those that relate to the potential – the appeal or attractiveness of a specific technology; and those related to one given firm set of competencies for the technology under study. Two sets of 16 criteria are presented, in which the second incorporates many more controllable factors than the first. The third section demonstrates the use of the method proposed in one small–medium sized high-tech company. The attractiveness and competitiveness of each technology of its portfolio are technologically evaluated, based on four company's project managers' views. The last section concludes with an emphasis on practical issues when implementing a technology audit.

EXISTING MODELS FOR AUDITING TECHNOLOGY

The audit process is usually organized along four steps. First, a complete list is drawn of the various technologies incorporated – or to be incorporated – by the firm in its product, processes, information and management systems. Second, the attractiveness of each technology is assessed, i.e. its importance for value creation. Third, the degree to which each technology is under the control of the company is assessed – the value accumulated into the start-up. Fourth, a map of each technology along two axes is plotted. Technology audit is useful for internal purposes, in defining where research and development (R&D) efforts should be directed and organized, as well as for external strategies, such as looking at potential licensing, forming alliances, and targeting acquisitions. This section starts with a definition of the concept of technology and follows with an examination of the shortcomings of different models for auditing technology.

What do we mean by technology?

Three elements delineate the concept of technology: the sources, the purpose and the fields of application. Technology is defined as any original and protected combination of scientific knowledge, technical knowledge and know-how, mastered by one firm – or a reduced set of companies – which is incorporated into a product, a service, a production process, an information system or even a management method, in order to serve economic purposes (Jolly and Thérin 1996). Figure 14.1 shows knowledge roots – science and technical knowledge – at the bottom, and know-how on the left. Areas of application are described like branches of a tree at the top of the drawing. It is important to stress that scientific and technical knowledge is, most of the time, developed in public bodies with a social purpose, while technologies are usually developed for economic purposes by private companies.

A frequent confusion, especially in the literature on new product development, is made between products and technologies. Several authors fail to recognize that technologies already exist before they embodied or manifested into products, materials, equipments, processes, or services. Technologies to be analysed include current technology development projects that a start-up might undertake – which will be embodied later in a future commercial offer – as well as the technologies that support current products and processes.

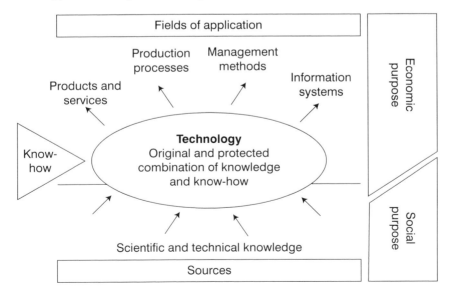

Figure 14.1 *Definition of technology*

Another confusion is between technology and technique. The use of the word 'technology' will be restricted to proprietary knowledge. The word 'technique' will be used for old technologies that finally became public. Managers should be sure that the technologies under study are not widely available to all in the industry. Finally, any audit should take into account that technologies differ according to their degree of innovativeness – radical versus incremental – compared to other technologies.

Feeding the decision process

The decision is served with an evaluation of the alternative projects, and an identification of independencies and interrelationships amongst projects. Different evaluation methods have been developed. Heidenberger and Stummer (1999) have identified six different approaches: benefit measurement, mathematical programming, decision and game theory, simulation, heuristics, and cognitive. Poh *et al.*'s (2001) comparison of different methods – based on weightings and ranking or on benefit-contribution – with an Analytic Hierarchy Process (AHP) shows that the scoring method – used for R&D project selection since the 1960s – is the most favourable method for R&D project evaluation.

Evaluation of alternative projects is not enough. Several authors have stressed that most conventional models evaluate individual projects in isolation, focusing on individual opportunities. They don't capture interdependencies when projects are highly coupled, where the success of A depends on the success of B and interrelationships between projects, such as mutual exclusion or overlap in resources utilization, which allow positive synergies (Stummer and Heidenberger 2003). Ouellet and Martel (1995) have proposed that synergies between projects are measured at three levels: in the use of resources, in technology and in payoffs. Dickinson *et al.* (2001) have suggested a – square – dependency matrix to capture interdependencies between projects.

Shortcomings of existing evaluation models

A number of shortcomings have been noted. The concept under study is not always clear. While many authors tend to focus on 'technology attractiveness' or 'technology value', many do not precisely define what they are looking at. Most of the models mix internal with external criteria, and controllable with non-controllable factors (see for example, Linton *et al.* 2002).

Many models are derived from financial analysis (see Spradlin and Kutoloski 1999; Kirchhoff *et al.* 2001). More sophisticated versions incorporate probabilities and uncertainties into the financial calculation. The objective is to maximize the potential return per unit of risk (Carter and Edwards 2001). Although financial measurements appear to be very clear-cut and elegant, they are very often based on highly subjective judgements with wide variance. Consequently, by focusing on financial and/or economic returns, these metrics fail to deal with non-monetary criteria. This is especially true if the project is in its early phase, where uncertainty is high, which makes this approach poorly fitted to young innovative companies.

Some authors (such as Yoon *et al.* 2002) suggest using patent statistics as a tool for decision-making at the micro-level – not only at the level of national technological capacity, as widely used by economists. Bibliometrics are used to identify potential research areas, to assess technological competitiveness and to set up priority in R&D investment. These techniques may be very useful, but unfortunately are too focused in their approach, because patent statistics considerably restrict the analysis.

Most of the models rely on a narrow set of criteria, or pay limited attention to the justification of the choice of criteria. Three variables were used by Ringuest *et al.* (1999) and later by Graves *et al.* (2000); four were used by Balachandra (2001); five by Dickinson *et al.* (2001); and six by Stummer and Heidenberger (2003). Ouellet and Martel (1995) use a more extensive list of 19 different criteria organized into three families – interdependencies, intrinsic value and risk.

Finally, some comparative models develop a sophisticated mathematical programming, but fail to input reliable data. A survey conducted by Cooper *et al.* (2000) highlighted a need for better information to feed the process of portfolio management.

So, in summary, existing models suffer from confusion between controllable and non-controllable factors, from excessively focused definition of variables – often financial or patent focused – and over-narrow set of indicators. Because of these limits, an effort was carried to draw an extensive list of criteria for technology auditing.

CRITERIA FOR ANALYSIS

We now suggest two sets of 16 criteria for evaluating technology attractiveness and technology competitiveness. These lists originated from literature review, experience, and several workshops conducted with managers involved in executive training.

Two distinct sets: controllable and non-controllable criteria

The dichotomy between controllable and non-controllable criteria is widespread in the management literature. It can be found in the field of strategy with the SWOT framework. The strengths and weaknesses of the company depend on its internal resources; the firm is free to adopt the behaviour it wants regarding these internal resources that are supposed to be under its control. Opportunities and threats depend mostly on what is happening in the environment. Firms have little impact on external elements such as the actions of competitors, suppliers and regulators or the choices made by customers, these are mostly non-controllable factors. Well known portfolio techniques used by strategists – BCG matrix, General Electric/McKinsey matrix, ADL matrix – are also all based on a two-dimension framework. These models are based on the same foundations: they differentiate between the sector attractiveness and the SBU position in its sector. The first dimension is mostly given and not under control while the second is supposed to be under the control of the firm.

In technology audit, some authors implicitly distinguish between controllable and non-controllable variables. Harris *et al.* (1981) refer to 'relative technology position' – which describes clearly controllable factors, such as patent position or key talents, and 'technology importance for competitive advantage', i.e. a dimension that can be traced back to factors such as the potential value added or the position in the life cycle – which are mostly given. Sethi *et al.* (1985) plot a technology on two dimensions: its 'technology importance' – in terms of value added, rate of change, potential market – and the 'corporate strengths regarding the technology and relative to its competitors' – in terms of patent, human resource strengths, technology expenditures.

Capon and Glazer (1987) also suggested establishing technology portfolios along two dimensions. First is the 'time' from technology inception to decline. It incorporates both technology and product life cycles by distinguishing pre and post market phases of technology exploitation. Second is the 'technology competitive position' of the firm. Brockhoff (1992) and later Ernst (1998) use two dimensions to draw patent applications: 'technology attractiveness' – as the growth rate of patent applications – and relative patent position for 'company's competitiveness'. The approach depicts external and internal features using objective, but narrow measurements. Hsuan (2001) has suggested mapping a given technology along the 'benefit provided to customers' and the 'competitive advantage', which allows portraying external vis-à-vis internal features.

In summary, there are things that are mainly under the firm's control, assets that depend on the firm's behaviour and decisions; these will be referred to as 'the company's technological competitiveness'. Criteria for auditing a firm's competitive position on a given technology express internal factors that are within the firm's control. So, on this axis, the position of a given company could be very different from the position of another.

There are other things that do not depend on the firm's actions, which are beyond its control: these will be referred to as the 'the attractiveness of the technology'. Criteria used for attractiveness of a given technology are important for value creation. These criteria refer mainly to external features that are idiosyncratic to the technology. They are intrinsically related to the technology and are beyond the control of the firm. This means that technological attractiveness is identical for all companies competing in this technology.

Evaluating technological attractiveness

The attractiveness of a technology is a function of many different factors; 16 criteria for depicting 'technological attractiveness' are given in Table 14.1. Semantic differential scales are given on the right for each criterion; they were co-constructed in the process of an executive seminar. It is possible to distinguish between four families: market, competition, technical factors and socio-political criteria.

Market volume opened by technology, and market sensitivity to technical factors are key drivers when it comes to making decisions about technology. Bond and Houston (2003) have stressed that it is essential to link technologies to the market. Factors in this category should express the expected commercial reward that can be gained from a given technology. Relying on the resource-based framework (Prahalad 1993), technological attractiveness should also emphasize the span of new applications, new functions and/or new customer segments that the technology opens, and its impact on the company's performance. Market attractiveness will be more or less easy to estimate, depending on its newness. Existing markets are relatively easy to estimate. But it is much more difficult to evaluate potential when the market is entirely new: there is much more uncertainty and many more unknowns about the potential uses or the size of the market.

Competition is a strong driver of technological development. Relying on competition analysis, as depicted by Porter (1980), criteria for evaluating technological attractiveness should emphasize the increase/decrease in competitors, the competitors' level of involvement, the competitive intensity, and the barriers to copying or imitation. Also very important is the impact of technology on competitive issues (Khalil 2000). The dimensions on which firms are competing are not so important – such as cost, quality, speed of development, speed of delivery, and performance. What is important is the contribution of technology to the building of a competitive edge. Relying on the work of Abernathy and Utterback (1978), and later of Utterback (1994), the absence or the existence of a dominant design – or de facto standard – either will or will not sustain technological attractiveness.

In situations of high-tech start-ups working at early stages of innovating, when technologies are radically new, rules still need to be written. This is why it is essential to include an evaluation criterion such as the dominant design in the analysis. This is because, in nascent businesses, competitive uncertainty arises from the existence of multiple standards. Firms compete to transform their own standard into a de facto standard.

Technical criteria rely on the work of Foster (1986), on the technology life-cycle and on the threat of substitution technologies. In the same vein, the concept of 'reserve for progress' has been studied by many authors (see Van Wyk *et al.* 1991). Technical criteria also include the performance gap vis-à-vis alternative technologies. This gap is limited in the case of an incremental innovation or significant in the case of a radical innovation, but a technology will always have to find its way in a

Table 14.1 *Evaluating technological attractiveness*

Environmental factors over which the company has a weak control		Weak attractiveness		High attractiveness
Market factors	Market volume opened by technology	low	☐☐☐☐☐☐	high
	Span of applications opened by technology	narrow	☐☐☐☐☐☐	wide
	Market sensitivity to technical factors	weak	☐☐☐☐☐☐	strong
	Number of competitors	decreasing	☐☐☐☐☐☐	increasing
	Competitors' level of involvement	high	☐☐☐☐☐☐	low
Competition factors	Competitive intensity	strong	☐☐☐☐☐☐	weak
	Impact of technology on competitive issues	low	☐☐☐☐☐☐	high
	Barriers to copy or imitation	low	☐☐☐☐☐☐	high
	Dominant design	exist	☐☐☐☐☐☐	don't exist
	Position of the technology in its own life-cycle	declining	☐☐☐☐☐☐	emerging
	Potential for progress	low	☐☐☐☐☐☐	high
Technical factors	Performance gap *vis-à-vis* alternative technologies	narrow	☐☐☐☐☐☐	wide
	Threat of substitution technologies	high	☐☐☐☐☐☐	low
	Potential for unit-to-unit transfers	difficult	☐☐☐☐☐☐	easy
Socio-political criteria	Societal stakes	threatening	☐☐☐☐☐☐	supportive
	Public support for development	spartan	☐☐☐☐☐☐	generous

Source: Jolly 2003

competitive world. A gap must be created to overcome barriers, or technological change might be difficult to implement. Finally, another technical criteria is the ability to implement horizontal transfers.

Evaluating technological attractiveness also calls for an examination of the negative by-products and societal pressures that can arise from the exploration of entirely new technical fields. Some major societal issues can arise from new technologies; the problem is that societal pressures might impede the development of the business. The financial support obtainable from public sources for some technologies, such as biotech and nanotechnologies, also needs to be taken into account.

Evaluating technological competitiveness

The criteria for evaluating a company's position on one specific technology should be broadly based. A list of 16 criteria for depicting 'technological competitiveness' is given in Table 14.2. Once again, semantic differential scales are given on the right for each criterion. Criteria can be grouped into two families. Some relate to the technical capabilities of the company, i.e. to the technological resources within its control. Others relate to complementary resources which are also within its control.

The evaluation of technological resources should take into account the origin of the assets. This relates to whether there is a dependence of the firm vis-à-vis external suppliers – such as another company, or a public research centre – or a total independence of the company. The relatedness to the core business is another important factor. This is the distance, the alignment, or the potential contribution of the technology to the firm's core competencies, as stressed by Coombs (1996), who relies again on the resource-based framework (Hamel and Prahalad 1990; Prahalad 1993). The hypothesis is that the closer the alignment between one technology and one core competence, the higher the R&D support should be. This argument coincides with the current trend of the resource-based theory (Jolly 2000), which is to refocus on core competencies rather than expand in several unrelated directions. The proprietariness captures the patents owned by the firm, and the protection issue, as analysed by Teece (1986) and Ernst (1998).

Other technical criteria include the firm's accumulated experience and familiarity in one given technological field, as well as the value of its labs and equipment, and the expertise of R&D staff, as stressed by Roussel et al. (1991). Development is known to be the most expensive when compared to research whether 'applied' or 'fundamental'. As such, the competencies of development teams are crucial for the success of the program. The last technical criterion – the diffusion of technological knowledge in the company – stems from the strong emphasis given over the last 10 or 15 years on the value of lateral transfer, through sharing knowledge within

Table 14.2 Evaluating technological competitiveness

Internal factors over which the company can exert a strong control		Weak position						Strong position
	Origin of the assets	external	☐	☐	☐	☐	☐	internal
	Relatedness to the core business	unrelated	☐	☐	☐	☐	☐	related
	Experience accumulated in the field	no experience	☐	☐	☐	☐	☐	world-class player
	Registered patents	none	☐	☐	☐	☐	☐	many
Technological resources	Value of laboratories and equipment	low	☐	☐	☐	☐	☐	high
	Fundamental research team competencies	low	☐	☐	☐	☐	☐	high
	Applied research team competencies	low	☐	☐	☐	☐	☐	high
	Development team competencies	low	☐	☐	☐	☐	☐	high
	Diffusion in the enterprise	undiffused	☐	☐	☐	☐	☐	diffused
	Capability to keep up with fundamental S&T knowledge	none	☐	☐	☐	☐	☐	strong links
	Financing capacity	low	☐	☐	☐	☐	☐	high
Complemen-tary resources	Quality of relationships between R&D and Production	weak	☐	☐	☐	☐	☐	strong
	Quality of relationships between R&D and Marketing	weak	☐	☐	☐	☐	☐	strong
	Capacity to protect against imitation	low	☐	☐	☐	☐	☐	high
	Market reaction to the company's design	unfavorable	☐	☐	☐	☐	☐	favorable
	Timetable relative to competition	behind	☐	☐	☐	☐	☐	ahead

Source: Jolly 2003

the group – such as by horizontal development, or learning and knowledge management.

Complementary resources include the links established by the firm with the scientific community in order to keep up with the latest developments; the ability of the company to finance the development of technology; the R&D-marketing and R&D-production interfaces. These are concerned with downstream coupling: R&D no longer lives in an ivory tower, and laboratories must not behave as independent units. Interfaces between R&D and marketing, as well as between R&D and production are intangible assets that need to be developed. Technological competitiveness depends on the strength of the link between R&D and marketing. The two functions could establish channels of communication so as to fluidify the transfer of knowledge between them, especially knowledge about consumer behaviour on one side, and functionalities offered by the technology on the other. Strong interfaces facilitate implementation whereas weak interfaces handicap business success.

Capacity to protect against imitation is important as any effort to build a technological competitive advantage might be ruined if the technology in question is not protected. The impact of the standard developed by the company on the market refers to the associated probability of the transformation of this design into a dominant one. R&D managers should understand that their technical choices have to be accepted by the market. Finally, timing exemplifies the importance of time in current competitive battles. It is well-known that being late in a technological race creates a competitive disadvantage. How to reduce the time to develop, to industrialize and to market are very common challenges.

Particular considerations for young companies

It can be hypothesized that the 32 criteria presented previously do not have the same importance. Some might be considered as having a greater impact than others. Some example of weightings in information technology can be found in Jolly (2003). In addition, when distinguishing between controllable and non-controllable factors, start-ups and larger firms might differ.

Regarding non-controllable factors, start-ups face a very similar situation to the one of larger companies, but differences might be faced in the controllable factors. Because their assets sometimes originate from a university or a public research centre, because their core business might still be uncertain, because they might have a limited experience, portfolio of patents, and R&D teams, young innovative companies frequently exhibit a weaker set of technological resources than large established companies. Nevertheless, start-ups might have some advantages regarding complementary resources. Their founders may be well acquainted with fundamental scientific and technical knowledge. Their limited size may help good quality relationships between functions – R&D-production, R&D-marketing – more than in larger companies.

ONE PRACTICAL EXAMPLE

The method described in the previous sections is now demonstrated on a small–medium sized high-tech company to evaluate the attractiveness and competitiveness of each technology of its portfolio. Technological evaluations are based on four company project managers' views. The example presented here is based on an unpublished report 'Technological evaluation of a high-tech company' written by 2003 MBA students at Newcastle-Upon-Tyne (UK) School of Management, Mei-Ling Queency Lo, Shi Dong Lei and Weinstock Liat.

The company is a software company involved in the development of network related software solutions. They employ approximately 60 employees, 40 of whom are R&D directly related engineers and the other 20 are administration staff. The company spends more than seven per cent of its annual turnover on R&D.

The company is currently engaged in the development of four technologies, all of which are the result of in-house R&D. All four belong to the same industry, where technologies A, B and C belong to what might be referred to as the 'old generation' and they are in their decline stage, while technology D is what one may refer to as the industry's 'next generation' and is in its emerging stage. Technologies A, B and C are interrelated and rely on the same know-how and competencies. Technologies A and C are used within technology B. Technology A is also a stand-alone technology and is marketed separately, while technology C is not and therefore not marketed separately.

None of these four technologies is the dominant design in its field, but all follow the dominant design, and are the outcome mainly of standards that are dictated from a higher authorized committee with the exclusion of developments that were made in what is known as the 'grey areas' in the standards. In these 'grey areas', the committee concerned dictates only an umbrella strategy for their development, allowing the companies involved to work out the details and to develop their own independent strategy. These areas constitute the basis for differentiation between the relevant technologies. Technology D, once marketed, will offer new functions which – being a market-pull technology – will reflect current market demands. This makes technologies A, B and C obsolete technologies, and their decline will come to an end, where their technologies will reach their physical limits.

Five different steps were undertaken. First, four project managers were asked to complete a questionnaire. Each project manager had to complete the questionnaire for all four technologies. Means for each of the criteria were calculated for each technology. Second, a Delphi round was performed in order to ensure the full understanding of all four project managers and the validation of their answers. Third, using the data from the four completed questionnaires after the Delphi, weighted scores were computed for each technology. This results in two coordinates for each of the four technologies, one for technological attractiveness and one for technological competitiveness. Fourth, a plotting of the four technologies in a two-dimensional framework gave a map of the portfolio, and in the fifth step, the results were analysed, and recommendations for technology strategy were formulated.

As Figure 14.2 shows, technologies A and B are regarded as the company's core technologies, while technology C is regarded as a leftover technology. All these three technologies are in quite a strong position – technological competitiveness – where A is the strongest technology and located in the technological frontier of the company, and technologies B and C are not far behind. Technology D, however, seems to be in a much weaker competitive position and is regarded as having an unstable position.

The company's technological attractiveness for technologies A, B and D is quite high. Technology A is considered as most attractive, and technologies B and D are very close. However, technology C is located far behind technologies A, B and D; perhaps the fact that technology C is not regarded as a stand-alone technology and is not marketed separately – rather it is only used within technology B – explains its weak position. Thus, one must wonder whether there is anything that the company can do in order to alter the situation of technology C, but one must also take into

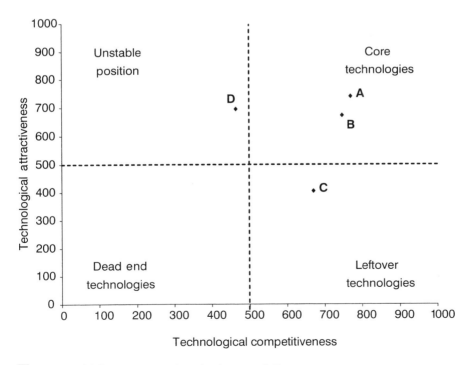

Figure 14.2 *The company's technology portfolio map*

account that perhaps such a change is not needed since this product is not marketed for itself, rather it is an internal technology within technology B.

The questionnaire data showed that the 'market volume that is opened' by technology C – as a stand-alone technology – received a mean of 3 out of 10; that the 'span of application' opened by technology C received a mean of 4 out of 10; that the 'impact of this technology on competitive issues' received a mean of 4 out of 10; and the 'potential for progress' received a mean of 3 out of 10.

Technologies A, B and C are declining; they have a mean of 6, 6 and 4 respectively for their 'position in their own life cycle'. They represent the 'old generation' of the industry while technology D represents the 'next generation'. This means that the current situation of technology D should be changed. Since it is considered to be emerging – as can be understood by the mean for its 'position of the technology on its own life cycle', which is 9 out of 10 – and since its overall technological attractiveness is relatively high, it might be worth while for the company to invest in this direction.

Technologies A, B and C are interrelated – technologies A and C are used within technology B – and all of the three are declining. Thus, the company should decrease the level of R&D investment in all three. At this stage, both technologies, A and B, should be exploited as much as possible, taking into account that both of them are regarded as the company's core technologies. Resources should be allocated to the marketing department to enable a further effort in gaining more contracts for the sale of technologies A and B. With time they both will move into the area of leftover technologies. Technology C is currently regarded as a leftover technology and is not marketed on its own, and it is not possible to recycle it into a different industry. Investment in technology C will be gradually and quickly reduced to mainly maintenance investment.

Technology D is only in the beginning of its industry's life cycle which may mean: high 'market volume opening' – rated 9 out of 10 – and wide 'span of applications opening up' – 8 out of 10. Moreover, it operates in a market where the 'increase in the number of competitors' is not high – 4 out of 10 – and competitors are not highly 'involved in the market' – 7 out of 10 – and the 'level of competition' is not highly intense – 7 out of 10. Having said all of the above, one must point out that the company's own 'fundamental competencies of its research team' and 'competences of its development team' are not as strong as needed – 3 and 5 out of 10, respectively – in the case of a technology that is emerging and which is in the early stages of its life cycle – 8 out of 10.

The company should either redirect its investment into a new direction, perhaps in the form of a new technology that may take advantage of the company's competencies, or increase its investments for the further development of this technology while entering into an alliance with a company that has the competencies that the company lacks about technology D. One decision might be to redirect resources from technologies A, B and C, allowing the same people that have developed these technologies to work on new projects while at the same time investing time in the previous technologies, but to a lesser extent; so working in a more efficient manner, avoiding idle time which could occur when the people that are still needed to further develop technologies A, B and C are idle since the work that is needed to be done on technologies A, B and C does not require the full-time attention of an engineer.

PRACTICAL ISSUES IN THE IMPLEMENTATION OF A TECHNOLOGY AUDIT

Who should participate to the assessment?

Participants should be able to give a professional judgment. The advantage of subjective ratings is explicitly to recognize the experience and the value of professional judgements made by R&D managers and others. These knowledgeable people are able to integrate factual data with intuitive perceptions in their analysis. Relying on such ratings partially overcomes the problem of (hard) data unavailability. The guiding principle is that the process should involve a wide variety of managers in order to avoid over-reliance on one specific group. Ideally, this includes operational as well as functional managers, at the business level and at the corporate level – if it exists.

Which methodology for data collection?

Managers from different departments might have different perceptions and interpretations. They might misunderstand the question and/or the scale, bias their evaluations in favour of their own technology, tend towards neutrality for technologies they do not know very well, over-estimate when they have too optimistic views, and under-estimate when they have too pessimistic views.

In order to deal with the subjectivity inherent to this kind of tool, and to increase the relevance of the audit, data collection should be organized along the following steps. First, there should be an explanation and definition of terms to participants in order to enhance comprehension of the questions. Second, each respondent should complete the questionnaire – first round – on an individual basis. Third, the data should be consolidated into one single document with individual scorings, group's means and standard deviations for each technology audited. Fourth, there should be a forum meeting with all the respondents, with the objective to share information, to unify understandings, to build consensus on strategic direction and to develop a shared vision. At this meeting, participants will have to identify similar answering patterns, contrast differences and discrepancies and finally discuss and argue for reducing variance into evaluations. In other words, they will be reconciling their divergent view points. Finally, after discussions in groups, there should be questionnaire resubmission – second round – for a new individual evaluation – original scores along with means scores – which should help to mitigate the possibility of skewed results and to paint a more homogeneous picture.

This means that the output and the process of the audit have to be distinguished. As stressed previously, the output is to assist the decision-making process regarding resource allocation across several internally competing technology projects. The results of the audit should not be taken for granted, but act as guidance to resource allocation. The audit is also interesting, however, for the process itself, as it allows the building of a shared and homogenous vision on the attractiveness and the competitiveness of each technology of the company's portfolio.

Formulating recommendations

Technology portfolio mapping gives insights into the directions where efforts should be made. Charting offers visual aid: a map of the technology portfolio allows viewing of all the projects together – as long as the number is not too high. By combining these two dimensions – technological competitiveness and technological attractiveness – resource allocation strategies for technology programs could be derived from the positioning of each technology on the portfolio map: no investment, redirection of resources, and dismantling of 'dead-end' technologies – low, low; very limited investment for recycling into other environments for 'leftover' technologies – high, low; strong and selective allocations for 'unstable' positions – low, high; and sustained commercial exploitation for 'core' technologies – high, high.

Two points should be stressed. First, mapping should exhibit the evaluations of the different respondents and highlight the average of these answers; this allows us to show the remaining variance amongst respondents. Second, respondents generally tend to over-emphasize their evaluations – especially competitiveness of their own programme. They tend as well not to use extreme figures. As a consequence, technologies are frequently mapped in a small square instead of using the entire available surface. It could be relevant to focus on this small square. This can be done by re-computing coordinates of each technology so as to expand differences.

CONCLUSION

High-tech start-ups need guidance when they allocate resources across an array of different investment opportunities or existing technology programs. Because not all projects can be financed, R&D efforts should be directed towards high value programs. The starting point for making the right choice is to audit all the technology development projects subject to internal competition for funding. Limited interest has been devoted in the literature to the design of auditing criteria and proper measurement techniques. Some models use financial metrics that are unfortunately oversimplified: they are exclusively monetary and use highly speculative inputs.

Other models restrict the perspective to patent statistics. Most models rely, without any justification of their choice, on a narrow set of criteria — frequently between three and six. And finally, the concept under study is not always clear.

Based on a review of several contributions to the field, this chapter suggested making a distinction between controllable and non-controllable criteria. The first set refers to the accumulated competencies and assets that depend on a firm's behaviour and decisions while the second set refers to the intrinsic potential, the appeal or attractiveness of one given technology that does not depend on the firm's action. 'Technological attractiveness' is identical for all companies competing in this technology while 'technological competitiveness' might differ from one company to another.

A list of two sets of 16 criteria for auditing 'technological competitiveness' and 'technological attractiveness' was proposed. Each of these factors was accompanied with appropriate measurement using semantic differential scales. Risks associated with 'technological attractiveness' represent some uncertainty that tend to reduce potential for value creation, while risks associated with 'technological competitiveness' look more like probabilities associated to accumulated value. A demonstration of the approach was given using real management assessments in a small–medium sized high-tech company. Practical issues in setting up a technology audit were inferred from this example and others. Interestingly, the audit process appeared to be as fruitful as the audit output.

Chapter 15

Networking for innovation
Managing through networks

Mette Moensted

In this chapter, innovation management in high-tech innovative firms is seen as being closely linked to uncertainty and networking is one of the means for gaining access to resources and for creating legitimacy for and for organizing for innovation. Networking is a new understanding of management and economy in which uncertainty and turbulence are the norms rather than the exception. Network management in an entrepreneurial turbulent environment is seen as a 'negotiated management' process, more than an established position in which power is exercized. The cases cited in this chapter are built on interviews in small Danish ICT and biotech firms, and ICT firms in Sophia Antipolis in France.

When firms are young and small, they have to deal with external complexity, and they do not have in-house control of important resources. To survive and grow, external resources have to be activated; the problem is one of organizing rather than structuring. It is therefore not so much about obtaining control and power, but to be a juggler in order to keep all the actors active. The question is how to create and maintain the role as project manager on joint projects with other – also large – firms. Networking is one way of mobilizing resources, through which resources for establishing high-tech firms are explored and exploited. The networking perspective helps us to understand the management and the growth of young high-tech firms.

To understand strategic networking, and the new challenges for management in networks, we have to understand networking processes and mechanisms as actions rather than as structures. Management becomes the relationships, and the social construction of a space for negotiated management. As the case biotech entrepreneur noted:

> As my firm is a network firm, I lose control, and how can I handle this uncertainty? I guess you just learn to live with it, as I live from it. This type of collaboration (in networks) is a delicate balance, as there are some things I have to try to keep secret. My basic knowledge, I have to keep for

myself, as this is what I survive on. It is a dilemma. On the one side, I need information from people in my network and to get some of that I have to provide knowledge, and this is the balancing which determines whether I survive.

With the bioavailability project, the secrecy is a problem. I try to split up information, and only in the final stage the know-how is open and vulnerable. At this stage, the involved person has to be contractually tied up. The secret processes of oxidation through necessitated encapsulation of the active drugs could be leaked when the manufacturing firm is very close to finishing the product.

The social construction of legitimacy is important, where legitimate partners – such as recognized peers – may be exploited as a viable strategy for establishing a good reputation. The fight to create legitimacy of ideas is a part of the strategy of small high-tech firms trying to overcome the barriers involved in radical innovation. Radical innovation and true entrepreneurship question existing orders.

> Entrepreneurs need to disguise the truly radical nature of their activity and the challenge it may pose to established organisations, while simultaneously making a case that they are different enough to hold a comparative advantage.
>
> (Aldrich and Fiol 1994: 652)

Customers, partners and investors have to be persuaded that knowledge is 'knowledge' and is not just 'a crazy idea'. Their knowledge and capacity is questioned all the time. When technology and markets are uncertain, persuasion via networks constitute legitimacy via other experts and recognized peers.

NETWORK CHARACTERISTICS

Smith-Doerr and Powell (1994) provide an excellent overview of network theory, with emphasis on structures, but in a relatively static perspective, they do not include action and fluidity in the strategic processes. Nohria's (1992) strategic perspective on networking establishes a new way of analysing organizations and organizing behaviour, in which the environment is constituted as an active part of the interaction. This goes beyond the primitive structural perspective on networks, and allows for action and processes of interaction. Research on entrepreneurship and small business highlights the crucial importance of the fluidity and action perspectives, in specifying various types of personal relations (as developed by Johannisson 1986, 1994). Structuration, as a process of networking, becomes a fundamental perspective.

Some studies of linkages between businesses focus only on one level, such as on pure economic relations and transaction costs (Williamson 1975), on regional business networks (Johannisson 2000; Grabher 1993; Bernasconi, Dibiaggio and Ferrary, Chapter 6 this volume), on systems of firms (Lundvall 1992; Williamson 1989), or on personal relations (Heimer 1992; Ibarra 1992; Cook 1982). Johannisson (2000), Nohria (1992), Burt (1992) and Grabher (2005) have developed the network concept as a strategic concept. The strategic level often combines business and personal relations, as happens in real life; business relations are used for personal contacts and personal networks are used for business.

The uniqueness of organizing via networking is that various contacts in different contexts refer to each other, which implies that a person's network does not have to comprise a group or an organization or be tied to one role. Organizing in these ways is not covered by other organization concepts, and is the most complex to study because the boundaries are fluid, fuzzy and uncertain, and because it is the 'opening' of opportunities rather than the 'closing' of decisions that is the interest of study. The focus and units of analysis are the interrelations and intermediaries, and the personal network is the main building stone for relationships and business change.

The basic idea is that people have different roles, and they interact with people while maintaining other roles. The communication will, therefore, not only be part of the organization, but will also have implications and relevance for other roles in life – such as sports, arts, family, friends, earlier students and colleagues. So people carry the knowledge, experience and reputation with them, from one role to another. This is why some contexts, such as golf or sports clubs, where 'the right people' can be met, are obvious platforms for establishing new personal contacts to be used in career development.

Networks are where one 'intermediary puts other intermediaries into circulation' (Callon 1991: 141); which is how networking can be seen as action. In this process, the intermediaries and their patterns transform and change. Some contacts – such as professors, student friends or earlier colleagues – can be dormant or latent for a long period, and then be revived in a recombination for a specific purpose.

Mechanisms in the functioning and characteristics of networks

A network is built up by dyads between nodes, i.e. the relations between individuals or enterprises. The dyad or the link thereby stresses the interrelations as the unit of analysis rather than the nodes, or actors themselves. Relations are transitive; the link may lead on to other links. When A knows B and B knows C, then A may get access to C. This is the basis for intermediaries, brokers and bridging (Marsden 1982; Burt 1992). This is shown in Figure 15.1.

Network relations are value loaded: positive or negative. Whether the relation is positive or negative determines whether and how the recommendation is carried

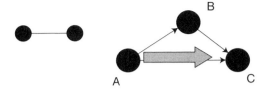

Figure 15.1 *Dyads and triads*

out. This aspect is often overlooked. In personal networks, it may be obvious, but the credibility of firms will depend on a positive evaluation, which is not evident for entrepreneurs or innovators. Commitment, trust and barriers in network may also be related to this emotional value. Recommendations from close network contacts may make busy people change their priorities. Negative value may block access, even if it is not 'fair', because it is based on attitudes and a subjective evaluation, and not on measures of performance. In Figure 15.2, B may receive mixed references from A via C and D.

A network is open and has no boundaries. There are various kinds of boundaries between subcultures, but networks may transcend these. Networks, however, have a tendency to align along demographic lines, and create sub-cultural barriers. The openness and the open-ended nature, however, are important for generating access to resources in a strategic way. Open-ended does not mean that no barriers to interaction exist, as suggested by the emotional value of network ties.

The network of a person does not form a group or an organization. The idea is that network contacts from different contexts may transfer references and information.

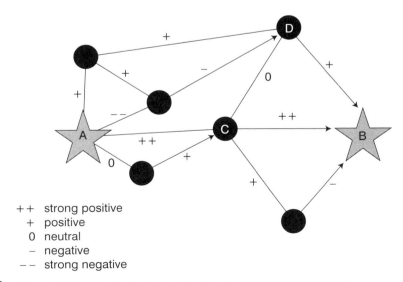

++ strong positive
 + positive
 0 neutral
 − negative
−− strong negative

Figure 15.2 *Value-loaded networks (Source: Moensted 2003: 127)*

A person's network does not create a homogeneous role or reputation, but a certain overflow of information and references from one role and context to another. A network combines personal relations from various roles and time. Colleagues, former colleagues, friends and family constitute a person's network, but not an organization or a group. The diversity and richness of the local network is important for its value. See Figure 15.3.

Network contacts may be both formal and informal. The boundary is not very clear, as some formal contacts develop to become informal and vice versa. As networks are created in different contexts and time, informal contacts may generate access to formal contacts, which may in turn develop into informal friendships.

Network services are not necessarily paid. Informal assistance among individuals has more resemblance to assistance from friends, which is usually expected to be balanced later. The principle is 'exchange', but with a delayed 'payment'. Strong networkers will build up credit, thereby specifying that 'you owe me one' in contexts where extraordinary assistance is provided. This may serve to 'jump a queue', or gain access to services and time from other nodes in the network. It is still related to a kind of barter trade based on 'What is in it for me?' and people would expect a balance in the long run.

Tight networks are mainly isomorphous groups or formations of homogeneous groups along demographical or other social criteria. Such sub-cultures form a good basis for trust building. Trust is easier to establish with people 'like me' as the frame of reference. Granovetter describes these as 'strong ties' (1973). Multiple relations

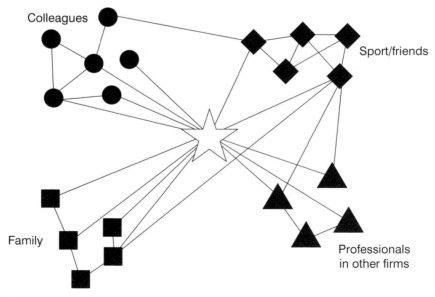

Figure 15.3 Segmented networks

create close ties. Multiple linkage-patterns, such as where several individuals have established relations between the same two firms, make the relationship stronger than just one connection. Tight networks are usually important for friendship, trust, support and social control. They may create the commitment and the 'glue' in the network. This is the support and social obligation and what constitutes the 'we' feeling and the mutual obligations. They may also be the basis for complex knowledge sharing as a 'community-of-practice' (Wenger 1998).

Network contacts that cross 'structural holes', or weak ties, are considered important for enabling access to new information and influence in the strategic search for complementary resources (Granovetter 1973). Ronald Burt (1992) has developed these arguments in a more strategic perspective, discussed later.

Socio-centred networks can be regarded – as viewed from the outside – as a spider's web, or as an infrastructure, when the actions and dynamics are frozen in time. Ego-centred networks describe the relations strategically from the point of view of the individual or the firm, and stress the social creation and fluidity of network relations, contrary to the stable structure. This perspective introduces networking as action, emphasizing the processes of creating networks and using them as infrastructures.

A network approach allows us to introduce dynamics and a concept of action and entrepreneurship, and to combine relations from various contexts and time in order to organize innovative projects. Networks provide entrepreneurial firms with the ability to establish and re-establish project teams, and to form partnerships for projects across firm boundaries. They give access to information, create alliances and also personal obligations. This process of enacting the environment as an infrastructure, however, introduces the complexity of organizing without boundaries. While this is interesting, it is difficult to grasp and to measure. As the case entrepreneur in biotech noted:

> I do not form network relations with former colleagues and friends from university. It is too much of a coincidence, if they should be working with issues relevant for me. But projects are initiated by building up networks of people with the relevant knowledge – like creating a 'package'. I use the phone and keep on until I am sure that I have talked to all the relevant people. The participants should fit the project, and also find themselves and their interests in the projects to get themselves committed. All projects start this way.

Some of the strategic mechanisms behind the process of networking are described. Two main forces of networks are essential for the understanding of strategic networking, access/complementarity/openness, and control/constraints/cohesion/closing.

Access/complementarity/openness embrace a number of characteristics. First, it involves access to resources outside the sub-culture and the strong ties. Second, it yields access to people and resources with a different background and other types of resources – as diversity management requires. Third, it involves surpassing the boundaries to create open doors and to keep options open, in which new opportunities and entrepreneurship are created.

Control/constraints/cohesion/closing includes a number of other characteristics. Control is a social form of exchange based on cohesion of nodes and a joint interest to use the personal relations as a social form of control. The cohesion and glue of the network create constraints in terms of mutual obligations, and moving external relations to internal. In a strictly economic perspective, the network can represent a constraint for options. On the other hand it is also 'closing of commitments', a kind of 'certainty feeling' beyond pure economic market relations. In Granovetter's words 'the necessity of trust and trustworthy behaviour for the normal functioning of economic action and institutions' (Granovetter 1992: 38).

These two forces or dimensions also show some of the paradoxes in networking for innovation. The need for openness and diversity for new ideas and knowledge about neighbouring fields of knowledge makes it more difficult to create the commitment, which is so much easier within the closed and homogeneous tight networks. The access to resources as a kind of connectivity (Grabher 2005), and is an essential feature of ICT and other types of communication and high-tech firms (Moensted 2003).

The constraints do limit options and new ideas, but provide a stability and commitment in turbulent settings. It moves relations from being 'external' to being much more 'internal'. With too many constraints and barriers, people cannot act, and entrepreneurship becomes difficult. Without social obligation and institutional frameworks of action, however, the foundation of the firm may be based on anarchy, in which economic transactions are hindered.

NETWORKING

The manager's position in an internal hierarchy is not the most important management role in small firms. In small high-tech firms, internal roles are diverse, being tied to decisions, to management, to research and development (R&D) or to production: it is not only an internal 'part time manager role'. The external roles involve management as a social construction, as in networking relations to sub-suppliers and customers. Jarillo's (1988) remark that the entrepreneur exploits more resources than he owns is a good starting point for evaluating the organizing of young high-tech firms. Small firms are weak in their own resources and have to organize beyond the firm to influence project development. By performing projects in networks, project management is enacted in and through the relationships.

The high level of technical uncertainty in many high-tech entrepreneurial firms creates a need for some kind of legitimacy or image of professionalism. The management of small firms is tied to self-organization, in which networking may be described as self-organized management in social constructions. Management of network ties does not provide a hierarchy or 'given' management structure. The ego-centred networker constitutes himself as the manager and manoeuvres to create the setting, and involve actors of management processes. As a manager in the case small biotech firm noted:

> I see myself as a spider that controls the web. The problem now is that many small, but potentially good projects are blocked by the time used on the large antioxidant project, i.e. in this early phase of the project I need more time, and the possibilities are immense. I have to concentrate, but also need new network contacts to evaluate the choices and need to find measures to control some of the relationships. Networking takes a lot of time.

The problem is how to handle the organizing of resources in parallel projects with different partners. Some partners may be involved in several projects, but others have to be found on the basis of their special expertise for particular projects. Management of these projects is an ongoing process of persuasion and motivation, as well as exchange. Entrepreneurial firms have to establish a network and create a networking behaviour, generating 'the meaning of management' within their network. They do not start by having authority: networking as action is very important. Networking is a type of organizing, and is how entrepreneurial high-tech firms develop projects. It is impossible to understand these firms without their networks. Tight and loose relations and the combination of these create the organizational set-up, and also the infrastructure in which confidence has to be generated in order that joint projects can be formed. As a manager of the case small bio-chemical firm noted:

> I am usually one of the people who organises people who usually do not work together to make joint projects. In one case, however, another leader of a small firm was the driving force in a good project, where all participants could see their interests. However, he could not see the project through. It became too big for the 'project-champion'. This resulted in a lot of wasted time for all partners, and it is often difficult to get someone else to play the role of the champion. It raises questions such as: where is the focus in networks? It has to be where the burden is carried. Marginal players can leave too easy, and when obligations are not taken serious all participants will lose.

249

In terms of implementation, this is more leadership than management, as various resources beyond their own firm are constantly involved and have to be motivated and to be kept active. There is no hierarchy to allocate the extra resources if projects take more time than scheduled, and the open space and fluidity in such loosely coupled projects is difficult to handle and requires a negotiated management approach.

Under innovative conditions, personal credibility becomes important for actors for them to earn legitimacy in the form of recommendations from others. If uncertainty is high, then personal credibility is in focus, and references from other credible peers may create the required legitimacy. In the personal evaluation involved in these networks, trust plays an important role. Collaboration is both based on trust, and also generates trust in the collaboration. Thus the links between trust, legitimacy and reputation provide for complexity in a process of circular explanatory factors. The process of building up trust in a relationship is a process of experience, which may build up gradually a spiral of trust, but it may be broken by just one 'mistrust' incident, as Figure 15.4 illustrates.

Trust is not timeless, but is based on experience, continuity, and evaluation of the person and of the project. Trust is built upon credibility and successful relations. A profile of contacts over time may provide an indication of how reputation, credibility and accessible resources develop outside the firm.

Technical cultures have a tradition for many ties among themselves and they make their own rules as to professional and personal ties. Networks that are 'communities of practice' seem to be tighter, and are based on personal evaluation of skill and trustworthiness (Wenger 1998). Engineers are quite direct in evaluating skills among themselves, and are often sceptical towards commercial and commercialized kinds of network, or to forms of rationality that are not their own. As a manager of the of measurement technology firm described:

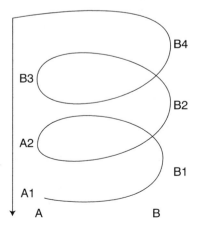

Figure 15.4 The virtuous circle of trust

Engineers' networks are very much based on trust. Sales people are very different and are too much 'suit and tie'. The problem at exhibitions (where he sells his technology) seems to be that suit-and-tie people are decision makers when it comes to purchasing environment-technology. They can create legitimacy and may be fascinated by the technique.

But how can the sales people get enough interest and knowledge to transmit a reliable message through to their technicians in their organisations? Transferring confidence between engineers via suit and tie is very difficult. I try to create small gadgets to attract the interest of the suit-and-tie people. But is it still a question as to who are the real customers in a large or a public institution.

Between professional cultures, there are barriers to communication and problems of legitimacy. There are some dilemmas and problems when high-tech firms seek complementary resources via networks. These happen when firms encounter serious barriers of trust and legitimacy in their search for possible network partners, for example, in export ventures. This raises the question as to how to create bridges, and transfer or create trust via a third party, is one of the functions of science parks.

It is the differences in complementary networks that create other forms of 'glue' in networks. The need for specialization, division of labour and the gradual experience of exchange can be linked to sociological theory. Tönnies describes the difference between 'Gemeinschaft', as solidarity based on communality and similarity, and 'Gesellschaft', where solidarity is based on complementarity and rich differences (Tönnies 1991 (1935); Asplund 1991). Important aspects of the solidarity concept could be interpreted as trust-building in network relations, even if the level of analysis is very different.

There are some paradoxes associated with the trust and homogeneity found in tight networks, which allow for close collaboration and joint experience which helps knowledge to be easily understood and applied. Burt (1992) raises the problem of the redundancy and lack of newness in knowledge from tight networks. The access to useful knowledge on the other hand is focused on complementary knowledge and complementary resources, but the easy understanding and trust could easily be a barrier to work on complex innovative projects where complex knowledge needs to be understood. The community of practice perspective (Wenger 1998) can be related to tight networks, where joint experience and easy understanding differences helps, but it does not relate to a discussion of how to get access to diversity in knowledge and resources, and to understand it sufficiently to act on it.

The paradox is between the necessity to get complementary knowledge and to be able to communicate with people of different backgrounds in order to form creative innovations, and the necessity to communicate about innovations which is so much easier within the homogeneous group of the community of practice. The strategic network solution might be to form teams and communities of practice based on diversity, in order to create the tight networks based on homogeneity on some of the social dimensions, or at least create bridges based on similarity.

ENTREPRENEURIAL FIRMS AND NETWORKS

The social psychological view of network structures indicates 'that power or reputation of leadership is attributed to actors in positions with high potential of communication activity and with high potential for control of such activity. Actors with a high level of communication activity are in positions to collect and synthesize information on the group task' (Marsden 1982: 205; Nohria 1992). This view is usually associated with the hierarchical type of communication control seen in large organizations. The most interesting aspects of the entrepreneurial firms, however, are their volatility, their opportunities to create new ties – thus to change their structures – and their readiness to 'exit'.

Burt's (1992) model uses a rational economic-perspective on networks. He diagnoses the network ties and the redundancy in networks, based on whether those in tight networks provide – and receive – the same information. The redundancy is then seen to be wasting time, but is a chance to revise networks in an almost surgical way. The strategic argument is that it is not necessary to maintain network contacts with several actors in a tight network, who know each other, as it consumes time but provides neither new information nor power positions. The strategy is to build up a role as broker between different tight networks, and to create a power base that makes the others dependent on the broker's role.

The method offers control and power via third persons and helps save time when maintaining and expanding network contacts. It is linked closely to power relations and the role as a strong 'player' as the spider of the web. Intermediaries are used both as bridges to access resources and for social control via third persons. The model presented (Figure 15.5) visualizes and introduces strategic thinking into network theory. These aspects of networking stress the connectivity to other resources, such as also shown by Grabher (2005). Power relations are also touched upon, even if they have been nearly taboo in the socio-psychological network theory. However, this model does not respect the mechanisms and foundations of social obligations and personal relations.

Using the model (Figure 15.5) in the pure form may be hazardous for small businesses, as they are very easy to be marginalized in networks. It is not possible clinically to cut out certain relations in the network, in order to have time for others that may be more interesting. Trust among 'friends' is challenged if perceived in an economic rational perspective. The model may be used, however, to increase consciousness of the use of networks. It is based on a diagnosis of where firms do not have access, but where they ought to have contacts. It may be relevant to find out who would be relevant as a contact in order to access new important networks.

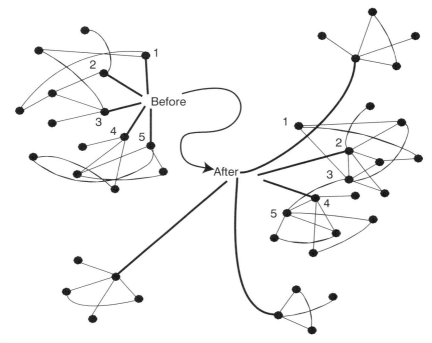

■ **Figure 15.5** *Structural holes in strategic networks (Source: Burt 1992: 22)*

The mutual exchange in the dyad is important for maintaining trust relations. Burt's perspective focuses on the powerful person in control of information, instead of looking into the dangers of having many secondary, professional or weak relations and only a few primary and tight relations. Many weak relations may rapidly change and leave an entrepreneur a very marginal situation, especially if the actor is not highly resourceful or has a committed network as well.

TRANSACTION BENEFITS AND STRATEGIC ALLIANCES

Strategic alliance can be seen as a special form of network. There are strategic objectives, and the alliances are relatively stable with mutual obligations for partners so as to create standards – even, for example, for large corporations in IT – and to manage supply chains and marketing efforts. The strategy and alliance concept combines two different paradigms and theoretical traditions. One is based on strategic economic thinking, closely tied to the classic economic business tradition (Ansoff 1977; Hamel and Prahalad 1994; Lorange and Roos 1992), largely developed in the context of large corporations. The other is based on networking as the creation of obligations and trust-based alliances.

Williamson's (1975, 1989) 'transaction costs' perspective presents network trans-actions within an economic framework, stressing 'transaction benefits'. 'Transaction cost economics suffers from not adequately exploring other available governance structures'. When costs of internalizing are too high and reliance on market too risky, it becomes economically 'rational' to organize in networks (Ring and Van der Ven 1994: 484). Furthermore, scanning ideas and relationships may itself create projects and alliances. As a project manager in small pharmaceutical firm noted:

> I do not look for ideas, but I maintain my contacts and I keep my eyes open for new options. I am good at collecting ideas and always have some new ideas in the pipeline partly on the basis of the relations.

There is a need to define the concept of strategic alliances as a form of alliance and networks, which differ from other collaboration forms. A strategic alliance is collaboration between two or more firms with the purpose of obtaining a goal of mutual and of high priority to both firms. Such an alliance could be formalized by a contract of stable collaborations where resources are vested from both parties or as long-term obligations. The strategic alliance perspective is mainly based on a perception of the benefits of economy of scale, but there are other objectives, including risk reduction, access to technology, learning, defence against competitors, commitment, and the creation of standards.

The same variables are used as arguments for mergers or acquisitions, but strategic alliances are loose relationships with less commitment than take-overs or mergers. A number of firms may benefit from this type of organizing, thereby maintaining the flexibility and creativity of individual firms. Grant and Baden-Fuller (2000: 116) stress that the inter-firm collaboration is most beneficial, 'when the firms' knowledge domains and product domains are incongruent, as this increases the efficiency of knowledge utilization, when uncertainty exists over future knowledge needs, collaboration offers risk spreading benefits, or when collaboration in developing new products and processes can exploit early-mover advantages'. Such alliances appear more beneficial to some sectors in the so-called new economy, and certainly within many types of ICT.

The network forces illustrated in Figure 15.6 should not be seen as dichotomies, but as a number of scales, where balancing in the act of networking may be needed. Networks for innovation include the combined and complex patterns of both 'poles' of these scales, combining tight and loose relations, and reflecting awareness of both openness and constraints.

A strategic alliance is not a form in itself, but is a hybrid that lies between a loose network and a joint venture, and between a state of not sharing information and firm merger. Such hybrid forms have a series of contradictory aspects, they create neither consistency nor theories, and they open a discussion concerning content and form. Content is about complementarity and innovation, and form concerns the kind of relationship and formality which is more fundamental for networking processes where known actors and similarity tend to be preferred.

Access	←———————→	Control
Complementarity	←———————→	Cohesion
Openness	←———————→	Closing
Options	←———————→	Constraints
Independent choice	←———————→	Obligation and dependency

Figure 15.6 *Network forces*

This raises a number of questions as to why firms want obligations and constraints. The need for small and vulnerable entrepreneurs is still to create obligations for partner firms as a kind of 'political non-aggression pact' (Mytelka 1991). So partner seeking firms need to have something to offer in a balanced exchange. This could be research, research capacity, or other resources that constitute some strengths or opportunities. Such strengths will make it possible to play the role as the stronger 'player' on some dimensions, as modelled by Burt (1992).

Collaborations among high-tech small firms often develop gradually into an arrangement that only ex-post-facto can be defined as a strategic alliance. In some projects the 'know-who' seems to be more important in the early stage than 'know-how'. In many ways this reflects a networking strategy, but not strategic alliance strategy, because it builds up gradually. Combining established network relations and new expertise is a way of creating new projects, as well as generating platforms for new projects. Some relationships may be contractual in the form of alliances, but others are informal. The management of the network is a special leadership-expertise capability that is essential if growth is to be achieved.

POWER AND MANAGEMENT

Looking at power in networks goes beyond the usual resource based view on power, to include patterns of relationships and dependencies, and various forms of social control in negotiated interrelationships. In a network perspective, power is not provided by the structure as a position, but rather is constituted in interaction in the relationships.

Small high-tech firms are not always weak partners in terms of competence, but are usually weak in terms of resources, which is especially important when faced with conflict. They are more often dependent on many external relationships, and therefore tend to have to balance their freedom with their constraints. At the network level, the convergence of those involved involves a combination of alignment and co-ordination. 'Thus the higher the degree of alignment and co-ordination of a network, the more its actors work together, and the less their very status as actors is in doubt' (Callon 1991: 148). They are not homogeneous in terms of production, but they have to fit together based on their complementarity (ibid.).

Power in networks is usually associated with having the power to control information or access routes, as Figure 15.7 illustrates. The star establishes a bridge, but also many contacts. If a, b and c need contacts to x, y, z, they have to involve the star at least for the first time, and accessing y, someone else as well. As soon as the contact is established, the figure changes, as the star is surpassed, and whether the star maintains his/her gatekeeper role, depends on other resources, contacts or power.

Nohria (1992) uses these aspects of sociometric relative power to represent influence in the network, tied to the idea of the control of resources. The problem is that the picture is not a stable picture or infrastructure: if 'a' knows that he has to get to 'y' and 'z', he may try to reach them directly. The power of the star is greater, at least the first time, if 'a', 'b' and 'c' do not know where to locate expertise. Power is created by combining information control with the role of broker.

The fluidity is embedded in the networking view. 'Those who search for laws and regularities overlook the way in which networks are not in the actors, but are produced by them. And they ignore the way in which networks only stabilize at certain places and at certain times' (Callon 1991: 155). Fuglsang (1997) characterizes the search for laws as 'killing the movement in order to measure it'. This is well illustrated by the manager of the small middleware firm:

> A small firm working on transferring data to new platforms often works with large mainframe producers. 'Reputation is everything in this business, and very much depend on avoiding failures. I have a close alliance to a few

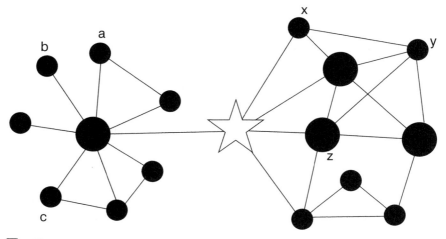

Figure 15.7 Power positions in networks

system-softwarehouses, where I can test the beta versions for comments. Some of the collaborators have offered to buy me, but I have rejected the offer. Then they try to create an alliance to tie me to one single supplier. But my strength is in being an independent actor, as I am invited as both the test-party and the necessary link to create middleware for hardware and software suppliers. For me tight alliances are dangerous.

The power concept is dynamic in the network perspective. The concepts of power and influence are based on a social construction and a process of negotiation. There are many ways of viewing and creating power relations, and of building management in networks. These include creating access to power (acting as if small firms have power and influence), generating power via persuasion in relationships (to create scale in networks or alliances), generating power and influence (to get recommendations and legitimacy), choosing interesting and resourceful partners (making sure both have interest and are complementary to create division of labour, so the strength of the partner reflects on the original actor), and choosing partners who are not dangerous (so do not compete on the main issues).

Power balancing involves a very complex evaluation of expertise, opportunities and strength, and in a dynamic way. The creation of power and influence is tied to the leadership role within the networks, and the extent to which the other actors depend on or find use in the leader.

MANAGING INNOVATION BY BUILDING ON EXPERTISE

The management of innovation may be seen as the creation or generation of meaning in context. Fragments of rapidly changing information may not necessarily create meaning. If the context does not cater for sense making, then new information does not create action because it remains passive as data, or even worse, as noise.

Expertise has to be accessible, in tight networks on a virtual basis, or locally where rich communication is possible. In Silicon Valley it could be that there is so much technological expertise in the area, someone can always be found to help on most technical problems – at least in the computer industry. Access to a rich resource network within the technical, management and finance areas is the foundation for using networking strategies for innovation and high-tech entrepreneurship. Networking to other people and business without resources just consumes time. Local access to resourceful people in the social and business worlds mean that networks create short-cuts in the solution of problems. Provided the networks are resourceful, they not only provide better solutions and contacts, but give quick access to knowledge. It is not only the form of organizing which is important, but also the content and resources in the network.

The starting point is seeing the entrepreneurial firms as weak, even if the entrepreneurs are strong as project leaders, because they need to organize resources beyond the boundaries of their own firms. 'Heavy experts' can be single consultants, managers, or partners in small firms. The expertise is therefore tied more to the finding of the people than to the firms involved in the solving of problems. Business alliances between small and large firms have to be seen in this way, where the organizational context for well-reputed experts is less important than the personal credibility of those involved. As an ICT firm manager in Sophia Antipolis noted:

> I have been a trainer in information technology for many years. Twenty years of experience during which I have taught at courses for firms. My personal network of knowledge covers both firms and system producers. We tend to keep relations with each other, whatever firm the people work for at present. We exchange information via the Internet, e-mail, fax, mail and telephone and maintain relations in Italy and the USA. I keep a close relationship to specialists, and we use each other. We exchange both services and work.

The case of the Danish artificial intelligence firm also illustrates this well. There is a strong professional board and a scientific panel of researchers tied to the firm. They have had between five and 10 employees between 1993 and 1997, physicists and data engineers, mainly recruited directly from the universities. A manager declared:

> In the early years, we were closer to the research world and had development projects with public funding. The network to the scientific world has remained very strong. In 1995, the basic core knowledge was developed to be more commercial. Core knowledge development has been very time consuming, but was necessary. The networks to customer groups are weak and a problem. It is difficult to obtain credibility in this technology.

One of the strengths and one of the weaknesses that small entrepreneurial firms face is in the ability to make 'bricolage' and being able to act in new contexts with the necessary means available. It may be a core competence to be creative and solve problems under difficult conditions, but this may also make a change from artisan to industrial thinking difficult. In ICT firms, time pressure pushes towards problem solving on an ad-hoc basis, rather than building strategic awareness. Articles and databases do not contain the newest knowledge. The learning is complex, as imitation and repetition are limited due to rapid changes in the tools of information technology, which creates a dependency of having personal contacts who know what is going on 'right now'. Within multimedia and software houses, the 'playing' and the exchange are part of both creating and playing the game. If firms are isolated, there is no game, no supplies, and no market, and in consequence, very soon, no firm.

STRATEGIES FOR COMBINING SECRECY AND INFORMATION EXCHANGE

The need to exchange information on new innovations is in a 'grey zone' for management (Kreiner and Schultz 1993). The exchange of information is important not only for moving on with an innovative project, but also to send signals to relevant professionals – scientists or development engineers – to create credibility and maybe create opportunities for later employment or collaboration. The case of a small biotechnological firm illustrates the tensions involved:

> The owner started up by carrying out pharmaceutical tests for other firms. This provided the generation of income and gave legitimacy and a personal network. It also provided occasions of small development projects from which he got a good reputation. He had been working on his patents in parallel projects. The innovative projects involved close collaboration with two university researchers, a supplier firm from the pharmaceutical industry and a sales company. The exchange of information with university researchers is a necessity, as the motivation and exciting ideas in a project are the most important. But he found that the only way he can protect his ideas is by 'leaking' part of the ideas to the collaborators. He is then the project-manager, holding it together and seeing the full range of the project.
>
> If university scientists find that he is hiding information, he is blocked. Their motivation is the scientific dimension only. This creates a dilemma, as the R&D bio-technical manager is dependent on exchange of information. He is both capable of strategic thinking, scientific development and of motivating and engaging scientists to work with his ideas. When the first patent began to result in sales – a nutrient antioxidant – then the awareness of his capacity increased, and vitamins-nutrient additions is a large drug market. The sales and promotion combined with discussion with scientists around other patents have opened the door for a collaboration with a very large international pharmaceutical, as a 'big-brother'.

Without trust, an 'exit' strategy would be a clear option, but in this case, the process managed to change opinions and interpretations of the actions (ibid.). This illustrates the complexity involved: whether trust is both the cause and the outcome. The story can be interpreted as a success story, or it can describe the risky balance of growth when depending on a large and powerful partner firm. The importance of creating credibility and legitimacy, and gradually creating confidence and reputation is apparent. For university researchers, trust is built on openness and having relevant research problems; hiding information blocks further collaboration. Some big firms and networks of researchers build up networks of support, based on trust.

It is not safe to lean on trust, and nothing ensures safety when very small young firms work with large corporations, but differentiated support networks can, when combined with patents, give the best possible chance. The collaboration is based on the partners having complementary competences. References, and the successes that occur, lead to many people referring the entrepreneur to other firms, beginning a virtuous circle of trust building.

A major strategic issue in high-tech concerns the protection of information. In many sectors, this can be through patents. In some sectors, however, patents are easy to get past or overtake, and they can provide recipes for competitors. Various combinations of strategies can be used to protect inventions and ideas, because small high-tech firms depend on other firms and are vulnerable both in development and sales. It is not viable for small firms to pursue law suits against large companies; for small innovative firms, new knowledge and innovations are never really protected. A strategy is to combine other measures with the development of personal relations and mutual obligations in partnering firms, leaning on social control.

The strategies that are appropriate, however, are very different in different sectors. In some pharmaceutical biotech sectors, patents have to be protected, but other network contacts usually supplement this protection. In the ICT sector, a lot of new development is not registered in patents, but protection comes from protecting the codes. None of these are safe strategies, but most small firms think not only about how to protect and hide knowledge, but also how to create different kinds of alliances with other forms of control. A single strategy is usually insufficient.

CONCLUSION

In this chapter, the focus is on the use of networks and decentralized acting (Fuglsang 1997) to create opportunities and innovations. The dilemmas are seen not as opposites, but more as an awareness of the combinations to form openness and closeness as the clue to innovations. The emphasis is not on transaction costs (Williamson 1979), but on transaction benefits. Even if networks are hard to manage and impossible to control, they create new organizational forms for innovations, and we see social innovation as the basis for the 'new economy', as well as for new perspectives on management.

Strategic perspectives on networking include a number of different business activities, where networking is the organizing form that both gives access to knowledge and protects social relations and knowledge. The creation of access to new and diverse knowledge is a very important aspect of strategic networking. Alliances and tight coherent networks are also treated as an important dimension of strategic networking, where there are many problems for small firms. They have to handle many uncertainties and loose ends, the teams or collaborations they form represent their kind of organization, and their external relations become seen as internal and 'safer'. The strategic view is to create working units larger than the firm itself, and to try to secure the commitment of partners.

The main way to create leadership in networks is through the two mechanisms of access and control. This is a new perspective management as leadership, based on acting as a leader, and being recognized as a leader by the network partners so that their commitment is retained. Exit is easy in networks, so network partners can leave at any time.

Strategic networking in innovation shows some of the paradoxes of working within a community or network of practice (Brown and Duguid 2000), but shows how the limits of the firm and its boundaries are not closed for new ideas from outside. The internal facilitation of communication and learning is not enough, but there has to be a capacity to communicate and learn across communities of practice.

Strategic networking is a way of understanding new demands for leadership within high-tech entrepreneurship. A leader's power is not given by the structure, but has to be gained by activities beneficial to the networking partners. Leadership and power in networks are created by the high-tech entrepreneurs themselves, through what they do and how they negotiate. The outcome is a high-tech entrepreneurial business that is, in itself, a social construction.

References

Abernathy, W. and Utterback, J. (1978) 'Patterns of industrial innovation', *Technology Review*, Vol. 80, No. 7: 40–7.

Acs, Z. J. and Audretsch, D. B. (1990) *Innovation and Small Firms*, Cambridge, MA: MIT Press.

Acs, Z. J. and Audretsch, D. B. (1993) 'Innovation and firm size', *International Journal of Technology Management* (special issue on small firms and innovation), Vol. 8, No. 5/6: 23–35.

Acs, Z. J., Audretsch, D. B. and Feldman, M. P. (1993a) 'R&D spillovers and recipient firm size', *Review of Economics and Statistics*, Vol. 69, No. 4: 567–75.

Acs, Z. J., Audretsch, D. B. and Feldman, M. P. (1993b) 'Real effects of academic research: comment', *American Economic Review*, Vol. 81, No. 3: 363–7.

Adizes, I. (1999) *Managing Corporate Lifecycles*, Englewood Cliffs, NJ: Prentice Hall.

Adler, P. S. and Kwon, S-W. (2002) 'Social capital: prospects for a new concept', *Academy of Management Review*, Vol. 27, No. 1: 17–40.

Ahuja, G. and Lampert, C. M. (2001) 'Entrepreneurship in the large corporation: a longitudinal study of how established firms create breakthrough inventions', *Strategic Management Journal*, Vol. 22, No. 6–7: 521–43.

Albert, M., Bernasconi, M. and Gaynor, L. (2004) *Incubation in Evolution: Strategies and lessons learned in four countries – France, Germany, United Kingdom, United States*, Athens, OH: NBIA.

Albert, P. and Gaynor, L. (2001) *Incubators – Growing up, Moving Out: A Review of the Literature*, Sophia Antipolis: CERAM.

Albert, P. and Mougenot, P. (1998) 'The creation of high tech companies', *Revue Française de Gestion*, March–April–May, No. 68: 106–18.

Albert, P., Fayolle, A. and Marion, S. (1994) 'L'évolution des systèmes d'appui à la création d'entreprise', *Revue Française de Gestion*, Vol. 101, Nov–Dec: 100–12.

Aldrich, H. (1999) *Organizations Evolving*, London: Sage.

Aldrich, H. and Fiol, C. M. (1994) 'Fools rush in? The institutional context of industry creation', *Academy of Management Review*, Vol. 19, No. 4: 645–70.

Allen, D. N. and McCluskey, R. (1990) 'Structure, policy, services, and performance in the business incubator industry', *Entrepreneurship Theory and Practice*, Vol. 14, Winter issue: 61–77.

Almeida, P., Dokko, G. and Rosenkopf, L. (2003) 'Start-up size and the mechanisms of external learning: Increasing opportunity and decreasing ability?', *Research Policy*, Vol. 32, No. 2: 301–15.

Amblard, H., Bernoux, P., Herreros, G. and Livian, Y. F. (1996) *Les nouvelles approches sociologiques des organisations*, Paris: Editions du seuil.

André, C. (2000) *Start-up Année 0*, Paris: Editions Village Mondial/Pearson Education France.

Ansoff, H. I. (1977) *Corporate Strategy: An Analytical Approach to Business Policy for Growth and Expansion*, London: John Wiley.

Aoki, M. and Takizawa, H. (2001) *Incentives and Option Value in the Silicon-Valley Tournament Game1*, RIETI Discussion Paper Series 02–E-001 Stanford, CA: Department of Economics, Stanford University.

APCE (2000), *Start-up in France – from Myths to Reality*, report available on the website www.apce.com: Agence Pour la Création d'Entreprises.

Arocena, J., Bernoux, P., Minguet, G., Paul-Cavallier, M. and Richard, P. (1983) *La création d'entreprise, un enjeu local*, Paris: La Documentation Française.

Arrow, K. (1962) 'Economic welfare and the allocation of resources of invention', in R. Nelson (ed.), *The Rate and Direction of Incentive Activity*, Princeton, NJ: Princeton University Press: 609–26.

Arrow, K. (1976) *Les limites de l'organisation*, Paris: Presses Universitaires de France.

Arrow, K. (1996) 'Technical information and industrial structure', *Industrial and Corporate Change*, Vol. 5, No. 2: 645–52.

Arthur, B. (1994) *Increasing Returns and Path Dependence in the Economy*, Ann Arbor, MI: The University of Michigan Press.

Arthur, D. L. (1981) *The Strategic Management of Technology*, London: European Management Forum.

Arthur, W. B. (1989) 'Competing echnologies, increasing returns, and lock-in by historical events', *Economic Journal*, Vol. 99, No. 394: 116–31.

Arthur, W. B. (1990) 'Silicon Valley locational clusters: when do increasing returns imply monopoly?', *Mathematical Social Science*, Vol. 19: 235–51.

Arthur, W. B. (1993) 'Pandora's marketplace', *New Scientist*, Vol. 6, February: 6–8.

Asplund, J. (1991) *Essä om Gemeinschaft och Gesellschaft*, Gothenburg: Bokforlaget Korpen.

Atherton, A. (1997) *Uncertain Worlds, Varying Views. An Exploration of the Concepts of Knowledge and Know-how in the Small Business*, Liteecemburg: Limburg University.

Atkinson, A. and Stiglitz, J. (1969) 'A new view of technical change', *Economic Journal*, Vol. 79, No. 315: 573–8.

Audretsch, D. B. and Feldman, M. P. (1996) 'Knowledge spillovers and the geography of innovation and production', *American Economic Review*, Vol. 86, No. 3: 630–40.

Autio, E. (1997) 'New technology-based firms in innovation networks: symplectic and generative impacts', *Research Policy*, Vol. 26, No. 2: 263–81.

Avenier, M.-J. (1997) *La stratégie chemin faisant*, Paris: Economica.

Axelsson, B. and Easton, G. (1992) *Industrial Networks: A New View of Reality*, London: Routledge.

Ayache, G. (1995) *Le développement de l'éolien en France et dans le monde: quelles perspectives en France?*, Sophia Antipolis: ADEME – SUD Consulting.

Ayache, G. (1998) 'Du management des ressources technologiques (MRT) au management des ressources informationnelles (MRI)', *Proceedings of the 1st of the Technological Resources Management Network workshop*, Senlis, France: Centre Technique des Industries Mécaniques (CETIM), 9–10 April.

Ayache, G. and Rey, C. (1999) *Voyage d'étude auprès des incubateurs israéliens*, Marseille: Marseille Innovation – Strateq Traders.

Aydalt, P. (1986) *Les milieux innovateurs*, Paris: GREMI CEE.

Balachandra, R. (2001) 'Optimal portfolio for R&D and NPD projects', Paper presented to the Portland International Conference on Management of Engineering & Technology (Picmet' 01), Portland, OR, July.

Barhami, H. and Evans, S. (1989) 'Strategy-making in high technology firms: the empiricist mode', *California Management Review*, Winter 89, Vol. 31, No. 2: 107–28.

Barney, J. (1991) 'Firm resources and sustained competitive advantage', *Journal of Management*, Vol. 17, No. 1: 99–120.

Barney, J. B. and Hansen, M. H. (1994) 'Trustworthiness: can it be a source of competitive advantage?' *Strategic Management Journal*, Vol. 15, Special issue S2: 175–203.

Bauer, M. and Bertin-Mourot, B. (1987) *Les 200. Comment devient-on un grand patron?*, Paris: Editions du Seuil.

Becattini, G. (1990) 'The Marshallian industrial district as a socio-economic notion', in: F. Pyke, G. Becattini and W. Sengenberger, *Industrial Districts and Inter-firm Cooperation in Italy*, Geneva: International Labor Office: 37–51.

Beckert, J. (1996) 'What is sociological about economic sociology? Uncertainty and the embeddedness of economic action', *Theory and Society,* Vol. 25, No. 6: 803–40.

Bell, G. C. and McNamara J. C. (1991) *High-Tech Ventures: The Guide for Entrepreneurial Success*, Reading, MA: Addison Wesley.

Ben-Ner, A. and Putterman, L. (2000) *Economics, Values, and Organisation*, Cambridge: Cambridge University Press.

Berle, A. A. and Means, G. C. (1932) *The Modern Corporation and Private Property*, New York: Macmillan.

Bernasconi, M., (1994) 'Enjeux interculturels et technologiques : le cas Français de la Silicon Valley', *Revue Organisation*, Special Edition: 25 ans de Sophia Antipolis, September: 39–46.

Bernasconi, M. (1995) 'The entrepreneur money and strategy in high-tech start-up: a Franco-American comparison', *Babson College Entrepreneur Review*, Babson Park, MA: Babson College, June.

Bernasconi, M. (2000) 'Models of development of high-tech companies', in M. Bernasconi and M. Monsted (eds), *Start-up High-Tech*, Paris: Dunod.

Bernasconi, M. (2004) 'The creation process of a technology company as an evolving project', paper presented to The 34th EISB Conference, Turku, Finland, September 2004.

Bernasconi, M. and Moensted, M. (2000) *Start-up high tech*, Paris: Dunod.

Bernasconi, M. and Moreau, F. (2003) 'L'évolution du projet des jeunes entreprises technologiques innovantes au cours des premières années: une méthode d'appréciation du cheminement stratégique' ('The evolution of young innovative technology companies during their first years: A method of appreciation of the strategic progression'), *Revue Internationale de la P.M.E.*, Vol. 16, No. 3: 11–29.

Bernoux, P. (1990) *La Sociologie des Organisations* (3rd edn), Paris: Editions du Seuil.

Besson, B. and Possin, J.-C. (1997) *Du Renseignement a l'Intelligence Economique, Détecter les menaces et les opportunities pour l'entreprise*, Paris: Dunod.

Besson, B. and Possin, J.-C. (1998) *L'audit de l'intelligence économique: Mettre en place et optimiser un dispositif coordonné d'intelligence collective*, Paris: Dunod.

Bhalla, A., Anderson, S. and Watkins, D. (2005) 'The origins and lessons of entrepreneurial achievement: a multi-paradigm perspective via the case method', in A. Fayolle, P. Kyrö and J. Ulijn, *Entrepreneurship Research in Europe*, Cheltenham: Edward Edgar: 150–73.

Bhidé, A. (2000) *The Origin and Evolution of New Businesses*, Oxford: Oxford University Press.

Blais, R. and Toulouse, J.-M. (1992) *Technological Entrepreneurship, 21 Cases of Successful SMEs*, Montréal, Canada: Editions Transcontinentales, Fondation Entrepreneurship.

Blais, R. and Toulouse, J.-M. (1993) 'La stratégie de développement des nouvelles entreprises technologiques', in ESC Lyon, *Création développement d'entreprises technologiques et innovante*, Lyon, France: ESC Lyon: 165–77.

Blomqvist, K. (2002) *Partnering in the Dynamic Environment: The Role of Trust in Asymmetric Technology Partnership Formation*, Acta Universitatis Lappeenrantaensis 122, Lappeenranta: Technical University of Lappeenranta,

Blyer, M. and Coff, R. W. (2003) 'Dynamic capabilities, social capital, and rent appropriation: ties that split pies', *Strategic Management Journal*, Vol. 24, No. 7: 677–86.

Boltanski, L. (1982) *Les cadres, la formation d'un groupe social*, Paris: Les éditions de Minuit.

Bond, E. U. and Houston, M. B. (2003) 'Barriers to matching new technologies and market opportunities in established firms', *Journal of Product Innovation Management*, Vol. 20, No. 2: 120–35.

Bouchikhi, H. and Kimberly, J. (1994) *Entrepreneurs et gestionnaires*, Paris: Editions d'Organisation.

Bouffartigue, P. (1994) 'Ingénieurs débutants à l'épreuve du modèle de carrière', *Revue Française de Sociologie*, Vol. 35, No. 1: 69–100.

Bouffartigue, P. (1995) *Les ingénieurs au cœur de la nébuleuse des cadres: quelques repères*, Working Paper, No. 38, Université d'Aix-en-Provence.

Bourdieu, P. (1980) *The Logic of Practice*, Stanford, CA: Stanford University Press.

Bourdieu, P. (1981) 'Social capital: provisional notes', *Actes de la Recherche en Sciences Sociales*, Vol. 3, No. 1: 2–3.

Bourdieu, P. (1989) *La noblesse d'Etat. Grandes Ecoles et esprit de corps*, Paris: Les éditions de minuit.

Bréchet, J.-P. (1994) 'From entrepreneurial project to company project', *Revue Française de Gestion*, Vol. No. 99, No. 1: 5–13.

Brockhoff, K. K. (1992) 'Instruments for patent data analyses in business firms', *Technovation*, Vol. 12, No. 1: 41–59.

Broder, A. (1990) 'Enseignement technique et croissance économique en Allemagne et en France, 1870–1914. Quelques éléments en vue d'une analyse approfondie', in Y. Cohen and K. Manfrass (eds), *Frankreich Deutschland forshung, tecnologie und industrielle entwicklung in 19 und 20*, Munich: Eul Verlag.

Bronckardt, J. P. and Mounoud, P. (eds) (1985) *Vygotsky aujourd'hui*, Paris: Delachaux & Niestlé.

Brown, J. S. (1997) 'Changing the game of corporate research: Learning to thrive in the fog of reality', in R. Garud, P. R. Nayyar, and Z. B. Shapira (eds), *Technological Innovation. Oversights and Foresights*, Cambridge: Cambridge University Press.

Brown, J. S. and Duguid, P. (1991) 'Organizational learning and communities-of-practice', *Organization Science*, Vol. 2, No. 1: 58–82.

Brown, J. S. and Duguid, P. (2000) 'Mysteries of the region: Knowledge dynamics in Silicon Valley', in C.-M. Lee, W. F. Miller, M. G. Hancock, and H. S. Rowen, *The Silicon Valley Edge. A Habitat for Innovation and Entrepreneurship*, Stanford, CA: Stanford University Press.

Brown, J. S., Collins, A. and Duguid, P. (1989) 'Situated cognition and culture of learning', *Education Research*, Vol. 18, No. 1: 32–42.

Brush, C. G., Greene, P. G., and Hart, M. M. (2001) 'From initial idea to unique advantage: The entrepreneurial challenge of constructing a resource base', *Academy of Management Review*, Vol. 15, No. 1: 64–78.

Brusoni, S., Prencipe, A. and Pavitt, K. (2001) 'Knowledge specialisation, organizational coupling, and the boundaries of the firm: Why do firms know more than they make?', *Administrative Science Quarterly*, Vol. 46, No. 4: 597–621.

Bruyat, C. (1993), *Création d'entreprise: contributions épistémologiques et modélisation* (Management Science Doctoral Thesis), Grenoble: Université Pierre Mendès France.

Bruyat, C. (1994) 'Epistemological contributions to the entrepreneurship sphere', *Revue Française de Gestion*, No. 101: 87–99.

Buckley, P. J. and Chapman, M. (1997) 'Theory and method in international business research', *International Business Review*, Vol. 5, No. 3: 243–55.

Bullock, M. (1983) *Academic Enterprise, Industrial Innovation and the Development of High Technology Financing in the United States*, London: Brand Brothers and Co.

Bunel, J. and Saglio, J. (1979) *L'action patronale, du CNPF au petit patron*, Paris: PUF.

Burns, T. and Stalker, G. M. (1961) *The Management of Innovation*, London: Tavistock Publications.

Burt, R. (1987) 'Social contagion and innovation: Cohesion versus structural equivalence', *American Journal of Sociology*, Vol. 92: 1287–335.

REFERENCES

Burt, R. (1992) *Structural Holes. The Social Structure of Competition*, Cambridge MA: Harvard University Press.

Business Week (1984) 'Composites have Sikorsky flying high', 9 July.

Bygrave, W. D. (1994) 'The entrepreneurial process', in W. D. Bygrave, *The Portable MBA in Entrepreneurship*, New York, NY: Wiley: 1–25.

Bygrave, W. D. and Hofer, C. W. (1991) 'Theorizing about entrepreneurship', *Entrepreneurship Theory & Practice*, Vol. 16, No. 2: 13–22.

Callon, M. (1991) 'Techno-economic networks and irreversibility', in J. Law (ed.), *A Sociology of Monsters: Essays on Power, Technology and Domination*, Sociological Review monograph 38, London: Routledge.

Callon, M. (1994) 'L'innovation technologique et ses mythes', *Annales des Mines – Gérer et Comprendre*, Vol. 34, March: 5–17.

Canion, R. (1989) 'America's fastest-growing company: Compaq's market creation strategy', in R. Smilor (ed.), *Customer-driven Marketing: Lessons from Entrepreneurial Technology Companies*, Toronto: Lexington Books

Capon, N. and Glazer, R. (1987) 'Marketing and technology: A strategic coalignment', *Journal of Marketing*, Vol. 51, No. 3: 1–14.

Carr, C. and Tomkins, C. (1998) 'Context, culture and the role of the finance function in strategic decisions. A comparative analysis of Britain, Germany, the U.S.A. and Japan', *Management Accounting Research*, Vol. 9, No. 1: 213–39.

Carter, N., Gartner, W. and Reynolds P. (1996) 'Exploring start-up event sequences', *Journal of Business Venturing*, Vol. 11, No. 3: 151–66.

Carter, R. and Edwards, D. (2001) 'Financial analysis extends management of R&D', *Research Technology Management*, Vol. 44, No. 5: 47–57.

Cassiman, B. and Veugeleurs, R. (1998) 'Complementarity between technology make and buy in innovation strategy: Evidence from Belgian manufacturing firms', University of Pompeu of Barcelona Working Paper, Mimeo, April.

Castells, M. (1985) (ed.) *High Technology, Space and Society*, Beverly Hills, CA: Sage Publications.

Castilla, E. J., Hwang, H., Granovetter, E. and Granovetter, M. (2000) 'Social networks in Silicon Valley', in C.-M. Lee, W. F. Miller, M. G. Hancock, and H. S. Rowen (eds), *The Silicon Valley Edge: A Habitat for Innovation and Entrepreneurship*, Palo Alto, CA: Stanford University Press.

Cayez, P. (1979) 'Quelques aspects du patronat lyonnais pendant la deuxième étape de l'industrialisation', in M. Levy-Leboyer (ed.), *Le patronat de la seconde industrialisation*, Paris: Les Editions Ouvrières: 193–200.

Chell, E. (2001) *Entrepreneurship: Globalization, Innovation and Development*, London: Thomson Learning.

Chesbrough, H. and Teece, D. J. (1996) 'When is virtual virtuous? Organizing for innovation', *Harvard Business Review*, Vol. 74, No. 1: 65–73.

Churchill, N. (1998) 'The six phases of growth', in S. Birley and D. F. Muzyka, *The Art of Entrepreneurship*, Paris: Les Echos-Village Mondial.

Churchill, N. and Lewis, V. (1983) 'The five stages of small business growth', *Harvard Business Review*, Vol. 61, May–June: 31–50.

Clugston, C. O. (1995) 'High-tech demands own new-product plan', *Electronic News*, 4 December.

Coase, R. H. (1937) 'The nature of the irm', *Economica*, Vol. 4, No. 4: 386–405.

Coase, R. H. (1988) *The Firm, the Market and the Law*, Chicago, IL: University of Chicago Press.

Cohen, E. (1988) 'Formation, modèles d'action et performance de l'élite industrielle: l'exemple des dirigeants issus du corps des Mines', *Revue de Sociologie du Travail*, Vol. 20, No. 4: 587–614.

Cohen, W. M. and Levin, R. C. (1987) 'Empirical studies of innovation and market structure', in R. Schmalensee and R. Willig (eds), *Handbook of Industrial Organization*, Vol. 2, Amsterdam: North Holland Press.

Cohen, W. M. and Levinthal, D. A. (1990) 'Absorptive capacity: a new perspective on learning and innovation', *Administrative Science Quarterly*, Vol. 35, No. 1: 128–52.

Cohen, W. M., Levin, R. C. and Mowery, D. C. (1987) 'Firm size and R&D intensity: a re-examination', *Journal of Industrial Economics*, Vol. 35, No. 4: 543–65.

Coleman, J. S. (1988) 'Social capital and the creation of human capital', *American Journal of Sociology*, Vol. 94, Supplement: S95–S120.

Coninck de, P. (1994) 'Pour une approche constructive de l'autonomie de la technique', in P. Troude-Chastenet (ed.), *Sur Jacques Ellul: un penseur de notre temps*, Bordeaux-le-Bouscat: l'Esprit du Temps.

Conover, W. J. (1999) *Practical Nonparametric Statistics*, New York: Wiley.

Constant, E. W. (1987) 'The social locus of technological practice: community, system, or organization?', in W. Bijker, T. Hughes, and T. Pinch (eds), *The Social Construction of Technological Systems*, Cambridge, MA, MIT Press.

Cook, K. S. (1982) 'Network Structures from an exchange perspective', in P. V. Marsden and N. Lin, *Social Structure and network analysis*, London: Sage

Cook, S. D. N. and Brown, J. S. (1999) 'Bridging epistemologies: The generative dance between organizational knowledge and organizational knowing', *Organization Science*, Vol. 10, No. 4: 381–400.

Coombs, R. (1996) 'Core competencies and the strategic management of R&D', *R&D Management*, Vol. 26, No. 4: 345–55.

Cooney, T. M. (1999) 'What is the relationship between entrepreneurial teams, structure and strategy in fast growing firms?', Proceedings of the ICSB 44th World Conference, Naples: 20–23 June.

Cooper, A. C. and Daily, C. M. (1997) 'Entrepreneurial teams', in D. L. Sexton and R. W. Smilor (eds), *Entrepreneurship 2000*, Chicago, IL: Upstart Publishing.

Cooper, R. G., Edgett, S. J. and Kleinschmidt, E. J. (1998) 'Best practices for managing R&D portfolios', *Research Technology Management*, Vol. 41, No. 4: 20–34.

Cooper, R. G., Edgett, S. J. and Kleinschmidt, E. J. (2000) 'New problems, new solutions: making portfolio management more efficient', *Research Technology Management*, Vol. 43, No. 2: 18–33.

Coser, R. L. (1975) 'The complexity of roles as a seedbed of individual autonomy', in L. A. Coser (ed.), *The Idea of Social Structure: Papers in Honor of Robert K. Merton*, New York: Harcourt Brace Jovanovich.

Crochet-Damais, A. (2004) 'Les standards RFID en quête de large diffusion', *LeJournalduNet, JDN Solutions*, online at http://solutions.journaldunet.com.

Crossan, M., Pina, E., Cunha, M., Vera, D. and Cunha, J. (2005) 'Time and organizational improvisation', *Academy of Management Review*, Vol. 30, No. 1: 129–45.

Crossley, N. (1996) *Intersubjectivity: The Fabric of Social Becoming*, Thousand Oaks, CA: Sage Publications.

Crozier, M. and Friedberg, E. (1977) *L'acteur et le système*, Paris: Editions du Seuil

Daft, R. L. and Lengel, R. H. (1992) 'Information richness: a new approach to managerial behavior and organizational design', *Management Science*, Vol. 38, No. 4: 554–71.

Dalloz, X., Géradon de Vera, O. and Portnoff A. Y. (2000) *Consommer, distribuer et produire en 2010: la création de valeur dans l'économie du XXIème siècle*, Paris: Gencod EAN France.

David, A. (1999) 'Logique, épistémologie et méthodologie en sciences de gestion', 8th A.I.M.S. Conference, Paris: l' Ecole Centrale de Paris, 26–28 May.

David, P. (1985) 'Clio and the economics of QWERTY', *American Economic Review*, Vol. 75, No. 2: 332–7.

REFERENCES

David, P. and Foray, D. (1996) 'Information distribution and the growth of economically valuable knowledge: a rationale for technological infrastructure policies', in M. Teubal, M. Justman and E. Zuscovitch (eds), *Technological Infrastructure Policy: An International Perspective*, Amsterdam, Kluwer Academic Publishers.

Davidow, W. H. (1986) *Marketing High Technology: An insider's view*, New York: The Free Press.

Davies, A., Hobday, M. and Prencipe A. (2004) *The Business of Systems Integration*, Oxford: Oxford University Press.

Day, C. R. (1978) 'The making of mechanical engineers in France, the Ecoles des Arts et Métiers: 1803–1914', *French Historical Studies*, Vol. 10, No. 3: 439–60.

de Boisanger, P. (1987) 'Du renseignement à l'action dans l'entreprise', *Management et Personnel*, Vol. 130–1: 49–72.

Deblock, F. (2003) 'RFID, ou l'identification par radiofréquences', *LeJournalduNet, JDN Solutions*, online at http://solutions.journaldunet.com.

Delmar, F. and Davidsson, P. (1998) 'A taxonomy of high-growth firms', *Frontiers of Entrepreneurship Research*, Babson Park, MA: Babson College.

Detoeuf, A. (1987) *Propos de O.L. Barenton, confiseur*, Paris: Editions d'Organisation.

Dibiaggio, L. (1998) *Information, connaissance et organisation*, PhD thesis, mimeo, University of Nice-Sophia Antipolis.

Dibiaggio, L. (1999) 'L'économie de la connaissance', *Revue d'Economie Industrielle*, Vol 88, Special issue: 67–88.

Dibiaggio L. (2004) 'Design complexity, vertical disintegration and knowledge organization in the semiconductor industry', Paper presented at the DRUID Conference, Copenhagen, June.

Dibiaggio, L. and Musso, P. (1998) 'Architecture informationnelle et apprentissage: un modèle de simulation', *Revue d'Economie industrielle*, Vol. 84, No. 1: 85–104.

Dickinson, M. W., Thornton, A. C. and Graves, S. (2001) 'Technology portfolio management: optimizing interdependent projects over multiple time periods', *IEEE Transactions on Engineering Management*, Vol. 48, No. 4: 518–27.

Divry, C. (2000) 'Organiser les compétences pour innover: arbitrage entre principes de division et d'intégration', *Revue Française de Gestion Industrielle*, Vol. 19, No. 1: 37–52.

Dosi, G. (1982) 'Technological paradigms and technological trajectories: a suggested interpretation of the determinants and directions of technical change', *Research Policy*, Vol. 11, No. 1: 1147–62.

Dosi, G. (1984) *Technical Change and Industrial Transformation*, London: Macmillan.

Dosi, G. and Fagiolo, G. (1997) 'Learning in evolutionary environments', Paper presented at the path dependency and path creation conference, Copenhagen, 19–22 August, Copenhagen Business School, Copenhagen, Denmark.

Dou, H. (1997) 'Technology watch and competitive intelligence: the European way', *NCE Review*, Vol. 8, No. 1: 78–84.

Dougherty, D. (1997) 'Organizational capacities for sustained product innovation', OECD workshop on the innovation performance of firms, 30 June – 1 July, Paris: OECD.

Douglas, M. (1978) *Cultural Bias*, Occasional Paper No 35, London: Royal Anthropological Institute.

Drucker, P. (1985) *Les entrepreneurs*, Paris: L'expansion Hachette.

Druilhe, C. (2003) *The Emergence and Process of Academic Enterprise: Cases from the University of Cambridge*, Cambridge: University of Cambridge.

Druilhe, C. and Garnsey, E. W. (2001) 'Academic spin-off ventures: a resource-opportunity approach', in W. During, R. Oakey, and S. Kauser (eds), *New Technology-Based Firms in the New Millennium*, Oxford: Pergamon.

Druilhe, C. and Garnsey, E. W. (2004) 'Do academic spin-outs differ and does it matter?', *Journal of Technology Transfer*, Vol. 29, No. 3/4: 269–85.

Durand, R. and Vargas, V. (2003) 'Ownership, organization and private firm's efficient use of resources', *Strategic Management Journal*, Vol. 24, No. 7: 667–75.

Dyer, J. H. and Chuh, W. (2000) 'The determinants of trust in supplier–auto-maker relationships in the US, Japan, and Korea', *Journal of International Business Studies*, Vol. 31, No. 2: 259–85.

Edquist, C. (1997) (ed.) *Systems of Innovation: Technologies, Institutions and Organizations*, London: Pinter-Cassell Academic.

Eggers, J., Leahy, K. and Churchill, N. (1994) 'Stages of small business growth revisited: insights into growth path and leadership/management skills in low-and high-growth companies', INSEAD Working Paper 94/63/ENT, Fontainebleau, France: INSEAD.

Eisenmann, T. R. (2002) 'The effects of CEO equity ownership and firm diversification on risk taking', *Strategic Management Journal*, Vol. 23, No. 6: 513–34.

Electronics Times (1998) 'Chips in the foundations', 29 June: 26.

Elfring, T. and Foss, N. J. (1997) 'Corporate renewal through internal venturing and spin-offs: perspectives from organizational economics', Working paper no. 1997–7, Copenhagen: Copenhagen Business School.

Ellis, P. (2000) 'Social ties and foreign market entry', *Journal of International Business Studies*, Vol. 31, No. 3: 443–69.

Ellul, J. (1990) *The Technological Bluff*, trans. G. W. Bromiley, Grand Rapids, MI: Eerdmans.

Ericsson, K. and Simon, H. (1985) *Protocol Analysis*, New York: Sage.

Ernst, H. (1998) 'Patent portfolios for strategic R&D planning', *Journal of Engineering and Technology Management*, Vol. 15, No. 2, September: 279–308.

European Commission (2001) *Benchmarking of Business Incubators*, Brussels: European Commission Centre for Strategy and Evaluation Services.

European Commission (2002) *University Spin-outs in Europe: Overview and Good Practice*, Brussels: European Commission DG Enterprise Innovation Policy.

Fayolle, A. (1994) 'La trajectoire de l'ingénieur entrepreneur', *Revue Française de Gestion*, No. 101: 113–25.

Fayolle, A. (2000) *Processus entrepreneurial et recherches en entrepreneuriat: vers une approche dynamique et globale des situations entrepreneuriales*, Grenoble, France: Habilitation à Diriger des Recherches en Sciences de Gestion, Univ. Grenoble II.

Fayolle, A. (2004) *Entrepreneurship*, Paris: Dunod.

Fayolle, A. and Livian, Y. F. (1995) 'Entrepreneurial behaviour of French engineers. An exploratory study', in S. Birley and I. MacMillan (eds), *International Entrepreneurship*, London: Routledge.

Fayolle, A., Ulijn, J. and Degeorge, J. M. (2005) 'The entrepreneurial and innovative orientation of French, German and Dutch engineers: the proposal of an European context based upon some empirical evidence from two studies', in A. Fayolle, P. Kyro and J. Ulijn (eds), *Entrepreneurship Research in Europe*, Cheltenham: Edward Elgar.

Ferrary, M. (1999) 'Confiance et accumulation de capital social dans la régulation des activités de crédit', *Revue Française de Sociologie*, Vol. 40, No. 3: 559–86.

Ferrary M. (2001) 'Pour une théorie de l'échange dans les réseaux sociaux: un essai sur le don dans les réseaux industriels de la Silicon Valley', *Cahiers Internationaux de Sociologie*, Vol. 111: 261–90.

Ferrary, M. (2002) 'Pour une théorie de l'échange dans les réseaux sociaux:u n essai sur le don dans les réseaux industriels de la Silicon Valley', in I. Huault (ed.), *La construction sociale de l'entreprise: autour des travaux de Mark Granovetter*, Paris: Éditions Management et Société.

Ferrary, M. (2003) 'The gift exchange in the social networks of Silicon Valley', *California Management Review*, Vol. 45, No. 4: 120–38.

Fischoff, B., Lanir, Z. and Johnson, S. (1997) 'Risky lessons: conditions for organizational learning', in R. Garud, P. Nayyar, and Z. Shapira (eds) *Technological Innovation: Oversights and Foresights*, Cambridge: Cambridge University Press.

Flamholtz, E. (1986) *How to Make the Transition from an Entrepreneurship to a Professionally Managed Firm*, San Francisco, CA: Josey-Bass.

Foster, R. N. (1981) 'Linking R&D to strategy', *The McKinsey Quarterly*: 35–52

Foster, R. N. (1986) *Innovation: The Attacker's Advantage*, New York, NY: Summit Books.

Freeman, C. (1987) *Technology Policy and Economic Performance: Lessons from Japan*, London: Pinter.

Fréry, F. (1998) 'Les réseaux d'entreprise: une approche transactionnelle', in H. Laroche and J. P. Nioche (eds), *Repenser la stratégie*, Paris: Librairie Vuibert.

Fuglsang, M. (1997) 'The dead organisation: the enigma of reflexivity', Paper presented at the 1st International Conference on Modes of Organizing/Knowledge Shifts, Warwick, UK, April.

Fukuyama, F. (1995) *Trust: The Social Virtues and the Creation of Prosperity*, London: Hamish Hamilton.

Galant, S., Ghiron, F. and Devalan, P. (1997) 'Technologies clés ou fonctions clés: le cas de l'industrie alimentaire', Internal document, Bertin et Cie, France.

Galbraith, J. K. (1982) 'The stages of growth', *Journal of Business Strategy*, Vol. 3, No. 1, summer: 70–9.

Garnsey, E. (1996) 'A new theory for the growth of the firm', in International Council for Small Business (ed.), *41st World Conference of the International Council for Small Business*, June 1996, Stockholm: International Council for Small Business.

Garnsey, E. (1998a) 'A theory of the early growth of the firm', *Industrial and Corporate change*, Vol. 7, No. 3: 523–56.

Garnsey, E. (1998b) 'The genesis of the high technology milieu: a study in complexity', *International Journal of Urban and Regional Research*, Vol. 22, No. 3: 361–77.

Garnsey, E. and Heffernan P. (2001) 'Growth setbacks in new firms', paper presented at ESRC Priority Network Conference on complex dynamic processes, 'Limits to Knowledge', Budapest, 23–24 June.

Garnsey, E. and Moore, I. (1993) 'Pre-competitive and near-market research and development: problems for policy', *International Journal of Technology Management*, Vol. 8, No. 5/6: 69–83.

Gartner, B. (1985) 'A conceptual framework for describing the phenomenon of new venture creation', *Academy of Management Review*, Vol. 10, No. 4: 696–706.

Garud, R. (1997) 'On the distinction between know-how, know-what and know-why', *Les Cahiers du Management Technologique*, No. 19, January–April: 5–30.

Garud, R. (2004) *3M Innovation as a process of mindful replication'*, CD-ROM teaching Case, New York, NY: Stern University.

Garud, R. and Lant, T. (1997) 'Navigating Silicon Valley: kaleidoscopic experiences', Paper presented to the path dependency and path creation conference, Copenhagen Business School, Copenhagen, DK, 19–22 August.

Garud, R., Nayyar, P. R. and Shapira, Z. B. (1997) 'Technological innovation: oversights and foresights', in R. Garud, P. R. Nayyar and Z. B. Shapira (eds), *Technological Innovation: Oversights and Foresights*, Cambridge: Cambridge University Press.

Gasiglia, C., Gueye, S., and Pistre, N., (2000) 'Valuation, the central stake in the financial reasoning of start-ups', in M. Bernasconi and M. Moensted (edsO, *Start-up High-Tech*, Paris: Dunod.

Gasse, Y. (2002) 'Technological entrepreneurs: profile of researcher-entrepreneurs', article available on www.fsa.ulaval.ca/dept/.

Gattaz, Y. (1970) *Les homes en gris*, Paris: Laffont.

Gattaz, Y. (1980) *La fin des patrons*, Paris: Laffont.

Gaudin, T. (1984) 'Les ingénieurs et l'innovation', *Culture Technique*, No. 12: 133–6.

Ghauri, P. N. and Usunier, J.-C. (eds) (1996) *International Business Negotiations*, Oxford: Pergamon.

Ghoshal, S. and Nahapiet, J. (1998) 'Social capital, intellectual capital and organizational advantage', *The Academy of Management Review*, Vol. 23, No. 2: 242–66.

Gibbons, M., Limoges, C., Nowotny, H., Schwartzman, S., Scott, P. and Trow, M. (1994) *The New Production of Knowledge. The Dynamics of Science and Research in Contemporary Societies*, London: Sage.

Giddens, A. (1987) *The Constitution of Society*, Berkeley, CA: University of California Press.

Gille, B. (1964) *Les ingénieurs de la renaissance*, Paris: COP.

Gipe, P. (1995) *Wind Energy Comes of Age*, New York: John Wiley & Sons.

Girvan, M. and Newman, M. E. (2002) 'Community structure in social and biological networks', *Proceedings of the National Academy of Science*, USA, Vol. 99: 8271–6.

Goffman, E. (1973) *La mise en scène de la vie quotidienne*, Paris: Editions de Minuit.

Goffman, E. (1974), *Les rites d'interaction*, Paris: Editions de Minuit.

Goffman, E. (1986) *Frame Analysis: An Essay on the Organization of Experience*, Boston, MA: Northeastern University Press.

Gordon Bell, C. and McNamara, J. (1991) *High-Tech Ventures*, Reading, MA: Addison Wesley.

Grabher, G. (1993) 'The weakness of strong ties.: the lock-in of regional development in the Ruhr area', in G. Grabher, *The Embedded Firm: On the Socioeconomics of Industrial Networks*, London: Routledge.

Grabher, G. (2005) 'The socio-economics of projects: a kaleidoscopic view on temporary organizations', in G. Matzner and G. Chaloupek (eds), *Recent Advances in Socio-Economics*, Marburg: Metropolis.

Granovetter, M. (1973) 'The strength of weak ties', *American Journal of Sociology*, Vol. 78, No.7: 1360–80.

Granovetter, M. (1982) 'The strength of weak ties: a network theory revisited', in P. V. Marsden and N. Lin (eds), *Social Structures and Network Analysis*, Beverly Hills, CA: Sage.

Granovetter, M. (1985) 'Economic action and social culture: the problem of embeddedness', *American Journal of Sociology*, Vol. 91, No. 3: 481–510.

Granovetter, M. (1992) 'Economic action and social structure: the problem of embeddedness', in M. Granovetter and R. Swedberg (eds), *The Sociology of Economic Life*, Boulder, CO: Westview Press.

Granovetter, M. and Swedberg, R. (1992) *The Sociology of Economic Life*, Boulder, CO: Westview Press.

Grant, R. (1991) 'The resource-based theory of competitive advantage: implications for strategy formulation', *California Management Review*, Vol. 33, No. 3: 114–35.

Grant, R. and Baden-Fuller, C. (2000) 'Knowledge and economic organization : an application to the analysis of interfirm collaboration', in G. von Krogh, I. Nonaka, and T. Nishiguchi (eds), *Knowledge Creation: A Source of Value*, London: Macmillan.

Graves, S. B., Ringuest, J. L. and Case, R. H. (2000) 'Formulating optimal R&D portfolios', *Research Technology Management*, Vol. 43, No. 3: 47–51.

Green, K. (1991) 'Shaping markets: creating demand for radically new products', Paper presented to the Workshop on the Management of Technology, Paris: September.

Greiner, L. E. (1972) 'Evolution and revolution as organizational grow', *Harvard Business Review*, Vol. 50, No. 4: 37–46.

Greiner, L. E. (1998) 'Evolution and revolution as organizations grow (2nd edition)', *Harvard Business Review*, Vol. 76, No. 3: 55–68.

Grelon, A. and Ternier, A. (1986) *Les ingénieurs de la crise: titre et profession entre les deux guerres*, Paris: Editions des Hautes Etudes en Sciences Sociales.

GREPME (1993) *Les PME: bilan et perspectives*, Paris: Economica.

Griffith, D. A., Hu, M. Y. and Ryans, J. K. (2000) 'Process standardization across inter- and inter-cultural relationships', *Journal of International Business Studies*, Vol. 31, No. 2: 303–24.

Grill, F. (1997) 'Anticiper pour agir : l'intelligence stratégique', *Paris Business Digest*, No. 67, September Supplement.

Grossetti, M. (1986) 'Trajectoires d'ingénieurs et territoires', *Les ingénieurs de la crise*, Paris: Editions de l'EHESS.

Grossetti, M. (2001) 'Les effets de proximité spatiale dans les relations entre organisations: une question d'encastrements', *Espaces & Société*, No. 101–102: 203–19.

Grosseti, M. and Bès, M.-P. (2002) 'Proximité spatiale et relations science-industrie: savoirs tacites ou encastrement ('Polanyi ou Polanyi')?', *Revue d'Economie Rurale et Urbaine*, No. 5: 777–88.

Grossman, S. and Hart, O. (1986) 'The cost and benefits of ownership: a theory of vertical integration', *Journal of Political Economy*, Vol. 94, No. 4: 691–719.

Guilhou, X. (2000) cited in Espitalier, S. *L'intégration d'internet en tant qu'outil de veille dans une entreprise internationale*, Marseille: Ecole Supérieure de Commerce de Marseille Provence

Gulati, R., Nohria, N. and Zaheer, A. (2000) 'Strategic networks', *Strategic Management Journal*, Vol. 21, No. 3: 203–16.

Guth, W. and Ginsberg, A. (1990) 'Guest editor's introduction: corporate entrepreneurship', *Strategic Management Journal*, Vol. 11, No. 4: 5–15.

Hackett, S. and Dilts, D. (2004) 'A systematic review of business incubation research', *Journal of Technology Transfer*, Vol. 29, No. 1: 55–82.

Hamel, G. and Prahalad, C. K. (1990) 'The core competence of the corporation', *Harvard Business Review*, Vol. 68, No. 3: 79–91.

Hamel, G. and Prahalad, C. K. (1994) *Competing for the Future*, Cambridge, MA: Harvard Business School Press.

Hanks, S., Watson, C., Jansen, E. and Chandler, G. (1993) 'Tightening the life-cycle construct: a taxonomic study of growth stage configurations in high-technology organizations', *Entrepreneurship Theory and Practice*, Vol. 18, No. 2: 5–29.

Hansen, E. and Bird, B. (1997) 'The stages model of high-tech venture founding: tried but true?', *Entrepreneurship Theory and Practice*, Vol. 22, No. 2: 111–23.

Harris, J. M., Shaw, R. W. Jr. and Sommers, W. P. (1981) 'The strategic management of technology', *Outlook*, Vol. 5, Fall/Winter: 20–6.

Harris, S. (2000) 'Reconciling positive and interpretative international management research: a native category approach', *International Business Review*, Vol. 9, No. 6: 755–70.

Harris, S. and Bovaird, C. (1996) *Enterprising Capital: A Study of Enterprise Development and the Institutions which Finance it*, Aldershot: Ashgate.

Harris, S. and Ghauri, P. N. (2000) 'Strategy formation by business leaders: exploring the influence of national values', *European Journal of Marketing*, Vol. 34, No. 1/2: 126–41.

Hastings, C. (1993) *The New Organization: Growing the culture of organizational networking*, London: McGraw-Hill.

Heidenberger, K. and Stummer, C. (1999) 'Research and development project selection and resource allocation: a review of quantitative modelling approaches', *International Journal of Management Reviews*, Vol. 1, No. 2: 197–224.

Heimer, C. A. (1992) 'Doing your job and helping your friends: universalistic norms about obligations to particular others in networks', in N. Nohria and R. G. Eccles (eds), *Networks and Organizations. Structure, Form, and Action*, Cambridge, MA: Harvard Business School Press.

Heirman, A. and Clarysse, B. (2004) 'How and why do research-based start-ups differ at founding? a resource-based configurational perspective', *Journal of Technology Transfer*, Vol. 29, No. 3/4: 247–68.

Heirman, A., Clarysse, B. and Van Den Haute, V. (2003) 'Resources of research-based start-ups and the influence of technology, institutional link and industry', Working Paper No. 22 Vlerick Leuven Gent Management School.

Henriksen, A. and Traynor, A. J. (1999) 'A practical R&D project-selection scoring tool', *IEEE Transactions on Engineering Management*, Vol. 46, No. 2: 158–70.

Herlau, H. and Tetzschner, H. (1999) *Fra Jobtager til jobmager. Model II*, Copenhagen: Samfundslitteratur.

Hernandez, E-M. (2001) *L'entrepreneuriat, approche théorique*, Paris: L'Harmattan.

Hickson, D. J. and Pugh, D. S. (1995) *Management Worldwide: the Impact of Societal Culture on Organisations around the Globe*, London: Penguin.

Hill, R. C. and Levenhagen, M. (1995) 'Metaphors and metal models: sensemaking and sensegiving in innovative and entrepreneurial activities', *Journal of Management*, Vol. 21, No. 6: 1057–74.

Hindle, K. (2004) 'Choosing qualitative methods for entrepreneurial cognition research', *Entrepreneurship Theory and Practice*, Vol. 28, No. 6: 575–607.

Hinkle, D. E., Wiersma, W. and Jurs, S. G. (1994) *Applied Statistics for the Behavioural Sciences*, 3rd edn, Boston, MA: Houghton-Mifflin.

Hite, J. M. (2005) 'Evolutionary processes and paths of relationally embedded network ties in emerging entrepreneurial firms', *Entrepreneurship Theory and Practice*, Vol. 29, No. 1: 113–44.

Hite, J. M. and Hesterly, W. S. (2001) 'The evolution of firm networks: from emergence to early growth of the firm', *Strategic Management Journal*, Vol. 22, No. 3: 275–86.

Hofstede, G. (2001) *Culture's Consequences: Comparing Values. Behaviors, Institutions and Organizations across Nations*, 2nd edn, Thousand Oaks, CA: Sage.

Holland, J. L. (1973) *Making Vocational Choices*, Englewood Cliffs, NJ: Prentice Hall.

Holland, J. L. (1992) *Making Vocational Choices, A Theory of Vocational Personalities and Work Environments*, Odessa: Psychological Assessment Resources Inc.

Hsuan M. J. (2001) 'Portfolio management of R&D projects: implications for innovation management', *Technovation*, Vol. 21, No. 7: 423–35.

Ibarra, H. (1992) 'Structural alignments, individual strategies, and managerial action: elements toward a network theory of getting things done', in N. Nohriaand and R. G. Eccles (eds), *Networks and Organizations: Structure, Form, and Action*, Cambridge, MA: Harvard Business School Press.

Jaffe, A., Trajtenberg, M. and Henderson, R. (1993) 'Geographic localization of knowledge spillovers as evidenced by patent citations', *Quarterly Journal of Economics*, Vol. 63, No. 3: 577–98.

Jarillo, J. C. (1988) 'On strategic networks', *Strategic Management Journal*, Vol. 9, No. 1: 31–41.

Jeffries, S. L. and Reed, R. (2000) 'Trust and adaptation in relational contracting', *Academy of Management Review*, Vol. 25, No. 4: 873–82.

Jensen, S., Siggard, M., Moensted, M., and Olsen, S. F. (2004) *Viden, Ledelse og Kommunikation*, Copenhagen: Samfundslitteratur.

Johannisson, B. (1986) 'Network strategies: management technology for entrepreneurship and change', *International Small Business Journal*, Vol. 5, No. 1: 19–30.

Johannisson, B. (1994) 'Building a "GLOCAL" strategy: internationalizing small firms through local networking', Proceedings of the 39th Annual ICSB Conference, Strasbourg, France, 27–29 June 1994: 127–35.

Johannisson, B. (2000) 'Networking and entrepreneurial growth', in D. L. Sexton and H. Landstrom (eds), *The Blackwell Handbook of Entrepreneurship*, Oxford: Blackwell.

Johannisson, B. and Moensted M. (1997) 'Contextualizing entrepreneurial networking: the case of Scandinavia', *International Studies of Management and Organization*, Vol. 27, No. 3: 109–36.

Johnson, B. and Lundvall, B. A. (1994) 'The learning economy', *Journal of Industry Studies*, Vol. 1, No. 2: 23–42.

Jolly, D. (2000) 'Three generic resource-based strategies', *International Journal of Technology Management*, Vol. 19, No. 7/8: 773–87.

Jolly, D. (2003) 'The issue of weightings in technology portfolio management', *Technovation*, Vol. 23, No. 5: 383–91.

Jolly, D. and Thérin, F. (1996) 'La stratégie technologique au service des stratégies basées sur les ressources', Proceedings of the 24th Congrès Annuel de l'Association des Sciences Administratives (Asac), Division Stratégies et Politiques, Montreal: 46–53.

Joule, R.-V. and Beauvois, J.-L. (1987) *Petit traité de manipulation à usage des honnêtes gens*, Grenoble: PUG.

Julien, P. A. (2002) *Les PME à forte croissance: l'exemple de 17 gazelles dans 8 régions du Québec*, Quebec, Canada: Presses de l'Université du Québec.

Julien, P. A. and Marchesnay, M. (1996) *L'entrepreneuriat*, Paris: Economica, Gestion Poche.

Kahaner, L. (1996) *Competitive Intelligence*, New York, NY: Simon & Schuster.

Kanter, R. M. (1983) *The Change Masters: Innovation and Entrepreneurship in the American Corporation*, New York: Touchstone.

Kasturirangan, R. (1999) 'Multiple scales in small-world graphs', MIT working paper, Cambridge, MA: Department of Brain and Cognitive Science, Massachusetts Institute of Technology.

Katzenbach, J. R. and Smith D. K. (1993) *The Wisdom of Teams: Creating the High-Performance Organization*, Boston MA: Harvard Business School Press.

Keeble, D., Lawson, C., Moore, B. and Wilkinson, F. (1999) 'Collective learning processes, networking and "institutional thickness" in the Cambridge region', *Regional Studies*, Vol. 33 No. 4: 319–32.

Kenney, M. (ed.) (2000) *Understanding Silicon Valley The Anatomy of an Entrepreneurial Region*, Palo Alto, CA: Stanford University Press.

Kenney, M. and Florida, R. (2000) 'Venture capital in Silicon Valley: fueling new firm formation', in M. Kenney (ed.), *Understanding Silicon Valley: The Anatomy of an Entrepreneurial Region*, Stanford, CA: Stanford University Press.

Khalil, T. (2000) *Management of Technology: The Key to Competitiveness and Wealth Creation*, New York: McGraw-Hill.

Kim, D. H. (1993) 'The link between individual and organizational learning', *Sloan Management Review*, Vol. 35, No. 1: 37–51.

Kirchhoff, B. A., Merges, M. J. and Morabito, J. (2001) 'A value creation model for measuring and managing the R&D portfolio', *Engineering Management Journal*, Vol. 13, No. 1: 19–22.

Kirman, A. (1992) 'Variety: the coexistence of techniques', *Revue d'Economie Industrielle*, Vol. 59: 62–74.

Klepper, S. (2002) 'The evolution of the U.S. automobile industry and Detroit as its capital', paper presented to the 2002 DRUID conference, Aalborg, Denmark, 17–19 January.

Kline, S. and Rosenberg, N. (1986) 'An overview of innovation', in R. Landau and N. Rosenberg (eds), *The Positive Sum Strategy*, Washington, DC: National Academy Press.

Klofsten, M. (1997) 'Management of the early development process in technology-based firms', in D. Jones-Evans and M. Klofsten (eds), *Technology, Innovation and Enterprise: The European Experience*, Basingstoke: Macmillan Press.

Kluckholn F. R. and Strotdbeck, F. L. (1961) *Variations in Value Orientations*, New York: Peterson.

Knight, F. R. (1921) *Risk, Uncertainty and Profit*, Boston, MA: Kelley.

Kogut, B. (2000) 'The network as knowledge: generative rules and the emergence of structure', *Strategic Management Journal*, Vol. 21, No. 3: 405–25.

Kogut, B. and Zander, U. (1992) 'Knowledge of the firm, combinative capabilities, and the replication of technology', *Organization Science*, Vol. 3, No. 3: 383–97.

Koka, B. R. and Prescott, J. E. (2002) 'Strategic alliances as social capital: a multidimensional view', *Strategic Management Journal*, Vol. 23, No. 9: 875–916.

Kostova, T. (1999) 'Transnational transfer of strategic organizational practices: a contextual perspective', *Academy of Management Review*, Vol. 24, No. 2: 308–24.

Kostova, T. and Roth, K. (2003) 'Social capital in multinational corporations and a micro-macro model of its formation', *Academy of Management Review*, Vol. 28, No. 2: 297–317.

Kotabe, M., Martin, X. and Domoto, H. (2003) 'Gaining from vertical partnerships: knowledge transfer, relationship duration, and supplier performance improvement in the U.S. and Japanese automotive industries', *Strategic Management Journal*, Vol. 24, No. 4: 293–316.

Krachardt, D. and Stern, R. (1988) 'Informal networks and organizational crisis: An experimental simulation', *Social Psychology Quarterly*, 51: 123–50.

Kreiner, K. and Schultz, M. (1993) 'Informal collaboration in R & D: the formation of networks across organizatons', *Organizational Studies*, Vol. 14, No. 2: 189–209.

Krieger, E. (1996) 'Trust and management: an application to innovative small companies', Proceedings of the 4th High Technology Small Firms Conference, Enchede: University of Twente: 373–88.

Krugman, P. (1991) *Geography and Trade*, Cambridge, MA: MIT Press.

Kumar, U. and Kumar, V. (1997) *Incubating Technology: Best Practices*, Ottowa, Canada: Federal Partners in Technology Transfer.

Kympers, L. (1992) 'Een Belgisch-Vlaamse kijk op Nederlands zakendoen', *Holland Management Review*, Vol. 33 No. 1: 59–69.

La Ville de, V. I. (1996) 'Apprentissages collectifs et structuration de la stratégie dans la jeune entreprise de haute technologie : etude de cas et éléments de modélisation procédurale', Ph.D dissertation, Lyon: Université Lyon III.

La Ville de, V. I. (2000) 'L'entrepreneuriat technologique comme processus de création collective', in M. Bernasconi and M. Moensted (eds), *Start-up high tech,* Paris: Dunod.

La Ville de, V. I. and Mounoud, E. (2003) 'Between discourse and narration: how can strategy be a practice?', in B. Czarniawska and P. Gagliardi (eds), *Narratives We Organize By*, Amsterdam: John Benjamins.

Laban, J. (1989) 'Le marketing des nouvelles technologies', *Revue Française de Gestion*, Vol. 72 (Jan–Feb): 88–96.

Laban, J. and Morin, J. (1988) 'Inventer le futur: les nouvelles offres technologiques', *Harvard l'Expansion*, Vol. 51 (Winter): 51–61.

Lanciano-Morandat, C. and Nohara, H. (2001) 'Academic spin-offs in the information technology sector in France: institutional effects or territorial effects?', *Revue d'Economie Regionale et Urbaine*, No. 2: 235–66.

Lange, C. (1993) *Etre ingénieur aujourd'hui*, Paris: Les Editions du Rocher.

Langlois, R. N. (1997) 'Cognition and capabilities: opportunities seized and missed in the history of the computer industry', in R. Garud, P. R. Nayyar and Z. B. Shapira (eds), *Technological Innovation: Oversights and Foresights*, Cambridge: Cambridge University Press.

Langlois, R. N. and Robertson, P. L. (1995) *Firms, Markets, and Economic Change: A Dynamic Theory of Business Institutions*, Routledge: London.

Lanthier, P. (1979) 'Les dirigeants des grandes entreprises électriques en France, 1911–1973' in M. Levy-Leboyer (ed.), *Le patronat de la seconde industrialisation*, Paris: Les Editions Ouvrières.

Larsen, A. F. (2001) *Giga-manden: Frontløberen i en dansk milliardsucces*, Copenhagen: Aschehoug Danske Forlag.

Larson, A. (1992) 'Network dyads in entrepreneurial settings: a study of the governance of exchange relationships', *Administrative Science Quarterly*, Vol. 37, No. 1: 76–104.

Lasserre, H. (1989) *Le pouvoir de l'ingénieur*, Paris: Editions l'Harmattan.

Laszlo, C. and Laugel, J.-F. (1998) *L'économie du chaos*, Paris: Les Editions d'Organisation.

Latour, B. (1987) *Science in Action: How to Follow Scientists and Engineers through Society*, Cambridge, MA: Harvard University Press.

Latour, B. (1998) 'Comment évaluer l'innovation?', *La Recherche*, No. 314, November: 1343–66.

Laurent, A. (1983) 'The cultural diversity of western conceptions of management', *International Studies of Management and Organisation*, Vol. 13, No. 1: 75–96.

Lave, J. and Wenger, E. (1990) *Situated Learning: Legitimate Periperal Participation*, Cambridge: Cambridge University Press.

Le Marois, H. (1985) 'Contribution à la mise en place de dispositifs de soutien aux entrepreneurs' Management Science Doctoral Thesis, Lille: Université de Lille.

Leavitt, H. J. (1986) *Corporate Pathfinders: Building vision and values into Organizations*, Homewood, IL: Dow Jones Irwin.

Lendner, C. (2002) *How University Business Incubators Help Start-ups to Succeed: An International Study*, 2002 Babson Kauffmann Entrepreneurship Research Conference, Babson College, MA, USA..

Leonard, D. and Sensiper, S. (1998) 'The role of tacit knowledge in group innovation', *California Management Review*, Vol. 40, No. 3: 112–32.

Levie, J. and Hay, M. (1998) 'Progress or just proliferation? A historical review of stages models of early corporate growth', London Business School Working Paper FEM WP 98.5, London: London Business School.

Levine, J. M., Resnick, L. B. and Higgins, E. T. (1993) 'Social foundations of cognition', *Annual Review of Psychology*, Vol. 44, No. 1: 585–612.

Levitt, T. (1983) 'The globalization of markets', *Harvard Business Review*, Vol. 61, May–June: 92–102.

Levy-Leboyer, M. (1979) 'Le patronat français, 1912–1973', in M. Levy-Leboyer (ed.), *Le patronat de la seconde industrialisation*, Paris: Les Editions Ouvrières.

Li, J., Lam, K. and Kuin, G. (2001) 'Does culture affect behaviour and performance of firms? The case of joint ventures in China', *Journal of International Business Studies*, Vol. 32, No. 1: 115–31.

Lichtenstein, G. A., and Lyons, T. S. (1996) *Incubating New Enterprises: A Guide to Successful Practice*, Washington, DC: Aspen Institute Rural Economic Policy Program.

Link, A. N. and Bozeman, B. (1991) 'Innovative behavior in small-sized firms', *Small Business Economics*, Vol. 3, No. 3: 179–84.

Linton, J. D., Walsh, S. T. and Morabito, J. (2002) 'Analysis, ranking and selection of R&D projects in a portfolio', *R & D Management*, Vol. 32, No. 2: 139–48.

Lojkine, J. (1992) *Les jeunes diplômés: un groupe social en quête d'identité*, Paris: PUF.

Longhi, C. and Masboungi, J.(1998) 'Sophia Antipolis, histoire et devenir', in M. Quere (ed.), *Les technopoles en Europe: enjeux et atouts de la diversité*, France: L'Association France Technopoles.

Longhi, C. and Quéré, M. (1991) 'La technopole comme système industriel localisé: éléments d'analyse and enseignements empiriques', *Economie and Société*, Vol. 8: 21–42.

Lorange, P. and Roos, J. (1992) *Strategic Alliances. Formation, Implementation, and Evolution*, London: Blackwell.

Luhmann, N. (1979) *Trust and Power*, London: Wiley.

Lundvall, B.-A. (1988) 'Innovation as an interactive process: from user-producer interaction to the National Innovation Systems', in G. Dosi, C. Freeman, R. R. Nelson, G. Silverberg, and L. Soete (eds), *Technology and Economic Theory*, London: Pinter.

Lundvall, B.-A .(1992), *National Systems of Innovation: Toward a Theory of Interactive Learning*, London: Pinter.

Lundvall, B.-A. and Johnson, B. (1994) 'The learning economy', *Journal of Industry Studies*, Vol. 1, No. 2: 23–42.

Lysaght, M. and Aebischer, P. (1999) 'Les cellules encapsulées', *Pour la science*, No. 266: 160–6.

McCann, J. (1991) 'Patterns of growth, competitive technology and financial strategies in young ventures', *Journal of Business Venturing*, Vol. 6, No. 3: 189–208.

McClelland, D. C. (1961) *The Achieving Society*, Princeton, NJ: Van Nostrand.

McClelland, D. C. (1979) 'That urge to achieve', in D. A. Kolb I. M. Rubin and J.M. McIntyre (eds), *Organizational Psychology: A Book of Readings*, Englewood Cliffs, NJ: Prentice Hall.

Macher, J. T. and Mowery, D. C. (2003) 'Managing learning by doing: an empirical study in semi-conductor manufacturing', *Journal of Product Innovation Management*, Vol. 20, No. 5: 391–410.

McKenna, R. (1985) *Le marketing selon McKenna*, Paris: InterEditions.

Magliulo, B. (1982) *Les Grandes Ecoles*, Paris: PUF.

Magretta, J. (2002) 'Why business models matter', *Harvard Business Review*, Vol. 80, No. 5: 86–92.

Malecki, E. (1991) *Technology and Economic Development: The Dynamics of Local, Regional and National Change*, Harlow: Longman.

Mansfield, E. (1985) 'How rapidly does new industrial technology leak out?', *The Journal of Industrial Economics*, Vol. 34, No. 2: 217–23.

Marcel, P., Meslif, A. and Domergue, Y. (1995) 'Le design dans l'innovation des plaques de cuisson gaz', in P. David and A. Pauche (eds), *L'innovation: actes des 6èmes entretiens de la Villette*, Paris: Cité des Sciences et de l'Industrie & Centre National de Documentation Pédagogique.

March, J. (1991) 'Exploration and exploitation in organizational learning', *Organization Science*, Vol. 2, No. 1: 71–87.

March, J. and Olsen, J. (1975) 'The uncertainty of the past: organizational learning under ambiguity', *European Journal of Political Research*, Vol. 3, No. 3: 147–71.

March, J. and Olsen, J. (1976) *Ambiguity and Choice in Organizations*, Bergen: Universitetsforlaget.

Marchesnay, M. (2002) *Pour une approche entrepreneuriale de la dynamique Ressources-Compétences: essai de praxéologie*, Lille, France: Editions de l'ADREG.

Marris, P. and Somerset, A. (1971) *African Businessmen: A Study of Entrepreneurship and Development in Kenya*, London: Routledge & Kegan Paul.

Marsden, P. V. (1982) 'Brokerage behaviour, restricted exchange networks', in P. V. Marsden and N. Lin (eds), *Social Structure and Network Analysis*, London: Sage: 201–18.

Marshall, A. (1920) *Principles of Economics* (8th edn), London: Macmillan.

Marshall, R. S. and Boush, D. M. (2001) 'Dynamic decision making: a cross-cultural comparison of us and Peruvian export managers', *Journal of International Business Studies*, Vol. 32, No. 4: 873–93.

Massacrier, G. and Rigaud, G. (1984) 'The start-up of new activities: vagaries and processes', *Revue Française de Gestion*, March–April–May, No. 45: 5–18.

Maurice, M., Sellier, F. and Silvestre, J. J. (1982) *Politique d'éducation et organisation industrielle en France et en Allemagne*, Paris: Presses Universitaires de France.

Meyer, M. (1993) *Questions de rhétorique: langage, raison et séduction*, Paris: Librairie Générale Française.

Mikkelsen, H. and Riis, J. O. (1998) *Grundbog i Projektledelse*, Copenhagen: Promet Aps.

Miller, D. and Friesen, P. (1983) 'Innovation in conservative and entrepreneurial firms: two models of strategic momentum', *Strategic Management Journal*, Vol. 3, No. 1: 1–25.

Miller, D. and Friesen, P. (1984) 'A longitudinal study of the corporate life cycle', *Management Science*, Vol. 30, No. 10: 1161–83.

Miller, R., Hobday, M., Leroux-Demers, T. and Olleros, X. (1995) 'Innovation in complex systems industries: the case of flight simulation', *Industrial and Corporate Change*, Vol. 4, No. 2: 363–400.

Miller, W. L. (1995) 'A broader mission for R&D', *Research Technology Management*, Vol. 38, No. 6: 24–36.

Millier, P. (1989) 'Le marketing de l'innovation technologique', Lyon: Groupe ESC Lyon Institut de Recherche de l'Entreprise.

Millier, P. (1995) *Développer les marchés industriels: principes de segmentation*, Paris: Dunod.

Millier, P. (1999) *Cas SPYMAG*, Paris: Centrale de Cas et des Moyens Pédagogiques.

Miner, A. S., Bassoff, P. and Moorman, C. (2001) 'Organisational improvisation and learning: a field study', *Administrative Science Quarterly*, Vol. 46, No. 2: 304–37.

Moensted, M. (2003) *Strategic Networking in Small High Tech Firms*, Copenhagen: Samfundslitteratur.

Montgomery, C. A. (1995) *Resource-Based and Evolutionary Theories of the Firm: Towards a Synthesis*, Boston, MA: Kluwer Academic Publishers.

Moreau, F. (2003) 'Proposition d'une typologie des modes de développement des jeunes entreprises technologiques innovantes à fort potentiel de croissance', PhD Thesis, Université Paris X, Paris: University of Paris.

Moreau, F. and Bernasconi, M. (2002) 'Modes de développement et gestion des risques', in F. Moreau (ed.), *Comprendre et gérer les risques*, Paris: Editions d'Organisation.

Moreau, F. and Tamarelle, F. (2004) 'L'intelligence commerciale dans les start-up high tech: le cas d'Infobjects', in A. Guilhon (ed.), *L'intelligence économique dans les PME-PMI*, Paris: L'Harmattan.

REFERENCES

Moriarty, R. T. and Kosnik, T. J. (1989) 'High-tech marketing: concepts, continuity, and change', *Sloan Management Review*, Vol. 30, No. 4: 7–17.

Morin, J. (1985) *L'excellence technologique*, Paris: Diffusion Publi-union – Editions Jean Picollec.

Morin, J. (1986) 'La maîtrise d'une ressource stratégique: l'information', *Le progrès technique*, May.

Morin, J. (1992) *Des technologies, des marchés et des hommes*, Paris: Les Editions d'Organisation.

Morin, J. and Seurat, R. (1989) *Le management des ressources technologiques*, Paris: Les Editions d'Organisation.

Moscovici, S. (ed.) (1994) *Psychologie sociale des relations à autrui*, Paris: Nathan.

Moutet, A. (1985) 'Ingénieurs et rationalisation en France de la guerre à la crise (1914–1929)', in A. Moutet, *L'ingénieur dans la société française*, Paris: Les Editions Ouvrières.

Mustar, P. (1994) 'L'entrepreneur Schumpétérien a-t-il jamais existé?', *Annales des Mines, Gérer et Comprendre*, Vol. 34, March: 30–7.

Mustar, P. (1997) 'Spin-off enterprises: how French academics create hi-tech companies: the conditions for success or failure', *Science and Public Policy*, Vol. 24, No. 1: 37–43.

Mustar, P. (2001) 'Diversité et unité des entreprises à forte croissance du secteur manufacturier en France', *Revue Internationale PME*, Vol. 14, No. 3–4 (Special issue): 67–89.

Mytelka, L. K. (1991) 'Crisis, technological change and the strategic alliance', in L. K. Mytelka (ed.), *Strategic Partnerships, States, Firms and International Competition*, London: Pinter.

Nachum, L. and Keeble, D. (2000) 'Localised clusters and the eclectic paradigm of foreign investment: film TNCs in central London', *Transnational Corporations*, Vol. 9, No. 1: 1–37.

Nelson, R. (1991) 'Why do firms differ, and how does it matter?', *Strategic Management Journal*, Vol. 12, No. 8: 61–74.

Nelson, R. (ed.) (1993) *National Innovation Systems: A Comparative Analysis*, Oxford: Oxford University Press.

Nelson, R. and Winter, S. (1982) *An Evolutionary Theory of Economic Change*, Belknap, MA: Harvard University Press.

Nesta, L. and Dibiaggio, L. (2003) 'Technology strategy and knowledge dynamics: the case of biotech', *Industry and Innovation,* Vol. 10, No. 3: 331–49.

Newbert, S. C. (2005) 'New firm formation: a dynamic capability perspective', *Journal of Small Business Management*, Vol. 43, No. 1: 55–77.

Nicolaou, N. and Birley, S. (2003) 'Academic networks in a trichotomous categorisation of university spinouts' *Journal of Business Venturing*, Vol. 18, No. 3: 333–59.

Nohria, N. (1992) 'Is a network perspective a useful way of studying organizations?', in N. Nohria and R. G. Eccles (eds), *Networks and Organizations: Structure, Form, and Action*, Cambridge, MA: Harvard Business School Press: 1–22.

Nohria, N. and Eccles, R. G. (eds) (1992) *Network Organizations*. Cambridge, MA: Harvard Business School Press.

Nonaka, I. (1994) 'A dynamic theory of organizational knowledge creation', *Organization Science*, Vol. 5, No. 1: 14–37.

Nonaka, I. and Takeuchi, H. (1995) *The Knowledge Creating Company*, Oxford: Oxford University Press.

Normann, R. (1984) *Service Management: Strategy and Leadership in Service Businesses*, New York: Wiley.

North, D. C. (1991) *Institutions, Institutional Change and Economic Performance*, Cambridge: Cambridge University Press.

North, D. C. (1994) *Institutions Matter*, Working Paper wuwpeh9411004, St Louis, WA: Washington University Department of Economics.

North, K. (1997) 'Travaux de recherche sur le knowledge management', PhD thesis, University of Wiesbaden.

Oakey, R. P., Faulkner W., Cooper S. Y. and Walsh V. (1990) *New Firms in the biotechnology Industry: Their Contribution to Innovation and Growth*, London: Pinter.

OECD (1999) *Boosting Innovation: The Cluster Approach*, Paris: OECD.

O'Farrell, P. and Hitchens, D. (1988) 'Alternative theories of small-firm growth: a critical review', *Environment and Planning*, Vol. 20, No. 10: 1365–83.

Ohmae, K. (1983) *The Mind of the Strategist*, New York: Penguin Books.

Ohmae, K. (1991) *Le génie du stratège*, Paris: Dunod.

Ouellet, F. and Martel, J. F. (1995) 'Méthode multicritère d'évaluation et de sélection de projets de R&D interdépendants', *Revue Canadienne des Sciences de l'Administration/Canadian Journal of Administrative Sciences*, Vol. 12, No. 3: 195–209.

Parsons, T. (1964) *Social Structure and Personality*, New York: Free Press.

Pavitt, K. (1990) 'What we know about strategic management of technology', *California Management Review*, Vol. 32, No. 1: 17–26.

Pedersen, T. and Thomsen, S. (2003) 'Ownership structure and value of the largest European firms: the importance of owner identity', *Journal of Management and Governance*, Vol. 7, No. 1: 27–55.

Penrose, E. T. (1995; 2nd edn 1959) *The Theory of the Growth of the Firm*, Oxford: Oxford University Press.

Perrow, C. (1984) *Normal Accidents. Living with High-risk technologies*, New York: Basic Books.

Perry-Smith, J. E. and Shalley, C.E. (2003) 'The social side of creativity: a static and dynamic social network perspective', *Academy of Management Review*, Vol. 28, No. 1: 89–106.

Peters, L., Rice, M. and Sundarajan M. (2004) 'Role of incubators in the entrepreneurial process', *Journal of Technology Transfer*, Vol. 29, No. 1: 83–91.

Pett, M. A. (1997) *Nonparametric Statistics for Health Care Research*, Thousand Oaks, CA: Sage.

Piore, M. J. and Sabel, C. F. (1989) *Les Chemins de la prosperité, de la production de masse a la specialization souple*, Paris: Hachette.

Pleitner, H. J. (1985) 'Entrepreneurs and new venture creation: some reflections of a conceptual nature', Economics, Law, Business and Public Administration Working Paper, St Gall: St Gall Graduate School.

Pleschak, F. (1997) 'Technology and incubator centres as aninstrument of regional economic promotion', in K. Koschatzky (ed.), *Technology-based Firms in the Innovation Process: Management, Financing, and Regional Networks*, Heidelberg: Physica-Verlag.

Pleschak, F., Werner, H. and Wupperfeld, U. (1997) 'Marketing in new technology-based firms', in K. Koschatzky (ed.), *Technology-Based Firms in the Innovation Process*, Heidelberg: Physica-Verlag.

Poh, K. L., Ang, B. W. and Bai, F. (2001) 'A comparative analysis of R&D project evaluation methods', *R & D Management*, Vol. 31, No. 1: 63–75.

Polanyi, M. (1966) *The Tacit Dimension*, Garden City, NY: Doubleday.

Poole, M. S., Van de Ven, A., Dooley, K. and Holmes, M. E. (2000), *Organizational Change and Innovation Processes: Theories and Methods for Research*, Oxford: Oxford University Press.

Porter, M. (1980) *Competitive Strategy*, New York: The Free Press.

Porter, M. (1998) *On Competition*, Boston, MA: Harvard Business Press.

Portes, A. (ed.) (1995) *The Economic Sociology of Immigration*, New York: Russell Sage.

Potter, J. (1996) *Representing Reality: Discourse, Rhetoric and Social Construction*, London: Sage Publications.

Powell, W. W. and Smith-Doerr, L. (1994) 'Networks and economic life', in N. J. Smelser and R. Swedberg (eds), *The Handbook of Economic Sociology*, Princeton, NJ: Princeton University Press: 368–402.

Prahalad, C. K. (1993) 'The role of core competences in the corporation', *Research-Technology Management*, Vol. 36, No. 6: 40–7.

Prevezer, M. (2001) 'Ingredients in the early development of the U.S. biotechnology industry', *Small Business Economics*, Vol. 17, No. 1: 17–29.

Price D. (1963) *Little Science, Big Science*, New York: Columbia University Press

Price, D. (1972) *Science and Suprascienceé*, (trans G. Lévy) Paris: Fayard.

Quinn, R. (1988) *Beyond Rational Management*, San Francisco, CA: Jossey-Bass.

Quinn, R. and Cameron, K. (1983) 'Organizational life cycles and shifting criteria of effectiveness: some preliminary evidence', *Management Science*, Vol. 29, No. 1: 33–52.

Ramsaswamy, K., Li, M. and Veliyath, R. (2002) 'Variations in ownership behaviour and propensity to diversify: a study of the Indian corporate context', *Strategic Management Journal*, Vol. 23, No. 4: 345–58.

Raveyre M. F. and Saglio J. (1990) 'Localized industrial systems: elements for a sociological analysis of industrial groups of SMEs', *International Studies of Management and Organization*, Vol. 20, No. 4: 77–92.

Raveyre, M. F. and Saglio, J. (1992) *Les herbes folles des friches industrielles*, Lyon: Rapport d'étude du Groupement Lyonnais de sociologie industrielle, No. 5.

Reagans, R. and Zuckerman, E.W. (2001) 'Networks, diversity, and productivity: the social capital of corporate R&D teams', *Organization Science*, Vol. 12, No. 3: 502–17.

Reuber, A. R. and Fischer, E. (2005) 'The company you keep: how young firms in different competitive contexts signal reputation through their customers', *Entrepreneurship Theory and Practice*, Vol. 29, No. 1: 57–78.

Reynolds, P. and Miller, B. (1992) 'New firm gestation: conception, birth, and implications for research', *Journal of Business Venturing*, Vol. 7, No. 5: 405–18.

Reynolds, P. D. and White, S. B. (1997) *The Entrepreneurial Process: Economic Growth, Men, Women, and Minorities*, Westport, CT: Quorum Books.

Ribeill, G. (1984) 'Entreprendre hier et aujourd'hui: la contribution des ingénieurs', *Culture Technique*, No. 12: 77–92.

Ring, P. S. (1996) 'Networked organization: a resource-based perspective', Acta Universitatis Upsaliensis, Studia Oeconomiae Negotiorum (No. 39), Upsala: University of Upsala.

Ring, P. S. and Van de Ven, A. H. (1994) 'Developmental processes of co-operative interorganizational relationships', *Academy of Management Review*, Vol. 19, No. 1: 90–118.

Ringuest, J. F., Graves, S. B. and Case, R. H. (1999) 'Formulating R&D portfolios that account for Risk', *Research Technology Management*, Vol. 42, No. 6: 40–3.

Rip, A. and de Velde, R. (1997) *The Dynamics of Innovation in Bio-engineering Catalysis. Cases and Analysis*, European Commission JRC EUR 17341 EN: Enchede, NL: University of Twente Centre for Studies of Science, Technology and Society.

Riverin-Simard, D. (1984) *Etapes de vie au travail*, Montréal: Editions Saint-Martin.

Robin, J.Y. (1994) *Radioscopie de cadres: itinéraire professionnel et biographie éducative*, Paris: Editions de l'Harmattan.

Roussel, P. A., Saad, K. N. and Erickson, T. J. (1991) *Third Generation R&D: Managing the Link to Corporate Strategy*, Boston, MA: Harvard Business School Press.

Saglio, J. (1984) 'Les ingénieurs sont-ils des patrons comme les autres?', *Culture Technique*, No. 12: 93–101.

Salais, R. and Storper, M. (1993) *Les mondes de production: enquête sur l'identité économique de la France*, Paris: l'EHESS.

Salmon, R. and Yolaine de, L. (1997) *L'intelligence compétitive*, Paris: Editions Economica.

Sammut, S. (1998) *Young Company: The Crucial Start-Up Phase*, Paris: L'Harmattan.

Sammut, S. (2001) 'Start-up phase in a small company: management system and scenarios', *Revue de l'Entrepreneuriat*, Vol. 2, No. 1: 61–76.

Sanchez, R. and Mahoney, J. (1996) 'Modularity, flexibility, and knowledge management in product and organization design', *Strategic Management Journal*, Vol. 17 (Winter special issue): 63–76.

Sanchez, R., Heene, A. and Thomas, H. (1996) *Dynamics of Competence-based Competition: Theory and Practice in the New Strategic Management*, Oxford: Elsevier.

Saporta, B. (1994) 'La création d'entreprise: enjeux et perspectives', *Revue Française de Gestion*, Vol. 74, Nov.–Dec.: 74–86.

Saxenian, A. (1994) *Regional Advantage: Culture and Competition in Silicon Valley and Route 128*, Cambridge, MA: Harvard University Press.

Saxenian, A. (1999) *The Silicon Valley–Hsinchu Connection: Technical Communities and Industrial Upgrading*, Stanford, CA: Stanford Institute for Economic Policy Research.

Saxenian, A. and Li, C.-H. (2003) 'Bay-to-bay strategic alliances: the networks linkages between Taiwan and the US venture capital industries', *International Journal of Technology Management*, Vol. 25, No. 1–2: 136–50.

Schein, E. H. (1978) 'Career anchors and career paths: panel study of management school graduates', in J. Van Maanen (ed.), *Organizational Careers: Some New Perspectives*, New York: John Wiley and Sons.

Schein, E. H. (1985) *Organizational Culture and Leadership*, San Francisco, CA: Jossey Bass.

Schulze, W. S., Lubatkin, M. H. and Dino, R. N. (2003) 'Exploring the agency consequences of ownership dispersion among the directors of private family firms', *Academy of Management Journal*, Vol. 46, No. 2: 179–95.

Schumpeter, J. (1934) *The Theory of Economic Development*, Cambridge, MA: Harvard University Press.

Schumpeter, J. (1935) *Théorie de l'évolution économique*, Paris: Dalloz.

Schumpeter, J. (1950) *Capitalism, Socialism and Democracy*, 3rd edn, New York: Harper and Row.

Scott, A. and Storper, M. (1987) 'High technology industry and regional development: a theoretical critique and reconstruction', *International Social Science Review*, Vol. 112, May: 215–32.

Scott, W. R. and Meyer, J. W. (eds) (1994) *Institutional Environments and Organisations: Structural Complexity and Individualism*, Thousand Oaks, CA: Sage Publications.

Segal Quince & Partners (1985) *The Cambridge Phenomenon: The Growth of High Technology Industry in a University Town'*, Cambridge: Segal Quince & Partners.

Segal Quince Wicksteed (2000) *The Cambridge Phenomenon Revisited*, Cambridge: Segal Quince Wicksteed.

Sethi, N. K., Movsesian, B. and Hickey, K. D. (1985) 'Can technology be managed strategically?', *Long Range Planning*, Vol. 18, No. 4: 89–99.

Seurat, R. (1986) 'L'entreprise aux aguets', *Management et Qualité*, March.

Seurat, R. (1994) 'Le management de l'innovation', *Futuribles*, Vol. 187 (May): 35–44.

Seurat, R. and Rougeaux, J. (1990) 'Intelligence service et marketing des projets industriels', *Revue Française du Marketing*, Vol. 127–8, Nos 2/3: 39–50.

Seurat, R. and Rougeaux, J. (1991) 'Comment mettre en place un système d'information et de veille performant?', *International Research Eurostart Conference*, Paris, June.

Shane, S. (2000) 'Prior knowledge and the discovery of entrepreneurial opportunities', *Organization Science*, Vol. 11, No. 4: 448–69.

Shane, S. (2004) *Academic Entrepreneurship: University Spinoffs and Wealth Creation*, Cheltenham: Edward Elgar.

Shankar, V. and Bayus, B. L. (2003) 'Network effects and competition: an empirical analysis of the home video game industry', *Strategic Management Journal*, Vol. 24, No. 4: 375–84.

Shanklin, W. L. and Ryans J. K. (1984) *Marketing High-technology*, Lexington, MA: Lexington Books.

Shapero, A. (1975) 'The displaced, uncomfortable entrepreneur', *Psychology Today*, Vol. 7, No. 11: 83–9.

Shapero, A. and Sokol, L. (1982) 'The social dimensions of entrepreneurship', in C. A. Kent, D. L. Sexton and K. H. Vesper (eds), *Encyclopedia of Entrepreneurship*, Englewood Cliffs, NJ: Prentice Hall.

Sherer, F. M. (1988) Testimony before the Subcommittee on Monopolies and Commercial Law', Committee on the Judiciary, US Representatives, 24 February 1988, cited in Acs and Audretsch (1993).

Sherer, F. M. (1991) 'Changing perspectives on the firm size problem', in Z. J. Acs and D. B. Audretsch (eds), *Innovation and Technological Change: An International Comparison*, Ann Arbor, MI: University of Michigan Press: 203–32.

Sherman, H. (1999) 'Assessing the intervention effectiveness of business incubation programs on new business start-ups', *Journal of Developmental Entrepreneurship*, Vol. 4, No. 2: 117–33.

Sherman, H. and Chappell, D. S. (1998) 'Methodological challenges in evaluating business incubator outcomes', *Economic Development Quarterly*, Vol. 12, No. 4: 313–21.

Shinn, T. (1978) 'Des corps de l'Etat au secteur industriel: génèse de la profession d'ingénieur, 1750–1920', *Revue Française de Sociologie*, Vol. 19, No. 1 39–71.

Shotter, J. (1990) 'The social construction of remembering and forgetting', in D. Middleton and D. Edwards (eds), *Collective Remembering*, London: Sage Publications.

Simon, H. A. (1976) 'From substantive to procedural rationality', in S. J. Latsis (ed.), *Method and Appraisal in Economics*, Cambridge, MA: Cambridge University Press.

Simon, H. A. (1981) *Science des systèmes, sciences de l'articifiel*, Paris: Dunod.

Simon, H. A. (1991) 'Bounded rationality and organizational learning', *Organization Science*, Vol. 2, No. 1: 125–34.

Simons, H. W. (ed.) (1989) *Rhetoric in the Human Sciences*, London: Sage Publications.

Slevin, D. and Covin, J. (1992) 'Creating and maintaining high performance teams', in D. Sexton and J. Kasarda (eds), *The State of the Art of Entrepreneurship*, Boston: PWS-Kent Publishing Company.

Slevin, D. and Covin, J. (1995) 'New ventures and total competitiveness: a conceptual model, empirical results, and case study examples', *Frontiers of Entrepreneurship Research*, Babson Park, MA: Babson College.

Smith-Doerr, L. and Powell, W. W. (1994) 'Networks and economic life', in N. J. Smelser and R. Swedberg (eds), *The Handbook of Economic Sociology*, Princeton, NJ: Princeton University Press.

Spence, M. (1984) 'Cost reduction, competition and industry performance', *Econometrica*, Vol. 52, No. 1: 101–21.

Spradlin, C. T. and Kutoloski, D. M. (1999) 'Action-oriented portfolio management', *Research Technology Management*, Vol. 42, No. 2.

Stacey, R. D. (1992) *Managing the Unknowable. Strategic Boundaries between Order and Chaos in Organizations*, San Francisco, CA: Jossey-Bass.

Stacey, R. D. (1996) *Complexity and Creativity in Organizations*, San Francisco, CA: Berrett-Keohler.

Stacey, R. D. (2001) *Complex Responsive Processes in Organizations. Learning and Knowledge Creation*, London: Routledge.

Stankiewicz, R. (1994) 'Spin-off companies from universities', *Science and Public Policy*, Vol. 21, No. 2: 99–107.

Stanworth, M. and Curran, J. (1976) 'Growth and the small firm: an alternative view', *Journal of Management Studies*, Vol. 13, No. 2: 95–110.

Stayaert, C. (1995) *Perpetuating Entrepreneurship through Dialogue: A Social Constructionist View*, Leuven: Catholic University of Leuven, Faculty of Psychology and Educational Sciences.

Steensma, H. K., Marino, L. and Weaver, K. N. (2000) 'Attitudes towards cooperative strategies: a cross-cultural analysis of entrepreneurs', *Journal of International Business Studies*, Vol. 31, No. 4: 591–609.

Steinmetz, L. (1969) 'Critical stages of small business growth: when they occur and how to survive them', *Business Horizons*, Vol. 7, No. 1: 29–36.

Stevenson, H. and Gumpert, D. E. (1985) 'The heart of entrepreneurship', *Harvard Business Review*, Vol. 63, No. 2: 85–92.

Stiglitz, J. (1987) 'Learning to learn, localized learning and technological progress', in P. Dasgupta and P. Stoneman (eds), *Economic Policy and Technological Performance*, Cambridge: Cambridge University Press: 125–46.

Storey, D. (1994) *Understanding the Small Business Sector*, London: Routledge.

Storper, M. (1995) 'The resurgence of regional economies, ten years later: the region as a nexus of untraded interdependencies', *European Urban and Regional Studies*, Vol. 2, No. 3: 191–221.

Storper, M. (1997) *The Regional World: Territorial Development in a Global Economy*, New York, NY: Guilford Press.

Strauss, A. and Corbin, J. (1991) *Basics of Qualitative Research: Grounded Theory Procedures and Techniques*, London: Sage.

Stummer, C. and Heidenberger, K. (2003) 'Interactive R&D portfolio analysis with project interdependencies and time profiles of multiple objectives', *IEEE Transactions on Engineering Management*, Vol. 50, No. 2: 175–83.

Tarondeau, J-C. (1998) *Stratégie industrielle*, 2nd edn, Paris: Vuibert.

Tatsuno, S. M. (1990) *Created in Japan: From Imitators to World-class Innovators*, New York: Harper and Row.

Tayeb, M. (1988) *Organizations and National Culture: A Comparative Analysis*, London: Sage.

Teece, D. J. (1986) 'Profiting from technological innovation: implications for integration, collaboration, licensing and public policy', *Research Policy*, Vol. 15: 285–305.

Teece, D. J. (1996) 'Firm organization, industrial structure, and technological innovation', *Journal of Economic Behavior and Organization*, Vol. 31, No. 2: 193–224.

Teece, D., Pisano, G. and Shan, W. (1987) *Joint Ventures and Collaborations in Biotechnology*, International Working Paper no. 1B-8, San Francisco, CA: Berkeley University.

Teece, D., Pisano, G. and Shuen, A. (1997) 'Dynamic capabilities and strategic management', *Strategic Management Journal*, Vol 18, No. 7: 27–43.

Teece, D., Rumelt, R., Dosi, G. and Winter, S. (1994) 'Understanding corporate coherence: theory and evidence', *Journal of Economic Behavior and Organization*, Vol. 23, No. 1: 1–30.

Ternier, A. (1984) 'Etre ingénieur d'hier à aujourd'hui', *Culture Technique*, No. 12: 337.

Tesfaye, B. (1997) 'Patterns of formation and development of high-technology entrepreneurs', in D. Jones-Evans and M. Klofsten (eds), *Technology, Innovation and Enterprise: The European Experience*, London: Macmillan.

Thépot, A. (1979) 'Les ingénieurs du corps des Mines', in M. Levy-Leboyer (ed.), *Le patronat de la seconde industrialisation*, Paris: Les Editions Ouvrières.

Thomsen, S. and Pedersen, T. (2000) 'Ownership structure and economic performance in the largest European companies', *Strategic Management Journal*, Vol. 21, No. 6: 689–705.

Tihani, L., Johnson, R. A., Hoskinsson, R. E. and Hitt, M. A. (2003) 'Institutional ownership differences and international diversification: the effects of boards of directors and technological change', *Academy of Management Journal*, Vol. 46, No. 2: 195–212.

Tönnies, F. (1955) *Community and Association* (trans. C. P. Loomis), London: Routledge & Kegan Paul.

Tönnies, F. (1991, 1935) *Gemeinschaft und Gesellschaft: Grundbegriffe der Reinen Soziologie*, Darmstadt: Bibliothek klassischer Text.

Tornatzky, L., Batts, Y., McCrea, N. and Quitman, L. (1996) *The Art and Craft of Technology Business Incubation*, Athens, OH: Southern Technology Council, and the NBIA publications.

Trompenaars, F. and Hampden-Turner, C. (1997) *Riding the Waves of Culture: Understanding Cultural Diversity in Business*, 2nd edn, London: Nicholas Brearly.

Tsai, W. (2000) 'Social capital, strategic relatedness and the formation of intraorganizational linkages', *Strategic Management Journal*, Vol. 21, No. 9: 925–39.

Tuschke, A. and Sanders, W. G. (2003) 'Antecedents and consequences of corporate governance reform: the case of Germany', *Strategic Management Journal*, Vol. 24, No. 7: 631–49.

Tushman, M. L. and O'Reilly III, C. A. (1997) *Winning Through Innovation*, Cambridge, MA: Harvard Business School Press.

Tzokas, N., Carter, S. and Kyriazopoulos, P. (2001) 'Marketing and entrepreneurial orientation in small firms', *Enterprise and Innovation Management Studies*, Vol. 2, No. 1: 19–33.

Utterback, J. M. (1994) *Mastering the Dynamics of Innovation*, Cambridge, MA: Harvard Business School Press.

Utterback, J. M. and Abernathy, W. J. (1975) 'A dynamic model of process and product innovation', *The International Journal of Management Science*, Vol. 3, No. 6: 639–56.

Van de Ven, A. H. (1992) 'Longitudinal methods for studying the process of entrepreneurship', in D. Sexton and J. Kasarda (eds), *The State of the Art of Entrepreneurship*, Boston, MA: PWS-Kent Publishing Company.

Van de Ven, A. H. and Garud, R. (1989) 'A framework for understanding the emergence of new industries', in R. S. Rosenbloom and R. A. Burgelman, *Research on Technological Innovation, Management and Policy*, Vol. 4, London: JAI press.

Van de Ven, A. H. and Grazman, D. N. (1997) 'Technological innovation, learning, and leadership', in R. Garud, P. R. Nayyar and Z. B. Shapira (eds), *Technological Innovation: Oversights and Foresights*, Cambridge: Cambridge University Press.

Van Wyk, R. J., Haour, G. and Japp, S. (1991) 'Permanent magnets: a technological analysis', *R&D Management*, Vol. 21, No. 4: 301–8.

Veblin, T. (1971) *Les ingénieurs et le capitalisme,* (trans. Gordon & Breach), Paris: L'Harmattan.

Venkataraman, S. (1997) 'The distinctive domain of entrepreneurship research: an editor's perspective', in J. Katz and J. Brockhaus (eds), *Advances in Entrepreneurship, Firm Emergence, and Growth*, Greenwich, CT: JAI Press.

Verin , H. (1984) 'Le mot ingénieur', *Culture Technique*, No. 12: 19–28.

Verin, H. (1993) *La gloire des ingénieurs, l'intelligence technique du XVIème au XVIIème siècle*, Paris: Albin Michel.

Vesper, K. H. (1980) *New Ventures Strategies*, Englewood Cliffs, NJ: Prentice Hall.

Vohora, A., Wright, M. and Lockett, A. (2004) 'Critical junctures in the development of university high-tech spinout companies', *Research Policy*, Vol. 33, No. 1: 147–75.

Von Hippel, E. (1989) 'A proposed change to the user-manufacturer interface with respect to new product and service development', Proceedings of the 16th International Research Seminar in Marketing – La Londe les Maures, IRET, 17–19 May: 174–87.

Waldman, D. and Bass, B. (1991) 'Transformational leadership at different phases of the innovation process', *The Journal of High Technology Management Research*, Vol. 2, No. 2: 169–80.

Walsh, J. and Ungson, G. R. (1991) 'Organizational memory', *Academy of Management Review*, Vol. 16, No. 1: 57–91.

Watts, D. J. (1999) *Small Worlds*, Princeton, NJ: Princeton University Press.

Watts D. J. and Strogatz, S. H. (1998) 'Collective dynamics of "small-worlds" networks', *Nature*, Vol. 393: 440–2.

Weatherston, J. (1993) 'Academic entrepreneurs', *Industry & Higher Education*, Vol. 7, No. 6: 235–43.

Weick, K. (1990) 'Technology as equivoque: sense-making in new technologies', in P. S. Goodman and L. S. Sproull (eds), *Technology and Organizations*, San Francisco, CA: Jossey Bass Publishers.

Weick, K. (1993a) 'The collapse of sense-making in organizations: the Mann Gluch disaster', *Administrative Science Quarterly*, Vol. 38, No. 4: 628–52.

Weick, K. (1993b) 'Organizational redesign as improvisation', in G. P. Huber and W. H. Glick (eds), *Organizational Change and Redesign*, New York, NY: Oxford University Press.

Weick, K. (1995) *Sensemaking in Organizations*, Thousand Oaks, CA: Sage.

Weick, K. (1998) 'Improvisation as a mindset for organizational analysis', *Organization Science*, Vol. 9, No. 5: 543–55.

Weick, K. E. (2002) 'Real-time reflexivity: prods to reflection', *Organization Studies*, Vol. 23, No. 6: 893–993.

Wenger, E. (1998) *Communities of Practice: Learning, Meaning, and Identity*, Cambridge: Cambridge University Press.

Wheelwright, C. and Clark, K. (1994) 'Accelerating the design-build-test cycle for effective new product development', *International Marketing Review*, Vol. 11, No. 1: 32–46.

Whitely, R. (1999) *Divergent Capitalisms: The Social Structuring and Change of Business Systems*, Oxford: Oxford University Press.

Williamson, O. (1975) *Market and Hierarchies*, New York: Free Press.

Williamson, O. (1979) 'Transaction-cost economics: the governance of contractual relations', *Journal of Law and Economics*, Vol. 22, No. 2: 223–61.

Williamson, O. (1985) *The Economic Institutions of Capitalism, Firms, Markets, Relational Contracting*, New York: The Free Press.

Williamson, O. (1989) 'The firm as a nexus of treaties: an introduction', in M. Aoki, B. Gustafsson and O. E. Williamson (eds), *The Firm as a Nexus of Treaties*, London: Sage.

Williamson, O. (1993) 'Calculativeness, trust and economic organization', *Journal of Law and Economics*, Vol. 36, No. 1: 453–86.

Wise, R. and Baumgartner, P. (1999) 'Go downstream: the new profit imperative in manufacturing', *Harvard Business Review*, Vol. 77, No. 5: 133–41.

Wong, P. L.-K. and Ellis, P. (2002) 'Social ties and partner identification in Sino-Hong-Kong international joint ventures', *Journal of International Business Studies*, Vol. 33, No. 2: 267–89.

Wright, M., Birley, S., and Mosey, S. (2004) 'Entrepreneurship and university technology transfer', *Journal of Technology Transfer*, Vol. 29, No. 3/4: 235–46.

Wright, P., Kroll, M., Lado, A. and Ness, B. V. (2002) 'The structure of ownership and corporate acquisition strategies', *Strategic Management Journal*, Vol. 23, No. 1: 41–53.

Yli-Renko, H., Autio, E. and Sapienza, H. J. (2001) 'Social capital, knowledge acquisition, and knowledge exploitation in young technology-based firms', *Strategic Management Journal*, Vol. 22, No. 6/7: 587–613.

Yoon, B., Yoon, C. and Park, Y. (2002) 'On the development and application of a self-organizing feature map-based patent map', *R & D Management*, Vol. 32, No. 4: 291–300.

Zimmermann, J.B. (2002) 'Grappes d'entreprises et "petits mondes": une affaire de proximité', *Revue Economique*, Vol. 53, No. 3: 517–24.

Zott, C. and Amit, R. (2003) 'Business model design and the performance of entrepreneurial firms', INSEAD-Wharton Alliance Center for Global Research and Development Working Paper 2003/94/ ENT/SM/ACGRD4, Fontainebleau: INSEAD.

Index

Abernathy, W. 231
accommodation 136–7
accountants firms 106
Acs, Z. J. 34, 35
Adizes, I. 144
ADL matrix 230
Aérospatiale 208
agency relationships 127–9
Ahuja, G. 71
Airbus 42
Albert, P. 131, 134, 144, 145
Aldrich, H. 243
Allen, D. N. 134
alliances 42, 49, 253–5
Almeida, P. 35
Amblard, H. 57–8
American Wind Energy Association 210
Amit, R. 164
André, C. 147
Ansoff, H. I. 253
APCE 176
appropriation (of knowledge) 39–40
Arocena, J. 57
Arrow, K. 39
Arthur, W. B. 95
artificial intelligence (AI) 22–4
Asplund, J. 251
Atherton, A. 17
Atkinson, A.. 37
Audretsch, D. B. 34, 35
Autio, E. 160, 161
Auto-ID 210–11

Balachandra, R. 229
banks 106
Barney, J. B. 115, 160
Bauer, M. 53
BCG matrix 230
Beckert, J. 16
Bell, G. C. 147, 164, 174
Benhamou, Eric 108
Berle, A. A. 34
Bernasconra, M. 131, 145, 155, 177
Bernoux, J. 57
Bernoux, P. 57
Bertin-Mourot, B. 53
Bès, M. 98
Besson, B. 223
Bhidé, A. 144
Biotech Organ 189–91, 192, 205
biotechnology 189–90
Bird, B. 144
Birley, S. 162
Blais, R. 144, 178
Boeing 208
Boisanger, P. de 218
Bond, E. U. 231
Bouffartigue, P. 57
Broder, A. 52
Brokhoff, K. K. 230
Brush, C. G. 160
Bruyat, C. 57, 176
Bullock, M. 160, 161
Burns, T. 76
Burt, R. 244, 247, 251, 252, 255
business buyouts 51, 53, 56, 58

Business Innovation Centres (BICs) 136; *see also* technology business incubation

business relationships: and institutional cultures 113, 118–20, 126–9; international differences in 116; and national cultures on 117–18, 122–6; *see also* networks

Bygrave, W. D. 174

Cable and Wireless 44

Callon, M. 24, 71, 244, 256–7

Cambridge University 159

Cameron, K. 178

Capon, N. 230

Carter, N. 145

Castells, M. 224

Castilla, E. J. 96

Chell, E. 144

Churchill, N. 178

Cisc 106

Clarysse, B. 162

cluster networks 93–101, 102–5, 107–11

CNISF 51, 53

Cohen, W. M. 33

Coleman, J. S. 96

collective creativity 70–2; memory 221

COM One 69, 72, 74–6, 77–8, 79–80

communication: in absence of knowledge 24–5; between decision and exploitation 38–9; collective learning through 76–8, 82–3; of communities of practice 12, 31; with customers 22–4; in development processes 147; with different mindsets 4, 12, 21; local networks of 16–17; in resource organization 4, 5; of track record 30; use of English 114

communities of practice: communication between 31; communication within 12; 107–8; defining 105–6; endogenous growth and 108, 111; expertise accumulation 87, 94, 101–5; generation of knowledge within 21, 93–4; and networks 211, 222, 257

companies *see* firms

Compaq 189

competences *see* skills and competences

competitive intelligence: confidentiality and secrecy 223, 259–60; deciphering signals 216–18; environmental scanning 207–14; evaluating technologies 231–5; management 221–4; organisation of surveillance process

219–21, 222; in strategic process 218–19; strategic vision 214–16 *see also* scanning networks

confidentiality 223; *see also* secrecy

consultancy 90, 106, 163, 166

consulting companies 106

Cook, K. S. 244

Coombs, R. 233

Cooney, T. M. 176

Cooper, A. C. 71, 176

Cooper, R. G. 225, 229

Coser, R. L. 94

Covin, J. 71, 144

creation processes: activity 178; dynamics of 181–6; entrepreneur typology 176–8; environment in 179–80, 182–3; financial resources for *see* financial resources; models 174–5; non-linear building 178–9; systemic approach to 175–80, 183

credibility: for data-access 21–2, 28; framework 22; through information exchange 259; and results 17; track record 31; trust and 12, 250–1

Crozier, M. 100

culture: Chinese 116; institutional 113, 118–20, 126–9; national 113, 116–18, 122–6; United States 116

Curran, J. 144

customer relations: in marketing 193–4, 201–2; trust 12, 21, 27

Daft, R. L. 16, 28

Daily, C. M. 71, 176

Dalloz, X 211

Danish Owners Association 210

data access 21–2

Davidow, W. H. 196

Davidsson, P. 144

decisions, knowledge basis for 18–19, 28; *see also* competitive intelligence

Delmar, F. 144

Deming's wheel 219

designers 44, 209–12

development stages 89–90

development through networks 114–15, 129

Dickinson, M. W. 228, 229

Dilts, D. 133, 134

dominant design 209–12

Dosi, G. 37

Douglas, M. 117
Druilhe, C. 160
Durand, R. 126–7
Dutch engineers 55–6

École Polytechnique 52
economics, sociology of *see* sociology of
    economics
economies of scale 33, 36, 41, 42, 45, 254
EDF 208
Eggers, J. 144
electronics industry 47, 210; business
    relationships of electronics engineers 120–6;
    microelectronics 20, 44, 47
Elfring, T. 20
Ellul, J. 69
Enercon 208, 215
engineers: as bearers of innovation 50; European
    55–6 *see also* French engineers; French
    see French engineers; study in business
    relationships of electronics engineers
    120–6
English language 114
entrepreneurs, typology of 58–67, 176–8
environment: for company creation 179–80,
    182–3; for cross-cultural relationships
    129–30; environmental scanning 207–14
    see also scanning networks; environmental
    uncertainty 35, 216; firms create own 42;
    of the high-tech entrepreneurship process
    1–2; high-tech world 7–9; in strategy
    development 156
EPC Global 210–11
equivocality 16
Ericsson 44
Ericsson, K. 121
Ernst, H. 230, 233
Espace 217
Essilor 211
ET 46–9, 177
Eurocopter 215
European Commission studies 141
European Technologies (ET) 46–9
evaluation of technology development projects:
    attractiveness 230–3; auditing models
    226–9, 240–1; competitiveness 230,
    233–5; criteria 229–36; portfolio mapping
    237, 240; serendipity 26; technology audit
    239–40; in young companies 235–9

expertise 27, 29; building on 257–8;
    codification of 223; communities of practice
    87, 94, 101–5; in development tools 46;
    of engineers 13, 60, 63, 64; legal expertise
    106; *see also* skills and competences

Fayolle, A. 53, 57, 145, 176
Ferrary, M. 96
financial resources 148, 151, 179, 233;
    financiers in high-tech environment 7; *see
    also* venture capitalists
Fiol, C. M. 243
focusing principle 199–200
foresight 216
Foss, N. J. 20
Foster, R. N. 211, 225, 231
France: engineers *see* French engineers; French
    community in Silicon Valley 108–10;
    network relationships 124–6;
French engineers: comparisons with other
    European engineers 55–6; entrepreneurial
    behaviour and career path 12–13, 51,
    58–68; innovative nature of 50; social
    position 52–3; training system 52, 54–5
Fréry, F. 224
Friedberg, E. 100
Fuglsang, M. 256

Galbraith, J. 147
Garnsey, E. W. 110, 144, 145, 160
Gartner, B. 71
Garud, R. 19, 20, 25
Gasse, Y. 176
Gassée, J.-L. 108
gate keeper networks 220, 221
General Electric/McKinsey matrix 230
geography: of high-tech firms 2–3; localized
    technological processes 37, 38, 100–11;
    model of industrial districts 95–7
Germany: German engineers 55–6
Gibbons, M. 23, 24, 25
Giddens, A. 78
Gillette 211
Ginsberg, A. 71
Glazer, R. 230
Goffman, E. 57, 76, 77
Google 105
Grabher, G. 244, 252
Granovetter, M. 30, 93, 94, 96, 98, 99, 248

Grant, R. M. 160
Graves, S. B. 229
Grazman, D. N. 3–4
Green, K. 190
Greiner, L. E. 178
Grossetti, M. 57, 98
Groupe de Recherche et Economie en Gestion des PME 34
Guilhou, X. 217
Guth, W. 71

Hackett, S. 133, 134
Hamel, G. 212, 233, 253
Hampden-Turner, C. 117, 123
Hanks, 144
Hansen, E. 144
Hansen, M. H. 115
Harris, J. M. 225, 230
Hastings, C. 25
Hay, M. 144
Hefferman, P. 144, 145
Heidenberger, K. 228, 229
Heimer, C. A. 244
Heirman, A. 160, 162
Henricksen, A. 225
Herlau, H. 2
Hernandez, E. M. 145
Hewlett-Packard 42
Hitchens, D. 144
Hofer, C. W. 174
Hofstede, G. 117, 118, 123
Holland, J. L. 56
Houston, M. B. 231
Hsuan, M. J. 230
human resources 105, 132

Ibarra, H. 244
IBM 44, 47, 210, 211
ICT: code protection 260; face-to-face communication 17; information exchange 258; strategic alliances 254
incubators see technology business incubation
India 127
industrial districts 95–7
information: asymmetric 8; collection, analysis and dissemination 220–1; exchange 147, 258–60 see also communication; information overflow 27–8; links in information flow

108–11; management of 221–4; see also knowledge
infrastructural services 136–7
initial public offering (IPO) 106
innovation: appropriation 39–40; autonomous 41; collective creativity in 71–2; collective improvisations 82–3; complexity of situation and 33, 36–7, 45–6, 49; constraints of 38; evolution of 72; firm size and 33–5, 40–9; interpretive blockages 83–4; learning process 36, 37–8; organizational structure and 40–6; patenting 34, 40; process characteristics 37–40; socio-cultural framework for 82–4, 85; systemic 41, 43, 44, 47
innovation management: through building on expertise 257–8; through networking 242–4, 248–57, 260–1; uncertainty and 17–24, 242
innovation projects 20–1
institutional setting 3; institutional cultures on business relationships 113, 118–20, 126–9
Intel 42
intellectual property 158, 159, 163, 166–7; see also patenting
international trade 113
investment banks 106
IRM (information resources management) 221–3
Israel 211

Jarillo, J. C. 248
JC Technology Ltd 211
Jeunes Chambres Economiques 110
Johannisson, B. 243, 244
Jolly, D. 2, 235
Julien, P. A. 4, 16, 144, 145
Juniper Network 105
JVC 210

Kahaner, L. 219
KAO 214
Kenney, M. 96
Kirchhoff, B. A. 228
Klofsten, M. 174
Kluckholn, F. R. 117
Knight, F. R. 16
knowledge: appropriation 39–40; as basis for decisions 18–19, 28 see also competitive

intelligence; codified and uncodified
40; criteria 27–8; domains of 212–14;
implicit 37–8, 40, 47–8; individual and
collective 76 *see also* learning; knowledge
creation dilemmas 24–6; knowledge
networks 46, 95, 251; knowledge services
163; obsolescence 43, 45; rigidity trap of
knowledge system 39, 41, 49, 215; tacit 17,
28, 38, 40, 82, 97
knowledge creation in firms 26
Kostova, T. 16
Kutoloski, D. M. 228
Kympers, L. 55

Laban, J. 207
labour division 25, 42–3, 47, 251, 257
Lampert, C. M. 71
Langlois, R. N. 43
Lant, T. 25
Lanthier, P. 53
large companies 33, 34, 49, 105
Latour, B. 24, 25, 71
Laurent, A. 117, 123
Le Marois, H. 57
learning: collective 69–70, 76–80; cumulative
37–8, 219; foundations of individual
learning 73–6; interpretive framing 76–8,
83–4 *see also* rhetorical dynamics; learning
processes in start-ups 34–5; localized 38
Leavitt, H. J. 16
legal expertise 106
Lendner, C. 131, 141
Lengel, R. H. 16, 28
Lenovo 211
Leonard, D. 26
Levie, J. 144
Levin, R. C. 33
Levy-Leboyer, M. 53
Lewis, V. 178
Li, C. 108–11
Linton, J. D. 228
Lojkine, J. 57
Lorange, P. 253
Lucent 44
Lundvall, B. A. 244

McCann, J. 144
McClelland, D. C. 56
McCluskey, R. 134

McNamara, J. C. 147, 164, 174
Mahoney, J. 43
Malecki, E. 15
management: incubation management 139–40,
141–3, 211; of information resources
221–4; of innovation *see* innovation
management; through networking *see*
networks; project management through
networking 248–52; strategy management
91
Mandala of creativity 212–13
March, J. 20, 75
Marchesnay, M. 4, 16
market: identifying market opportunities
163; international 112, 114; linking of
technologies to 231; new markets 4, 205 *see
also* marketing; uncertainty in 30, 31
market analysis 19, 205
market information 38
marketing: capitalising on experience 203–4;
constructing the market 205; customer
relations 193–4; entrepreneur 200–1;
for growth 203–4; high-tech marketing
194–7; in high-tech start-ups 189–94;
marketing models 11; principle of
proliferation/segmentation/focus 197–200,
203, 205; R&D interface with 235; setting
intermediary objectives 203; technology
192–3; during a transitory state 201–2, 206
Marks & Spencer 211
Marsden, P. V. 252
Marshall, A. 95
Martel, J. F. 228, 229
Massacrier, G. 174
Means, G. C. 34
media coverage 106
merchant banks 106
Meyer, M. 80
microelectronics 20, 44, 47; *see also* electronics
industry
Microsoft 33, 211
Miller, B. 144
Minnesota Innovation Research Program
(MIRP) 71
MITI 210
models 5, 11, 17
Moensted, M. 145, 155
Montgomery, C. A. 160
Moore's Law 37

Moreau, F. 145, 147
Morin, J. 208–9, 221
Moscovici, S. 74
Motorola 42, 44, 47
Mougenot, P. 131
Mustar, P. 145, 161

NASA 210
NASA-DOE 208
National Association/Council of French
   Engineers and Scientists (CNISF) 51, 53
Nelson, R. 71, 72, 80
Netherlands: engineers 55–6; network
   relationships 122–6
networks: access through incubators 138;
   broker role 252; characteristics 243–8; of
   communication 16–17; of competencies
   48–9; exploitation 38–9; gate keeper
   networks 220, 221; high-tech clusters 93–
   101, 102–5, 107–11; information-scanning
   212–21, 223, 224; institutional cultures
   and 113, 118–20, 126–9; international
   network relationships 113, 116–18,
   122–6; of knowledge 46, 95, 251; network
   formation 88, 252–3; network relationships
   for development 114–15, 129, 188, 211;
   power relations 252, 255–7; project
   management through networking 248–52;
   qualities of network relationships 115; social
   see social networks; socio-economic 94,
   97, 99, 106, 110; strategic alliance 253–5;
   transaction benefits 253–4, 260; as virtual
   communities of partners 211, 222, 257; of
   weak and virtual links 108–11
newspapers 106
Nicolaou, N. 162
Nohria, N. 243, 244, 252, 256
Nonaka, I. 214, 223
North, D. C. 119

O'Farrell, P. 144
O'Reilly III, C. A. 211
Oakey, R. P. 20–1, 28
obsolescence: of knowledge 43, 45; of products
   43; technological 203
Olsen, J. 20, 75
organizational memory 78
organizational structure and innovation 40–6,
   48–9

Oullet, F. 228, 229
owner-entrepreneurs, network relationships
   127–8

Packards 95
Parsons, T. 105
partner seeking 255
patenting 34, 40, 163
Patir Research Centre 211
Paul, W. F. 215
Pedersen, T. 126
Penrose, E. T. 160, 162–4
PeopleSoft 211
Perrow, C. 16
Perry-Smith, J. E. 94
Peters, L. 133
Philips 44
planning in scanning 220
Pleitner, H. J. 57
Pleschak, F. 176
Poh, K. L. 228
Porter, M. E. 231
Portes, A. 108
Possin, J. C. 223
Powell, W. W. 243
power relations 252, 255–7
Prahalad, C. K. 212, 233, 253
Prevezer, M. 176
problem-solving: innovation in 36;
   organizational forms adapted to 41, 45
Proctor & Gamble 211
product standardization 113–14
projects: creation processes in see creation;
   evaluation see evaluation of technology
   development projects; domains of
   knowledge 212–14; through networking
   248–52; project teams 44; project types
   154–5; selection 18
proliferation principle 197–8

Quebec 176
Quinn, R. 178

R&D (research and development): constraints
   38; direction through technology audit
   226, 229, 233, 239, 240; and firm size 33,
   34; and geographical cognitive proximity
   95; investment in 38, 39; marketing and
   production interfaces with 235; military

25; place in knowledge generation 24; in university spin-out typology 166; *see also* research centres
R&D intensity 33, 34
Ramsaswamy, K. 127
Ratier Figeac 208
recruitment agencies 106
Remington 211
research centres 105, 132, 134, 141; *see also* universities
research and development *see* R&D
resources: communication in resource organization 4, 5, 163–4, 169; evaluation of 140, 222; exhaustion of 81; external 4, 41, 138, 142; financial *see* financial resources; generation of 142; human 105, 132; incubation 88, 142, 143; internal 139; managed through networking 242, 248–52; management of information resources 221–4; mobilization of 71, 90, 108, 109, 160, 163; new combinations of 90, 163; resource advantage of large firms 12; resource-based approach 160; in shared services 137; tangible and intangible 112
Reynolds, P. 144, 160
RFID (radio frequency identification) 210–11
rhetorical dynamics 80–5
Ribeill, G. 53, 54
Rigaud, G. 174
Ringuest, J. F. 229
Rip, A. 20–1
risk: agency effects 126; limitation through alliances 42; from limited appropriation possibilities 39–40; opportunity and 23, 26; in start-up models 148, 149; uncertainty and 16
Riverin-Simard, D. 57
Robertson, P. L. 43
Robin, J. Y. 57
Roos, J. 253
Roth, K. 116
Rougeaux, J. 219
Roussel, P. A. 233
routinization of practices 79–80

Sammut, S. 144, 176
Sanchez, R. 43
Sanders, W. G. 127
SAP 211

Saporta, B. 144
Saxenian, A. 96, 108–11
scanning networks 212–24; *see also* environment: environmental scanning
Schein, E. H. 56, 117
Schumpeter, J. 50, 62, 70; 'small is beautiful' hypothesis 33, 41, 49
Science & Mesure 192
science parks 132, 141, 180, 251
secrecy 259–60; *see also* confidentiality
segmentation principle in marketing 198–9
SEMATECH 42
Sensiper, S. 26
serendipity 19, 26, 29, 35
Sethi, N. K. 230
Seurat, R. 217, 219
Shalley, C. E. 94
Shane, S. 158, 160
Shapero, A. 57
Sherer, F. M. 33
Shockley 95
Sikorsky 215
Silicon Valley 42, 43, 94–97, 100–9, 149, 257
Simon, H. 73–4, 121
size and innovation 33–5, 40–9
skills and competences 26–9; dialogical 82–5; in-house and external 40–1; mobilization of 46, 48; networks of 48–9; teamwork 39
Slevin, D. 71, 144
small and medium-sized enterprises *see* SMEs (small and medium-sized enterprises)
small high-tech firm characteristics 44–6
SMEs (small and medium-sized enterprises) 34, 54, 70, 141; characteristics 44–6; sales of 106; technology evaluation 236–9
Smith, A. 42
Smith-Doerr, L. 243
social foundations of technological entrepreneurship 72–80
social networks 71, 93–100, 108–11; cultural effects on 118, 125–6, 128
sociological theory 251
sociology of economics 95–8; *see also* networks: socio-economic
Soft Method 193–4
software 47–8, 167, 193; software editors 211
Sokol, L. 57
Sony 210
Sophia Antipolis 87–8, 100–11

Sophia Professional Women's Network 110
Sophia Start up 110
specialization 42, 43; short-sightedness from 216; within business incubators 136
spill-overs 34
spin-offs 34, 177
spin-out firms *see* university spin-out firms
Spradlin, C. T. 228
Spymag 200–1
Stacey, R. D. 28
Stalker, G. M. 76
Stanford University 105, 108
Stankiewicz, R. 161
Stanworth, M. 144
Stiglitz, J. 37
Storey, D. 144
strategic networking *see* networks
strategic services 137–9
strategy development: chaotic 153–4, 155, 156; competitive intelligence in 218–19; complex 151–3, 155, 156, 211–14; development modes 154–6; integration criteria 146–7; interprocessural integration 89; learning processes in 34–5; management 91; operational models 147–54; overview 89; simple development 147–9, 155, 156; start-up models 144–5; strategic alliances 253–5; strategic vision 214–16; temporal criteria 145–6, 235; traditional 149–51, 155, 156
Strotdbeck, F. L. 117
Stummer, C. 228, 229
sub-contracting 40–1
Sun 211
surveillance 219–21, 222; *see also* competetive intelligence: environmental scanning
Swatch 217
Swedberg, R. 30
systems *see* technical systems

Tacke 215
Takeuchi, H. 214, 223
Tatsuno, S. M. 212
technical dynamics 78–80
technical systems: decomposition of 42–3, 215; modules 43; system architecture 43–4; system integration 43, 44
technicians 1; marketing by 193; technical support of incubators 137; *see also* engineers
technological idiosyncrasies 81–2

technological improvisation 82–4
technological scanning 207–14
technology: as a borderless phenomenon 112; as constraint on innovation 38, 47; definition 2, 227–8; distinction from product 194–6, 227; functional approach to 215; high-tech products defined 2; marketing 192–3; mastering of 39; standardization 38; technique and 228; transfer of 209 *see also* technology transfer advisers; uncertainty in 4, 7, 22, 29
technology business incubation: incubator profile and practices 135–40; incubator roles 7, 88–9, 131–4; Israeli incubators 211; management of 141–3; resources for 88, 142, 143; sponsors of 134–5; strategic tasks of 139–40, 211; transitory states 201–2, 206, 219
technology transfer advisers 172
Teece, D. J. 37, 41, 42, 233
Terman 95
Tesco 211
Tesfaye, B. 174
Tetzschner, H. 20
Thépot, A. 53
Thérin, F. 2
Thomsen, S. 126
Tönnies, F. 251
Tornatzky, L. 134
Toulouse, J. M. 144, 178
training for firms 138–9
transitory state of products 201–2, 206, 219
Traynor, A. J. 225
Trompenaars, F. 117, 123
trust: creation of 17; cultural differences in 117; of customer 12, 21, 27; as factor in networks 115; and geographical proximity 97; in hybrid organizational forms 44; in information exchange 259–60; results crucial to 17, 30; from shared understandings 113; uncertainty and 29–31, 250–1
Tuschke, A. 127
Tushman, M. L. 211
Tzokas, N. 144

uncertainty: as a basis for innovation 16–17; decision-making in the face of 18–19, 28; environmental 35, 216; innovation

management and 17–24, 242; managing technical uncertainty 80–4; overcoming uncertainty 204; overview 3–5, 6–7; radical 35–6; strategic 35; trust and 29–31, 250–1
United Kingdom, network relationships 122–6
United States: agency effects on risk taken 126; culture 116; start-ups 176
universities 105, 132, 134, 141, 211
university spin-out firms 164–71; academic entrepreneurial process 160–4, 172; definition of 158–9; diversity 160, 172–3; typology of business activities 164–71
Utterback, J. M. 209–10, 211, 231

Van de Ven, A. H. 3–4, 20, 70, 71
Van Wyk, R. J. 231
Vargas, V. 126–7
Varian 95
variety: in business activities 164–71; created by network links 12, 110; in incubators 143; overview 2–3, 5–7; in types of entrepreneur 176–8; wealth generated 64
VCR recorders 210
Veblin, T. 53
Velde, R. 20–1
Venkataraman, S. 160
venture capitalists: advantage of local relationships to 97; business development models 11; communication with 21; French 109; network relationships 127–8; roles of 106
venture creation 50, 51, 53, 54, 56–8
Verin, H. 50
Vesper, K. H. 71
Vestas 208
virtual companies 42, 43
Visionnix 211
VLSI Technologies 47
Vygotsky, L. 73

Wal-Mart 211
Weick, K. 28, 76, 78, 82
White, S. B. 160
Williamson, O. 244, 253
wind technology 208
Winter, S. 71–2, 80
world of high-tech 7–9
Wright, M. 160

Xerox/Parc 105

Yahoo 105
Yoon, B. 229

Zodiac 215
Zond 208
Zott, C. 164